The Toyota Way Fieldbook

The Toyota Way Fieldbook

A Practical Guide for Implementing Toyota's 4Ps

Jeffrey K. Liker
David Meier

McGraw-Hill

New York   Chicago   San Francisco   Lisbon   London   Madrid
Mexico City   Milan   New Delhi   San Juan
Seoul   Singapore   Sydney   Toronto

Contents

Acknowledgments

It is always difficult for an author to narrow the list of acknowledgments, let alone for coauthors. So many people have affected the learning and writing process. We decided to list them separately within this section, which also gives us the opportunity to thank each other and those who helped bring us together.

From David Meier

As I began to reflect on the various people who have helped me in some way, I was overwhelmed by the large number of individuals who had a part in bringing me to the point where I could contribute to this book. It really would not be possible to mention each person by name here. I want to say that any achievement I have reached is based on two broad groups: the individuals who trained me to think and worked patiently with me, and the people whom I have been teaching, and from whom I have learned a great deal.

I wish to thank the many teachers and trainers at Toyota who made great sacrifices to help all of us at Toyota Motor Manufacturing, Kentucky. The legacy of understanding and ability has been passed along from generation to generation, like a special family recipe, within Toyota. I hope that my efforts honor the spirit of those who have struggled and persevered to develop this process. I would like to give special thanks to: Takeuchi-san, Kusukabi-san, Kidokoro-san, Nakano-san, Ito-san, Honda-san, Miyagowa-san, and Ohno-san. I know that at times I was a great challenge, and I appreciate your patience.

After leaving Toyota, I have continued on my journey of discovery and growth, and I owe that largely to the people who have been students—and thus my teachers. I am listing them in chronological order, as that is how I see my personal development.

My first foray outside the walls of Toyota as a lean advisor was with Cedar Works, in Peebles, Ohio. It may be that the first time is always the best, but the experience at Cedar Works was good enough to encourage me to take a larger leap.

I would like to thank John Beakes and Dr. Robert Deutch of RWD Technologies, Inc. for taking the first chance on me as a consultant. My wife and I are especially grateful for the wonderful insurance coverage, which provided in-vitro-fertilization services. We were blessed with two wonderful boys as a result.

Thanks to Mike Scarpello and the folks at Ford for making my transition away from the comfort of Toyota a pleasant one. Thanks also to my colleagues at Total Systems Development, and especially John and Charlie for providing the opportunity to learn the ropes and develop my skills as a consultant.

To all my friends at Hoffman—it was a big challenge, but everyone made it worthwhile. Special thanks to Dennis Spiess and his family for sharing your "home away from home." Thanks to Ray, Michelle, Mark, Al, and Lyle for providing challenging situations and opportunities to try new ideas. To Don Westman: I appreciate your confidence in me and your willingness to "stay the course." The Kentucky Management team—Diane, Duane, Mark, Bill, and Gene—was one of the most unified management teams I have worked with.

Paul Kenrick has provided opportunities to challenge my abilities and to continuously improve my methods. To the many folks at Parker-Hannifin—Dave, Diane, Joe, Tim, Alex, Millie, Phil, Donnie, Glenn, Greg, and everyone in the plants—who are working hard and facing the challenges of lean.

This acknowledgement would not be complete without a special thank-you to my good friend, and fellow "guru," Bill Costantino. Our paths have been aligned from the first day at Toyota in 1987. I appreciate your continued support, guidance, and many exciting opportunities along the way. It was Bill who connected me with Jeff Liker for this book. I will always cherish your friendship and insights.

I am grateful to Jeff Liker for trusting in Bill's recommendation and taking on a novice writer in this process. It is a great bounty to work with an accomplished author on such a great project.

Most importantly, I must thank my family—my wife Kimberly, who provided life support while I was working, my daughter Jennifer, and my sons Matthew and Michael. Each of them has made sacrifices while I have been busy with this project. They heard me say over the years that I was going to "write a book." Now I finally have! My mother, Patricia Meier, spent countless hours reviewing and editing my work, utilizing her great attention to detail to find the countless punctuation errors. She has always been there to support me as I pursued my crazy dreams.

From Jeff Liker

It was great working with David and sharing his insider Toyota perspective with my outsider view of the Toyota Way. As an outsider, I depend on the kindness of strangers inside Toyota for access to the constantly evolving system we call the Toyota Way. Actually, I have developed many close relationships over the years and continually learn through my visits to Toyota and its affiliates, as well as intense discussions with my friends and colleagues inside and outside of Toyota. I also continually learn from my experiences consulting to companies throughout the world that try to learn from the Toyota Way. Indirectly, I am constantly learning from the consultants who work for me through Optiprise, which is on the front lines of implementing lean and transforming culture in many different types of organizations.

Since I wrote the book, I have spent a good deal of time at the Toyota plant in Georgetown, Kentucky (TMMK), at NUMMI in California, and at Denso in Battlecreek, Michigan. I had a similar epiphany in each case. All three have struggled and had to work really hard to maintain the Toyota Way culture and become self-sufficient from their early Japanese mentors. There are case studies from all three of these Toyota group sites in this book. Many people spent a great deal of time patiently showing me and teaching me, in particular, Gary Convis, president of TMMK, and Wil James, vice president of manufacturing, despite the intense demands on their own time. Mike Brewer, who has the distinction of being the only NUMMI alumni who worked for General Motors to be brought back to NUMMI as a Toyota Production System (TPS) advisor, showed me the progress being made at that continuing TPS success story. Andris Staltmanis, assistant general manager of Denso in Battlecreek, is helping to lead that location to a new level of TPS, and he shared generously his insights.

I was able to draw on companies that I advise to develop case examples that illustrate the struggles and victories of American companies outside Toyota learning to think lean. Pasquali Digirolamo personally has helped lead Tenneco Automotive toward a global transformation with endless passion and energy. Mike Butler has been working tirelessly as a civil servant to make the Jacksonville Naval Air Depot one of the benchmarks for lean to better serve the American defense effort through quicker turnaround of aircraft. John Matheson has led the U.S. operations of Framatome Technologies into lean models to teach its French parent what lean can do in the very customized nuclear fuel industry. David Nelson took his deep learning from Honda to John Deere and then to Delphi Automotive Systems to try to teach American companies what true lean supplier partnerships are all about.

I am also grateful to Bill Costantino for bringing David Meier and me together on this important applied volume on the Toyota Way.

Last but most, I am blessed with a wonderful family, my wife Deborah and children Jesse and Emma. They have been remarkably supportive and resilient in the wake of all the demands on my time since the success of *The Toyota Way.*

Foreword

John Shook
Former Toyota Manager

WHEN JEFF LIKER AND DAVID MEIER asked me to write a foreword for this fieldbook, I immediately and enthusiastically replied yes, but then had an immediate and nagging feeling of concern. A "fieldbook" on the Toyota Way? What exactly is a fieldbook, and how would it describe the Toyota Way? A cookbook with recipes? A roadmap?

But what you the reader will find in these pages is no cookbook or roadmap, but more of a compass to set direction and help you steer your own course. Your guides Jeff and David are fellow travelers and well-equipped to help you, a fact I know well. Somewhat coincidentally, I was on the ground with both Jeff and David the first time they set foot on Gemba in Toyota City, though in quite different circumstances for each. I met Jeff Liker when I was still with Toyota and Jeff was a professor at the University of Michigan continuing the research into socio-technical systems that he had begun years earlier as a student at the University of Massachusetts. I met David Meier in Toyota City when I was introducing many new American employees of Toyota to the Toyota Production System and he was there to began learning the Toyota Way the way you're really supposed to learn it—on the plant floor.

Jeff found Toyota through a formal education and subsequent research path that combined equal interest and experience in the "soft side" of industry with the "hard side." As an industrial engineering major and co-op student at Northeastern University, Jeff worked for General Foods Corporation, doing industrial engineering work such as operations research, plant layout, and so forth, but what came to interest him most was the Topeka dog food plant that was organized around self-directed work teams using a socio-technical systems (STS) approach—joint design of the social and technical systems. After getting a Ph.D. in sociology at University of Massachusetts, Jeff joined the faculty of the

Department of Industrial and Operations Engineering where he has remained since. Jeff's study of the auto industry and Japan developed through involvement with David Cole and Robert Cole through the famous University of Michigan US-Japan auto study. This led him to Toyota and the Toyota Production System, where he found actual application of the STS approach he had begun studying many years before. At Toyota, he felt he had at last found an organization in which the social and technical systems were truly integrated.

Jeff, along with John Campbell, professor of political science, and Brian Talbot, professor at the Michigan Business School, created the Japan Technology Management Program—where I was also privileged to work for several years—which had as its mission the study of how successful organizations in Japan *managed* technology, recognizing that the competitive advantage that many Japanese firms had gained in their respective industries came not from advantages in "hard" technology—Toyota purchases stamping machines and robots from the same sources available to GM or Ford—but from the *way they managed* the same technology. The program focused particularly on the way some firms, notably Toyota, attained holistic integration of technology with people, organization, product, and strategy. While few Japanese firms would have explained it in these terms, the difference lay in their socio-technical system.

David's hands-on learning began on the plant floor when he was in the first group of front-line supervisors from Toyota's Georgetown, Kentucky, Camry plant (TMMK) to visit Toyota City for supervisor's training in the Summer of 1987. Toyota had "practiced" on NUMMI, and Georgetown was the company's first full-blown solo operation outside Japan. Working with the Commonwealth of Kentucky, Toyota developed a comprehensive assessment that evaluated 100,000 applicants for an initial 3,000 jobs! David was one of a highly select group of individuals chosen to be shop floor leaders. The selection process was extensive, but it was just a prelude to the training and development process that David would experience in the subsequent years. Toyota knew from the start that the key to success at TMMK was going to be the degree to which the company could—in short—establish the Toyota Way.

They didn't call it "the Toyota Way" then. It was just "the way Toyota did things." The Toyota Production System was fully articulated by then, as was basic company philosophy, especially in such areas as quality and human resources. But the philosophy didn't stop with those key functions; it played out in each and every company activity. Just as David underwent training as a production group leader, every leader at the new Georgetown operation, paid a similar visit to Toyota City, spending time not only at Tsutsumi, the Camry production plant, but also in their counterpart department at the company's headquarters, in such areas as accounting, purchasing, community relations, and facilities management. TMMK community relations professionals learned how Toyota the company works and cooperates with Toyota City the city. Why? Did Toyota think it's relationship with Toyota City was a benchmark of best practice? Or that the relationship the company had with the local community outside Nagoya, Japan, was somehow something to emulate in central Kentucky?

No, of course not. What Toyota knew was that its culture—its corporate culture not its "Japaneseness"—was what defined it, what gave definition to how it operates at every level, in every function. David and his colleagues didn't hear the phrase "the Toyota Way" at that time, but "Toyota's way" was precisely what was being passed on, in all its aspects, both technical and social.

That's what makes Jeff and David a great team to produce this fieldbook. Jeff's years of academic study of socio-technical systems in general, and Toyota in particular, combined with David's front-line experience of living the Toyota Way on the plant floor add up to the practical, yet conceptually insightful guide you are holding now.

Among experienced Toyota Production System sensei, any attempt such as this one to "write down" the Toyota Way is a controversial undertaking. It is difficult to capture in words the essence of any system laced extensively with tacit knowledge, as is the Toyota Way. This is *not*, however, because the Toyota Way is so *mysterious* that it has to be intuited but simply because it is a "learn through doing" system. As such, even if you are successful at writing it down accurately, there is still a danger of misleading some readers. Corporate executives are smart people, often highly educated, accustomed to keeping up with the latest management fads through books, seminars, executive education. The danger with attempts at learning TPS through such means is that some readers have a tendency to think that if they've read about something they know it.

The Toyota Way is deceptively simple. It can be too easy to read one of the simple principles and say, "Sure, I know that. . . ." Jeff and David have chosen an approach with this Fieldbook that will try to help you avoid that tendency. Rather than putting the book down with a sigh of relief thinking "I got it," you will be encouraged to embody in practice what you are reading: read, try, reflect . . . and learn.

John Shook

Preface

A PARADOX OF THE TOYOTA WAY is that though it is continually improving and changing, the core concepts remain consistent. We are continuously learning new aspects of the process and seeing different applications in different situations. Yet as our understanding deepens, the "basics" continually resurface, guiding decisions and methods.

One thing that seems to shock many of the people we teach and advise is the difficulty even Toyota has had in globalizing the Toyota Way. Consider some of the icons of the Toyota Production System in North America: the Toyota plant in Georgetown, Kentucky; Toyota's joint venture with General Motors, NUMMI in California; and Toyota's largest supplier, Denso, in Battlecreek, Michigan. All three locations went through a dip on the Toyota Way around 2000 as they were rapidly expanding and dealing with a changing workforce and management team, and all three have made heroic efforts to bring the level of Toyota Way thinking back up and are now moving to even higher levels of self-sufficiency in the Toyota Way.

This is important because it suggests the culture underlying all the neat lean systems many companies are busily working to implement does not necessarily come naturally, particularly outside of Japan, and takes constant effort to maintain. Even Toyota group companies in America, with their lean tools that are the envy of most other companies, slip back and must work to move forward.

We have had many experiences in observing, teaching, and consulting throughout the world. At each step we realize that the core concepts and philosophies are applicable in every situation and are truly the most important aspects to learn. The greatest challenge in facing each new and unique situation is to understand how to flexibly apply the methods of the Toyota Way, yet remain true to the core concepts.

Outside Toyota, the challenge becomes the explanation of concepts that were learned through continuous repetition but never described in terms of "absolutes."

There is no "one way" to do any of the lean processes. We have finally concluded that there are certain things that a good Toyota Production System (TPS) sensei instinctively knows and understands but they "don't know how they know." This provides an ongoing challenge to effectively communicate with and teach others.

The Toyota Way is passed from person to person through a process of repeated suggestions to "just do," multiple attempts, reflections, and review, further attempts and reviews, and so on, continuing again and again until intuitional ability is achieved. This method of learning creates a challenge when it comes to explaining "why" something is done, or why it is important. How do we know what we know? How do we know what to do next? How do we see traps? The answer is: It seems intuitive and right.

We always insist in any company we work with that individuals be assigned full-time as disciples of the Toyota Way. They must be coached by a lean expert one-on-one, much as anyone experienced at a craft (cooking, sewing, sports) would pass on his or her accumulated wisdom to a student. This method is slow and tedious; however, it develops individuals capable of facing any condition and understanding an appropriate course of action. It develops individuals who believe in their gut and "know" the right thing to do next. This is important, since they will continually have to convince others who do not believe, and do not know, and wish to continue the old ways.

This book is an attempt to clarify the thought process used by Toyota and how those ideas are applied and used to create the tremendous success Toyota has achieved. We focus on how to think about the process and about solutions. This process will provide many challenges along the way. Always remember the frequent admonitions and challenge that is issued at Toyota: "Please try" and "Do your best."

Part I

Learning from Toyota

Chapter 1

Background to the Fieldbook

Why *The Toyota Way Fieldbook?*

Toyota's success as a company has been well documented. It has a well-earned reputation for excellence in quality, cost reduction, and hitting the market with vehicles that sell. The result has been a highly profitable company by any standards. Earning billions of dollars per year and amassing at any point in time $30 to $50 billion in cash reserves would be enough to convince anyone this company must be doing something right. Since *The Toyota Way* initially hit the shelves in January 2004, Toyota has continued to break records, earning over ¥10 trillion (about $10 billion) that year and becoming the most profitable company in the history of Japan. That pattern continues into 2005 breaking continuing profitability records while many of its competitors are losing market share and struggling to earn a profit. In 2005 Toyota in North America also won top honors in the coveted J.D. Power Initial Quality Award winning first place in 10 of 18 categories. Toyota then was recognized by Harbour Associates as having the most productive plants in North America. All this was accomplished while steadily increasing sales volume in North America at a time while its domestic competitors were losing volume.

But Toyota's impact on the world has gone beyond making money. It has even gone beyond making excellent vehicles people can enjoy driving. Toyota has contributed a new paradigm of manufacturing. "Lean production," a term coined in *The Machine That Changed the World*, is widely considered the next big step in the evolution of manufacturing beyond Ford's mass production. Who would have thought that Sakichi Toyoda, working in the rural hinterlands of what is now Toyota City in Japan, would have wrought a global powerhouse that has changed the face of manufacturing? And it has gone way beyond mass production of automobiles to all types of manufacturing: chemical processing, pharmaceuticals, nuclear fuel, ship and aircraft construction, medical products, building construction, shoemaking, sewing, defense bases that repair planes and ships and tanks, and on and on. And if that's not enough, there is a revolution in service industries working to apply lean thinking to drive out waste, including banks, insurance companies, hospitals, post offices, and more.

The Toyota Way became an international best-seller beyond expectations. We knew that those who were already committed to adopting lean manufacturing and to spreading lean beyond the shop floor would find something of interest in the book. But we did not realize how far lean thinking was spreading and how many people simply admired Toyota and wanted to see what they could learn from this corporate icon. Readers described feeling in awe when reading the book, inspired to go out and improve their organizations and their own personal lives. People read the book in just a few sittings and did not want to put it down. And all this for a business book?

The most common feedback from people who read the book was that it opened their eyes to a much broader view of what they could learn from Toyota. For them, it was more than the tools and methodologies of lean production or even lean applied to the office. They realized that Toyota had created an entire system of organization that focused on adding value to customers through people.

The sum total of Toyota's approach creates a unique culture that people throughout the world in many different kinds of organizations believe they can learn from. An overwhelming number of business leaders have written saying that they are adopting *The Toyota Way* as a blueprint for remaking their organizations. While they have reported taking away many different kinds of lessons, we cannot help wondering if the original book is enough to provide that blueprint. Our purpose had been to describe Toyota's management principles with case examples to bring them to life. The book was not written as a guide on how to apply the principles to your organization.

A fieldbook is intended to provide practical recipes for success, right? It should have tools, techniques, and methods that you can follow step by step. Well, maybe by some definitions. But then that posed a dilemma for us. On the one hand, the whole premise of *The Toyota Way* was that Toyota's system was much more than tools and techniques. Those tools and techniques—cells, *kanban*, mistake proofing, and quick changeover, among others—have already been well documented, and there is no shortage of detailed technical descriptions of these methods. On the other hand, the punch line of the book was that Toyota's main contribution has been to create a true learning organization. And the way they pass on the DNA of this learning organization as they expand globally is through dedicated *sensei* who act as personal tutors to new associates.

The Toyota Way is about tacit knowledge, not explicit procedural knowledge. "Tacit" knowledge is the craft type of knowledge that you gain from experience and reflection, not from reading a recipe. This tacit knowledge includes know-how and a philosophy of continuous improvement that is learned by doing with a coach who already has been enlightened through hard work and experience. The obvious implication is that the book should be reduced to one sentence: Go find a sensei to learn from and enjoy the journey!

We thought there was still value to writing a "fieldbook," but we struggled to define its purpose. We began by ruling out writing a "how-to" book that gives checklists and assessment instruments and step-by-step procedures. There are some in here, but those by themselves would not do justice to the profound insights we have gotten from our experiences with Toyota. Jeffrey Liker has spent over 20 years visiting and studying Toyota. David Meier spent almost 10 years with personal Japanese mentors at Toyota's Georgetown, Kentucky plant and could easily imagine their disapproving grunts and head shaking if he reduced Toyota's way to a cookbook format.

So we decided to take a different approach. *The Toyota Way* documented Toyota's Way. We decided the fieldbook should provide practical advice to those attempting to learn from *The Toyota Way*. We have both had years of experience in teaching Toyota's methods and philosophies to thousands of companies by lecture and hands-on consulting. We are constantly learning what works and what does not work. We are constantly facing misunderstandings about how to learn from Toyota. We also occasionally have the good fortune of seeing the lightbulbs go on, and people do amazingly innovative things based on what they learn. So we decided to share our experiences from hands-on efforts to help companies learn from Toyota.

We still realize this book is a long way from a how-to guide. We have many examples from Toyota to bring the concepts to life. And we can share many lessons we have had the good fortune to learn. But we've taken our understanding of Toyota one step further, providing advice on how to learn from the Toyota Way. The learning journey must be your own personal journey. Treat this book as picking up on the lessons of the Toyota Way and applying it to how you can learn from Toyota. But these are just ideas. You have to apply the ideas in your situation in your way.

Some of the ideas we present here may generate some disagreement in the lean manufacturing community. There are as many specific approaches to a particular situation as there are lean "experts." You may look at one of our examples and think, "They should have done it this way," or "There is another possible method." If you make these observations, great! That means you understand the concepts well enough to realize the various possible solutions to any situation.

The one reality of the Toyota Way is that there is *always* more than one way to achieve the desired result. The important thing is to learn, to think about what you have learned, to apply it, and to reflect on the process and continuously improve in such a way as to strengthen your organization for the long term.

You may think that we have left out or completely missed some important aspects of the Toyota Way. There is no question that this is the case. An entire book could easily be written about any topic covered here. We have attempted to distill the information to those things that are most critical and often overlooked elsewhere. We are fully aware that we ourselves might have overlooked some key items, and we would love to hear from you so those items may be considered for future work.

How the Book Is Organized

The starting point for this book is the 4P model developed in *The Toyota Way*. The four Ps are Philosophy, Process, People/Partners, and Problem Solving (all right, there are kind of five Ps). In this book we have also used the 4P structure, but we did not exactly stick to the original principles. We found a somewhat different list, one more amenable to teaching others how to apply the principles.

We still stuck with the high-level organization of the 4P model. Here's a brief description of the 4Ps and what makes them somewhat unique to Toyota:

◆ **Philosophy.** At the most fundamental level, Toyota's leaders see the company as a vehicle for adding value to customers, society, the community, and its associates. This is not naive political mumbo jumbo. It's real. It goes back to the founder, Sakichi Toyoda, and his desire to invent power looms to make life simpler for women in the farming community in which he grew up. It continued when Sakichi asked his son Kiichiro Toyoda to make his own contribution to the world by starting an automobile company. It is imprinted in all of Toyota's leaders today. It sets the foundation for all the other principles.

◆ **Process.** Toyota leaders have learned through mentorship and experience that when they follow the right process, they get the right results. While some of the things you should do in the name of the Toyota Way bring immediate dollars to the bottom line, such as shedding inventory or eliminating wasted human motion in jobs, others are investments that in the long term enable cost reduction and quality improvement. It is the long-term investments that are the most difficult. Some are quantifiable in a clear cause and effect way, while in other cases you have to believe they will pay off. For example, bringing parts to an assembly line every hour can seem wasteful, yet it supports the principle of creating flow. Spending time on developing consensus and getting input from those affected can seem wasteful, but if you short-circuit this process some of the time, you will short-circuit it most of the time.

◆ **People and Partners.** Add value to your organization by challenging your people and partners to grow. The Toyota Production System (TPS) was at one time called the "respect for humanity" system. We often think respecting people means creating a stress-free environment that provides lots of amenities and is employee friendly. But many of the tools of TPS aim to raise problems to the surface, creating challenging environments that force people to think and grow. Thinking, learning, growing, and being challenged are not always fun. Nor is Toyota's environment always fun. But people and Toyota's partners, including suppliers, grow and become better and more confident.

◆ **Problem solving.** Continuously solve root problems to drive organizational learning. We all solve problems every day whether we like it or not. Usually we do not like it because problems are really crises—fires to fight. The same problems come back because we do not get to the root cause and put in place true countermeasures. In Toyota, even when it would seem a product launch or a team project has gone flawlessly and achieved all of the objectives, there were always many problems that had to be solved. There are always opportunities to learn, so at least those problems are less apt to come up again. Moreover, when someone in Toyota learns an important lesson, they are expected to share it with others facing similar problems so the company can learn.

The 4P model was intended, to some degree, to be hierarchical, with higher levels building on lower levels. Without a long-term philosophy, a company will simply not do all the things the other Ps imply. The technical process provides the setting in which to challenge and develop your people, which is necessary if you ever hope to achieve a true learning organization focused on continuous improvement through problem solving.

We organized the chapters within each of the four Ps into prescriptive lessons. In each chapter we go into some depth about the lesson. We will emphasize main points through a variety of vehicles:

Tip
This is a tip from our experience that can help you practice the concept effectively.

Trap
Common traps we have experienced that lead people and organizations to miss the boat in effectively learning a Toyota Way principle.

Go and See

Genchi genbutsu is a central Toyota Way principle that means the actual place, the actual part. The principle is to go and see the actual place and understand the real situation through direct observation. We could not bring you to real-life cases, so we bring some real-life case studies to you.

Reflection

A key to learning in Toyota is reflection. It is the driver of *kaizen*. In all chapters, we pause to ask reflection questions to help you apply the lessons to your organization.

Overview of the Toyota Way Principles

While we did not organize the book around these principles exactly in this way, it is worth reviewing the principles as background for the *The Toyota Way Fieldbook*.

I. Philosophy as the Foundation

1. Base your management decisions on a long-term philosophy, even at the expense of short-term financial goals.

Cost reduction has been a passion since Taiichi Ohno created the famous Toyota Production System on the shop floor. Yet cost reduction is not what drives Toyota. There is a philosophical sense of purpose that supercedes any short-term decision making. Toyota executives understand their place in the history of the company and are working to bring the company to the next level. The sense of purpose is like that of an organism working to grow and developing itself and its offspring. In this day and age of cynicism about the morals and ethics of corporate officers and the place of large capitalistic corporations in civilized society, Toyota gives us a glimpse of an alternative, provides a model of what happens when tens of thousands of people are aligned toward a common purpose that is bigger than making money.

Toyota always starts with the goal of generating value for the customer, society, and the economy. This principle should always be the starting point, not just for product/service design efforts, but for every function in the company. An important subtext for this mission orientation is that Toyota sees itself as responsible. Leaders must all take responsibility. This goes back to the beginning of the auto company, when Kiichiro Toyoda resigned from the company he founded because economic conditions forced him to lay off many associates.

This strong philosophical mission orientation has defined Toyota from their beginnings as a manufacturing company, and often separated them from their competitors. It is the foundation for all the other principles . . . and the missing ingredient in most companies trying to emulate Toyota.

II. The Right Process Will Produce the Right Results

2. Create a continuous process flow to bring problems to the surface.

"Flow" means cutting back to zero the amount of time that any work project is sitting idle, waiting for someone to work on it. Redesigning work processes to achieve "flow" typically results in products or projects being completed in one-tenth the time that was previously required. Flow is most evident in the Toyota Production System, but it is also evident throughout Toyota in the organizational culture, which has a focus on value-added flow as an alternative to the normal stop/start approach to working on projects a little bit at a time. But the reason to create flow is not just to have material or information moving fast. It is to link processes and people together so that problems surface right away. Flow is a key to a true continuous improvement process and to developing people.

3. Use "pull" systems to avoid overproduction.

Your customers have extremely demanding service requirements. They want parts when they want them, in the amount they want, and missed shipments are unacceptable. So what can you do about this? The obvious answer is to rent a warehouse and hold lots of inventory so you have the maximum of anything they might possibly want. Toyota's experience has proven that to be the wrong answer. In fact, stocking inventory based on forecasted or even promised demand almost always leads to chaos, firefighting, and running out of the very products the customer wants. Toyota found a better approach, modeled after the American supermarket system. Stock relatively small amounts of each product and restock the supermarket shelf frequently, based on what the customer actually takes away. The *kanban* system is often viewed as the signature of the Toyota Production System. But the underlying principles and the systems needed to make it work effectively are often misunderstood. And the *kanban* system is itself waste which should be eliminated over time.

4. Level out the workload (work like the tortoise, not the hare).

The only way to realistically create a continuous flow is to have some stability in the workload, or *heijunka*. If the demand on an organization rises and falls dramatically, it will force the organization into a reactive mode. Waste will naturally rear its ugly head. Standardization will be impossible. Many companies believe unevenness in workload is simply the natural order of things created by an unstable environment. Toyota works to find many clever ways to level the workload to the degree possible. Spikes and peaks are handled through flexible workforces brought in from contracting companies and suppliers.

5. Build a culture of stopping to fix problems, to get quality right the first time.

Toyota has won the highly prestigious Deming Award for quality in Japan and won about every award J.D. Power and Associates offers as well. Quality for the customer drives the value proposition of Toyota. Of course, Toyota uses all the modern quality assurance methods that have become standard in the industry. But what sets them apart goes back to the founder of the company, Sakichi Toyoda watching his grandmother slave away at a manual loom, working her fingers to the bone. Eventually Sakichi invented a power loom, and ultimately he solved a nagging problem with power looms.

The problem was, if a single thread broke, then all the material woven after that was waste until somebody noticed the problem and reset the loom. The solution was to build into the loom the human capability to detect the problem and to stop itself. To alert the operator that the loom needed assistance, he developed the *andon* system, which signaled the need for help. This invention became the basis for one of the main pillars of the Toyota Production System—*jidoka* (machines with human intelligence). It is the foundation to Toyota's philosophy of building in quality. When there is a problem, do not just keep going with the intention of fixing it later. Stop and fix the problem now. Productivity may suffer now, but in the long run productivity will be enhanced as problems are found and countermeasures put in place.

6. Standardized tasks and processes are the foundation for continuous improvement and employee empowerment.

You cannot predict the timing and output of your processes unless you have stable, repeatable processes. The foundation for flow and pull is predictable and repeatable processes. But standardization is often confused with rigidity, and the assumption is that creative, individual expression is stifled. In fact what Toyota has found is the exact opposite. By standardizing today's best practices, they capture the learning up to this point. The task of continuous improvement is then to improve upon this standard, and the improvements are then incorporated into the new standard. Without this standardization process, individuals can make great improvements in their own approach to the work but no one will learn from them except through impromptu discussion. When an individual moves on from that job, all of the learning is lost. Standards provide a launching point for true and lasting innovation.

7. Use visual control so no problems are hidden.

In these days of computerization, the ideal is the paperless office and paperless factory. Put everything online. Yet, go to any Toyota manufacturing plant and you will see paper kanban circulating through the factory, paper flip charts used for problem solving, paper charts and graphs being updated every day by work teams. Even in service parts warehouses with hundreds of thousands of parts being moved about, physical visual aids abound. There are signs and labels everyplace in a Toyota environment. Why? Because people are visual creatures. They need to be able to look at their work, look at the parts rack, look at the supermarket of parts, and easily see whether they are in a standard condition or a deviation from the standard. People looking at well-designed charts on a wall can have very effective discussions. Going to a computer screen moves the workers' focus from the workplace to the computer screen. Robots do not care if the factory is visual, but people do, and Toyota will always design systems to support people.

8. Use only reliable, thoroughly tested technology that serves your people and process.

Technology enables people doing work according to a standard process; people should not be subservient to technology. The process always takes precedence over technology. Toyota has had experience with pushing the latest and greatest technology, and now avoids repeating this mistake. Since Toyota focuses so heavily on stability, reliability, and predictability, the organization is very cautious about introducing untested technology in business processes, manufacturing systems, or in products. Nor is Toyota willing to jump on the technology bandwagon until a clear need has been articulated in detail and the technology has been thoroughly investigated. Technologies that conflict with Toyota's philosophies and operating principles will be rejected.

On the other hand, Toyota is always interested in being current in their technology and encourages their people to "think outside the box" when considering new approaches to work. A thoroughly considered technology that has been carefully investigated and proven through trials will be implemented quickly and very effectively.

III. Add Value to the Organization by Developing Your People and Partners

9. Grow leaders who thoroughly understand the work, live the philosophy, and teach it to others.

Leaders at Toyota are grown; they are not bought. If the goal is to get some leader to manage a part of the business, and the criteria for selecting the leader is his or her technical understanding of the business specialty (e.g., logistics) and general management skills, many good managers can be hired and hit the ground running. Toyota in Japan rarely hires managers from outside, except for overseas where they have to hire from the outside as they grow. Gary Convis, president of the plant in Georgetown, Kentucky, estimates that it takes 10 years to train a new manager from the outside to the point where the manager can be trusted and autonomous. At the Toyota Technical Center in Ann Arbor they describe as "painful" the process of bringing in managers from the outside.

The reason for these difficulties is that Toyota does not view the manager's job as simply accomplishing tasks and having good people skills. Managers are viewed as bearers of the Toyota Way. More than anyone, they must exemplify the philosophy in everything they do: the decisions they make and how they go about making the decisions. They must be teachers of the Toyota Way. They also must understand the actual work at a level of detail that most American managers do not feel is necessary to do the job.

10. Develop exceptional people and teams who follow your company's philosophy.

One thing that is obvious in talking to a lot of different Toyota employees—or "team associates," as they call them—is that they are more similar than different in the way they talk about Toyota, its philosophy, and their work. We often think about "cults" negatively—people, who are brainwashed into a strong, often counterculture, belief system. But any strong organization that has survived through centuries, like the Catholic Church, has a strong sense of shared purpose and a strong culture shared by members. The definition of a strong culture is one in which values and beliefs are well-aligned among members. Toyota has a strong internal culture that they often refer to as their DNA. Toyota is very conscious of the importance of maintaining this DNA in all their associates and works hard to continually reinforce the culture.

The essence of the Toyota Way is exceptional individuals and teams who work within the philosophy of the Toyota Production System to achieve outstanding results. The tools are just tools that can be picked up by any company. But the gifted carpenter who carelessly leaves his tools lying around so someone else can steal them does not have to worry about being replaced by an amateur who finds his tools. And picking up kanban and andon from Toyota will not make you a world-class lean enterprise. The people using the tools, and how they use them, are what bring the Toyota Production System to life.

11. Respect your extended network of partners and suppliers by challenging them and helping them improve.

Toyota does not use and abuse their partners, extracting whatever value they can for the lowest possible price. A partner becomes an extension of Toyota. Part of contributing to society is supporting partners so that they become better as a result of working with Toyota. It is part of "Respect for Humanity," a concept that has a far different implication than terms like "human resource management," which imply making the most productive use of resources, almost like you would a piece of equipment. Challenge is a core value within the Toyota Way and central to the way people and business partners are developed.

IV: Continuously Solving Root Problems Drives Organizational Learning

12. Go and see for yourself to thoroughly understand the situation.

You cannot solve problems and improve unless you fully understand the actual situation—which means going to the source, observing, and deeply analyzing what is going on, or *genchi genbutsu*. Do not solve the problem remotely by theorizing only on the basis of reported data or looking at computer screens. If you are responsible for a problem and make recommendations on possible solutions, you might be asked whether you went and looked at the situation yourself in person. If the answer is, "No, but I saw the reports," you better be prepared for an assignment to go and see for yourself. There is a basic belief in Toyota that people solving problems and making decisions need to have a deep understanding that can only come from personally verified data: seeing for yourself. Even high-level managers and executives should go and see for themselves as much as possible. Summarizing reports by subordinates when you yourself have only a superficial understanding is not acceptable in the Toyota culture.

13. Make decisions slowly by consensus, thoroughly considering all options; implement decisions rapidly.

It has become a truism in the literature that Japanese management moves slowly in decision making to generate consensus, which allows them to move fast in execution. While this is certainly true of Toyota, the real key is not consensus but exploring potential problems and solutions to get to the best possible answer. The method of asking "Why?" five times is a way to thoroughly analyze the root cause of the problem. The surface problem is seldom the true cause. When a Toyota member brings a solution to the boss, the first question might be: "How do you know what the real problem is?" The second question is: "Who have you spoken to, and are they in agreement with the solution?" *Nemawashi* is the process of bringing problems and potential solutions to all of those affected to gather their ideas and get agreement on a solution. This is a time-consuming process, but it helps broaden the search for solutions as well as setting the stage for rapid implementation once a decision is made.

14. Become a learning organization through relentless reflection and continuous improvement.

Continuous improvement follows immediately after having achieved stable processes. It includes Toyota's famous "Five-Why Analysis" and the "Plan, Do Check, Act" tool for determining the root cause of inefficiencies or slowness, as well as effective countermeasures. When you have stable processes, and waste and inefficiencies are publicly visible, you have an opportunity to continually learn. But learning happens through people, and it is also necessary to have stability of personnel, slow promotion, and very careful succession systems to protect the organizational knowledge base. Learning means moving forward and building on your past rather than starting over with each new project . . . and each new manager.

Westerners seem to see criticism as something negative and self-admission of our limitations as a sign of weakness. It is just the opposite within Toyota. The greatest sign of strength is when an individual can openly identify things that did not go right, along with "countermeasures" to prevent these things from happening again. *Hansei* is a broader concept in Japan, which is not peculiar to Toyota. Parents may ask their children to reflect when they have done something wrong. It implies that you feel bad about your shortcomings and vow to never make the same mistake again. Even after a successful vehicle launch, Toyota engineers take time to reflect on shortcomings of the program they just completed and develop countermeasures so they will not make the same mistakes again. Hansei is an attitude and philosophy, which is at the core of *kaizen*, or continuous improvement.

How to Use This Book

Writing a fieldbook on the Toyota Way is itself a challenging task. As we noted earlier, in some ways it seems to run counter to the Toyota philosophy of learning by doing. And it seems to imply that it is possible to follow simple lessons and recipes. What we are in fact trying to do is offer some of the lessons we learned through trying to help companies become lean learning organizations. A lean learning organization seeks to achieve its objectives with minimum waste by continually getting better. The best sports teams get a little better every day— from practice, from games, and from reflecting on tapes. No athlete is ever done learning. And no organization should ever be finished learning and improving. Toyota is always far from where it wants to be.

We hope this book will inspire, provide useful tips, make some lightbulbs go on, and even lead to direct application. But it is just a book. The real learning takes place every day. The real lessons are life lessons. If we motivate you to try some things differently, to reflect a little bit more on some life lessons, to put a few of the concepts you have learned into a broader perspective, we will consider ourselves successful. In any case, you can be certain that we will practice *hansei* to reflect on ways that we can correct any shortcomings and to improve our abilities in the future. We hope that you will do the same. We wish you all the best on your lean learning journey.

Part II

Why Does Your Company Exist?

Chapter 2

Define Your Company Purpose and Begin to Live It

What Is Your Company's Philosophy?

Ask this simple question at work and watch the eyes glaze over. It is a bit like asking why humans exist on this earth. Leave that to the philosophers. Let's get down to the work we have to do today. Companies regularly have retreats where plans are made for the next year, and some forward-thinking companies even develop five-year plans. But then we hear about the mysterious 500-year plans of Japanese companies. It is not necessary to know what your company will be doing in 500 years. The question is whether your vision includes being around that long.

Toyota's vision certainly does include being around for the long term. Starting as a family company, it has evolved into a living organism that wants first and foremost to survive in order to continue contributing. Contributing to whom? Contributing to society, the community, and all of its associates and partners.

If we ask why most private companies exist, the answer comes down to a single word: profit. Any economist can tell you that in a market-driven economy the only thing a company needs to worry about is making money—as much as possible, within legal constraints, of course. That is the goal. In fact, any other goal will lead to a distortion of the free market.

Let's consider a simple thought experiment. If a sound financial analysis demonstrated that your company could be more financially valuable if it were broken up and the assets sold off rather than continuing as a company, would your leaders do it? Would they be fulfilling the purpose of the company by dissolving it and selling off the pieces?

From a pure market-economics perspective they should dissolve the company and sell it off. Of course, one could argue that it depends on the terms being considered. Perhaps with a change in strategy the company could be more profitable in a 10-year period compared to dissolving it. Or perhaps one has to look out 15 years. But the time period is not the issue. The issue is: Why does the company exist? If it is purely a financial endeavor, it could achieve its purpose by being profitably dissolved and sold off based on risk-reward calculations over some time horizon. If the company exists for other reasons, then selling it off, even at a tidy profit, may be admitting failure.

If Toyota were broken into pieces and sold off at a handsome profit, it would be an utter failure based on its purpose. It could not continue to benefit society, let alone its internal associates or external partners, if it were dissolved as a company. It would only benefit a few individual owners in the short term. This is an important fact as a foundation for building a lean learning enterprise because it leads to the fundamental question: What is it worth investing to achieve the purpose of the company? For every business transaction this question will come to the fore. For every investment in improving the company, its people, and its partners, this question will loom large. In fact, if you can't answer this question, it may not be worth learning to be lean. You might want to pull a few of the lean tools out of the lean bag of tricks and map your process, eliminate some waste, and grab the cost savings. But you won't become a lean learning enterprise by taking that path. And most of the good advice and tips in this book will not apply to your company. Read a book on financial analysis instead.

So at some point you need to face the tough question: Why do we exist as a company? It need not be an abstract, unanswerable, philosophical debate. In this chapter we discuss a way of thinking about your company's purpose and some tips on what it takes to develop the foundation for building a lean learning enterprise.

A Sense of Purpose Inside and Out

What does it mean for an organization to have a sense of purpose? If it's simply to make money, put a big dollar sign on a poster for the employees and managers to see and forget the elaborate mission statement. If it's more than that, you should consider what you're trying to accomplish both internally and externally. What are you trying to build for your internal stakeholders? What are you trying to help them contribute, and what will they get in return? What impact are you trying to have on the outside world? Furthermore, your mission should have two parts—one part about people and the other about the business.

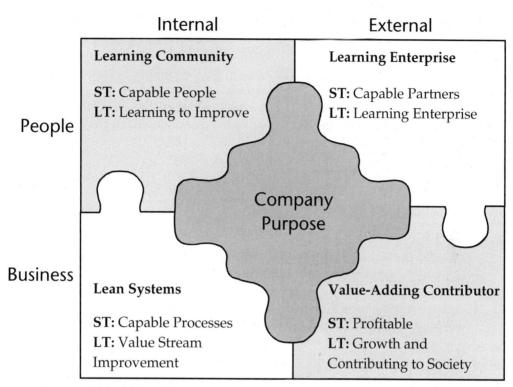

Key: ST=Short term   LT=Long term

Figure 2-1. Defining the company purpose

Figure 2-1 represents company purpose as a matrix combining internal and external goals as they relate to people and business. It includes simple statements based on Toyota's purpose and shows both the short-term goal and the longer term purpose of the company.

The short-term goals for each cell are what every company wants: capable internal processes, capable people who can do the work, capable partners who can do their jobs, and they want to make money. That's pretty straightforward. More challenging is getting a sincere commitment by top management to long-term thinking. Let's consider what long-term thinking means in each of the four cells.

Lean Systems

Let's keep it simple and start with what most of the world knows best about Toyota—the technical part of the Toyota Production System. It reduces the time between a customer order and delivery by eliminating non-value-added waste. The result is a lean process that delivers high quality to customers at a low cost, on time, and allows Toyota to get paid without holding enormous amounts of inventory. Similar lean processes can be found in product development, where Toyota has the fastest development times in the industry, getting updated styling and features to customers faster, with higher quality, and at a lower cost than competitors. And lean internal processes even extend throughout Toyota's business support functions, to sales, purchasing, production engineering, and planning, though the lean processes are not as formalized as in manufacturing and product development.

What is less understood is that lean systems are not just about tools and techniques, but about philosophy. For example, it's easy to understand how eliminating waste using lean tools will lead to immediate financial returns. But what about the necessity of creating some waste in the short term in order to eliminate waste in the long term? Consider the following scenarios:

1. To treat the value-added worker as a surgeon and get him or her all the tools and parts needed to do the job without distracting the worker from value-added work may require some non-value-added preparation. Tools and parts may need to be prepared in advance in right-sized containers or kits, and a material handler might need to bring these frequently to the place where value-added work is being done.

2. To reduce batch size and improve the flow of parts through the system may require changing over the tooling on a piece of equipment more frequently, incurring additional setup costs. SMED (single minute exchange of dies) procedures can dramatically reduce the setup time and cost, but many companies want to use that saved time to produce more parts, adding to overproduction instead of using the time to reduce batch size.

3. To improve the quality and reduce the lead time of the product development process may require investing in dedicated chief engineers who run the programs but do not manage the people working on the programs. This is an additional role beyond that of the more typical program manager role. Chief engineers have a lot of responsibility and need to be well paid.

4. Improving the quality of a product launch may require involving suppliers early in the process and partnering with suppliers that are highly competent technically, thus paying more money per piece initially, rather than seeking the lowest cost commodity producer.

In other words, it may be necessary to invest some money in the short term to get the high-quality lean processes needed to save money in the long term. And to make matters worse, it may not be easy to exactly calculate the savings attributable to a particular action that costs some money. For example, what is the benefit of producing smaller batch sizes compared to the cost of changing over more frequently?

One can calculate the labor cost, but the benefits of smaller batch size are more elusive. In fact, if one could calculate the benefits of each change piece by piece, we wouldn't be talking about lean as a system. Therefore, lean systems are a matter of philosophy, though on the surface it seems to be a straightforward technical issue.

TRAP

STOP

Viewing Lean Systems as Piecemeal Technical Projects

The tools of lean can be very powerful. For example, many companies have done one-week kaizen workshops and found they can save space, improve productivity, and get better quality all in one fell swoop—great stuff! Some companies even calculate return on investment at the end of each workshop. Unfortunately, to get a true lean system requires a connected value stream that goes beyond what is typically done in individual kaizen workshops. And some of the returns on investment are more elusive. Do not attempt to develop a lean system by justifying every improvement piecemeal. You will find the low hanging fruit but you won't get a sustainable system that continues to drive out waste, leaving a lot of money on the table.

Learning Community

Within many parts of Toyota, TPS is referred to as the "Thinking Production System." When Taiichi Ohno started connecting operations to eliminate the waste in and between the operations, he made a startling discovery. When processes are connected, problems become immediately visible and people have to think or the processes shut down. Once the discovery was made, it was no longer accidental. The real power of lean systems, Ohno found, is that they bring problems to the surface and force people to think.

But this has a limited impact on the company unless what individuals learn is shared with others. Reinvention is its own waste. Thus, investments must be made in learning systems in order to capture the knowledge gained in trying out countermeasures, so this knowledge can be used again. And learning creates a new standard and a new plateau to build on for further learning.

Building a learning *community* means having individuals with the capacity to learn. This is the basic starting point. Beyond this, a community suggests belonging, and individuals cannot belong if they are short-term labor to be fired at will as soon as there is an economic downturn. Belonging to a community suggests reciprocity: a commitment by the individual to the community, and a commitment by the community to the individual.

In fact, Toyota makes very large investments in its people, as we will further discuss in Chapter 11. For example, it takes about a three-year investment to develop a first-class engineer who can do the basic work Toyota expects. Thus, an engineer who leaves in three years is a completely lost investment. The reason for the three-year investment is that Toyota is teaching the engineer to think, solve problems, communicate, and do engineering in the Toyota Way. It is not simply a matter of learning basic technical skills.

We see that Toyota views its own people in light of the broader philosophy of the Toyota Way. This leads to long-term investments they would not otherwise make. The philosophy provides the framework in which individual actions are taken.

Lean Enterprise

The philosophy just keeps building. Since 70 to 80 percent of Toyota's vehicles are engineered and built by outside suppliers, a Toyota product is only as good as the supply base. Toyota realizes customers do not excuse it for faulty parts just because an outside supplier made them. Toyota itself is responsible. And the only way to be responsible is to ensure that suppliers have the same level of commitment to lean systems, a learning community, and the lean enterprise as Toyota does. It's all part of the value stream—part of the system.

Therefore, Toyota makes investments in its partners that often seem to defy common sense. But consider what was learned several years ago when a plant that produced p-valves for Toyota burned down. P-valves are a critical brake system component in every car sold in the world, and Toyota had made the mistake of sourcing to one supplier and one plant. With just a three-day supply of p-valves in the supply chain after the fire, a total of 200 suppliers and affiliates had to self-organize and have p-valve production up and running before the supply ran out. Sixty-three different firms were making p-valves on their own without Toyota even asking. How much is loyalty like this worth? It allows Toyota to run a very lean supply chain with confidence that in a crisis it can mobilize vast problem-solving resources. This dramatic example illustrates the powerful strategic weapon Toyota has amassed by investing in a lean enterprise.

Value-Adding Contributor

What drives Toyota executives to get up in the morning, go to work, and make the right decisions for the long term? If their goal were to simply maximize their own personal utility, as some of the economics theories presume, they would not do the things they do. Jim Press, executive vice president and chief executive officer of Toyota Motor Sales, admitted that his total compensation was much less than his counterparts in American automobile companies. When asked why he put up with it, he said: "I get paid well. I am having a ball. I am so fortunate that I am able to do this. The purpose [of the money] is so we can reinvest in the future, so we can continue to do this . . . and to help society and to help the community."

Coming from most people, we would just smile and say what a lovely and completely unrealistic thought. But Jim Press meant it. He believes it. And as one of the top Toyota executives in North America, he can influence an awful lot of people based on that belief.

If returning a dividend to shareholders and paying fat bonuses to key executives was the only purpose of the company, there would be no reason to strive to become a lean enterprise. There would be no reason to invest in a learning community. Even lean systems would amount to short-term cost reduction through slash-and-burn lean. So the philosophy interrelates everything. And without all of the pieces, the 4P pyramid collapses.

TIP

Developing a lean system is similar to saving money for retirement. Effort and sacrifice must be made in the near term in order to reap the benefit in the future. The implementation process will require the sacrifice of time and resources now for the *potential* gains in the future. Like investing, the key to success is to start early and to make contributions regularly.

Creating Your Philosophy

Unfortunately, simply writing down Toyota's philosophy will not get you there. It is a bit like trying to get the benefits of the Toyota Production System (TPS) by imitating a kanban system or replicating a cell you saw at a Toyota supplier. It comes to life in the Toyota Way culture. So the hard work still remains. You must develop your own philosophy.

Certainly you do not have to start from scratch. You can build on what you have learned about Toyota—a superb role model. And there are many other companies and organizations you can learn from. But just as watching a great tennis player does not make you a great tennis player, what counts is what you do and the skills you develop. It is about how you behave every day . . . and what you learn.

A starting point is to get together and take stock of the current situation. This is always the basis of any Toyota improvement process. What is our culture today? What are its roots? The principle of genchi genbutsu says you must go and see for yourself and understand the actual situation. So some legwork is required. You have to go and see and talk to employees and managers. What is our real culture? How does it match our stated philosophy? There will be a gap. There is a gap at Toyota—we suspect smaller than most.

Now, what is the future state vision? What do you want your philosophy to look like? What is your way? The four-box model in Figure 2-1 can help you focus on all the essential elements. What do you want to look like internally and externally, in terms of people and the business?

For the business, you need to think about this in the context of a broader corporate strategy. You cannot be a profitable, financially healthy business without a well-developed strategy. Just the citations to the literature on strategy would fill this book. One of the chief gurus of strategy is Michael Porter. In a *Harvard Business Review* article (Nov.–Dec., 1996) he posed the straightforward question: "What is strategy?" He observed:

> Under pressure to improve productivity, quality, and speed, managers have embraced tools such as TQM, benchmarking, and reengineering. Dramatic operational improvements have resulted, but rarely have these gains translated into sustainable profitability. And gradually, the tools have taken the place of strategy. Operational effectiveness, although necessary to superior performance, is not sufficient, because its techniques are easy to imitate. In contrast, the essence of strategy is choosing a unique and valuable position rooted in systems of activities that are much more difficult to match.

He makes many interesting observations in this article. For example, he notes that you do not really have a strategy unless the strategy states what you will *not* do. What are profitable business ventures you would pass on because they do not fit your strategy? If the answer is none, you do not have a strategy, according to Porter. He also talks about systems of activities that translate the strategy into action, and an alignment of the systems of activity with the strategy—something that is very visible in Toyota's system.

If you have a great strategy that defines how you will be a unique value-adding contributor, you need to fill in the other three boxes. These speak to Porter's "systems of activities." To achieve this strategic vision for the business, what does operational excellence look like? That is, what lean systems are required to satisfy the outside business purpose? What kinds of people are needed to support this vision inside the company and in your partners? The totality of the answers to these questions will define the philosophy of your company.

Going off-site and getting top leadership to agree on your way is a great start and certainly worth doing. You should do some groundwork to look at your current state. You should look back in history at your company's heritage and what has shaped your culture. But having come out of such an off-site meeting with a feeling of renewal and a commitment to a grand vision is just the starting point.

Living Your Philosophy

The preface to *The Toyota Way* quotes Mr. Cho, who was president of Toyota and an Ohno disciple:

> What is important is having all the elements together as a system. It must be practiced every day in a very consistent manner—not in spurts.

How could he be so cruel as to raise the bar so high? Turning a philosophy into practice in spurts is tough enough, but making it so natural that it's practiced consistently every day can seem downright impossible.

To make matters worse, the responsibility for living the philosophy falls straight on the shoulders of a particular and easily identifiable group: leadership. All executives, managers, directors, supervisors, group leaders, or whatever else you call them have to live the philosophy "every day in a very consistent manner." Leaders have to lead by example . . . consistently.

To do this requires a major commitment, starting from the very top of the company. It is not just an abstract philosophical commitment to support "lean." It is a commitment to a "way"—a way of looking at the business purpose, of looking at processes, of looking at people, and a way forward in learning to learn as an organization.

The various commitments that leaders must be prepared to make are summarized in the 4P model in Figure 2-2, below. We show the Toyota Way management principles as a set of leadership commitments essential to moving forward in learning from the Toyota Way. Each of the management principles is associated with a philosophy—a way of thinking about purpose, process, people, and problem solving. When President Cho issued the "Toyota Way 2001" as an internal document, he was reinforcing the needed commitment of all leaders. Toyota then proceeded to develop a comprehensive training program to help leaders think in the Toyota Way. The training includes detailed case studies where managers critique a plant manager's approach to a plant launch based on all of the Toyota Way principles. It includes managers leading projects to improve processes using appropriate Toyota Way methods. No manager is exempt. It takes about six months, and it is one small part of reinforcing commitment to the Toyota Way.

Making a Social Pact with Employees and Partners

On the people side, if this is to be a community of learning together for the long term, then some long-term agreements need to be made. In Japan there is much less reliance on formal documents and litigation than we see in the United States. In Japan face-to-face meetings, word of mouth, and basic understandings between people play a larger role in commerce. Toyota has never written down an employment guarantee or a guarantee that suppliers will retain the business if they are doing a good job. But there is certainly a strong and well-understood social pact.

The social pact was clarified in 1948 when Toyota Motor Company president and founder Kiichiro Toyoda resigned. The Japanese economy was in terrible shape, and Toyota's debt was eight times its capital. Kiichiro tried to solve the

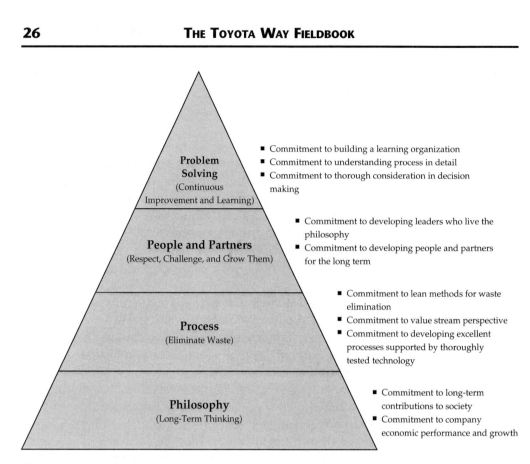

Figure 2-2. Top leadership commitment required

problem with voluntary wage concessions but concluded that he needed to lay off 1,600 workers to keep the company afloat. But he did it in an unusual way. He personally took responsibility and resigned first. He then got agreements from 1,600 workers to voluntarily "retire." This was very painful for the company, but the Toyota leadership vowed at the time never to get into that dire situation again. This is one reason why Toyota is such a fiscally conservative company, with tens of billions of dollars in cash reserves.

In *The Toyota Way* you will find the example of TABC in Long Beach, California, which was set up to make truck beds in 1972. In 2002, Toyota decided to move truck bed production to a new plant in Mexico. Cheaper labor you assume? Go to the Web page for TABC and you find that "in 2004, when truck bed production shifts to TMMBC, TABC will assemble commercial trucks for Hino Motors to be sold in North America, and beginning in 2005, TABC will assemble four-cylinder engines." Since that was written, it in fact happened. TABC is alive and there were no layoffs. There were a variety of reasons to move truck bed production to Mexico, but Toyota would not close down TABC and fire the workers who had done a good job for the company.

The commitment is clear: Toyota will not lay off employees who are doing good work for the company except as a last resort to save the company. Employees who are not performing get warnings and must show that they are seriously trying to improve.

Like all companies, Toyota deals with ups and downs in the marketplace. They use flexible staffing as a shock absorber. First, they have considerable numbers of "temporary workers" from contract companies. This can be 20 percent or more of the workforce. They do not have the same commitment to temporary workers as they do to regular workers. But they do have long-term relationships with the contract labor companies who understand their requirements, and Toyota gives these outside partners steady business. They also have affiliated companies in the broader Toyota group and can add and subtract labor through transfers of personnel.

The question for your company is very simple: What type of social pact will you make with your employees? Again, start with your historical understanding, which may be just fine as is. But if the reality is that employees are added and subtracted at will based on market conditions and simple ROI calculations on plant closings, something will have to give. Either change the pact or forget about becoming a lean learning enterprise in the true sense.

Maintaining Continuity of Purpose

A number of major corporations have made significant progress on the lean journey. It typically starts when someone with operational responsibility—a vice president or even a middle manager—decides to seriously investigate what lean can do for the company's operations. It's often driven by a real business concern, such as shrinking margins forcing severe cost reduction, or it can be opportunities to expand the business and a desire to minimize major capital investments. Consultants are brought in, someone is assigned to lead the lean initiative, and lo and behold, it works! It works in the sense that processes are improved, material flows better, and the needle on performance indicators moves—at least for the areas where lean is applied.

Success motivates, and there is nothing better than achieving the business objective. This can lead down several paths. One is to spread lean and strive to get even more of the good results. Teach more employees the lean tools, and find more projects. Companies that have done this find that they keep on getting improvements here or there but at some point realize it is not coming together as a system. They also realize that the gains are not sustained and technical changes are slipping back to the old way of doing things. To make it come together as a sustainable system requires another major leap forward. Top management must realize that lean is more than a set of tools and techniques. It is a way of thinking about the very process of management.

Companies that have made this next big leap forward from tools and techniques to a management philosophy and a system start shifting attention to culture change. What do we mean by culture? It is a *shared* set of values, beliefs, and assumptions. The key is that it is shared. And strong cultures last beyond particular leaders. Constancy of purpose comes from having a strong company culture starting at the top leadership level, and sticking with it across generations of leaders. Arguably, Toyota's basic management culture began when Sakichi Toyoda started Toyoda Automatic Loom Works in 1926. Since then, the management principles of the Toyota Way have evolved, but have not deviated in any fundamental way from what Sakichi believed. We are talking about almost 80 years of an evolving culture—of constancy of purpose. In historical terms that still is a tiny slice of time. But it beats most companies that turn over leadership every one to three years, and with each new leader comes a new philosophy.

So how can you get what Edward Deming called "constancy of purpose"? The answer is simply that it has to come through continuity of leaders. You need a set of aligned leaders who truly believe in a common vision for the company. You need to act on it in a consistent way over time. Eventually, if you do this, it will become your culture. Then, to keep the culture going, leaders who live the culture must be grown from within. This requires a succession system. Any leaders brought in from the outside have to start somewhere below the top of the company and be carefully developed and nurtured over years in your way.

What if you do not have committed leaders? You have to start someplace. And the best place to start is through actions that improve processes and deliver bottom-line results. Use that to gain management attention and start building support from the grass roots level up. If you do not succeed in changing the thinking of top leaders at least you will have some improved processes, and you will have learned a lot.

TRAP

STOP

Faking a Valiant Purpose

Many companies have off-site meetings where they proclaim motherhood and apple pie mission statements—satisfying customers, empowering employees, continuous improvement, and on and on. While a good first step, the second step is to take the mission statement seriously. Behavior that is contrary to the mission statement immediately signals to the ever weary employee that the commitment is not real. Credibility is lost and the mission statement is worthless . . . actually doing more harm than good to morale.

Reflection Questions

1. Gather statements of your company's values (Hint: The mission statement is one source).

2. Evaluate the relationship between stated values, beliefs, mission, and what the company actually seems to stand for. Consider the model in Figure 2.1. Evaluate your company's values and mission in light of this model.

   a. Is the purpose of your company narrowly stated in one of the four boxes, or across all the boxes—internal, external, people, and business?

   b. Do you have a clear and consistent social pact with team associates?

   c. Are team associates partners or variable costs?

   d. Does the company philosophy change with each CEO or is there continuity of purpose?

3 Take the opportunity in an off-site meeting, or arrange an off-site meeting, to discuss and write down your company's way. It should build on the strengths and unique history of your company.

4. Begin the process of educating all your leaders on your company's way.

Part III

Creating Lean Processes Throughout Your Enterprise

Chapter 3

Starting the Journey of Waste Reduction

Lean Means Eliminating Waste

Getting "lean" has become a corporate buzzword. A corporate executive hearing about the success of his competitors with a lean program might say to a subordinate, "We must get lean to survive in this competitive market. Go take a course and get certified on this lean stuff and come back and do it." If only it were so easy. The subordinate, often a middle manager or engineer, goes through the certification course, starts to sort out the bewildering array of terms like "kanban," "andon," "jidoka," "heijunka," "takt time," and on and on, and comes back charged up and overwhelmed. "Where do I start?" he asks. "Our processes don't look like the case examples they used in class."

Unfortunately, every process is different, and simply learning a template for setting up a kanban system or building a cell may not transfer in a straightforward way to your operation. Quite possibly a tool used by Toyota, as they use it, may not even make sense in your environment. This leads many people to conclude that "lean does not work here."

When we hear this, we ask our students or clients to step back a bit. We might both agree that building a supermarket and using kanban is not the solution. But do not give up just yet. Let's go back to first principles. The starting point on creating a lean flow for us is Taiichi Ohno's description, in 1988, of what he was trying to accomplish:

> All we are doing is looking at the time line from the moment the customer gives us an order to the point when we collect the cash. And we are reducing that time line by removing the non-value-added wastes.

We then ask, "Are you interested in reducing your lead time? Do you have non-value-added wastes that you can start to eliminate?" Obviously the answer is yes, every process has waste, or *muda* in Japanese.

The foundation of the Toyota Way is based upon this simple yet elusive goal of identifying and eliminating waste in all work activities. In fact, when you look at a process as a time line of activities, material, and information flows, and chart the process from start to end, you find a depressing amount of waste—usually far more waste than value-added activity. But seeing the waste is not the same as eliminating it. The challenge is to develop a systematic method for continuously identifying and eliminating waste. A sporadic removal will yield pockets of improvement, but the system-wide benefits that Toyota enjoys are achieved by following a cyclical method of continuous improvement.

The key to forcing waste from the organization lies in this paradox: In order to improve, the condition must be made worse. There is no way to become truly lean without a certain amount of discomfort. Unfortunately, there is no "magic pill" or "silver bullet" that will produce the desired result without sacrifice. As we will learn later, when we link operations together, as in creating a cell, when one process shuts down, the next immediately shuts down. The pain in any part of the process immediately causes pain for the rest of the process.

You might ask, "What could Ohno-san possibly have been thinking?" Some level of improvement can surely be gained without discomfort. There is always "big waste" that can be removed because there is no rational reason for its existence. As an example, we recently heard of a manufacturing company that wanted to "get lean" because of the enormous amounts of inventory after every step of their process. They hired a consultant who sold them scheduling software that figured out how much inventory they needed to sustain flow in their process at each step. They then made it a policy to limit inventory following the computer model. Inventory went down, and the consultant was a hero. Nothing else changed in the process, and there was no pain. Who can beat that?

Unfortunately, nothing else did improve. They got some savings based on the inventory reduction, but nagging problems of equipment downtime, long changeover times that limited flexibility, delays due to shortages of the parts the customer needed, and tons of firefighting were still the order of the day. So waste was reduced, but the root cause problems that accounted for the waste were not. And by the way, over time, the inventory levels began to creep back up.

Real success comes from an improvement *process* for identifying waste—understanding the root cause and putting in place true countermeasures to this cause. Unfortunately, this is much more difficult than installing a piece of software. Complete success is dependent on three things:

1. A focus on understanding the concepts that support the philosophies of lean, strategies for implementation, and the effective use of lean method-

ologies, rather than focusing on mindless application of lean tools [kan-ban, 5S (see page 64), etc.].

2. An unwavering acceptance of all aspects of the lean process, including those that produce undesirable short-term effects. This prevents "cherry picking" only those elements that do not push beyond the comfort zone.

3. Carefully conceived implementation plans that contain a systematic, cyclical, and continuous eradication of waste.

TRAP

STOP

We often tour plants that have put in place beautifully laid out cells, without a deep understanding of the purpose. In one exhaust system plant a cell assembled a complete muffler out of an assortment of parts. It was a "one piece flow." Unfortunately, when we happened to tour the plant certain operations had gotten ahead of others, and they did not have space for the subassemblies they were building. So they began to pile them up on the floor. Rather than stop producing, they continued to overproduce and pile parts on the floor. The plant manager smiled nervously and said, "We try to train them but they do not understand the concept of one piece flow." He went over and yelled at the offending worker, and then we continued walking. This indicated a lack of clearly defined procedures (standards), an unwillingness to deal with uncomfortable situations, and a lack of "stop and fix problems immediately" mentality. The plant manager did not truly understand or embrace the philosophies of the Toyota Way. He had gotten the form but not the substance of flow.

Toyota has identified seven major types of non-value-adding activities in business or manufacturing processes, which we describe below. You can apply these to product development, order taking, and the office, not just a production line. There is also an eighth waste, which we have included in our list.

1. **Overproduction.** Producing items earlier or in greater quantities than needed by the customer. Producing earlier or more than is needed generates other wastes, such as overstaffing, storage, and transportation costs because of excess inventory. Inventory can be physical inventory or a queue of information.

2. **Waiting (time on hand).** Workers merely serving as watch persons for an automated machine, or having to stand around waiting for the next

processing step, tool, supply, part, etc., or just plain having no work because of no stock, lot processing delays, equipment downtime, and capacity bottlenecks.

3. **Transportation or conveyance.** Moving work in process (WIP) from place to place in a process, even if it is only a short distance. Or having to move materials, parts, or finished goods into or out of storage or between processes.

4. **Overprocessing or incorrect processing.** Taking unneeded steps to process the parts. Inefficiently processing due to poor tool and product design, causing unnecessary motion and producing defects. Waste is generated when providing higher quality products than is necessary. At times extra "work" is done to fill excess time rather than spend it waiting.

5. **Excess inventory.** Excess raw material, WIP, or finished goods causing longer lead times, obsolescence, damaged goods, transportation and storage costs, and delay. Also, extra inventory hides problems such as production imbalances, late deliveries from suppliers, defects, equipment downtime, and long setup times.

6. **Unnecessary movement.** Any motion employees have to perform during the course of their work other than adding value to the part, such as reaching for, looking for, or stacking parts, tools, etc. Also, walking is waste.

7. **Defects.** Production of defective parts or correction. Repairing of rework, scrap, replacement production, and inspection means wasteful handling, time, and effort.

8. **Unused employee creativity.** Losing time, ideas, skills, improvements, and learning opportunities by not engaging or listening to your employees.

Ohno considered the fundamental waste to be overproduction, since it causes most of the other wastes. Producing earlier or more than the customer wants by any operation in the manufacturing process necessarily leads to a buildup of inventory somewhere downstream. The material is just sitting around waiting to be processed in the next operation. We should note that the main reason the first seven wastes are so critical, according to Ohno, is because of their impact on what we are calling the eighth waste. Overproducing, inventory, etc., hide problems, and then team associates are not forced to think. Reducing waste exposes problems and forces team associates to use their creativity to solve problems.

The remainder of this chapter presents a big picture view of waste reduction. We discuss it in relation to the broader philosophy of the Toyota Way. We also discuss value stream mapping as a methodology for building a big picture view of waste reduction. In Chapters 4 through 9 we go into more detail about specific tools and methodologies for waste reduction in the value stream.

Developing a Long-Term Philosophy of Waste Reduction

In recent years there seems to be an almost maniacal rush to "get lean," as if there is a finish line in the process. Rapid results and large gains are, of course, part of the allure of the Toyota Way, and there is nothing wrong with the expectation of large benefits. The problem occurs when the short-term push for results crosses paths with some of the philosophical elements, which require a long-term view.

For example, we have led many focused improvement activities, sometimes called the "kaizen blitz" or rapid improvement event. It is exhilarating to see the waste, come up with innovative ideas for waste reduction, and actually make the changes right then and there. The results are almost always astounding to the participants. The new process takes a fraction of the space, there is a clearer understanding of flow, often fewer people are needed, and equipment that had been overproducing is often surplused. The team disbands after a big celebration. But two weeks later the process keeps stopping, some operations are overproducing, the visual management board is not kept up, and it's business as usual, fighting one fire after another.

The typical problem is that none of the support systems were put in place to sustain what was accomplished in the one-week event. Skilled leadership is absent, for example. Standardized plans for reacting to breakdowns are lacking. There is no good process for daily equipment maintenance. Standardized work may be posted, but it is not understood or followed. The unseasoned manager who does not understand will start to revert to the old process, allowing inventory to build up and trying to drive production through brute force methods to chase the schedule.

The Toyota Way is to build a lasting learning organization in which problems are constantly surfaced and team associates are equipped with the tools to eliminate waste. When this occurs, you are developing a long-term capability for improvement and adaptation to the environment. A well-executed kaizen workshop can be a step in teaching people what is possible. But it should be part of a longer term strategy for developing lean value streams and ultimately a lean enterprise. One useful tool for guiding improvements based on a carefully thought-through plan is value stream mapping.

Value Stream Mapping Approach

Improving isolated processes seems to come more naturally than improving flow across value streams. You can see this in the way most plant tours are conducted. The tour usually starts at the raw material receiving dock, and we might see trucks being unloaded and then walk to the first process that adds value. The tour guide gives a detailed explanation of that manufacturing process, marveling at any new technology like machine vision inspection or laser welding. We walk past piles of inventory, hardly noticing, then take a detailed look at the next value-added process.

Often, a lean expert will ask to conduct the tour in reverse, starting with the shipping dock. This is not just a gimmick or a clever trick. Beginning at the end of the flow allows the lean expert to understand material flow from the customer's perspective. They do not want to know where material is going next, they want to know where it comes from. Is it being pulled from this process or is an earlier process pushing it whether it is needed or not? This will be the basis for the development of the "future state."

Lean experts will ask questions about the rate of customer demand [*takt* in the Toyota Production System (TPS)] and how many days of finished goods inventory is being held. They go to the final operation that adds value, often an assembly operation, and ask how the operator knows what to make, in what quantity, and when to make it. They quickly lose interest in the tour guide's detailed discussion of the nifty automated process that is continuously monitored by computer.

The lean experts are looking at the operation from a value stream perspective. Individual processes need to be stabilized, but the reason for that is to support the flow needed to give the customers what they want, in the amount they want, when they want it. Toyota's Operation Management Consulting Division (OMCD) was created by Taiichi Ohno to lead major TPS projects and teach TPS by doing. He wanted a tool to visually represent the flow of material and information and pull people back from dwelling on individual processes. Ultimately, that led to what we now call "value stream mapping," and what Toyota calls the "Material and Information Flow Diagram."

Originally, this methodology was passed on within Toyota through the learning by doing process—mentors trained mentees by assigning them to work on projects. There was no documentation on how to develop the Material and Information Flow Diagram, and in fact the name didn't come until long after the method was being used. Mike Rother and John Shook changed that by writing *Learning to See* (Lean Enterprise Institute, version 1.3, 2004), in which they teach the methodology by walking the reader through a case study on Acme Stamping. You learn how to develop a current state map on one piece of paper that shows your material flow and the information flow that triggers the material flow, and you can see the waste in your value stream. You calculate the value-added ratio—the ratio of value-added time to total lead time—then learn how to develop a future state map: material and information flow based on flow and pull and building to the customer rate of demand, or the takt time. From there you develop a detailed action plan and do it.

There have been a number of books building on *Learning to See*. Kevin Duggan, in *Mixed Model Value Streams* (Productivity Press, 2002), presents in a similar format how to map a process in which there is a great deal of variety in your products and they have different cycle times—for instance, variation in the amount of time needed to machine parts for different products. And for improving repetitive business-office processes, Beau Keyte and Drew Locher, in *The Complete Lean Enterprise* (Productivity Press, 2004), work through a case in a similar way to *Learning to See*, except the case is a business process instead of a manufacturing process.

TIP

Management Must Lead Value Stream Improvement

Use teams led by high-level managers to do your mapping. Value stream mapping can be narrowly viewed as a technical tool to design your lean system. But the real power is as an organizational intervention to get the right people to become dissatisfied with the waste in their system, develop a shared, realistic vision for the future, and develop an action plan they are enthusiastic about. A well-facilitated two to four day workshop can have wondrous results. The workshop should have all the key functional specialists represented who are touched by the process. It could be facilitated by a lean expert but in terms of content should be led by a high-level manager. The manager should be someone with responsibility and authority over all the main processes in the value stream being worked on. In many cases that means the plant manager. Some companies have organized by product family with "value stream managers," and they are the obvious candidates to be the content leaders for the workshop.

We will not try to teach value stream mapping in this book. However, we would like to share a number of tips we have learned in teaching and doing value stream mapping:

1. **Use the current state map only as a foundation for the future state map.** We are so excited about fixing individual processes when we look at the current state map with all the waste revealed that we want to immediately go to work attacking the waste. Fixing problems in the current value stream simply brings us back to point kaizen (see "Trap: Fixing Problems in the Current Value Stream"). You do not get true flow. The power of lean is in the *future state system*.

2. **The future state map represents the *concept* of what you are trying to achieve.** The map does not show the specific details of how it will be constructed. For example, the symbol for a supermarket *represents* the customer and the storage of materials to satisfy the needs of the customer. The actual setup of the supermarket may vary, depending upon the specific needs of the customer. We will explain the primary lean concepts that are depicted on future state maps below.

3. **The future state mapping needs to be facilitated by someone with deep lean expertise.** Unfortunately, the simplicity of the mapping method can lead us to believe that anyone who can draw a truck or a stick figure of a person can develop a good future state vision. This is no truer than assuming that anyone capable of using architectural software can design a great house or building. A group should develop the future state map, but someone in the group needs to have real experience with lean and understand deeply what is being drawn on the map.

4. **The purpose of mapping is action.** Often overlooked when companies do mapping is that little section at the end of *Learning to See* that talks about developing an action plan. Too often we see great-looking maps lining a conference room, but then go out onto the floor and see little evidence of anything we saw on the map. Our tour guide, the lean coordinator, explains that they just spent the last six months on the mapping phase and are now up to the implementation phase. We call this "creating value stream mapping wallpaper."

5. **Don't develop any map before its time.** Its time is when you plan on using it for action. It is better to develop one map for one product family and then implement the map for that product family than to have a mapping phase for a whole plant followed by spotty, inconsistent implementation. Start with one map, implement it, then work on your next map and work to implement that. At some point you will have covered all your value streams much more deeply than if you simply blanket your organization with maps and scattered activity.

6. **Someone with management clout has to lead.** The reason for value stream mapping is to get away from point kaizen, not only to improve individual processes. But who has responsibility for the whole value stream that cuts across individual processes? Generally, it would be a high-level manager; perhaps a plant or division manager. That person must be passionate about leading the transformation and be personally involved in the entire mapping process.

7. **Don't just plan and do, also check and act.** It's tempting after working so hard on the map and then on implementation, to sit back and feel like we're done with this lean stuff. Unfortunately, we've just gotten started. Whatever is put in place will fall back to a non-lean state unless we're

vigilant about auditing, going to see, and improving further. Once we have achieved much of our future state map, it's time to develop another current state map on where we are now, and then develop yet another future state map. You should choose time periods for the mapping horizon that encourage concrete action, for example, looking six months to one year into the future is more realistic than five years into the future.

TRAP

Fixing Problems in the Current Value Stream

The real benefit of value stream mapping is that it gets us away from isolated point kaizen and we can build toward a true *system* based on the flow of materials and information across the entire value stream. We teach this methodology a lot and can recall numerous cases in which we followed up with a student and heard the following:

> That value stream mapping is great. I developed a map of one of our processes we wanted to improve, and it revealed all sorts of waste. We did a couple of kaizen workshops, and the improvements were remarkable—we took out three people, we reduced inventory by 80 percent, and freed up half the floor space.
>
> We ask: "What do you mean you developed a map of a process? Didn't you develop a current and future state map of the entire value stream?"
>
> Answer: "We did not get that far. There was so much waste in our stamping department we started there and developed a current state map to show the waste and went to work right away. At some point we will get to the future state."

In other words, value stream mapping is being subverted as a tool for point kaizen. You will get a fraction of the benefit by improving isolated processes.

Benefits of the Value Stream Mapping Approach

Value stream mapping is more than a neat tool to draw pictures that highlight waste, though that is certainly valuable. It helps us see linked chains of processes and to envision future lean value streams. Underlying value stream mapping is a philosophy of how to approach improvement. The philosophy is that we need to straighten out the overall flow of the value stream before we deep dive into fixing individual processes. The point of improving individual processes is to support the flow.

The maps also provide a "common language" and understanding so that everyone has the same vision. Like a road map, the value stream mapping tool shows the road for the journey, but it is only a guide. It does not detail what you will find along the way. You must have a thorough understanding of the basic concepts and how to create processes that adhere to them. This is when it is very helpful to have someone who has previously made the journey. They not only know where they're going, but they can save countless hours otherwise wasted by taking wrong turns!

Developing a Current State Map

Developing a current state map seems a simple enough task. Just go out and document what you see. Show the processes and the flow of material from one process to another. That sounds easy enough! What we see in reality is people getting "stuck" in a mapping quagmire. Many people try to make the map "right" when in fact the purpose of mapping is to see that things are far from right. As we will see in Chapter 6, lack of standardization in the work area will at times make the process of capturing reality very difficult. Don't despair! The purpose of the current state map is to understand the nature of the processes so that an effective future state can be created.

TIP

Make the Level of Detail Fit the State of the Process

During the initial cycle through the continuous improvement spiral, data collected from the process may not be completely "clean." This is often the case prior to achieving a baseline of standardization (on the first pass). Many hours can be wasted in futile attempts to gather data at a detailed level.

For the initial current state mapping activity, keep data at a high level or "overall" for the process. Use rough estimates of key parameters. Process-specific detailed data can be gathered later, when activity is initiated in a particular area.

The main purpose of the first mapping of the current state is to understand the condition of material flow in the value stream and the inhibitors to the flow, as well as understanding the information flow process and the level of activity necessary to sustain it. The future state then provides a high level picture of the flow of material and information, which can be later refined when the process is stabilized.

Understand Your Objectives When Mapping the Current State

As you map the current state, it is important to evaluate the processes with the creation of a future state in mind. It is necessary to understand what you want to achieve when you get "lean" in order to know what the current obstacles are (this is the problem-solving method outlined in Part IV—define the current situation, identify the goal, and recognize the gap between where you are and where you want to be). There may be several goals that you would like to achieve with your lean effort. Here are a few of the higher-level objectives that are typical characteristics of a lean value stream. For your initial efforts in creating a connected value stream, these should be your primary objectives. Subsequent activities can focus on more specific point-kaizen improvements and continued elimination of waste.

1. Flexible processes to respond quickly to changing customer requirements, especially increased variety of products. Is the process capable of producing any part at any time?
2. Short lead-time from customer order to completion and delivery of the product.
3. Connected processes (see Chapter 5) with continuous flow and pull of materials.
4. Each value stream may have separate "flow loops" within the value stream that are identified by points when flow is not possible. These are dictated by the current process limitations.
5. Simplified information flow within the value stream that comes from internal customers (the following process).
6. A clear awareness of the customer requirement (the "voice of the customer"). In a pull environment, the customer (next operation) dictates what is done and when. The voice of the customer should provide:
   a. Required rate (takt time)
   b. Required volume (quantity)
   c. Required model mix
   d. Required sequence of production
7. Every value stream and flow loop within the value stream will have a "pacesetter" process that will establish the rate (per takt time) for all other operations.

With these items in mind as you map your current state, you will be looking for the opposite indicators of these conditions, or places where you can create the desired condition. For example, as you look at each process ask, "Is this process flexible—capable of changing from one product to another quickly (within a few minutes)?" Indicators of inflexibility include long setup times and high volume production runs. It's also important to evaluate whether the previous process is capable of delivering product in the required variety. As you observe the operations, identify the method currently used to compensate for the process incapability.

Inventory is commonly used to compensate for inflexibility. Toyota considers inventory to be an indicator of "weakness" in the process, and the inventory is a constant reminder of the need to strengthen the process. Many people misinterpret this concept to mean that there should be no inventory within the process. Ideally this would be the case, but realistically some processes are currently not capable of operating without some inventory. Toyota is always striving toward the "just in time" ideal; however, in the meantime, the philosophy is to utilize inventory strategically for the best performance results. This strategic use of inventory includes specific rules and controls, as well as location within the flow.

TIP

The Paradox of Inventory

One idea that is difficult to grasp is that in lean systems inventory *may* be useful (at least in the short term). We all know that inventory is one of the eight forms of waste, and therefore the goal should be to eliminate it. In fact, until processes are capable, the careful use of inventory may be advantageous. One paradox of the eight wastes is that it may be preferable to *substitute* one form of waste for another (like trading cards).

The key is to think about *where* the waste is and in *what state* it is. In other words, is it in finished goods? Is it in WIP? Does the inventory serve the process to achieve one of the larger objectives? Are you minimizing the waste as much as possible? It is preferable to push inventory back "upstream" toward the beginning of the value stream and to use inventory in those situations where it is currently not feasible to flow. Examples include processes that have multiple products and customers, and processes that are inflexible.

As you study and map your operation, identify inventory locations as well as the category (work in process, finished goods, purchased components, and raw materials). Each category of inventory is typically used to compensate for a specific weakness.

Identify where in the value stream the customer order enters the stream (where do you schedule?). How long does it take the product to reach the end of the stream from that point? If you are "scheduling" at multiple points, note that as well. Multiple scheduling points are an indicator of "push" manufacturing. You will likely see indicators of disconnected processes as well. Look for accumulation of inventory before and after processes. Is it moved forward (pushed) without regard as to whether the next process requested it?

Observe the processes within the value stream that are scheduled by someone from outside the process (normally someone from production control). Also evaluate whether there are any "informal" scheduling methods used. Supervisors often carry a notepad with the "real" schedule based on requests from other supervisors.

TRAP

STOP

DANGER!

As you begin to see the "problems" within your value streams there is a tendency to want to "fix" them. If you run out and start fixing these issues, you will be sidetracked from the primary goal—to create a lean value stream. Just because you have finally taken the time to look at your processes and have seen them with their flaws does not mean that you can suddenly expect everyone else to immediately correct the issues. The point here is to see the process as it is today and to understand what will be required to make it better in the future.

If you see people working outside the defined process (as with supervisors and informal scheduling), it is important that you recognize the real issues. People work around systems for two reasons: (1) because they can and (2) because they need to get the job done and the current method does not work (at least they think it doesn't).

Note: The exceptions are any safety concerns or immediate quality problems that cannot wait.

As you map you are also developing an understanding of current process capabilities. One of the objectives for the future is to create connected flow in the value stream. Observe each process, and determine if it is a "flow through" process: that it is capable of producing any product at any time without consideration or limitation. These processes are not constrained by long setup times or specific conditions that hinder the ability to process various models, sizes, or orders. Indicators of flow-through processes are the ability to "take it as it comes," and the work is not typically batched into similar groups for processing.

A good example of a flow-through process is parts washing since all parts can be processed similarly with only minor modifications to the operating parameters.

Identify the operation in your value stream where the specific part gets its identity. Toward the beginning of the value stream a part may be a "base model" for many finished goods parts. For example, an automobile body in the welding department can become any color vehicle with any interior colors to match. As the body is painted a specific color, it has a color identity. In assembly, each subsequent operation may change the identity to the specific features, such as interior material and option packages. Operations that create part identity will typically receive information regarding what to produce. Depending on the situation, this operation may get an external schedule (from Production Control) or an internal signal, such as a kanban returned from the following operation. Understanding these conditions will be important for developing a future-state-connected value stream.

The future state map in Figure 3-1 shows the seven fundamental aspects mentioned above. If we consider the basic flow, production control takes customer data and the amount of finished goods inventory kept as a supermarket and creates a leveled schedule for the final flow-through processes. This is the one point in the value stream that is scheduled. That process then pulls material from a supermarket, which then creates a production pull two steps back to a process that flows through first in, first out, to the next process. That process pulls from the supplier. This has the desirable properties of a leveled schedule sent to one point and flows connected by pull from the supplier through to the customer.

Your future map will not look exactly like this one. Do not compare this example to your situation and assume that you are unable to implement certain aspects of the process. You should strive to achieve the best result possible for your value stream and create a process that matches your operational needs. Rest assured, however, that all seven elements are to some extent possible in your value stream.

1. **Flexibility.** In this value stream the finished goods supermarket at the end of the process is applied to improve flexibility. It is used strategically to shorten the time from order to delivery as well (by shipping high-volume items from inventory). If you are a high-variety manufacturer, the use of supermarkets may be possible in some situations (e.g., for the highest volume products). Note in this case that Production Control considers both what is in finished goods inventory and the actual customer demand in developing a leveled schedule (see Chapter 7).

2. **Short lead-time.** A key characteristic of lean value stream is a very short lead-time. Note that in Figure 3-2 below the lead time is reduced by strategically locating a supermarket of components after the first flow loop. While inventory is considered waste, utilizing it in this manner both improves the flexibility of the value stream and shortens the lead-time. The inventory level in

the supermarket is maintained at the lowest possible level, and is eliminated when the value stream operations are capable of true flow.

3. **Connected processes.** Notice that the supermarket illustrates connecting two processes together through pull. The lane with a triangle, circle, and square also shows a connection. This indicates a "sequenced flow"—the flow of material from operation to operation in the same sequence. This is sometimes referred to as a FIFO (first in, first out) lane. These connections are specifically defined in Chapter 5.

4. **Flow loops.** The supermarkets will delineate the beginning and end of a flow loop. They also become the "customer" for each flow loop. The objective is to always satisfy the customer. Although the "true" customer is the operation withdrawing from the supermarket, the consumption from the supermarket represents the demand. In the case of a custom or high variety producer, there may not be a supermarket. The value stream in that case might be one flow loop from beginning to end.

5. **Simplified information flow.** A key aspect of a lean value stream is the simplification of information flow within the stream. Information is either external or internal. External information from the customer enters the value stream at one point only. All other information about what's needed to complete the work is generated internally. If supermarkets are used, the supermarket is the source of information. If sequenced flow is used, the information flows with the product. "Schedules" are dictated by one of these processes. We see below, in Figure 3-2, that some mechanisms act as the "voice of the customer." This information flows to the process to dictate what is to be done and when.

6. **Awareness of the customer requirement.** Awareness means an actual physical awareness in the work area. It is not a schedule on a sheet of paper. This will be explained further in Chapter 5, but briefly, it includes the use of signals (kanban), and physically defined connections between operations.

7. **Pacesetter.** Every value stream must have a pacesetter (called the "pace-maker" in *Learning to See*), and within the value stream, each flow loop must have a pacesetter. The value stream pacesetter will ultimately dictate the pace for all operations, but supermarkets act as a divider of flow loops, and thus require a separate pacesetter.

Limitations of the Value Stream Mapping Approach

When Mike Rother and John Shook wrote *Learning to See*, they realized there was a danger in getting this book out to the public. They were afraid it would appear to be a cookbook, making lean as easy as following steps 1, 2, 3. Unfortunately, the reality is far more complex. There is a reason that within Toyota you spend

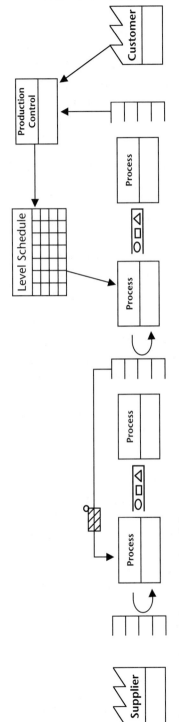

Figure 3-1. Basic example of future state

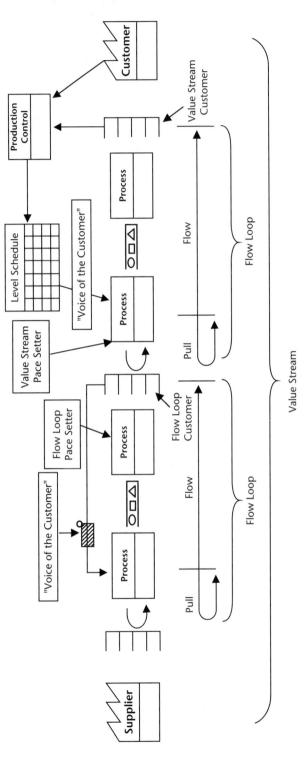

Figure 3-2. Future state value stream with elements defined

years in the plant working on improvement projects before you even reach novice status in the Toyota Production System. There is a lot to learn that can only be learned by doing. Mapping makes people feel like they're doing lean, but it is simply drawing pictures. To push an earlier analogy further, if I hand you a blueprint, it does not mean you can build the house. There are many skills involved.

Creating Flow Step by Step

Value stream mapping gives us a picture of how to put the pieces of the puzzle together to get a connected value stream. When we do specific point kaizen, we can reduce changeover time here, set up a cell there, put in a few mistake-proofing devices across the plant, and end up with little islands of improvement. But the big bang comes from setting up a system where material flows smoothly across processes based on the takt time—the rate of customer demand. The operations should be synchronized like a fine symphony orchestra. But how do we get to this point? Once the future state map is drawn, how should we proceed to implement it?

The creation of lean processes requires a methodical, step-by-step approach. The first step prior to setting up one-piece flow is to create a stable process capable of meeting customer requirements. The creation of flow, and the subsequent connecting of operations, forces problems to surface, and any abnormalities will shut down production. It is imperative that all operations achieve a basic level of consistent capability prior to the establishment of flow. If flow is attempted before this basic readiness, the result could be catastrophic. Do not aim for perfection, since improvement should continue once you have set up good flow. After one operation has reached this level, a second process is stabilized, and then the two processes are "connected," or "linked," making each process dependent on the other. This continues over and over until all operations in the value stream are connected, and flow with minimal stoppages is continuous from the first operation to the last. The continuous improvement cycle is shown in Figure 3-3.

This process is typically introduced in a "phased" or "staged" implementation. Initially each operation in the value stream progresses through the phases independently. After successfully connecting to other operations, the entire chain progresses concurrently. With a step-by-step compression of the time frame representing the customer requirement—weekly schedules become daily, become hourly, and so on—the process with the greatest weakness (most waste) will appear.

This repeated loop could be thought of as a spiral of deepening flow as illustrated in Figure 3-4. Each cycle through the phases results in ever smaller

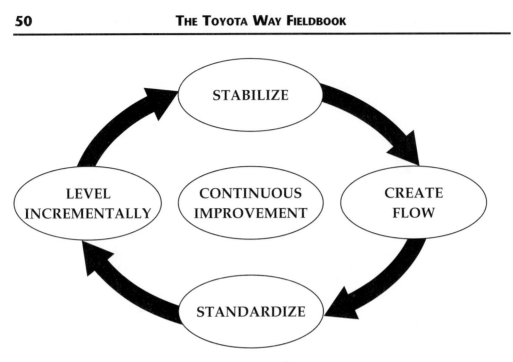

Figure 3-3. Continuous improvement cycle

TRAP

🛑 **STOP**

Don't Outrun Your Headlights

It is important to keep these dramatic improvements in context. Toyota has a deep bench. They are able to focus and leverage resources to create major improvements in a short time. If you attempt to duplicate Toyota's achievements, you may find that you have to "outrun your headlights." It is crucial to focus on the depth of skills within your organization rather than on a short-term dramatic push to results. Rushing to short-term gains will surely end in disaster.

---

quantities of waste, and in "tighter," more efficient work. At some point continuous improvement becomes a series of small, incremental improvements. However, periodic major changes in the environment or in the product will create instability, and then large improvements will be needed, starting all over down the spiral. For example, product model changes, the introduction of new products and processes, and changes in plant facilities will naturally create more variation, and thus instability, in the process.

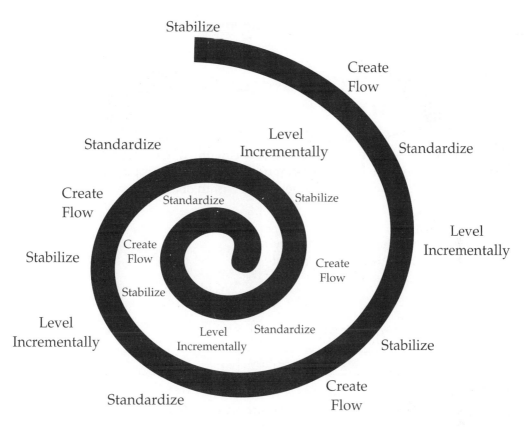

Figure 3-4. Continuous improvement spiral

Toyota senior executives in the period of 2002-04 intentionally created instability because they believed that intensified competition from low wage countries like China and Korea could threaten Toyota's global leadership. They requested major cost reductions of 30 to 40 percent over two to three years in their own plants and the plants of suppliers. Small, incremental changes could not possibly achieve these targets. Managers who had grown accustomed to fine-tuning stable operations had to take a fresh look at all processes and make big changes that created instability when moving up the spiral. We saw this while visiting the first American Toyota plant in Georgetown, Kentucky, in 2004. They had been so focused on growth in the 1990s that some of the TPS discipline had slipped. In 2002 they received severe marching orders from Japan to improve. The engine plant, for one, was asked to reduce total costs by 40 percent—an astounding number. But by 2004, they were well on the way to achieving these aggressive goals. And in the process, TPS was tightening up across the operations, leading to major improvements in productivity, quality, and safety.

Sequential and Concurrent Continuous Improvement

Initially the implementation begins with reaching a basic level of stability within one cell or line—known as "disconnected stability" (see Figure 3-5, below)—which is not connected to its customer process or its supplier process. If the process is a cell or line (multiple operations within one area), the flow phase can

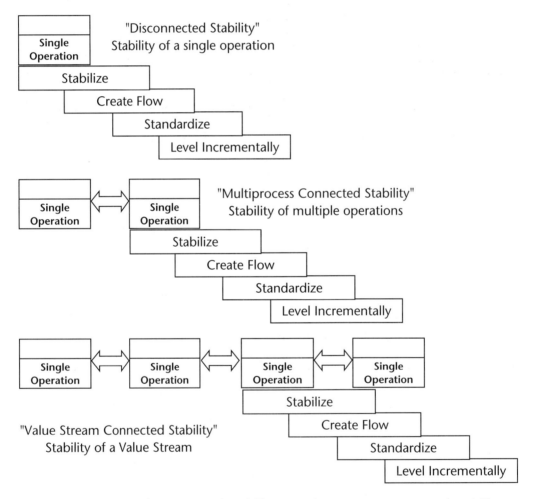

Figure 3-5. From disconnected stability to value stream connected stability

be initiated within the process. If the operation is independent of others, the flow phase is not initiated until "connection" is made with additional operations. This is "multiprocess connected stability." Connecting two or more individual operations, cells or lines, may create new stability challenges that need to be corrected prior to advancing.

Finally, as all processes pass through the first phase of stability and reach a capability level to support connection, they are connected across the entire value stream. This is "Value Stream Connected Stability." The initial process of moving through the Continuous Improvement Cycle to achieve system-wide stability and flow can take years of effort.

We generally recommend creating a fully connected value stream within your own plant or operation before moving out to your customers and suppliers. Once you have your house in order, you can begin to work with suppliers to help connect them to your lean processes. The same approach applies. They need some level of internal stability before it is valuable to connect their operations to yours through pull systems. And then you still face a problem if your customer is not lean and does not understand the Toyota Way philosophy. Educating your customer is certainly challenging since they hold the purse strings. But this can be done in small steps, and when they see the benefits, they'll want to learn more and you will become even more valuable to them. The ultimate goal is a connected lean enterprise.

In sum, waste reduction sounds easy but there is actually much to it. The purpose is not to simply make one pass over your operation to seek and destroy waste. The purpose is to create a connected value stream in which all team associates are being forced to think, solve problems, and eliminate waste. In the chapters that follow we will go into more detail on the process of creating connected value streams.

TIP

Multitask for Speedier Results

The time frame for creating a connected value stream can be accelerated by working in multiple process areas simultaneously. Think of it as building a chain, link by link. After each link is stable, the connections between them can be made. After a value stream is connected, an incremental reduction in pitch time (small leveling) within the entire value stream will cause the weakest link to "break" and become unstable again. This is the link that will require focused attention and a return through the continuous improvement cycle.

Reflect and Learn from the Process

1. Before you begin your waste reduction journey, take time to assess the potential challenges you will face compared to the potential rewards of success. Don't make the mistake of counting only the rewards. The road to riches is filled with many obstacles.

   a. Carefully consider potential financial gains (see Lean Thinking in Table 5-1 on page 89, Table 6-1 on page 118, Table 7-1 on page 138 and Table 8-1 on page 179 for estimates of potential gains). Develop a five-year financial statement that reflects the potential financial rewards and opportunities for growth.

   b. In every company there is a link between the employees, the customers, and the company. Employees who feel a sense of purpose and belonging are more fulfilled, and this will affect customer service and ultimately company performance. It is difficult to measure these items (the so called soft side benefits) from a direct financial standpoint.

      i. Identify at least two other potential benefits of implementing the Toyota Way that are not financial in nature.

      ii. What are the likely longer term financial benefits that will come from these nonfinancial benefits?

      iii. What are the specific challenges of attaining these benefits?

   c. Reflect on the biggest personal challenge you will face on this journey. What personal changes will you need to make?

   d. Reflect on your organization in terms of philosophy. Does long-term thinking exist or will you need to make changes?

      i. Identify specific changes that will need to be made. Incorporate action items into your lean journey plan (at least a five-year plan).

      ii. How will you avoid the "flavor of the month" syndrome?

2. Will the culture of your company support your waste reduction efforts?

   a. Identify the three strongest aspects of your culture in terms of cooperation, creativity, perseverance, communication, energy, commitment, vision, team spirit, and so forth.

   b. How can you leverage each of these strengths?

c. Identify the three greatest weaknesses of your culture (lack of items above) that may hinder your waste reduction journey.
d. Develop a specific plan for overcoming these weaknesses and incorporate them into your lean journey plan. Assign members of the management team specific responsibilities for improvement.

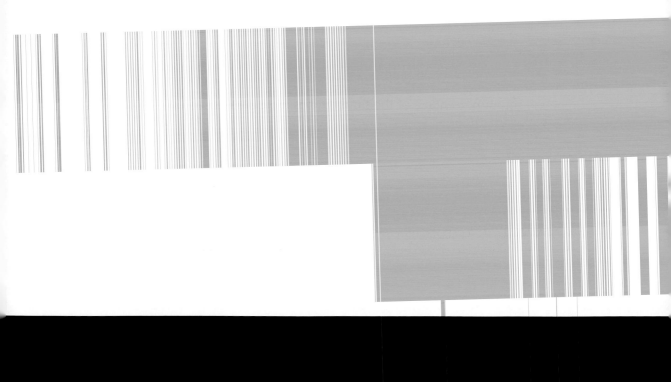

Create Initial
Process Stability

First Get to Basic Stability

If you have not already been using lean methods and improving processes, in all likelihood your individual processes are unstable. Stability is defined as the capability to produce consistent results over time. Instability is the result of variability in your process. It could be that equipment is not well maintained and so breaks down regularly. It could be that for any number of reasons defects are regularly produced. Or perhaps there is no standard work, and the amount of time it takes to perform a given process varies tremendously from person to person, across shifts, or over time.

The first step in creating lean processes is to achieve a basic level of process stability. The primary objective in developing stable processes is to reach a consistent level of capability. Based on the spiral model of continuous improvement presented in the last chapter, there are increasing degrees of stability. The initial level of stability is generally defined as the capability to produce consistent results some minimum percentage of the time. This is measured based on the outcome and is related to producing the same quantity of products, with the same amount of resource time (people and equipment), with a high degree of reliability (the exact level may vary according to the process and conditions, but a reasonable rule of thumb is 80 percent or better). A simpler indicator would be the ability to meet the customer requirements with quality products the first time through on time (again, 80 percent or better). In many cases the "customer requirement" is not clearly defined and becomes one of the first tasks of the stability phase.

Indicators of Instability

There is a wide belief that stability is indicated mainly by equipment performance. As a result, the pursuit of certain lean tools—like "quick changeover"—and attacking equipment failures through preventative maintenance become primary activities. Developing process stability is not an end onto itself. In fact, it's more about creating a foundation for further aspects of a lean process. Through direct observation, an unstable process is indicated by the following conditions:

- A high degree of variation in performance measures—either pieces produced or pieces per labor hour.
- Changing the "plan" often when a problem occurs. This includes relocating labor or leaving a position vacant when an absence occurs, moving product to another machine when a breakdown occurs (and thus not producing the planned product), and stopping work in the middle of an order to change to another order.
- It is not possible to observe a consistent pattern or method to the work.
- Batches or piles of work in process (WIP) that are random—sometimes more, sometimes less.
- Sequential operations that operate independently (island processes).
- Inconsistent or nonexistent flow (also indicated by random WIP piles).
- Frequent use of the words *usually, basically, normally, typically, generally, most of the time*, when describing the operation, followed by *except when*, as in: "Normally we do this . . . except when . . . happens, then we do this. . . ." (By its very nature, an unstable operation does not often experience "normal" in terms of consistent method. In fact, the abnormal becomes the normal.)
- Statements such as, "We trust the operators to make decisions about how the work is done" (part of a misguided application of employee empowerment).

It's important to realize that no operation will ever achieve a perfect level of stability, and thus to some degree these conditions will always exist. In fact, stability is not only a requirement for flow, but developing flow helps motivate disciplined approaches to stability—they go hand in hand. The main consideration is how unstable the process is, and how stable it needs to become in order to move into the next phase of achieving some degree of flow. Based on the spiral model of continuous improvement, during the incremental leveling phase the operation will be "squeezed" and a higher level of stability will be necessary to meet the tighter requirements. This, in turn, will force a refinement in the methods, beginning a new turn around the spiral in ever tightening cycles.

Clearing the Clouds

The Japanese are prone to using metaphors to describe situations. Toyota Production System (TPS) masters often refer to "clearing the clouds" when discussing the initial creation of a lean process. This was often compared to a photograph that was cloudy or unclear. Many issues often cloud processes that have not achieved a basic level of stability. They may or may not be truly related to the process; however, the *cloudiness* makes it difficult to determine this. Most important, these "clouds" obscure our view, and our ability to see and understand the true underlying image. On more than one occasion a TPS trainer was seen circling his hand, palm down, around his head and muttering, "Very confused," indicating the effect of many obfuscating issues.

Upon initially observing an operation, it's easy to confuse the activity seen with beneficial or necessary (value adding) work. People are busy, they're moving quickly, they're "doing" things, and it can be challenging to ascertain what the underlying true image should be.

Processes fraught with randomness and chaos tend to lead us to incorrect conclusions about what is real, what is possible and what's not. The ability to adapt to surrounding conditions is a human characteristic necessary for survival, which is fortunate, and yet it makes creating lean processes especially difficult.

By our nature, we adapt to our surrounding conditions and within a short time come to accept them as "normal" and no longer give them consideration. In many cases we even come to consider these conditions part of what we "have to do." Fortunately, we can be shaken from this paradigm, and when the situation is considered from a different angle, understanding is developed. Utilization of the lean philosophies and tools will force us to take a fresh look from a different perspective, and if we allow our minds to accept the new information, real transformation can occur. And then—human nature again—once the transformation occurs and we become accustomed to the new condition, it may never occur to us to reevaluate again and to seek another level. This is the challenge of continuous improvement. Diligent application of the lean transformation spiral model will force continual evaluation and removal of another layer of cloudiness in pursuit of the underlying crystal clear image.

Objectives of Stability

The primary objective of the stability phase is to create a basis for consistency so the "reality" can be seen and random activities removed, thus establishing a foundation for true improvement. This includes reducing the variability of the demand rate (prior to the establishment of takt time, rate of customer demand) and the creation of basic daily volume leveling. Additionally, each phase in the continuous improvement spiral provides necessary preparation for the development of succeeding phases. Thus, the stability phase is crucial for the preparation of the flow phase. Major impediments to flow must be targeted and removed. If connected flow is attempted prior to achieving stability, the impediments may be too large and the creation of smooth, consistent flow will be impossible. A stable process will also have a higher degree of flexibility and capability of meeting varied customer requirements.

TRAP

STOP

The Fallacy of Perfect Stability

We were involved as consultants in the early day of the implementation of the Ford Production System, modeled after the Toyota Production System. There was general agreement on the importance of process stability before moving to the higher levels of lean. There was also a strong belief that all plants around the world (over 130) had to move forward in roughly the same time frame. So the first year was spent on process stability issues in one model area that each plant selected, including 5S (see page 64), preventive maintenance, and standardized work. The first year extended into year two. It became clear that these seemingly simple tools required a great deal of discipline and understanding and the plants had little incentive other than "corporate wants us to do it and is going to check up on it." In later years this moved at Ford to a more integrated approach where flow, pull, and stability were better integrated in model areas. Process stability should have a reason—to support value-added flow. Reducing waste and creating flow will make stability a necessity instead of a necessary evil to please the corporate lean group.

On the other hand, it's possible to spend years trying to achieve perfect stability without moving to higher levels of flow and pull. Experience suggests that this will lead to cycles of stability: dropping back to instability, reattaining stability, and on and on. The reason is that there is no motivation to sustain the higher levels of capability because the system is not tightened to require the improved level. In a large batch operation without flow, a high level of stability is actually not needed and thus the only motivation to continue using disciplined processes is to keep "lean managers" off your back.

Strategies to Create Stability

Table 4-1 shows the strategies utilized during the stability phase, as well as the primary and secondary lean tools often utilized. Any particular tool may or may not be used, depending on the circumstances of the operation. The objectives and strategies, however, *always* apply.

Strategies	Primary Lean Tools	Secondary Lean Tools
• Eliminate "big" waste • Consolidate multiple waste activities to make it visible and provide focus • Improve operational availability (OA) • Eliminate or reduce variability	• Standing in the circle • Standardized work (as an analysis tool) • 5S • Workplace organization • Quick changeover • Preventative maintenance • Problem solving • Basic heijunka (level to daily customer requirement)	• Data collection and measurements • Story boards (dashboard, glass wall, etc.)

Table 4-1. Strategies and Tools Used in the Stability Phase

As we noted earlier, it is not our intent for this to be a "how to implement lean tools" book. There are already numerous books filled with excellent descriptions of each of these tools. Our objective is to focus on the philosophy and an understanding of the process.

Identify and Eliminate Large Waste

As mentioned previously, the identification and elimination of waste is a primary philosophy of lean. If this is a virgin site for lean, there's a lot of low hanging fruit. For example, simply using 5S to label where inventory should be held and setting visible maximum and minimum levels can have a large impact. Standardized work and 5S can significantly improve manual operations. Improvements in equipment uptime and reductions in lost time by reducing changeover times will add capacity and improve process throughput.

Removing the first, large layer of waste generally yields significant improvements in overall performance. At this point most of the improvements are at the individual process level, not at the level of flow-connecting processes. Subsequent cycles through the continuous improvement spiral will connect processes and can have even larger impacts, and reinforce motivation to maintain the stability of individual processes.

Standing in the Circle Exercise

Learning to identify the seven types of waste begins immediately during the stability phase and is reinforced by "standing in the circle," the exercise used by Taiichi Ohno to train new members. This is part of the philosophy of *genchi genbutsu*, which emphasizes going to the actual place to observe and understand. During this exercise, the member is directed to stand and observe an operation carefully, and to identify the waste within the operation and the conditions that cause the waste to exist. Members are often left standing for 8 hours or more before the *sensei* is satisfied that they have seriously seen the waste. Ironically, this is even harder to do when you're already familiar with the operation. Because you understand the "reason" that the waste exists, you will be inclined to rationalize its existence (why it is that way) and to conclude that nothing can be done to improve it. During the circle exercise it is best to simply acknowledge that the waste exists, without the need to explain it or to try to figure out how to "fix" it.

If the exercise is taken seriously, the amount of waste observed can be overwhelming. A common reaction is to immediately seek out solutions to remedy the situation. In Part IV, which deals with problem solving, we explain that the first step is to develop a thorough understanding of the situation prior to beginning corrective action. Standing in the circle for many hours will allow a thorough understanding, which is necessary before any true countermeasures can be identified.

The circle exercise may be likened to a distance race, such as the marathon. (Though we have never run anything close, we all know people who have.) About 20 miles into the 26.2 mile race, runners describe a sensation known as "hitting the wall." Some have described the physical aspect as a sort of "transcendence" of the body. The circle exercise is similar in nature. During the first few minutes to an hour, the mind is observing the larger issues and capturing the "big picture" and might conclude that everything has been seen and there is no need to continue. Stand some more! The real learning is just beginning. Depending on the individual, it may take four to eight hours before "hitting the wall" and transcending to a higher level of awareness. This is an extremely powerful exercise. Do not view it as merely "standing around." Rather, use it as a method of "tuning" your awareness skill. Once this skill is mastered, a shorter observation will provide a clear understanding of the details of an operation. Fortunately, it will not require eight hours every time!

Standardized Work as a Tool to Identify and Eliminate Waste

After you have mastered the ability to observe and identify waste, it is possible to document the situation using the standardized work tools. Often standardized work is thought to be mainly a set of instructions for the operator. In reality one of the most powerful uses of standardized work is for analyzing and understanding waste in the operation. The documented work procedure will be a visual representation of the waste (opportunity for improvement) that exists. It is part of the analysis that helps to remove the "clouds" and see the underlying image. It will also provide beneficial information for establishing balanced work flow during the creation of continuous flow.

In Chapter 6 we will provide greater detail on standardized work and how it's used to establish and document the standard method, but at this phase suffice it to say that the tools are simply used to aid in identifying waste. There are three critical elements in analyzing the work and identifying waste during the stability phase:

1. Identify the basic work steps.
2. Record the time for each step.
3. Draw a picture of the work area and the operator's flow within the area.

Bear in mind that the intent is to identify waste, and it is important to start with the "big" waste first. As an analysis tool, standardized work will primarily aid in the identification of motion (walking, reaching) and waiting (when the work cycle is below takt rate). It's best to first analyze from a higher level and then work down to a detailed level. If the work requires the operator to walk out of the work area, we begin by identifying this major component. If the operator walks within the work area, we begin with the walking pattern. If the operator is stationary (in a chair, or does not walk), we begin by observing his or her hand motions.

There are no hard rules about how to document the work at this stage. The objective is to record what is happening in such a way that the big waste can be seen and understood by everyone. The level of detail for describing the work steps is relatively basic. It is not intended to prescribe *how* the work is to be performed; rather, it is a description of *what* is happening.

Since we're looking for big waste, the general rule of thumb is to record each time the operator takes a step from place to place for walking jobs or moves his or her hands for stationary jobs. We are looking for the waste, and not necessarily the details of what is being done at each step.

After the steps have been identified, the amount of time for each step is captured and recorded. Separate the time into two basic categories: work time, and walking (or reaching) time. Finally, a bird's-eye drawing of the work area is made, the location of the work steps is added, and the steps are connected with a line. This drawing is very important, and visually powerful. Make it large enough to get a clear picture. Do not worry if the drawing looks "messy" with too many lines and circles. That's the point! When the picture is completed, look at it and ask, "What does it look like?" Perhaps the answers will be, "Messy, lots of moving around, lots of crisscrossing, backtracking, etc." Visually, people will see that the work flow is not good. If you are fortunate to have good work flow at this stage and do not see a messy picture, you're ready to go a level deeper and analyze for smaller hand motions.

Figure 4-1 shows a completed waste analysis, including the work steps, the work and walking time (in seconds), and the pictorial view of the operator work

Work Step	Work Time	Walk Time
1. Pick up A Bracket	1	2
2. Load Fixture (walk to fixture)	6	2
3. Pick up B Bracket	1	3
4. Load Fixture	5	3
5. Pick up Side Support	1	1
6. Load Fixture	3	1
7. Pick up Stiffener	1	2
8. Load Fixture	8	2
9. Pick up Brace	1	3
10. Load Fixture (start over)	5	3
Total Seconds	32	22

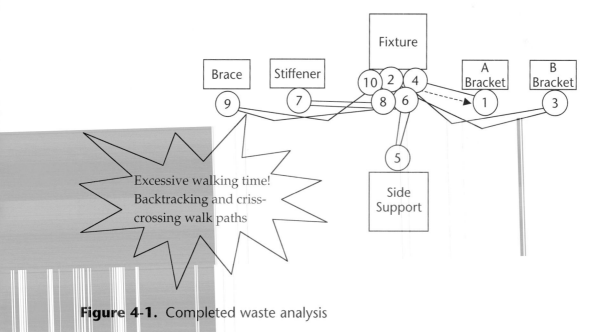

Figure 4-1. Completed waste analysis

flow. As you can see, the walking time is two-thirds as long as the work time, and the picture shows a nonlinear work pattern with significant distances, back-tracking, and crisscrossing paths.

Remember, the first step is to thoroughly understand the current situation. Only then should you start to identify an optimal condition (reduced walking time) and then work toward how to create it. There are many options and techniques, but the basic idea is to have the work "flow" in a continuous fashion with no moving back over tracks already made. (See Chapter 6 for more on the use of standardized work, including examples of the documents used.) During the stability phase the process is used primarily to identify the waste rather than to establish "standardized work," which is not possible until a certain degree of stability is established.

5S and Workplace Organization

We group 5S (Figure 4-2) and workplace organization together, and some would argue they are in fact one and the same, being primary methods for clearing the first layer of "clouds" by physically removing the clutter in a work area. Many people mistakenly believe that 5S is merely a clean-up initiative, perhaps because a clean work area is one outcome. The primary purpose of the first S in 5S is to clear the clouds, which involves eliminating the waste of motion from moving things and the waste of looking for tools and materials. However, other components of the 5S process—Straighten or Set in order, and Standardize—develop disciplined work habits that are crucial in later phases of lean implementation.

TRAP

Making 5S a Stand-alone Program

Doing 5S is fun. Doing 5S is liberating. Anyone who has experienced the joy of cleaning the basement or garage in the spring after a year of garbage has accumulated knows the feeling. But 5S is just one tool that enables stability that enables flow. We have seen too many companies make 5S into a stand-alone program with fanfare and rewards and signs everywhere. Stand in one place too long and you are apt to get a circle drawn around where you are standing. There is nothing wrong with being diligent about 5S. But well-organized and sparkling clean waste is still waste. You need to move on down the spiral and get to true leveled flow. Getting bogged down in 5S can be an avoidance pattern—avoiding the hard work of thinking about how to create flow and solve the real root cause problems inhibiting flow.

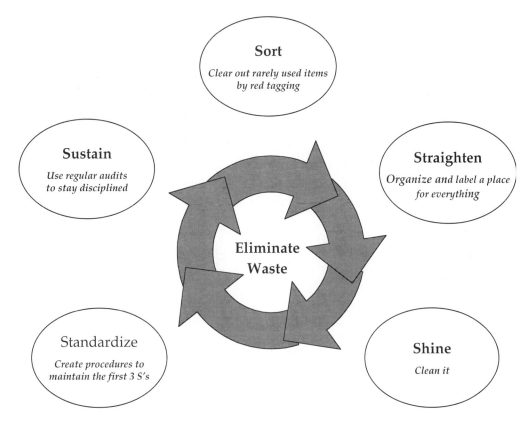

Figure 4-2. The 5S process

Consolidate Waste Activities to Capture Benefits

This strategy is often overlooked because of misguided beliefs. One such belief is that individual efficiencies can be maximized if each person works independently. In this way the problems encountered by one operation do not negatively influence others. As we will see in the next chapter, this philosophy will allow problems to be minimized, which makes the urgency to correct them also minimal. In addition this thinking allows for isolated waste activities that are absorbed by each person. Each operation then carries a high waste burden, and in many cases the waste is identical to wasteful procedures required at other operations.

Case Example: Consolidate and Conquer the Waste

In this example several operations were working independently to assemble various models of a product. Each operator had non-value-added activities in common with all other operations, such as retrieving material from the storage area, preparing the material for assembly, completing the shipping documents, and transporting the completed orders to the shipping area. Operators did this for themselves. Standing in the circle and carefully observing all operations revealed that about 20 percent of each operator's total time was consumed by these activities (see Figure 4-3). Multiply this across all operators and the waste was enormous. This did not include other non-value-adding activities within the work process.

Utilizing standardized work charts to analyze the work indicated that these waste activities could be consolidated to one "line support" operator, who would be able to minimize the waste by performing those activities collectively, thereby reducing the waste of conveyance. This meant that one operator was removed from the line to perform this "consolidated waste," which was at first resisted by management (see Figure 4-4). By streamlining these consolidated activities, the time required for these tasks was reduced. The line support function then had free time available to perform other duties, such as data collection and reporting, and problem solving.

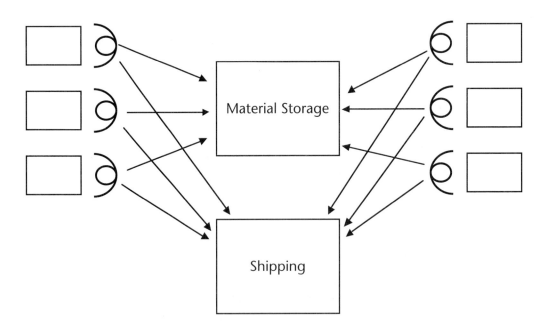

Figure 4-3. Each operator wastes effort getting materials

Line Support

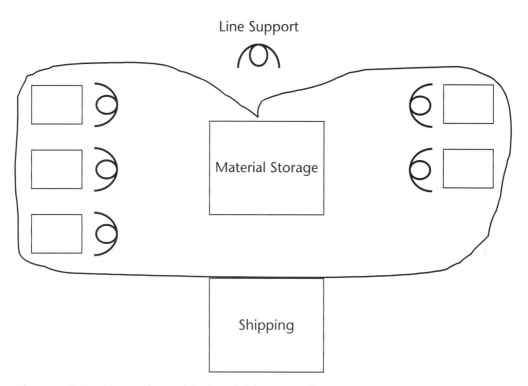

Figure 4-4. Non-value-added activities consolidated

In addition to establishing an available resource, the consolidation of non-value-added tasks creates a cyclical, repeated process for the pickup and delivery of material. This activity should be performed on a timed cycle, or pitch. This pitch is defined based on the needs of the operations and other factors and is the foundation for standardizing the movement of material.

Standardizing this activity includes what will be done, who will do it, and when it will be done. It is important that these tasks be cyclical and repeatable so the foundation is established for standardization. Once it is established, additional improvements can be added, such as specific containers and delivery carts, and racks for presenting material to the operator. Many companies get the cart before the horse and attempt to create the devices (carts, racks, containers) before they establish the process—a standardized repeatable method. Once the process is standardized we can then look for opportunities to reduce the labor required by rebalancing the work among other operators. Ultimately we usually find labor savings both in direct labor and in material handling.

Another misguided belief is that it's preferable to perform certain activities less frequently so that waste is minimized. This is most commonly applied to the movement and delivery of materials in a facility. There are additional factors that contribute to this belief, namely the distinction between "direct" and "indirect" labor. Within Toyota, all manufacturing employees have the same classification. They are all called "production team member," and there is no distinction regarding the type of work performed. All employees are viewed as assets, and the cost of the asset is the same regardless of the type of work being performed. Waste is waste, and the cost effect is the same regardless of job function.

In contrast, managers of other companies are more often evaluated based on their ability to control indirect labor costs, which means fewer material handlers. If there are fewer material handlers, the obvious solution is to deliver larger quantities to the line less frequently. In many ways, this method increases the overall waste, and the net result is a higher "total cost." (Most cost accounting systems are focused on the individual cost of labor, or piece production costs rather than the overall cost for the entire system.)

The case example below compares the two thought processes. The Toyota Way is to always focus on optimizing value-adding activity, and any system established begins with consideration for the operator and minimizing waste. We use the expression, "Treat the value-adding operator as a surgeon." A surgeon needs to focus exclusively on the patient, and when reaching out to request a scalpel, an assistant places the right tool directly in his or her hand. This philosophy leads to increased quality and generally lower overall waste.

 Case Example: Consolidation of Common Waste in an Assembly Plant

At an assembly plant of a major automotive manufacturer, the manager directed a continuous improvement team to focus on reducing indirect labor costs by minimizing the number of times parts were moved from a warehouse area to the assembly line. The plant manager was intent upon bringing the material from the truck to the line directly, with a minimum number of trips. It was hard to understand why he focused on this. It's likely this was driven by years of being beaten up by upper management to reduce labor cost as the primary directive. This narrow objective can often lead to eliminating one waste but creating other more serious wastes. In this case the plant manager was convinced that producing in larger batches and putting product in large containers would save material handling costs. But what are the other consequences of this "big box" mentality?

Reviewing Figure 4-5 below, and beginning with the value-adding operator, we see that the overall length of this one sample work zone

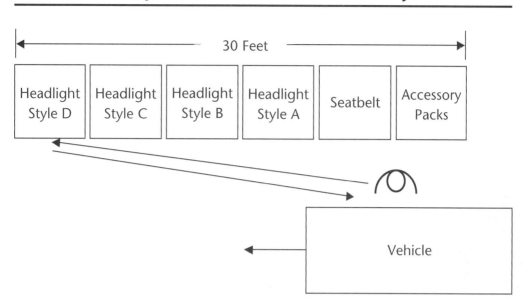

Figure 4-5. Long work area dictated by large containers

on the assembly line is 30 feet long. The reason for the length is a combination of the variety of parts the operator is responsible for installing and the size of each container. The containers are approximately four feet wide by four feet deep by four feet high. Because of this size and weight, only one box of each type part can be placed on a heavy-duty roller conveyor. Keeping one box for each type of part creates a huge amount of inventory line side.

Because of the long work space (three times the length of the vehicle), the operator has an excessive amount of walking. When there are about 20 pieces remaining in the box, the operator contacts the material handler, who is driving back and forth waiting for an empty container. The material handler brings the new container to the line, sets it down, and removes the empty container. Because the timing is not exact, the operator must remove any remaining parts from the container and set them on top of one of the neighboring containers. (Aside from the fact that this is wasteful activity, there's a good chance of product damage as well as mixing up similar products, leading to the installation of incorrect items.) The old container is removed and set aside, the new container picked up and set on the line, and the operator replaces the parts previously removed from the old container (again wasteful, and potential for damage).

A closer look reveals another problem. The indirect labor, which is the focus of attention, is actually not very effective. In this case the material handler is only able to service one customer at a time (the operator), and only one item (part) because the material is delivered in large heavy containers requiring a forklift. There is substantial waste in the material handler's job going back and forth throughout the day.

Also, the work method in this situation is impossible to standardize. Since the line will only hold one box of each type of part, the timing of the exchange is driven by the consumption of each part (which is driven by the model mix), and that timing will therefore never be consistent. It is impossible to dictate a specific time to deliver a certain part to the line.

Anytime it's not possible to standardize a job task, the result will be a less efficient operation. It is impossible to define cyclical work and to ensure that the methods are refined. Consolidating this waste allows the creation of a standardized process for material handling that also allows the delivery of a large variety of parts to many operators.

The Toyota Way is to begin with a focus on the value-adding operation. This view would conclude that for the operator to be most effective, there would have to be a minimum of walking and the operator should be able to install a greater variety of parts. This leads to the understanding that a greater variety of parts need to be delivered to the work area, in a smaller space, and that the replenishment of parts should not require the operator to remove parts from containers before they are needed on the vehicle.

A lightweight "flow rack" can be constructed that will accommodate a large variety of parts in a much smaller space. Since the containers are smaller in height, the rack is designed to handle multiple levels, as shown in a front view in Figure 4-6, and provides for the return of

← 10 Feet →			
Headlight Style A	Headlight Style B	Headlight Style C	Headlight Style D
Seatbelt	Access.	Washer Bottle	Rad. Overflow
Empty Return	Empty Return	Empty Return	Empty Return

Figure 4-6. Front view of flow rack

empty containers that are collected by the material handler. The rack is also deep enough to hold several containers of each part type, and the exchange and replenishment of material is handled without interrupting the operator.

Since each operator is not required to walk long distances, they can install additional parts. This consolidation will reduce the number of operators on the line by about 20 percent.

If these non-value-adding activities of many operators are consolidated and "pushed" out of the work area, the resulting waste becomes the burden of the material handler, who is now required to service many customers simultaneously and must create an efficient work pattern that will meet their needs. The material handler can drive a small electric cart that pulls a chain of dollies carrying a large variety of "right sized" containers for a large number of operators. Because this method requires smaller containers with lower quantities per container, the frequency of replenishment will be increased, which will increase inventory turnover, a desirable characteristic; however, it will not increase the labor needed. In fact, it is likely to reduce the overall labor requirement for material handling.

Improve Operational Availability

Often, we find processes that struggle to meet the requirements of the customer. The root causes are generally attributable to production opportunities that are lost due to the unavailability of equipment. The causes for lost time are numerous; however, they fall into two main categories:

1. **In-cycle losses.** These are losses that occur during the work cycle (as the equipment is operating). They may include excessive motion and equipment travel distance. One such case involved a spot welder who had a six-inch stroke when only three inches was necessary to clear the work piece. This extra distance traveled required two seconds *every* cycle. Cycle losses are generally considered first because they may be easily corrected, the improvement is immediate, and it is gained each and every cycle. Multiplying the small amount of time by the frequency of occurrence (every cycle), these small changes can amount to significant gains in operational availability.

2. **Out-of-cycle losses**. These generally occur when the equipment is not operational. The losses per occurrence tend to be significant, but the frequency of occurrence is less. One of the significant losses is equipment setup or a tooling changeover. The principles pioneered by Shigeo Shingo, known as SMED or Single Minute Exchange of Dies, can be used to

dramatically reduce this time. Also known as "quick changeover," or "rapid changeover," this method can be applied any time equipment is "changed" from one physical state to another. This may include tool changes, material changes, or changing to a different product or configuration. Additional causes for out-of-cycle losses are easily identified using a simple comparison of value-adding and non-value-adding activities as shown in the following case example.

Case Example: Improving Operational Availability at the Cedar Works

The Cedar Works produces wood birdhouses. The first step of the operation involves slicing the raw wood stock into thin slabs using a band saw. As a result of a sharp increase in demand, this operation was running seven days a week, 24 hours a day, in an attempt to maintain production levels. After four hours of standing in the circle, it was estimated, however, that only about 30 percent of the saw capacity was being utilized. The department manager, was incredulous. "That's crazy!" he said. "We're working 24/7! How can we get more out of this operation?" Having not had the opportunity to stand in the circle, he'd fallen into the trap of confusing "work" and "activity" with value-adding time, confusing the activities of the person and the machine.

To improve his understanding, we first reviewed the concept of the seven forms of waste (non-value-adding) and value-adding activities. Beginning with the easier side of the comparison, we identified the value-adding activity and agreed that the saw added value when the blade was cutting wood. We also agreed that there are other "necessary" activities performed, though they do not help achieve the end goal of cutting more wood. We then agreed that only when the blade is cutting wood is value truly added by the saw. Now the comparison was simple: On the value-added side we had "blade cuts wood," and on the non-value-added side, "everything else."

By standing in the circle and observing, we saw many situations when the blade was not cutting wood. This list was shared with the operators, who were asked to add any additional items that were not observed. We suggest standing in the circle at various times of the day and on multiple days to get a fairly complete understanding of the situation.

Figure 4-7 shows a side-by-side comparison of value-added and non-value-added activities. It shows a typical situation for any operation. There will generally be few items on the value-added side and many on the non-value-added side. This provides a large selection to capture

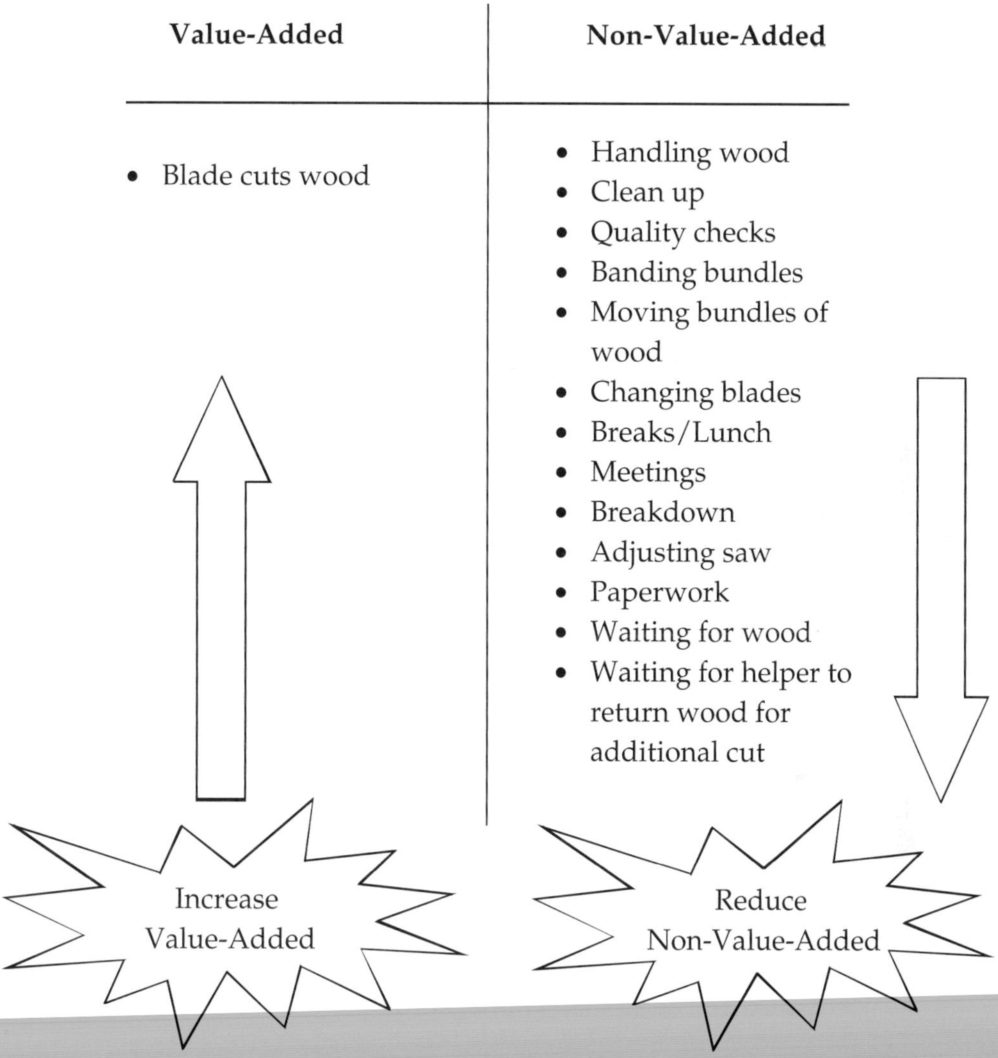

Value-Added	Non-Value-Added
• Blade cuts wood	• Handling wood • Clean up • Quality checks • Banding bundles • Moving bundles of wood • Changing blades • Breaks/Lunch • Meetings • Breakdown • Adjusting saw • Paperwork • Waiting for wood • Waiting for helper to return wood for additional cut

Increase Value-Added

Reduce Non-Value-Added

Figure 4-7. Comparison of value-added and non-value-added activities

lost time opportunity by shifting from the non-value-added to the value-added side.

From the non-value-added list we first focused on in-cycle losses—those occurring during the operation of the saw. The operators realized that simply changing the wood-handling method would increase the value-adding time nearly 25 percent. In addition, shifting activities that were currently performed "internally" (while the saw was stopped) to "external" (performed while the saw continues to add value) was borrowed from the quick changeover technique. These changes were easy to implement, and the cost was minimal.

Out-of-cycle losses were the secondary focus: primarily, reductions in time for blade change (quick changeover) and in cleaning time. The blade change time was reduced from 10 minutes per change (average two times per shift) to 2 minutes, and cleanup time was reduced from 30 minutes to 15 minutes per shift.

Reduce Variability by Isolating It

Reduction of variability is the key to achieving stability. Variability comes in two forms:

1. Self-inflicted variability—that which you control.
2. External variability, which is primarily related to the customers, but also to suppliers and to the variation that is inherent to the product itself (different sizes, shapes, and complexities). External variability may not be within your ability to *change*. However, you can build systems to compensate for the effects of the variability, mitigating the impact.

A common example of self-inflicted variability is the way many companies apply resources—people and equipment. Many companies that operate with the "island" method—with each operation working independently of others—have no way to fill a position if an employee is absent. This includes *vacation*, which is a *planned* occurrence. In most companies, planned and unplanned absences amount to between 10 and 20 percent of workdays. During these occurrences, planned work is not completed, workers are shifted around to the "hot" jobs, and other work—much of it already in process, thus wasting the time and effort already expended—is left to wait. Once this first domino falls, a chain reaction begins of chasing the hottest jobs and shifting resources (now people *and* machines), all of which magnifies the variation.

The problem with variation is that once it gets started and an "adjustment" is made, it sets off additional waves of variation, making it difficult to return to "normal." We should note here that many people incorrectly believe that a lean process is rigid and inflexible because the ability to make "adjustments" randomly is removed. We will explore this in Chapter 6, but for now we can say that the idea is that a standard condition will manage planned occurrences such as absences, and that response plans will handle unplanned events such as equipment failure—without negative consequence to the customer, and with a quick return to the standard method.

A common example of external variability is product demand, or model mix. The reality in today's manufacturing environment is a shift from high volume, low variety (HVLV) to low volume, high variety (LVHV). This creates many challenges since the different products require varying amounts of time and/or processing steps to manufacture. Balancing the resources (people, machines, and material) with this inherent product variation is virtually impossible without employing the concept of *isolating variability*. If you are unable to control the variability, the next best option is to isolate it, which reduces the impact on the whole. In the last chapter, where we discussed value stream mapping, we brought up the concept of a product family. In fact, separating products into "similar families" that belong to a common value stream is an example of isolating variation.

In considering methods for isolating variation, it's important to think about future steps. These will include the creation of flow and pull, as well as standardizing. The value stream mapping process is a useful tool for developing an understanding of the relationship of the different processing steps and times, and the effect on creating balanced flow later.

The 80/20 Rule

The 80/20 rule is useful when considering divisions in products that will isolate variation. The *time* required to complete the product at each operation is the critical element for the creation of future flow, so look at the products to determine where the variation occurs relative to time. To reduce variability in processing time we consolidate similar products based on the required processing time. Time is also the important factor in establishing the alignment of resources.

In fact, some operations are not affected by product variability. (We call these operations "flow through" processes, because all products flow through without any change in time required.) For example, a washing or cleaning operation is not affected by the variation-in-part complexity, or model type, and thus requires the same amount of time regardless of what is produced. We are looking for the operations that are most affected by the product variation, especially if they create a bottleneck.

The tricky thing about variation is that 20 percent (the minority) of the product often provides 80 percent of the total variation. This may be difficult to see, because the ripples of prior variation create new ripples. A great deal of variation can seemingly be "removed" from the overall results of an operation by simply isolating this minority—"seemingly" because the variation is in fact not removed at all, but the magnifying effects are reduced, providing greater consistency.

Case Example: Isolating Variability in a Low Volume Aerospace Supplier

This company produced welded tube sections for the aircraft industry, an operation with a spectrum near the extreme end of low volume (average order, about five pieces) and high variety (in the thousands). Long lead times are the norm in this industry, and the desired outcome was to reduce the throughput time through the bending and welding portion of the operation. Figure 4-8 shows the average throughput time by month. It indicates an unstable process, and the range in time is between 14.5 and 21 days, with the average near 17.5 days.

Using a value stream map, it was determined that the welding area was the controlling point in the flow. Observation and discussion revealed that the complexity of the tubes caused significant variance in the welding time per tube. This contributed to the fact that daily output in pieces varied greatly as well. Also, in reviewing the entire value stream, it was determined that the welding operation is the most critical, time-consuming, and difficult process, and is most affected by the variation in product complexity. These characteristics made the welding area a good choice as the initial work area for achieving stability, since performance in the other processes in the value stream were more capable and stable.

Evaluation of the products showed that while each tube is unique (high variety), they fell into common groupings in regard to the *time* required to weld. On the low end, tubes required less than 10 minutes per piece; the middle range was between 10 and 30 minutes;

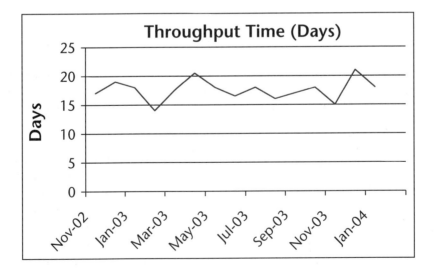

Figure 4-8. Throughput time prior to isolating variation of welding time

and on the high end, tubes required 30 minutes to several hours to complete (some could take *days*). From this perspective, the low-end tubes had a narrow range of variation and the high end had a large range. On a volume basis, 80 percent of all tubes were in the low to middle range, allowing the variation in time, relative to the total range, to be isolated within a narrow range.

This narrow range provided an opportunity to effectively align resources to the workload. The narrow range on the low and middle time tubes allowed us to establish a takt rate and then to determine the number of welders needed to meet the rate.

Since the mix of product varies as a result of customer requirements, it's necessary to be able to determine the alignment of resources with the workload on an ongoing basis. The "standard" was determined based on average volume history, which is a fair indicator, but current reality rarely matches the average. In this case, current "real-time" indicators were needed so that everyone could see the actual product mix at any time and adjust accordingly, in order to maintain flow.

During the creation of lean processes, it's often necessary to bring forward concepts from subsequent phases and to introduce them "early." Utilizing basic concepts of connected flow and pull (to be described in the next chapter), the team created visual awareness of actual demand by setting up defined locations and quantities of work in process (WIP) for each category (low, mid, high). Minimum and maximum quantities were defined for each location, providing a standardized indicator—brought forward from the standardize phase—for the team so they could make decisions about allocating resources. These visual indicators were added throughout the value stream so that each operator worked to maintain consistent flow.

Defining and controlling the WIP at each operation reduced the range of throughput time, and decreasing the quantities further will drive down the overall time. Figure 4-9 plots the results. Clearly, the process is more consistently achieving a throughput time of 15 days, and the graph indicates that the process is "stable" in terms of this performance. Having achieved a basic level of stability, this value stream is ready to move forward in the continuous improvement cycle.

Level the Workload to Create a Foundation for Flow and Standardization

As we saw in the previous case example, the establishment of product groupings in order to isolate variation is a crucial step in the development of stability and

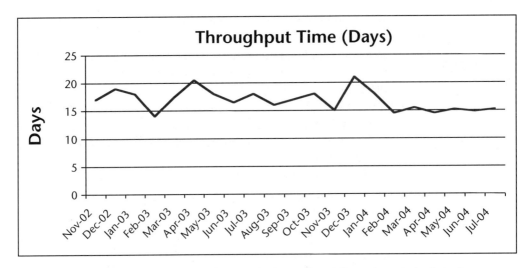

Figure 4-9. Process stability after variation of welding time is isolated

a foundation for creating flow and establishing standardization. In essence, this isolation of variation is a basic application of *heijunka,* or leveling. By grouping similar products, we were able to level the workload for the majority of the process. The highly variable work is still difficult to standardize, but in this case 80 percent of the total is possible. This is an important aspect of creating stability. Some basic applications of leveling can be done in the stability phase, and there are advanced applications of heijunka as well, that will incrementally tighten the timing and pressure on the system in later phases. (We will discuss this in detail in Chapter 7.)

One common mistake is to attempt to establish flow or standardization too soon. As we will go into in the next chapter, creating flow between operations is designed to surface any issues quickly and to make them critical in nature (ignoring them would be disastrous). If this step is taken before eliminating major obstacles, the result will be too many problems and a consequent retreat to the "old way." Likewise, an attempt to standardize a chaotic process with a high level of variability will most certainly cause frustration, since it is not possible to standardize variation.

If we liken the creation of lean processes to building a house, we understand that in order to support the roof, we will need walls and trusses. Foundations and subfloors, in turn, support the walls. This is easy to see and understand because a house is a real, visible, tangible object with common elements (they all have roofs of some type). A lean system, on the other hand, is not so clear. If you focus your effort on developing an understanding of the *intent* of each phase, rather than the application of lean tools, this process will be more successful. Understand the *what* before trying to apply the *how*. The lean tools are applied to address specific needs, and should not be applied simply because they are in the toolbox.

Reflect and Learn from the Process

1. Develop a current state map of your operation. The primary purpose is not to complete a map, but to *see* what is actually happening in your organization.
   a. List at least 50 examples of waste that you observed while developing the map. At this time do not be concerned with "fixing" the problems you see. Simply look and notice the opportunities.
   b. If you cannot identify at least 50 examples, walk through the process again, taking more time to stop and observe (repeat as necessary).
2. Identify one specific operation from your current state map where you believe the greatest need for improvement exists.
   a. Complete the "stand in the circle" activity at this operation for at least two hours or more (longer is better).
   b. List at least 50 examples of waste within this single operation. This should be a simple task. If you have trouble identifying 50 items, you're overlooking many examples of waste. Take time away from the process; then return with a fresh mind. Begin with the most obvious examples (big waste), and then become more focused on smaller and smaller examples of waste. If 50 examples is a simple task, keep adding to the list until you are challenged to find additional examples. This is when you will develop your powers of observation.
3. Identify indicators of instability in this one operation (chaos, variation, firefighting, inconsistent performance). Do not think about why these conditions exist or how to correct them. The purpose is simply to observe the current condition.
   a. Make a list of the indicators of instability that you observed.
   b. Separate the list into two categories based on whether the instability is caused by external issues (customer demand and product variation) or by internal issues (changes made that are within your control).
   c. Review the suggestions in this chapter and determine the strategies and lean tools needed to address the issues.

Chapter 5

Create Connected Process Flow

One-Piece Flow Is the Ideal

Taiichi Ohno taught us that one-piece flow is the ideal. In school when you have the right answer for the test you get an A. The right answer is one-piece flow. So just go out and implement one-piece flow and you are doing lean. What could be easier? In fact, Ohno also taught that achieving one-piece flow is extremely difficult and, in fact, not always even practical; he said:

> In 1947 we arranged machines in parallel lines or in an L-shape and tried having one worker operate three or four machines along the processing route. We encountered strong resistance among the production workers, however, even though there was no increase in work or hours. Our craftsmen did not like the new arrangement requiring them to function as multiskilled operators. . . . Furthermore, our efforts revealed various problems. As these problems became clearer, they showed me the direction to continue moving in. Although young and eager to push, I decided not to press for quick, drastic changes, but to be patient.

Ohno learned to be patient and deliberate about reducing waste while moving in the direction of one-piece flow, also called "continuous flow." Products that move continuously through the processing steps with minimal waiting time in between, and the shortest distance traveled, will be produced with the highest efficiency. Flowing reduces throughput time, which shortens the cost to cash cycle and can lead to quality improvements. But Ohno learned that one-piece flow is fragile.

Sustaining continuous flow also serves to surface any problem that would inhibit that flow. In essence, the creation of flow *forces* the correction of problems, resulting in reduced waste. We often use the analogy of a ship on a sea filled with dangerous rocks. As long as the rocks, like problems, are covered with water, like inventory, it's smooth sailing. But if the water level is lowered, the ship can quickly be demolished by running into the rocks. In most operations there are boulders hovering just under the surface, so naturally we keep enough inventory to hide the problems.

Ohno discovered that if he reduced the inventory, the problems surfaced, and people were forced to solve them or the system was forced to stop producing. This was a good thing, as long as the damage was not too severe and the people had the capability to improve the process so that the problems did not recur. He also learned that the system needed some minimal level of stability, or the reduction of inventory would just result in a loss of production, as we saw in Chapter 4.

Connecting two or more processes into a continuous flow will increase the severity of any problems and necessitate their elimination. Connected flow across the enterprise means that production in the *entire* facility—and perhaps across multiple facilities—will be shut down if the problems are not corrected effectively. Imagine the importance of equipment readiness, manpower availability, and material supply when thousands of people all stop working if there is a failure! At Toyota this occurs from time to time. The entire operation is connected, and so within a few hours a problem with a main component will halt the entire facility.

Many organizations believe that this type of production stoppage is unacceptable. Stopping production is a sure ticket to the unemployment office. But Toyota sees it as an opportunity to identify a weakness within the system, to attack the weakness, and to strengthen the overall system. It is this counterintuitive thinking that perplexes bottom-line thinkers. The Toyota Way suggests that "failing" and correcting the shortcoming is a way to improve results for the long term. Traditional thinking, in contrast, is that success is achieved by never allowing "failure" to affect the short-term result.

That said, the objective is not to entirely jeopardize performance. It is wise to prepare for flow by eliminating major issues, and to move with careful intent and understanding, beginning with planning, and developing the discipline for solving problems. As the process improves, and develops capability, the control parameters are compressed during the leveling phase to surface the next layer of issues in an ongoing cycle of continuous improvement.

Why Flow?

Most often the failure of implementation stems from a misguided belief that success is rooted in the application of lean tools (such as setting up the cell). We often tour clients through lean plants, in some cases Toyota plants, and it's interesting to hear what they get out of the tour. They have overall impressions of cleanliness, orderliness, precision, and people engaged by their work. But their eyes light up when they see something they can directly apply in their plants.

One time, someone noted how a lean plant kept small cabinets of expendable materials by each work cell and the cell leader signed out materials as needed. A kanban system was used to replenish things like plastic gloves. The "industrial tourist" was excited about going back and setting up a similar system for expendable materials in his plant. Unfortunately, he had noticed only one specific tool, and failed to see the interconnectedness and interdependence of all the various elements. Successful creation of lean processes is derived from a deep understanding of how each tool is utilized to accomplish an end objective. A trained mechanic does not bring a wrench to the car and then find a nut to loosen. He first determines the nature of the problem, what will need to be done to correct it, and then selects the appropriate tools to complete the job.

Yet we often see organizations place the tool before the understanding. "We are going to implement visual control," managers say, as if it were an individual piece of a jigsaw puzzle to be added. A key to long-term success is a combined effort that includes understanding the primary philosophy or concept, an effective strategy that necessitates the concept (it must become mandatory), a methodology for applying the concept, lean tools that support the method, and an effective way to measure the overall result.

We find it helpful to think about the relationship between one-piece flow and waste reduction in the context of a broader model as shown in Figure 5-1. Rather than leap into implementing tools for flow and pull, step back and understand the purpose. This model emphasizes the relationship between the primary principle of lean—the identification and elimination of waste—and the method for achieving that objective—reducing batch size to move toward continuous flow. The creation of continuous flow is often thought to be a primary objective when creating a lean process, but in reality, the creation of continuous flow is designed to drive waste from any operation: Waste elimination is the primary objective.

When material and information flow continuously, there is less waste in the operation. This is true by definition. If there were a lot of waste, material and information would not be flowing. However, there is something more profound happening here. Maintaining continuous flow between processes will create a linkage, making each process dependent on the other. This interdependency and the relatively small amount of buffering make any condition that interrupts the flow more critical.

Anyone who has attempted to implement one-piece flow (a difficult task indeed!) understands that heightening the level of problems can be of great benefit . . . or of great harm. If effective systems are not in place to support the operation, the severity of problems will surely spell doom. This is the time when lean tools must be applied to provide the necessary structure to ensure success rather than failure. The lean tools can help by providing both support systems and control methods to react appropriately to the problems that surface.

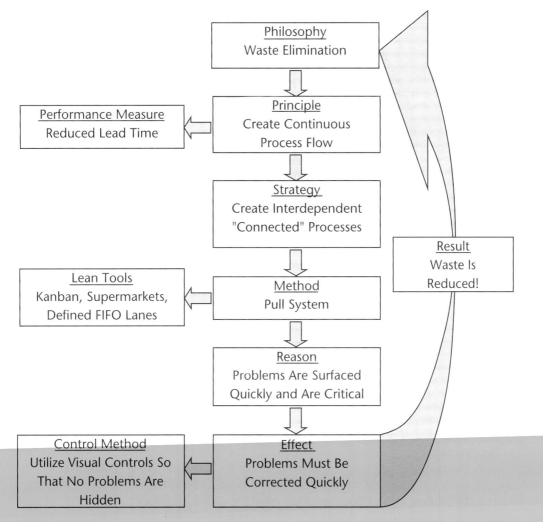

Figure 5-1. Waste reduction model

Less Is More: Reduce Waste by Controlling Overproduction

In a true one-piece flow, each operation only builds what the next operation needs. If the next operation gets backed up for some reason, then preceding operations actually stop. It seems that nothing can be more uncomfortable in a traditional manufacturing operation than stopping. Yet the alternative to stopping is overproducing—producing more, sooner, or in greater quantity than the next operation requires. Toyota considers overproduction to be the worst of the seven types of waste because it leads to the other six types of waste (inventory, movement, handling, hidden defects, etc.). This is the key to understanding how less can be more (less means fewer parts produced in some individual steps in the process, more means getting more value-added activity done from the overall process). The case example below explains a typical situation of overproduction that reduced the ability to meet the customer requirement.

Case Example: Control Overproduction to Improve Operational Availability

While standing in the circle and observing a fabrication line, it was clear that overproduction was rampant. The line was filled with product, much of it stacked two and three layers deep. The workers were all busy, but we could see that the operators overproducing were engaged in "busy work" such as stacking and positioning the excess product. Operators typically reached a point when no additional work would fit on the line, and then excess time was spent care-tending the overproduction (inventory). Cycle time comparisons to takt time revealed— no surprise—that these operations were below the takt time and had extra time available. Since they were not provided with additional value-adding tasks, the operators filled their extra time by overproducing and care tending.

Observation also showed that the process downstream of the overproduction (the customer) had to spend additional time moving and unstacking the product that was poorly presented in large batches. The cycle time of this operation was at takt time, but with the additional work required to move and unstack product, the total time actually exceeded the takt time. It could not achieve customer demand during scheduled work hours. In this case, the supplier process created the excess waste, but the negative effect was realized at the customer process.

We asked the operators at the initial operations to stop, and to stand doing *nothing*, rather than to continue producing when the next process had more than enough material to work with. It is, of course, very uncomfortable for operators to do nothing because they've been conditioned by management to "keep busy." Toyota stresses the importance of this concept because it allows everyone to see and understand the amount of opportunity available. Everyone can see the idle time because it is not being *clouded* by busy work (overproduction).

By having these operators do *less* (make fewer parts), the customer operations also had less wasted time and were able to convert that time to *more* production. The total output of the entire operation increased significantly by simply controlling overproduction.

Of course, we were not satisfied to have operators standing around with idle time—the waste of waiting. The next step was to determine how to eliminate additional waste from these operations, and to combine operations and achieve "full work." For this task standardized work analysis similar to the example described in Chapter 4 was used.

Case Example: Making Aircraft Repair Flow at Jacksonville Naval Air Depot

Repair operations have even more variability than manufacturing. Until you break into the equipment, you don't exactly know what the problem is or how long it will take. So repair is often treated as a craft process: Get a team of expert repair persons to work on each piece of equipment. It is a return to the old days of the Model T, when a team of craftsmen stood around a stand and built the car in place.

The U.S. Department of Defense does a tremendous amount of repair and overhaul of ships, submarines, tanks, weapon systems, and aircraft. These are very large things. There is almost always urgency getting a plane out. A fighter plane being repaired in a hangar is one less plane available for combat.

The largest employer in Jacksonville, Florida, is a Naval Air Depot where aircraft is repaired for the Navy. Aircraft need to be completely overhauled at periodic intervals, and some aircraft have serious weaknesses that require specific repairs. Because of the urgency of getting planes overhauled, repaired, and back in service, when a plane comes in, it's brought into a hanger, and skilled personnel attack it, taking it apart. Each plane sits in position and is dismantled, parts are repaired or replaced, everything is tested piece by piece, and it is finally reassembled and flown back into the field. Another motivation to get to work on the plane immediately is to get paid. The base gets paid based on charging hours for working on planes.

While the base had decades of experience repairing aircraft, the pressure to reduce the time aircraft spend on the ground was intense. In some cases aircraft are discontinued, and there are then a limited number available in service. If the planes spend too much time in the repair hangar, there won't be enough to fly the scheduled missions. A program called

"Air Speed" was started at headquarters to speed up the process of repairing aircraft at NAVAIR facilities.

Two aircraft repaired at Jacksonville were the F18 and the P3 fighters, worked on in different hangers. Lean manufacturing experts were hired as consultants to lead internal lean teams and develop internal expertise. Independently, they analyzed the current situation for the P3 and F18. Their conclusions were the same:

♦ Each plane was treated as a unique project, with craftsmen working in place, in no particular standardized process.

♦ The work area around the plane was disorganized with tools and parts lying every which way.

♦ Repair people spent an inordinate amount of time walking to get tools and parts and indirect materials.

♦ When the plane was disassembled, parts were tossed into boxes that were sent to storage (e.g., an automated storage and retrieval system), and then when the parts were brought out for reassembly, much time was spent sorting through boxes, looking for parts. Parts were often missing because they were "robbed" to work on another plane.

♦ Many planes were being worked on at once, and when they got stuck on one for some reason (e.g., needed key parts), they shifted to work on another.

♦ There was a belief that the planes came in for repair unpredictably and that it was impossible to plan for a stable, leveled amount of work.

Value stream mapping revealed a huge amount of waste in the current processes. Future state maps were developed and similar solutions were presented for all the aircraft:

♦ The process of disassembly, inspection, repair, and reassembly needed to be separated into distinct phases.

♦ A flow line needed to be set up with planes at different stations, and specific work done at each station.

♦ The line then needed to be balanced to a takt time. Analysis of actual data showed the arrival of planes was far more stable than previously believed.

♦ Standardized work needed to be developed at each station.

♦ 5S was needed to stabilize the process and reduce much of the non-value-added walking and getting stuff.

♦ A "hospital" position was needed so that if the workers got stuck on one of the planes (e.g., waiting for a long-lead-time part), the plane could be set aside in the hospital and the flow would not stop.

◆ Management needed to be educated in the process and stop the practice of bringing in additional aircraft whenever one arrived. They needed to control the work in process limiting aircraft to the number of stations in the flow lines (discussed later).

The work areas were laid out into workstations. There was a technical challenge in moving the plane from station to station. At some point the plane was taken apart and the center barrel and wings were removed, along with the wheels. The F18 was a new aircraft for the base, and they were able to purchase a system that held the plane together on a big fixture on wheels so it could be moved from position to position. This was not the case with the P3, so in its case a decision was made to use a "virtual flow line." That is, teams of repair persons would come to each aircraft at fixed intervals of time to perform a stage of work. This meant they would have to bring in the tools and materials needed for each phase of the process.

Kaizen workshops were used to set up each piece of the overall system. There were 5S workshops to lay out the area, find places for everything, and label standard positions. There were material flow workshops to take parts off the plane and put them into "shadow boxes" or kits, so when they were brought back for reassembly they were organized. Hazardous materials were set out on carts in kits. All the kits and parts and materials were set up on pull systems to be replenished as they were utilized. The slow and complex process of analyzing each procedure in detail to develop standardized work was started so that each station could be aligned with the takt time.

The P3 is an older plane soon to be retired. The Navy decided to reduce the available planes in the fleet by over 50, from 200 to 150, yet wanted a constant number in the field (about 120). This required less time tied up in maintenance to keep the planes needed in the fleet available. Due to some fuel tank and structural integrity problems associated with aging, additional stress testing and repair requirements were added, increasing the pressure—doing more in less time. In short, from the Navy's perspective this was a crisis, and from a lean perspective an ideal opportunity to show the value of waste elimination.

Repairing these aircraft prior to the additional testing and repair requirements took 247 calendar days. To meet the 120 planes needed in the field at all times required a reduction in turnaround to 173 days, a 30 percent improvement.

In April 2004 the lean activities formally started under the direction of an experienced lean consultant.[1] After value stream mapping and

---

[1] The consultant was Ed Kemmerling, who was later joined by Sam Talerico, both with many years of experience applying lean methods at Ford Motor Company.

numerous kaizen events, significant results were already evident by February 2005, less than one year later, as can be seen in the table below.

	Pre-Lean (4/04)	Post Lean (2/05)
Planes in hanger (WIP)	10 planes	8 planes
Takt time	Nonexistent	15 days
Lead time when takt achieved	—	120 days
Actual lead time (calendar days)	247 days	200 days (on track for target of 173 days)
Additional Results		Reduced cost and manpower

Setting up the process was one thing. Managing it was another. It required a different approach to management than the current leaders were used to. While there were many different things to manage—5S, standardized work, problem resolution processes, etc.—one of the toughest challenges was fighting the urge to bring in more aircraft. The flow concept was based on a fixed amount of WIP (work in process). That is, there were a certain number of positions and a hospital, and there should be no other aircraft in the hangar. When one plane was finished and taken out of the hanger, one more could be brought in.

This was counter to just about every instinct of the leaders and counter to the measurement system. First, they believed if they left a plane outside, it would take longer to get it fixed. The lean project in fact had shown the opposite—lead time could be reduced in a major way by working on a specific number of aircraft and leaving any additional outside of the hanger until there was a place opened up at the beginning of the line. Second, there were times when people were not busy working on the planes, since all the work that needed to get done was done on the aircraft in process. This was feared because the leaders were judged based on charging direct labor hours, which also justified having indirect labor in the hangar. At various times when a new plane came in, some higher level leader would at first order the plane to be taken into the shop. The lean consultants had to use their influence to get the plane taken back out. It was clearly a major cultural clash.

The results were quite astounding to the Navy. The Jacksonville base quickly became a preferred tour site for personnel from the Navy, Naval Air Depots, Air Force, and others to see real lean in action. Jacksonville was emerging as a benchmark. Perhaps most dramatic was to see planes being repaired in assembly-line fashion. Setting up a flow line with a takt time drove tremendous continuous improvement to eliminate waste and balance the line. Stability and control immediately began to replace chaos and disorganization.

Strategies to Create Connected Process Flow

Table 5-1, below, shows the strategies that guide the creation of connected process flow, as well as the primary and secondary lean tools often utilized. The same tools that were used during the stability phase may be used (continually refining the result), as well as additional tools, depending on the circumstances of the operation. The objectives and strategies, however, *always* apply.

Single-Piece Flow

This is the epitome of flow, and in fact the move toward single-piece flow has reached fad status, with many companies failing in their attempts to reach this level. Achieving single-piece flow is extremely difficult and requires a highly refined process and very specific conditions. It will not ever be possible in many

Strategies	Primary Lean Tools	Secondary Lean Tools
• Continued elimination of waste • Force problems to surface • Make problems uncomfortable • Establish connected processes to create interdependency • Identify weak links in the flow and strengthen them	• Workplace/Cell design • Pull techniques • Clearly defined customer/supplier relationships • Visual controls	• Kanban • Kanban boards • Supermarkets • FIFO lanes • Problem solving

Table 5-1. Strategies and Tools Used in Creating Connected Process Flow

situations, and in many others several iterations through the continuous improvement spiral would be required before attaining this level of capability.

As an analogy, imagine a bucket brigade line where the bucket is passed from person to person one at a time. The ultimate single-piece flow would allow the passing of a single piece from one member directly to the next. This would require perfect synchronicity between all members of the brigade. After handing off one bucket to the following member, a turn is made to the previous member to retrieve another bucket. Unless the timing between the two members is absolutely the same, one of the members will wait on the other, which is a form of waste. This level of precision would be exceptionally difficult, and only possible in cases where the cycle time balance is perfect. Any slight falter or misstep by one person on the line would throw off all the others, and the house could burn down in the meantime.

In most manufacturing operations utilizing one-piece flow, a single piece is placed between the workstations, allowing for minor variance in each worker's cycle time without causing waiting time. Even at this level, the cycle time balance between operations needs to be exceptionally high. Additional pieces between each operation allow for greater variation in cycle times from operation to operation; however, this also increases the waste of overproduction. This is the conundrum. Decrease the buffer between operations to reduce overproduction, and increase the losses due to imbalanced work times.

There is a happy medium as you move forward with the creation of lean processes. That medium point will provide a certain degree of urgency for problems, so they're not ignored, and also a degree of cushion until the capability of the operation is improved and a tighter level can be sustained. The continuous improvement spiral model outlined in this section moves this cycle forward. The

---

TIP

When Is a Problem Not a Problem?

Within Toyota, leaders are conditioned to not only stop and fix problems, but also to continuously be on the lookout for problems *before* they occur. A well-established lean operation with continuous, connected flow provides signals, which give everyone an "early warning indicator" prior to complete system failure. The ability to find problems before they occur allows leaders to take preemptive corrective action, thus averting the failure.

Note: Within Toyota, "failure" is not considered to be a "bad" thing. In fact, lack of failure is considered to be an indication that the system has too much waste. Not knowing when and where the failure will occur is an indication of a poorly designed system.

incremental leveling phase will require a reduction in buffer quantities throughout the flow stream, thus driving ever-smaller problems to the surface, where they demand attention. This will create new instability, and the cycle spirals toward a tighter level of performance.

Key Criteria for Achieving Flow

As we discussed in the last chapter, foundational elements are necessary for achieving smooth flow. These key criteria are generally met during the stability phase, but bear repeating here.

- Ensure consistent capability, which is the primary intent of the stability phase. At the very least, the level of capability should be on a daily basis. During each day the operation must be capable of fulfilling the requirements of the customer.
- Consistent capability requires consistent application and availability of resources—people, materials, and equipment. The inconsistent availability of these resources is the primary reason that flow is unsuccessful. Methods must be put in place to ensure availability of resources (not by simply adding resources, which is added cost).
- Reliability of processes and equipment is imperative. Initially this would encompass the larger issues such as downtime, or changeover, but as the process is refined it would include lesser issues such as ease and simplicity of use.
- Operation cycle times must be balanced (equal) to the takt time. Uneven work times will create waiting time and overproduction.

TRAP

The Risk of One-Piece Flow Before Its Time

We have seen companies coming back from training classes excited about one-piece flow immediately create a cell, discover the cell is shut down most of the time, and conclude that lean does not work in the real world. They are suffering from a problem known as "rolled throughput yield." Take the case where five machines are linked together in a one-piece flow and each machine independently breaks down 10 percent of the time—that is 90 percent uptime. In this case the uptime of the cell will be:

$$.9^5 = .9 \times .9 \times .9 \times .9 \times .9 = 59 \text{ percent uptime of the cell!}$$

The solution: Keeping a few pieces of WIP between operations in carefully selected locations can increase this to 90 percent.

Case Study: The Danger of Single-Piece Flow for Short Cycle-Time Jobs

The move to making material flow from traditional "batch and queue" methods has become somewhat of a fad. As with most fads, they can be taken to an extreme, and negative consequences ensue. The single-piece flow "fad" has, in many cases created reduced performance results. Single-piece flow may not be the most efficient method for short cycle-time operations (30 seconds or less).

A kaizen workshop was held with the objective of establishing single-piece flow capability in the assembly operation. The product was an assembled fitting requiring 13 seconds to complete. The takt time was determined to be 5 seconds, based on the customer demand. The work was divided among three operators, and a work cell (another fad) was created to facilitate the passing of product between operators, which is necessary for flow.

Several months later this work area was struggling to meet the customer demand, and operators had returned to batching product between operations. Observation revealed two major issues. First, as the cycle balance chart in Figure 5-2 shows, the cycle times for the operators were not well balanced.

This imbalance in work cycle times is a major reason operators begin to deviate from the "no batching" rule. When operators deviate from the original plan, it's a strong indication that there is a flaw in the plan. Unfortunately, a struggle usually ensues as management attempts to enforce the rules of flow rather than to stop and consider where the

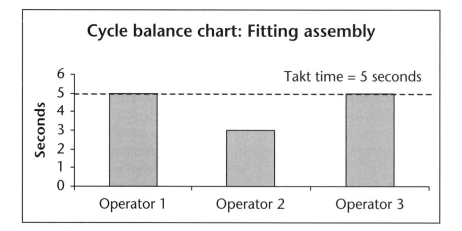

Figure 5-2. Original cycle balance chart for fitting assembly

process is flawed. Learn to see operator deviation as a positive! Stop and observe and find the real cause, which if corrected will yield a stronger process.

If the cycle times were properly balanced and smooth flow achieved, there is another less noticeable problem. Attempting single-piece flow when the work cycle time is very short creates a high ratio of waste to value-added. Here's why: During any work process there is inherently some amount of necessary waste, such as picking up the part and setting the part down for the next operation. This waste can be minimized, but in the best-case scenario will still require one-half to one second for each motion (pick up, and put down). Assuming the best case, this would require a total of one second per work cycle—a half second to pick up, a half second to put down—of motion waste. If the work cycle time is five seconds total, one second for handling amounts to 20 percent of the total time! This comes to over 30 percent on a three-second operation. That is a huge amount of inevitable waste. Yet this waste is often overlooked because of the assumption that if the material is flowing and the operators are moving continuously, it is "lean." As we see here, that is simply not the case.

This operation would be improved by having two operators pick up a part and complete it entirely, rather than breaking the operation into multiple jobs in an attempt to create "flow." The time would be reduced by two seconds, and the result is 11 seconds to complete (Figure 5-3). The net time per piece is 5.5 seconds (two people working simultaneously produce two parts every 11 seconds and 11 seconds divided by 2 pieces = 5.5 seconds per piece), which is

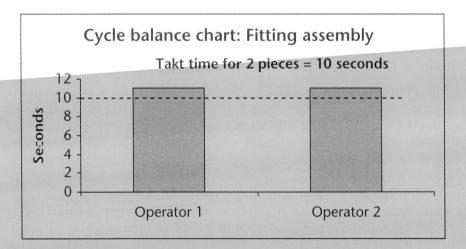

Figure 5-3. Cycle balance chart for improved fitting assembly

0.5 seconds over takt. The next step would be to reduce other waste and simplify the operation so it can be completed in 10 seconds or less, resulting in a net time per piece below takt time (5 seconds).

In this example, the creation of flow actually reduced performance by 33 percent (three operations rather than two). Also, in the scope of the entire value stream, this operation was a very small portion of the total material flow. There were much greater opportunities to create flow and reduce the throughput time in other areas by connecting operations utilizing the pull methods described below.

Pull

The terms "pull" or "pull system" are often used interchangeably with flow. It should be understood that, like flow, pull is a concept, and the two are linked, but not the same. Flow defines that state of material as it moves from process to process. Pull dictates when material is moved and who (the customer) determines that it is to be moved.

Many people are confused about the difference between the "push" method and the "pull" method. Some erroneously think they are "pulling" because the material continues to move or flow. It is possible to flow without having pull. There are three primary elements of pull that distinguish it from push:

1. **Defined.** A defined agreement with specified limits pertaining to volume of product, model mix, and the sequence of model mix between the two parties (supplier and customer).
2. **Dedicated.** Items that are shared between the two parties must be dedicated to them. This includes resources, locations, storage, containers, and so forth, and a common reference time (takt time).
3. **Controlled.** Simple control methods, which are visually apparent and physically constraining, maintain the defined agreement.

In a push system there is no defined agreement between the supplier and the customer regarding the quantity of work to be supplied and when. The supplier works at his own pace and completes work according to his own schedule. This material is then delivered to the customer whether the customer requested it or not. Locations are not defined and dedicated, and material is placed where there is an opening. Since there is no definition, or dedication, there is no clear way to understand what to control or how to control it.

Of course, some element of control does happen through expediting, changing the schedule, and moving people, but this only leads to additional waste and variation. It could be argued as well that the agreement is defined based on the schedule. All processes are working to the "same" schedule. In fact they may be on the same schedule, but they are not on the same page.

A "pull system" is an aggregation of several elements that support the process of pulling. The kanban "sign" is one of the tools used as part of a pull system. The kanban is simply the communication method and could be a card, an empty space, a cart, or any other signaling method for the customer to say, "I am ready for more." There are many other elements as well, including visual control and standardized work. If the three elements of pull are properly installed, a "connection" is formed between the supplier and customer processes. The three elements dictate the parameters of the connection and its relative strength and "tightness."

The case example below illustrates the three distinct requirements for pull. Single-piece flow is the easiest to explain and understand, but the same principles apply for any variation whatever the situation. For example, the same principles apply to high-mix, low-volume operations, and to batching operations where the quantities between processes may be much larger. This following example is the easiest to understand, but the principles can be applied to any situation.

Case Example: Creating One-Piece Flow

Operation A supplies parts to Operation B, which supplies parts to Operation C.

Is the agreement defined and specified?

Yes. We said it was single-piece flow, so in this case the defined quantity is *implied* in the name. (As we will see, implied definition is not sufficient).

What is the specified agreement?

Provide one piece at a time.

When is the piece provided?

When the next operation takes the previous piece (remember the bucket brigade).

Upon observation, we can determine whether the agreement is being followed. In this case we see in Figure 5-4 that Operation B is not following the agreement and has exceeded the defined limit of one piece.

How do we know this is a violation of the agreement?

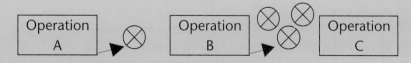

Figure 5-4. Flow that is not defined

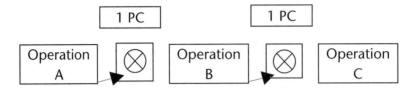

Figure 5-5. Single-piece flow with visually defined agreement

It is implied in the term "single-piece flow" that only one piece will be between operations. THIS IS NOT GOOD ENOUGH! The agreement needs to be *distinct* and *visible* to everyone.

If it is not distinct and visible, what will happen?

The agreement will not be followed, which is a deviation (creates variation) from the agreed-upon standard (we see that in establishing pull we begin to create a structure to support the next phase—standardization).

How do we make it visual so that it is *easily controlled*?

Define and *dedicate* the space for one piece. The space is outlined with tape or paint to show that only one piece is permitted, and a sign or label is added to further clarify this (a taped square on the table is not completely clear, so a sign is added for clarification of what the square means), as shown in Figure 5-5.

In addition to the visual markings, the space could be physically limited (controlled) by allowing only enough room for a single piece. This technique is especially effective when the parts are oriented vertically and can be placed into a slot, thus controlling the quantity.

One of the primary benefits of creating flow and establishing defined agreements is that the effect of problems can now be seen easily. In the example above, if consistent deviation from the agreement occurs and the visual controls are in place, there is another problem.

When deviation is occurring, this is a clear message of an underlying problem that needs to be addressed. In this situation managers often state, "They know what they're supposed to do, but we can't get them to do it." Many managers make the mistake of blaming the operator for not following the rules, and in fact the operator is compensating for a problem that needs to be corrected. Stop, and "stand in the circle" to identify what the operator is compensating for.

There are generally two reasons for this condition. The first thing to evaluate is whether the agreement is visual and easily understood by everyone; the second is to look for additional problems that the operators feel compelled to "work around."

The primary causes of deviation by operators are:

1. Imbalanced work cycle times that may be due to normal variation in work content, operator skill, or machine cycle times. Typically, the person with extra time will deviate.
2. Intermittent work stoppages due to lack of parts or (the fear of) operators leaving the work area to perform additional tasks—such as retrieving parts or performing quality checks—machine failures, or correction of defects.
3. Intermittent work delays due to struggles with machines or fixtures, or overly difficult or complex tasks.
4. Miscellaneous issues such as "building ahead" to "buy time" for change-over, an operator leaving the line for some reason, or to stagger break or lunchtimes, or such.

In some situations the correct course of action would be to adjust the defined quantity of WIP between operations. Single-piece flow requires *perfect* operation time balance, which is extremely difficult to achieve. Consider an operation that will incur natural variations in the work cycle time, such as deflashing an injection-molded part.

The cycle time will vary slightly each time because this is largely a manual task, and no one can complete work cycles with exact precision (Olympic athletes, after all, do not run every race in the exact time every race). These minor variations may cause intermittent interruption in the flow. Operators do not like to wait with nothing to do, so they will naturally add buffer to compensate. The addition of buffer is the logical choice to compensate for *minor* time variation; however, the quantity to add needs to be defined as the standard. Perhaps the defined buffer to allow for the minor time variations should be two or at most three pieces.

TIP

The Value of Outside Eyes

The problem with communication is that it is hard to understand why others misunderstand what we clearly understand. The point of an agreement on a standard is for everyone to have the same understanding. One simple way to test this is to find someone who is not familiar with the work area, show her the standard, and ask her to explain the agreement. You may be surprised to discover how challenging it is to clearly communicate agreements visually!

Complex Flow Situations

If we consider a different example with a higher degree of complexity, we can see that it is a derivation of the same concepts. In this example, there are three different models of product to produce——Models 1, 2, and 3—and we need the flexibility to produce any of the models at any time, one at a time. The layout is shown below in Figure 5-6.

Suppose Operation C is required to produce Model 2. They would remove the single piece from the defined location between Operation B and Operation C. This provides a signal to Operation B in accordance with the agreement—an empty space serves as a signal, and the agreement is that when the customer pulls a part, it is replaced—to produce a Model 2 part. The layout would now look like Figure 5-7.

Operation B then removes part 2 between himself and Operation A, causing Operation A to respond by beginning a Model 2 part. When completed, Operation B will replenish the defined location between himself and Operation C. The layout would now look like Figure 5-8.

Again, this is a simplistic model; however, the three required conditions exist and are supported by visual methods. This basic model works well for producing high-volume or low-variety products, or for stock items. The primary advantage is the flexibility to produce any of the models at any time and to change between the models quickly.

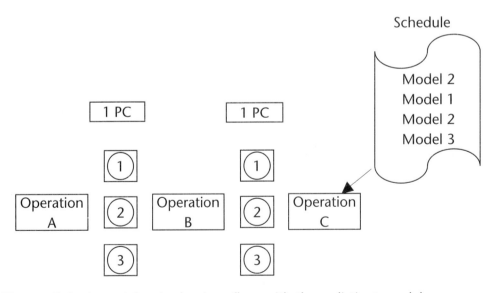

Figure 5-6. Layout for single-piece flow with three distinct models

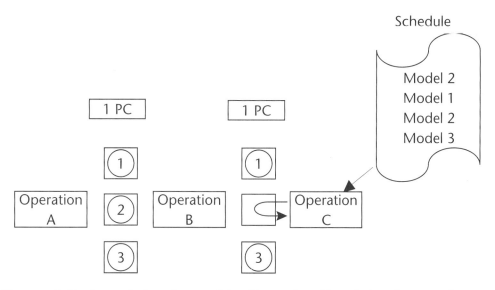

Figure 5-7. Layout showing pull by Operation C and signal to produce Model 2

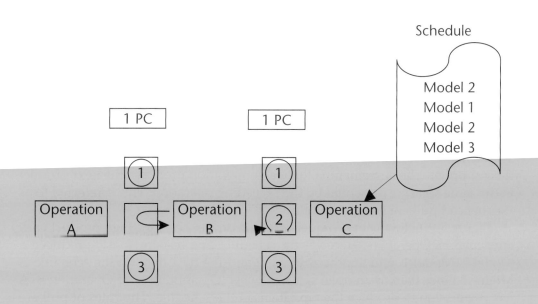

Figure 5-8. Layout showing replenishment of part, and pull from customer

Pull in a Custom Manufacturing Environment

Because of the simple model (see Figure 5-8), which is based upon the production of the same three models of parts again and again, many people believe that pull in a high-variety or custom production environment is not possible. This is based on the incorrect assumption that when Operation C produces a specific model, they will send a "pull signal" to the preceding operation (B) to make a replacement for that same model. Operation C uses a "1" and Operation B makes a replacement version of "1."

What if you have thousands of possible items and some may be used only once per month? In a high-variety, high-mix, or custom production situation the instruction on what to produce next (the custom order) would be given to Operation A rather than C. After completion, Operation A passes the part to Operation B. Then Operation B would work on this part, complete it, and pass it to Operation C. In this manner the work "flows through" the subsequent operations. Remember that flow and pull are not the same thing. The common assumption is that the work must be *pushed* to Operation B and Operation C if the instruction to produce is provided to the beginning of the line (Operation A).

Look back at the distinctions between push and pull. The first element is a defined agreement between the two parties. Is there a defined agreement between Operation A and Operation B in a custom production situation? Yes, it is still one piece of work in process. The second element requires that the location be defined in accordance with the agreement and then dedicated. The space is dedicated just as in the previous example. The third element requires a method to control the production to satisfy the agreement (the standard). How is the production controlled? It is controlled the same way—visually.

What is the difference? The only difference is in the agreement of "what the customer wants." In this case, the quantity is the same, but what about the model? The customer processes (B and C) do not dictate the specific model produced by their supplier. The agreement is that each operation produces the next product in the same *sequence* presented by the preceding operation. This is referred to as "sequenced pull" or "sequenced flow."

Figure 5-9, below, shows sequenced flow production for a high product variety situation. Operation A receives the schedule, and has previously produced a Model 2, Model 1, and another Model 2; and the next item on the schedule is Model 3. Since there is an open space between Operation A and Operation B, A has permission to produce the next item on the schedule. The rules of pull are still followed in that Operation A would not produce if the space were full. The rule states that an operation can complete the part in process if the customer space is full, but will not pass the part to the space. The part will remain in the

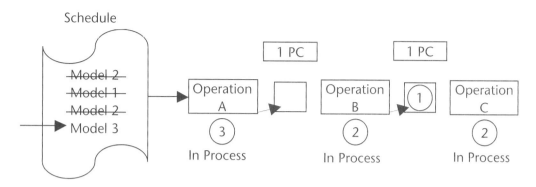

Figure 5-9. Sequenced flow for high product variety production

workstation. In effect, Operation B still dictates what to do (build the next item on the schedule) and when to do it (when the space is empty). If Operation B completes the part before the signal space for Operation C is empty, the operator will hold it in the workstation and wait for a signal from Operation C to replenish the space.

In a high model-mix environment, the level of flexibility is limited by the lead time from the point-of-schedule introduction to the completion of the product. This is dictated by the number of operations that must be "flowed through." Instant changes to the schedule will not yield instant changes in the output because of the flow-through time delay.

For this type of flow to work well, each operator must have the capability to produce any model that comes at any time. Often the greatest challenge in establishing sequenced flow in a custom environment is achieving a balance of operation times. Refer to the case study in the previous chapter for an example of reducing the high degree of variation often found in a custom production facility, and how better balance is achieved by defining the time requirements more narrowly.

What if there is not a perfect balance in cycle times across Operations A, B, and C? First, ask: "Can each operation consistently perform the task in less than the customer requirement time—the takt?" Second, if on average the answer is yes but because of variability, the takt time is often missed, we need to put in some buffer. The buffer does not have to be an unmanaged push system. It can be defined with a specific visual arrangement showing the number of pieces allowed, e.g., three between stations. And the principle of first in-first out (FIFO) should be used to prevent a particular part from "cutting in line."

So we see that flow and pull work hand in hand. Establishing the three elements necessary for pull then creates defined connections between operations. These connections are important to surface and highlight problems. They create a singular process in which all operations are interdependent. This step will significantly increase the level of urgency to resolve any interruptions to flow. If a problem occurs in any operation, it will quickly affect all other operations. Working around the problem by shifting manpower or machinery, or changing the schedule, will cause additional problems throughout the entire system because all operations are linked.

Creating Pull Between Separate Operations

From this understanding of the basics of pull it is possible to design a system that will be effective in any situation. The single-piece flow model above is specifically for line- or cell-type operations where the workers pass the product down the line.

How are the basics applied in operations that are separated physically, or for operations that produce parts in batches? First of all, it is important to understand the inherent nature of an operation. Someone well trained in TPS will understand that at the current time some operations are not conducive to single-piece flow for some reason. It may be the size of the part (very large or small), a resource that is shared (has multiple suppliers and/or customers), or has a limitation in the process, such as changeover times.

For example, the stamping operations at Toyota are not currently capable of producing one fender, then changing to a hood, and then back to a fender one piece at a time. The stamping operation has multiple constraints preventing single-piece flow, and the parts are produced in "lot size" quantities. First, the size of the equipment prohibits placement next to the customer operation (the body welding department). Second, the machine ("shared resource") produces multiple part models that are required by different customers (the fender is installed at a different location than the hood), so it is not possible to place the equipment in proximity to all customers. Also the changeover time, while it is very good, still limits the ability to make one piece, change over, make another, and change over again.

How do the basic concepts of define, dedicate, and control apply in this situation? Start with an understanding of the agreement between the supplier and the customers. Supply the correct material when requested. All operations must adhere to the basic rule: "Always satisfy the customer," or put another way, "Never short the customer." This is Rule 1. Always follow Rule 1! (Note the paradox of this statement. While it is the goal to always satisfy the customer we have stated previously that a process that never stops a customer operation is likely to have excessive waste built in.)

Is the agreement defined? The first step is to establish the correct amount of WIP between supplier and customer to buffer the time requirement of the supplier to changeover and also to supply the second customer. Many operations currently have loosely defined (not visual and controlled) agreements that are a good starting point for the quantity needed.

Are the locations for the storage of WIP defined? Are they dedicated, and are they clearly marked? This should include information defining the maximum allowable amount, and the minimum. The maximum serves as a visual indication that overproduction has occurred, and the minimum serves as an "early warning indicator" that a problem with supply may occur and should be investigated (find the potential problem early, before it becomes a problem). Are the containers used to transport material dedicated? In our stamping example the containers are specifically designed to hold a certain part. A fender will not fit in a hood container.

The final piece is visual awareness of the needs of the customer. If the customer process is not within visual sight distance, a mechanism must be used to provide visual awareness of the customer needs and status. The visual mechanism used to provide a signal from customer to supplier is the kanban. Traditionally when dealing with suppliers that are physically separated but close enough to send truckloads throughout the day, Toyota used a physical card as the kanban. A kanban that has been returned from the customer represents the consumption of material, and as kanbans are accumulated at the supplier, they are a visual representation of the WIP agreement. The kanbans represent an inverse of the WIP quantity. More kanbans at the supplier equals less WIP at the customer.

We do not intend to completely explain the workings of kanban here, but the principles are easily understood. The kanban is a control mechanism. It can be a space on the floor if two operations are near each other. If customer and supplier are separated by line of sight, it can be a card, or return of an empty rack, or an electronic signal. The kanban must contain information relevant to the agreement, such as the supplier and customer locations, machinery utilized, material, and of course quantity and model.

Refer back to the single-piece flow example above. How did Operation B know that Operation C needed another Model 1? Operation C removed the part, and the empty space signaled Operation B of the need to replace it. The space serves as a kanban, with the pertinent information regarding quantity and model specified by visual indicators. Any kanban system is simply a derivative of this basic concept.

Case Example: Connecting Operations to Surface Waste in Engineering

An automotive seat supplier had a very elaborate "phase-gate process" for developing new products. Each phase in the process of developing a vehicle had been defined in detail. The criteria for predefined "gates" for the product design was clear, and if upon review the design did not meet all those criteria, it would not pass to the next step in the process. This process was taught to everyone so they knew what to do in the process and when to do it.

One of our associates worked with them as a consultant to develop a value stream map of the current process and discovered that it did not match the phase-gate process on paper very well (a common finding). There were constant delays causing backups in the system and no good flow. A future state vision was developed, and they went to work stabilizing subprocesses and then, somewhat crudely, connecting them together.

One of the bottlenecks in the current state was the process of producing and testing prototypes. Seats were designed, parts were ordered, and hundreds of prototypes built and tested.

When that process was mapped, it became clear that this was a classic case of batch and scheduled push (see Figure 5-10). All the seats were completely designed, including heated, not heated, bench, captain's chairs, power, and so on. Based on the designs, parts were ordered. The parts arrived at various times from suppliers. The prototype group waited as long as they could for all the parts they needed and then started building whatever seats they could with the parts they had. Then they released lots of seats to testing. Seats that failed testing had to be redesigned to correct the problems.

A future state map was developed. It became clear that the fundamental problem was batching. Each step in the process developed large batches and pushed to the next process. The inventory triangles in the current state diagram show the result—inventory. In the case of seat designs, it was an inventory of information—the designs—accumulating in front of parts ordering. The solution: Create a sequenced pull system. But

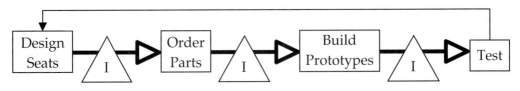

Figure 5-10. Current state map of prototyping process

how do you do this with an information process like engineering, where each design is unique?

The answer was to schedule the releases at each step based on a "staggered release." Don't wait to design all the different seat varieties. Design one and release it to parts ordering so they can get started ordering parts. Get all the parts for that seat to build prototypes, and get prototypes for that one seat to the test department so they can give feedback as quickly as possible to the seat engineers.

A key tool to enable this was something they called a "pull board." It was a simple visual management tool: a white board with key information about each of the seats in process. Each department had one. So parts ordering could see when they ordered parts, when the parts were due to arrive, whether they came in on time, as well as when the next seat design could be expected. If they started to get backed up with seat designs before getting the parts in, they could inform engineering of this. If they were ready for more, they could inform engineering of this as well.

The result was significant time reductions for this process. It was no longer a bottleneck, and feedback was faster and improved the quality of designs. Suddenly the process gained some semblance of control.

Case Example: Creating Flow in Order Processing

The creation of flow is an effective method that will provide benefits to any operation that produces a "product." (We often think in terms of a manufactured product, but these concepts apply to anything that moves from person to person as it is being processed. It could be a purchase order, an insurance policy, or a sandwich being prepared at Subway.) In this case, the "product" was a customer order that required data entry into the computer system, modifications to the order for special customization, ordering of materials for custom work, CAD drawing work to design custom elements, and a review process.

Similar to typical manufacturing operations, each of these functions was separated into different departments, each with a specific task. The order would move from department to department, each time landing in an "in basket" pile. Elaborate systems had been developed to track dates and to ensure that orders were processed FIFO, but in reality this was not the case. Some orders were more complex, requiring more time, and others were simpler jobs and "finish up" jobs that needed to move more quickly because they were related to completing jobs that had already been shipped to customers. The result was long lead times for order processing, which left little time for manufacturing and also left the stress of dealing with the complexity.

As with any situation where flow is attempted, the balance of work time and content was a major challenge. Any particular job might take longer to complete in order entry than in CAD, or vice versa. Bottlenecks shifted continuously, and as a result the lead time through the process varied considerably. This problem was compounded when associates were absent from work (especially if the current order mix was such that more time was required in the department with an absent associate).

The process was first mapped, and the product was evaluated for separation into product families (value streams). The decision to split the product into families was necessitated by the need to isolate variation, as described in Chapter 4. The product was divided into three value streams based on the complexity and time required to process each order. The most complex orders with the greatest degree of variation became one value stream, and the simpler finish-up jobs with the least amount of variation became another. The final value stream (the majority of orders) included orders that were more "standard" in terms of complexity and time required.

The group realized that the associates could be aligned in "teams" to create work cells dedicated to the particular product value stream. The office was rearranged so members in the teams were sitting next to each other. This facilitated the flow of orders. The separation of orders according to complexity and time required also allowed for a defined standard number of associates for each value stream. When this is defined it is often discovered that there are "extra" people in the process. In fact they are not "extra" per se, since the time is utilized to "cover" for any variation, including absences. It is preferable to define the correct number of associates required (based on takt time and work content) for standardized work and the desired flow. If each position is standardized, it is *essential* that it be filled *continuously!* In this case the "extra" associates become team leaders, and fulfill many important functions that will be described in Chapter 10, including filling in for associates who are absent.

As explained earlier in the chapter, it was necessary to define the agreement between operations for flow, to dedicate the resources, space, and method, and to develop a control mechanism so that each value stream could achieve connected flow. An important aspect of these elements is the visual awareness of status within each cell. After receipt, each order was identified, placed in a colored folder according to the designated value stream, and put in a queue rack. The leader was able to see the workload and make adjustments as necessary to shift some work to other value streams if the "backlog" exceeded the agreed-upon limit (the standard). Agreements were established (standards) regarding the allowance of shifting work (e.g., the simple jobs could shift to the medium value stream, but the complex jobs could not shift to the simple stream). Also, clear rules were established regarding who was allowed to make the shift. If all teams fell behind based on the defined limits, overtime was used to support the workload.

Within each team, the elements of flow were established between each operation. Because of the inherent variation in time required from order to order, a connection mechanism was needed to buffer the variation in work times, but also to support flow and surface problems. Single-piece flow was not possible. In this case a sequenced queue (sometimes referred to as a FIFO lane) was utilized. The queue rack had a defined number of spaces to indicate the status of flow and balance between operations. The team leader monitored the queue levels and made minor adjustments within the cell (e.g., completing an order "off line" and reinserting it) to support balance. As always, these adjustments were only made when the condition exceeded the defined agreement, and after careful assessment of the situation.

For example, if the defined agreement was a maximum of five orders between team members, and the maximum level was reached, the team leader would be notified by the team member to evaluate the situation. If the team leader determined that the subsequent orders were simpler for the downstream operator (the one who is "behind"), he or she might decide to take no action. The imbalance could be temporary and correct itself on the following orders. If the product mix had complex orders downstream at the bottleneck, an automatic correction was not likely, and the team leader would make adjustments.

In addition to improving flow, the teams realized that separating orders according to complexity and difficulty provided an opportunity to train new associates on simpler jobs before progressing to more complex work. Associates from different departments became part of one team, and cross training was done to facilitate flexibility within the team. Locating operations in close proximity facilitated quicker feedback on problems as well, and the "rework" required was reduced significantly.

This group was able to create a dramatic reduction in the lead time for orders, especially the crucial "finish-up" jobs. As the business grew, the order-processing group consistently processed a much greater number of orders without the addition of associates or the need for overtime.

Traditional   Ideal State
Batch & Queue   of Lean

$\longleftarrow \hspace{6cm} \longrightarrow$

Push or Scheduled	Supermarket Pull (Kanban)	Sequenced Pull (broadcast)	FIFO Sequenced Flow	Continuous Flow (1 pc Flow)
Schedule each process and push to the next	Upstream process replenishes what downstream customer took away	Pull from a feeder in sequence	Defined lane with defined standard WIP between unlinked processes in FIFO sequence	Physically link process steps with no inventory between

Figure 5-11. Continuum of flow

Flow, Pull, and Eliminate Waste

The most common perception of lean is that it is about "just in time"—the right part, the right amount, the right time, the right place. As we see, there is a lot more to it. The key to eliminating waste is creating flow, and the principles of pull require the production in a "just in time" manner.

It is best to think of flow on a continuum, as shown in figure 5-11. Even the dreaded schedules create some degree of flow. At the other extreme is a one-piece flow process with no inventory between operations. Between, you can have a supermarket that is being replenished, you can pull parts in sequence from one process to the next, or you can flow through a lane with a defined amount of inventory without breaking the FIFO order. Notice that the famous kanban system in which a supermarket is replenished is not the preferred choice, but the next worst choice besides scheduling. Kanban is an admission that inventory is needed and must be managed. Waste is designed into the system. Both sequenced pull and FIFO generally require less inventory than supermarket systems and have better flow.

The main point is not that you either use one-piece flow or you're not lean. The point is that the focus should be on waste elimination. If you have a supermarket replenishment process, take out a kanban and stress the system. If you have a FIFO lane, reduce the lane by one piece and it will force continuous improvement.

Reflect and Learn from the Process

1. Using your current state map as a guide, walk the path of the material flow once again. During this walk identify processes that are inherently inflexible where continuous flow is not currently possible. Do not attempt this exercise from your office. You must see each of these processes to understand the cause and effect relationships that prevent flow.
   a. Identify the inflexible processes on your map.
   b. List the cause of the inflexibility for these processes, such as long setup times or shared resources that supply multiple parts or processes.

2. Evaluate each customer-supplier relationship in the value stream.
   a. Determine whether each connection will utilize a FIFO-style connection (if flow-through is possible), or a supermarket-style connection.
   b. Develop a plan to define each connection in terms of what will be included, how many (define the unit of measure), and where the material will be.
   c. Determine whether the space needs to be dedicated, whether containers or carts are dedicated, and whether the resources are dedicated to this connection.
   d. Identify the control mechanism for each connection and how you plan to make it visual and easy to verify adherence.

3. Good flow depends upon good balancing of cycle times along the value stream.
   a. Measure the cycle times of each operation in your value stream, and create a cycle balance chart to determine the current operation balance.
   b. As you walk the value stream, identify the physical signs of work imbalance (such as waiting, or inventory accumulation), and highlight these on the current state map.

4. The following questions apply to any operation that is a low-volume, high-variety (custom, semicustom, or make-to-order) producer. Your objective is the same as any other company—to create the best possible flow. In relative terms your flow may never be perfectly balanced or smooth, but it can be improved.

   a. Evaluate the grouping of your product into "families" based on the work content time required at each operation (short time, medium time, and long time).

   b. Is it possible to achieve a better work flow by controlling the product mix introduced into the value stream (to even out the work content time)?

   c. Graph the part numbers by the quantity ordered in a year from highest to lowest volume (P-Q chart), and identify product families based on volume and frequency of orders. High- and medium-volume parts are candidates for cells. You may also be able to use these to level the schedule (see Chapter 7).

   d. In a custom production environment the defined agreement is based on an agreed-upon "unit." What will your defined unit be? (It may be part-by-part, or order-by-order, an increment of time, or another common element.)

5. The following questions pertain to nonmanufacturing processes. The result of your work may be less tangible than a manufactured product, but work is being done and there is an end result. The end result is your "product."

   a. Define the product. Identify and map the flow of the product through the various processes.

   b. In nonmanufacturing processes the product is often not easy to see as it moves through the operations. It may be paperwork or information in a computer. These create unique challenges in trying to make the process visual.

      i. Do you have visual awareness of the product flow (product that is "in the system" or stacked in an in-basket is not visual)?

      ii. If the product itself is not visual, how can you create visual awareness of its progress?

Chapter 6

Establish Standardized Processes and Procedures

Is Standardization Coercive?

Standardized work evokes images of industrial engineers with stopwatches terrorizing the workforce by squeezing out every second of productivity. It brings to mind a highly regimented existence in which "big brother" is watching to make sure you follow each and every rule. It is bureaucracy run rampant where human will and creativity are wiped out and people become automatons.

But there are other views of standardization. Masaki Imai in his seminal work says he learned that there can be no kaizen without standardization.[1] Standardization is actually the starting point for continuous improvement. As discussed in *The Toyota Way*, Paul Adler took an organizational theory perspective and looked in depth at the Toyota Production System (TPS).[2] He discovered that much of what had been written on the unintended negative consequences of bureaucracy were avoided by Toyota, which used the standardization of bureaucracy along with employee empowerment to create an "enabling" bureaucracy. We think of bureaucracy as "coercive"—limiting the ability of people to be flexible and improve. Yet Toyota's enabling bureaucracy has the opposite effect—allowing for flexibility and true innovation that makes a lasting impact.

The establishment of standardized processes and procedures is the greatest key to creating consistent performance. It is only when the process is stable that

[1] Masaki Imai, *Kaizen: The Key to Japan's Competitive Success*, New York: McGraw-Hill/Irwin, 1986.

[2] Paul S. Adler, "Building Better Bureaucracies," *Academy of Management Executive*, 13:4, November 1999, 36-47.

you can begin the creative progression of continuous improvement. As we've shown in the previous chapters, the work of developing standards begins early in a lean implementation and is a common thread throughout the development of lean operations. The creation of standardized processes is based on defining, clarifying (making visual), and consistently utilizing the methods that will ensure the best possible results. As such, standardization is not applied as a stand-alone element at specific intervals. Rather, it is part of the ongoing activity of identifying problems, establishing effective methods, and defining the way those methods are to be performed. And it is *driven* by people, not *done to* people. People doing the work understand it in sufficient detail to make the biggest contributions to standardization.

We have stated throughout that our objective is to teach the core philosophies and concepts of the Toyota Way. Again, this is not intended to be another "how to" lean tools book. The process Toyota refers to as "standardized work" is so important to the overall production system that one third of Toyota's internal *TPS Handbook* is devoted to it.[3] Quite simply, standardized work and other work standards are the baseline for continuous improvement.

This is another one of those misunderstood points about TPS. Until standards are defined in any operation, it is not possible to truly make improvements. Think about it this way: If a process is not standardized (it is random and chaotic), and improvements are made, what was improved? Did you improve the randomness? Or did you just add one more version of how the work can be done to further increase the chaos? If a person creatively improves the work but it does not become a standard, then the work is only improved while that particular person is doing it. And nobody else will build on that improvement. If the improvement was to create standardization, then you created a platform from which to enable teams to continuously improve the process. You have the foundation for a learning organization.

Unfortunately, it is not uncommon in our work with companies that are implementing lean processes to be asked to "do standardized work" as if it were a stand-alone tool to be applied according to an implementation schedule ("Our road map says we need to do standardized work now"). One such request went something like this: "We need to get standardized work done by October." To which was replied: "We can certainly do that, but standardized work is a tool, and like any tool, it has specific uses and is used to accomplish specific objectives."

In one company, standardized work was behind schedule according to the lean implementation plan. The solution: Hire a schoolteacher over the summer to write out the standardized work for all jobs. The result: very nice looking, posted standardized work that no one followed. If you just want to fill out sheets, laminate and hang them in the work area and create no real value, you can do that. If you are interested in using standardized work to reduce waste, define a

---

[3] *TPS Handbook,* 1989 by Toyota Motor Corporation.

better work process, and continually improve process, you can do that as well. Which would you prefer?

We are introducing standardization as one of the "phases," but in reality this concept is applied throughout the journey and is the one concept that should be considered during the development of any work method. As with most elements of TPS, the concept is key, and an understanding of the concept will improve your ability to apply it. Standardization is not a set of documents that are prepared and carefully controlled. It is a *means* of creating the most consistent performance possible. It is the basis for process stability. Without it, tools like Six Sigma and other advanced variation reduction methods are worthless.

Standardized Work or Work Standards?

Standardization may be the most misunderstood and most often misapplied of all lean concepts. The root of this problem may extend back as far as the early studies by Frederic Taylor and the desire to maximize profits by carefully defining the work elements and holding employees accountable for achieving them. Work standards have a long embattled history in some industries (particularly the automotive industry), and the objective has been to "beat up" employees for nonperformance.

This has created certain recognizable "games" and ways to beat the system. Most of all it's created an antagonistic relationship between workers and management, instead of a mutual objective of creating the best possible product for the customer, we find an environment of one-upsmanship. This is a game in which management more carefully defines the work method in order to determine costing standards and to ensure that each employee is putting forth the required effort. Employees know this game and intentionally change work methods when observed, in order to create artificially low requirements that are easy to achieve. Management then utilizes the "standards" to make manufacturing decisions based on "earned hours" or "absorption" or a similar measure based on the work standards, with the goal of making sure that manufacturing employees "earn" the correct amount of hours for the amount of product produced. If this occurs, the overhead cost of employees is "absorbed," the correct standard cost is achieved (or exceeded), and the desired profit is theoretically generated.

Employees view work standards as a measure of how "hard" they have to work, or the amount of effort that will be exerted. In addition, they inherently understand that everyone has different capabilities and the system is based on the lowest capability. In this way low performers can be successful and high performers can exceed performance, or if they choose, work faster to create extra "free time."

In this model, a work standard is established based on the wrong objective. It is based on creating a cost standard rather than creating the best possible work method, with the least amount of waste, producing the best quality product at the lowest cost. This work standard is then used as either a club to beat employees for nonperformance or as a carrot to entice them to exceed the standard (as in pay-for-performance derivatives of this method). Since these ideas are so ingrained in the minds of management and employees, the establishment of standardized work as defined by Toyota can be one of the greatest challenges during lean implementation. It is extremely difficult for all parties to let go of the current process because everyone has learned how to survive or thrive under that system. Managers fear that the Toyota Way will allow employees to run amuck, deciding their own work methods and therefore not working hard enough. They also fear the loss of a measurement system that they have learned how to manipulate and control to achieve success. Everyone is familiar with this conversation:

> *Production manager (to supervisor):* "The earned hours are down in your department. What are you going to do to get them back up?"
>
> *Supervisor:* "We had some tough jobs coming through the shop, which hurt our hours. We are going to come in Saturday to work on some of the easy jobs to get them out. That will help."
>
> *Production Manager:* "Okay. I have to report to the plant manager on this, so I'm going to tell him that the product mix has not been good and that it should get better after this week."

Clearly this is a misguided focus on the measurement and not a focus on creating a truly efficient process that will consistently deliver performance results. Notice that the supervisor will work on "easy jobs" to get the numbers up. A part is a part according to the numbers. But are the easy jobs the parts that the customer wants? That seems secondary. It is a shame how much time and effort is wasted trying to "make the numbers" rather than trying to create the best possible process. Management is caught in a vicious cycle and can't seem to break free because their own performance is measured on their ability to deliver the desired numbers.

Objective of Standardization

The traditional manufacturing model has an initial focus on achieving the lowest possible unit cost and then creating work method standards to achieve the cost objective (Figure 6-1). This model considers individual efforts and "cost per piece," while the Toyota Way seeks to maximize the entire system and considers "total cost" via waste reduction as the primary indicator of success. The traditional method utilizes time and motion studies to determine the most "efficient" work procedure, and a "standard" time is allotted for the designated task. Typically, an operator is observed and the work elements and times are recorded. This is not necessarily the best method; it is just the method that the operator happens to be using when being observed. This process creates a "false standard" that is then utilized to determine "efficiency."

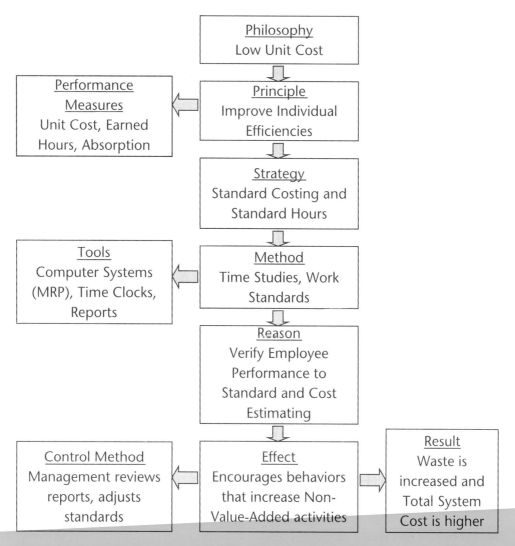

Figure 6-1. Traditional unit-cost-focused manufacturing

The Toyota Way seeks the same objective in terms of low cost; however, the primary focus is on reducing the waste within the system (Figure 6-2). As such, Toyota considers the development of standardization to be a baseline for continuous improvement, meaning that future results are expected to improve from the standard. The traditional method considers standards as the objective to achieve, as if the standard were the ultimate level of performance, which precludes the possibility of improvement. This fundamental difference in thinking is the basis for many of the paradoxical elements of a lean system. The objectives

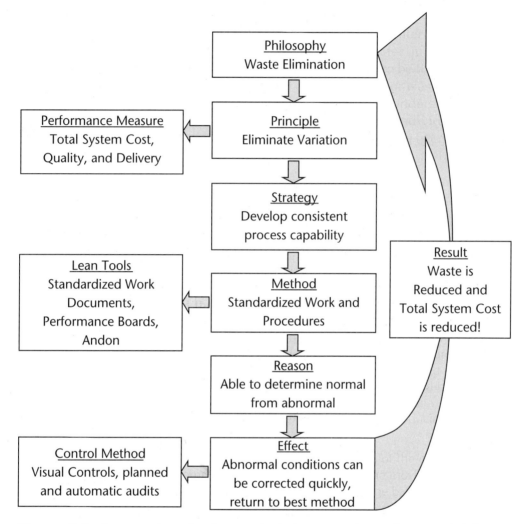

Figure 6-2. Lean waste reduction results in lower total cost, improved delivery, and quality

are the same; namely, to provide the highest quality product at the lowest possible cost within the shortest time possible; however, the thought process to achieve these results is opposite the one used by mass manufacturers for the past 100 years. And the mass production approach limits the ability to achieve these objectives.

The lean waste reduction model begins with a philosophy focused on waste reduction. In most organizations there is a substantial amount of waste that is caused by random activities and inconsistent methods. To eliminate waste, we must reduce or eliminate variation within processes. Variation is the antithesis of standardization. By definition, variation implies the inability to standardize. As discussed in Chapters 4 and 5, the isolation of variation is a key to the establishment of standardized work methods and procedures. This will also establish a baseline and the ability to distinguish the (normal) standard method from (abnormal) nonstandard methods. Visual control methods and other lean tools are utilized to provide instant recognition of performance, and adjustments can be made in real time so performance objectives are achieved consistently.

Strategies to Establish Standardized Processes and Procedures

The primary tools in establishing standardized processes and procedures are standardized work documents and many of the lean tools that were used during the previous phases are also used in the development of workplace standards (Table 6-1).

Traditional policies and procedures often work against standardization. Consider attendance policies. With standardized work processes it's *mandatory* that every work position be filled at all times. This means that when a person is absent, he or she must be replaced in order for the process to function correctly. It can't function correctly when there are no contingencies as to how the position will be filled in the event of absence. Yet, in traditional systems absenteeism is rarely a top management focus and supervisors scramble around to fill positions due to absences each day without a standardized approach.

TIP

Create a Structure to Support Standardized Work

Toyota has a system of group leaders and team leaders. The team leaders are hourly and are responsible for supporting about five to seven associates. They audit the work procedures of employees to detect deviations from standard work (see Chapter 11 here and page 191 of *The Toyota Way*) and provide the necessary structure to fill in for absences. They are often involved in developing standard work for new models. They are a key to turning standard work from good looking wall hangings to true tools for continuous improvement. Interestingly, the team leader role is exactly what is missing in most companies.

Strategies	Primary Lean Tools	Secondary Lean Tools

• Create a repeatable work method that becomes the foundation for kaizen
• Establish clearly defined expectations
• Develop processes to insure consistency for all elements of the work
  • Labor needs
  • Work Methods
  • Materials
  • Machinery
	• Standardized work documents
	  • Standardized work chart
	  • Production capacity sheet
	  • Work Combination Table
		• Visual controls
		• Policies and procedures
		• Boundary samples
		• Process check sheets
		• Job Instruction Training

Table 6-1. Stategies and Tools for Standardized Processes and Procedures

Types of Standardization

There's often confusion regarding the establishment of the process Toyota broadly refers to as "standardized work." This seemingly simple method is deceivingly difficult for other companies to mimic. Since the intent of standardized work is different from the traditional process of creating work standards, it is not possible to make a direct correlation. Companies have methods they call "standards," but it's not what Toyota means by using the term "standardized work" to define the method used to perform work tasks with the least amount of waste. In fact there are many types of standards that are consolidated into one overriding method used to dictate the best work procedure. Within Toyota, the primary tool that dictates the work method is standardized work, which defines who, what, when, and where work is to be performed.

Figure 6-3 uses a house model to show the relationship of the different types of standards and how they support the primary objectives of providing a defined method to perform the work with the least waste, as well as to provide detailed information to the employees about developing the highest knowledge and skill level possible.

Notice that each standard serves a separate function, but they all must be incorporated into the standardized work method. This does not mean that the standardized work document includes all the standards. It simply includes the work steps that will produce the desired result (achievement of other standards). The details of other standards are included in operator instruction and training, as can be seen in Figure 6-4.

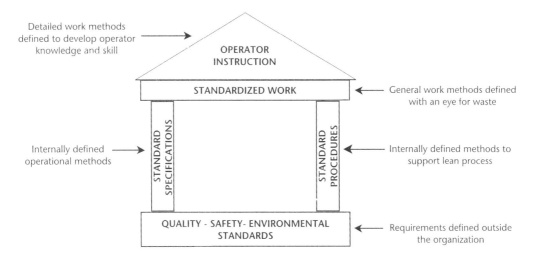

Figure 6-3. Relationship and purpose of standards

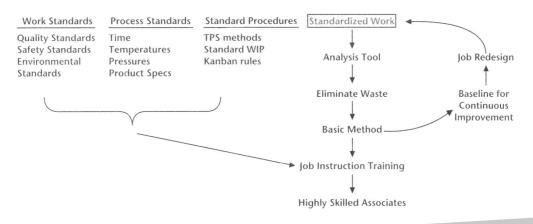

Figure 6-4. Relationship between standardized work and other standards

Quality, Safety, and Environmental Standards

Quality standards are based on customer expectations that have to do with items such as fit and finish, and establish the cosmetic requirements of a product. Examples include:

◆ General appearance
◆ Color matching
◆ Deformities, abnormalities (rounded edges, depressions, etc.)
◆ Gaps or tolerances
◆ Surface quality
◆ Limitations of defect size and quantity

TIP

Store Your Valuables for Safekeeping

Boundary samples are very important items and must be treated with a degree of care. They should be stored in a safe place, and possibly locked, with access limited to a supervisor. They are not used frequently once operators develop judgment ability. Boundary samples must be signed and dated by the authorized quality representative, and it is manufacturing's responsibility to request and maintain them. Treat them like an investment!

Quality standards are generally incorporated into operator instruction sheets for detailed description of what type of condition to look for, where specifically to look, and how to make a judgment determination of good/no good. Operations people use the feedback from quality audits to determine the primary conditions to look for, as well as the most common areas of occurrence. This provides the ability to create a specific inspection method that can be incorporated into the work to ensure that key areas are checked for the most common problems. It promotes a higher level of quality at the source. The inspection step is not spelled out in detail in the standardized work documents but is shown as a single element (inspect the part).

Written quality standards that require a visual disposition of a product are subject to interpretation and are somewhat subjective. For example, the interpretation of "acceptable surface appearance" depends on the subjective opinion of "acceptable." In these situations it is essential that the quality department provide tangible examples of the desired quality levels. These are referred to as "boundary samples," and they represent the limit of acceptability for a particular issue.

The company generally establishes safety and environmental standards to follow state and federal regulations. These standards are usually created by the specific engineering departments and are not modifiable by other employees or management without approval from that engineering department. However, these requirements are provided to the employees who will develop standardized work methods to achieve the necessary operator and environmental safety. The work team or management for that area may develop safety requirements specific to a particular job. Examples would include specific injury risk, such as lacerations, or equipment pinch points. These potential safety concerns are noted by the safety cross on the standardized work document.

Standard Specifications

These specifications provide the technical information on the correct operation of equipment and certain process specifications required for producing a product. Examples include:

- Dimensions and tolerances
- Processing method (welding method, finishing method, etc.)
- Equipment operation parameters (time, temperature, pressure,
- Equipment operation sequence
- Corrective action information

Standard specifications are not detailed on the standardized work documents. They are included in the operator instruction documents only if not previously specified on other documents such as blueprints (there is no need to document standards previously specified).

Equipment operation parameters are used to develop equipment verification processes that become a task assignment for a specific individual and a routine standardized process. In Toyota's case, the team leader most often does this. The equipment verification process is completed at various intervals during the day to ensure correct operating conditions. In many cases it is completed prior to the start of the shift, and again during the shift, depending on the critical nature of the equipment. The intent of the "preshift" verification is to ensure that all process parameters are in the correct operating range and that equipment is operational and ready for production.

Corrective action information is handled similarly to the specifications for equipment verification. It provides detailed step-by-step actions to be taken in the event of equipment failure or process problems and includes contingency plans such as alternative equipment that may be used or the manual operation of equipment.

Standard specifications are typically provided by industrial or manufacturing engineering, and manufacturing uses the information to develop standard procedures and operator instruction sheets, as necessary. Some companies confuse these specifications with standard work for the operator, but the standard specifications do not tell the operator anything about work steps, timing, or how to optimally perform the job.

Standard Procedures

These are developed by the manufacturing group and are used to define operating rules. The procedures may be necessitated by the other sources of standards or may be the sole responsibility of manufacturing. Examples include:

- Standard work in process
- Kanban rules and parameters (inventory levels, number of cards, etc.)
- Material flow routes within the facility
- Defined 5S requirements
- Production result boards
- Color coding

These standard procedures should be *visually* defined in the work area and, thus, are self-explanatory and need not be documented in the standard work. For example, a kanban card includes all the information related to its use, and the standards are defined within the content of the card. Likewise, the defined agreements between operations will be visually apparent in the work area. Note that the items mentioned here are likely to change often as process improvements are made. It would become a paperwork nightmare to attempt to document these standards and constantly update them as conditions in the work area change. Develop a visual system to convey the standards, and maintain the visual awareness.

Myths of Standardized Work

There are many myths regarding standardized work in the world outside of Toyota. It is frustrating to see the amount of time and effort wasted by companies that fall into one or more of these myth traps and attempt to create a system based on them. We will attempt to debunk as many of these myths as possible in the hope that your efforts can be directed effectively toward the goal of process improvement.

Myth 1: If we have standardized work, anyone can learn everything about the job by looking at the documents.

We're not sure how this myth originated, but it is probably caused by Toyota's description of standardized work. During Toyota plant tours, standardized work is touted as the process used by operators to define their work method, and of course it is documented and posted. Perhaps this is misinterpreted as a fully detailed description of the work and associated standards. Anyone who has read the sheets would see that the work description explains the work elements in basic terms—not nearly enough information to read and fully understand the job.

Within Toyota, the job instruction method (explained in Chapter 11) is used to transfer complete knowledge of a job to a team member. This is a lengthy process, since there is much to learn to become an exceptionally qualified associate. Anyone who believes that a job is simple enough to distill down to a few sheets of paper underestimates the competency level necessary of their employees. We have never been in any work environment where the work is so simple that "everything you need to know" is on a few sheets of paper.

Myth 2: If we have standardized work, we can bring anyone off the street and train them to do the job in a few minutes.

Refer to Myth 1. This may be possible for a small portion of a job or for a specific task, but to become a "complete" employee with a full understanding of the work takes considerable effort. We often hear this myth in conjunction with a reference to bringing "monkeys" off the street that could be trained quickly.

Not only does this reference display a complete lack of respect for employees and their abilities, it mistakenly assumes the simplicity of the work done by employees. This mind-set will need to be adjusted in order to create the right culture for developing a lean operation.

Myth 3: We can incorporate all details of the work and standards into the standardized work sheet.

This is a classic case of trying to make a Swiss army knife out of a specific tool. Standardized work is not an all-inclusive tool. It is specifically used as a tool to identify and eliminate waste. After the most effective work method is established, the documented process is used as a visual reference to ensure adherence to the standard.

Myth 4: We will post the document so operators can look at the sheet each day to remember how to do the job.

This is a complete misunderstanding of the purpose of a visual standard. In this case, after the operator has been trained—a carefully controlled process that ensures the employee's capability before he or she is fully released to the job—and after the first few hundred repetitions, a reminder of the proper method is not necessary. The visual reference is utilized by *management* for adherence to the standard, which we'll discuss later when we describe "auditing the standardized work."

Myth 5: Employees develop their own standardized work.

This myth is partially true. Toyota does not want individual employees to "own" their standardized work, and uses job rotation so no one employee owns any one job. The initial standard work is developed by engineers working with representative operators who are part of a "pilot team," and this team assists in the launch of the next new model. Group leaders and team leaders then have responsibility for training employees on the standard work and soliciting their input. Once the process is operating at some level of stability, employees are challenged to develop better methods, but the methods are always reviewed by others, including management. So it is the work team with their team leader and group leader that collectively "own" the tasks to be accomplished.

This myth is often combined with a misguided attempt to institute "employee empowerment," whereby employees are free to develop their own work methods. It's this notion that creates fear in the hearts of managers who envision employees creating work that is inefficient and who worry that employees will take advantage of the situation.

Nothing could be further from the truth. If everyone is in agreement that the objective is to create a work method that meets the needs of the customer with the least amount of waste possible, it does not mean that employees have free will to create the work any way they would like. They still have to follow specific rules and guidelines. It is analogous to a sports team. Players at specific positions know their jobs in detail, but the coach does not simply say to players, "Do your own thing—you are empowered." The coach has specific ideas about the team's strategy and how specific individuals need to fulfill their roles. On the other hand, a coach who simply dictates how each player should play generally ends up with a player revolt and also does not capitalize on the unique talents and knowledge of each player. Similarly at Toyota, the work methods are not created in a vacuum. Everyone is looking at the work with the same intent. There are many possible alternatives. The idea is to find a method that is better than the current one. (Note that "better" is not subjective. It must be quantifiable and measurable.) Management has the responsibility to set the objectives for the employees and to provide the tools and resources necessary to achieve them. These objectives are most realistic if management has a deep understanding of the process, and of the lean philosophy, and is acting as an effective coach.

Myth 6: If we have standardized work, operators will do the job properly and will not deviate from the standard.

This may be the most preposterous myth. Defining work and documenting it on paper is still a great distance from good performance. There is nothing in standardized work that will prevent deviation by the operator except the visual awareness of others. To ensure compliance to the standard, it's necessary to remove options from the work area and to remove the "clouds." If any deviation from standard is immediately recognizable, and there is a negative consequence, the standard will be followed.

At Toyota work is so carefully defined and requirements for performance so stringent that a deviation from the standard will generally produce immediate recognition. Suppose an operator elects to perform a task out of sequence, and as a result the time required increases. This operator would likely exceed the takt time and need to "stop the line" using the andon cord. If this happened several times it would attract immediate attention, and when investigating the condition, the team leader or supervisor would verify adherence to the standard.

Standardized Work

Toyota says that the purpose of standardized work is as a "foundation for kaizen." If the work is not standardized and it is different each time, there is "no basis for evaluation," meaning no reference point from which to compare. Many companies are dismayed to discover that sometime after "improvements" are made, the work has returned to the "old way" and there has been no sustained

improvement. Doing kaizen before standardizing would be analogous to build
ing a house on quicksand. You may get it built, but it will be sinking fast!

You may ask, "If standardized work is the foundation for continuous improvement, why don't we do it first?" This is a good question. Toyota points out that
there are some prerequisites to developing standardized work. They are typically dealt with during the stability phase, and bear repeating here in case you're
tempted to skip the appetizer and head to the main course. Putting standardized
work ahead of stability will surely create a condition similar to a dog chasing its
tail—you will go round and round but never get the result you want.

Prerequisites of Standardized Work

A degree of stability is needed in each of the three areas listed below before
moving on to standardized work. Unfortunately, there are no definitive measures
that say, "Now you are ready for standardized work." The best advice we can
give is that if you feel like the dog chasing its tail, the process is not stabilized
enough for standardized work.

1.   The work task must be repeatable. If the work is described in "If . . . then"
     terms, it will not be possible to standardize. For example, if the task is
     described by saying, "If A happens, then do B, but if C happens, do D,"
     and so on, it is not possible to standardize unless these are just a few very
     simple rules.
2.   The line and equipment must be reliable, and downtime should be minimal.
     It is not possible to standardize if the work is constantly interrupted and
     the worker is sidetracked.
3.   Quality issues must be minimal. The product must have minimal defects
     and be consistent in its key parameters. If the worker is constantly correct-
     ing defects or struggling with the effects of poor product uniformity—
     such as size variation that affects the fit of the part, and thus the time
     required—it is not possible to see the true picture of the work.

TRAP

A frequent mistake when implementing an "improvement" to
the work is to leave an operator with a new process and withdraw support too soon, or worse—not to be present when the new
process is tried for the first time! The operator feels dumped on,
is not confident in what to do with the new procedure, and will
view "process improvements" as negative, stressful events.

Standardized Work Documents

There are three primary documents used for developing standardized work, and many other related or supporting documents. It is not the purpose of this book to go in to detail on how to use each of these tools but it is worth saying a bit about each of the following:

1. Standardized Work Chart
2. Standardized Work Combination Table
3. Production Capacity Sheet

Standardized Work Chart

Originally the document that Toyota used for the Standardized Work Chart was primarily a diagram of the work area and worker flow. There was no verbal description of the work method and no element times associated with each step. The detailed element times were a separate document, such as the Standardized Work Combination Table. Somewhere along the line in many operations the Standardized Work Chart and the Standardized Work Combination Table were blended into one simplified document that is often referred to (outside of Toyota at least) as a "Standardized Work Sheet," or "Standardized Work Chart."

The Standardized Work Sheet is used initially as a tool to identify and eliminate waste. After improvements are made, the new method becomes the baseline for improvement. Then it is posted in the work area as a method of visual control for management to verify adherence to the standard.

As with any tool, its use is dependent upon the circumstances. What is the skill of the user? What condition is being corrected? Do not worry about trying to achieve a perfect result or using the sheet "correctly." During the initial application of standardized work in a process, the first step is to create a baseline for improvement. The steps of the process are:

1. Record the sequence of the job (the work steps)
2. Diagram the work movement.
3. Identify waste
4. Determine improvements needed to achieve desired results (meeting the takt time is an objective that is explained below)
5. Incorporate material usage and flow (standard in-process stock)
6. Document improved method

Figure 6-5, below, provides an example of a Standardized Work Sheet. The main elements are the work sequence and the diagram of the work movement. Once the steps and diagram of the work flow are completed we ask the question, "What do you see?" Look at the diagram and describe your initial impression.

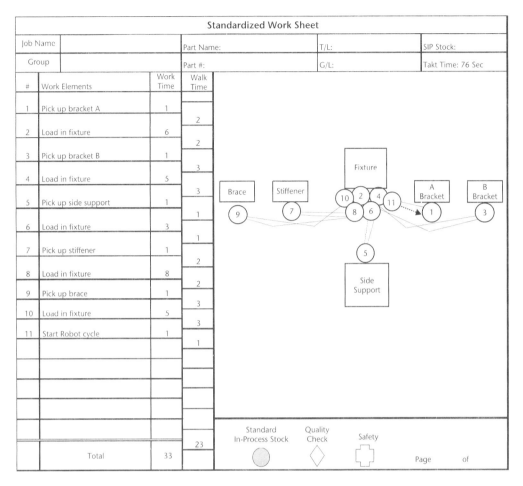

Figure 6-5. Standardized Work Sheet

Your initial impression is of the waste! If we ask the question regarding the job depicted in the figure we might get the answers: "It is a mess," and "Look at the long distance between operations," or "The operator has to crisscross his work pattern." These are observations of the waste. Once the waste is understood we can ask: "Is there a better method?"

As you progress through the improvement cycle your use of the Standardized Work Chart will change. The initial effort to achieve standardization and eliminate waste within a single operation shifts to creating operations that are aligned and balanced with other operations in the flow. This alignment is achieved by designing jobs that are aligned to a common pace known as takt time (explained below).

TIP

Focus on the Work, Not the Operator

One advantage of documenting the work flow and showing it to operators is that it removes the "fault" for a poor method from the operator. If you see waste and point it out to operators, they will likely explain why it is necessary (defending the method, which they own). If you diagram the work and show operators the diagram, they are likely to respond, "Look at the poor work pattern. We should change that!"

Standardized Work Combination Table

As the name implies, this table (also called the Standardized Work Combination Sheet) is used for analyzing jobs that have combined work. The intent is to show the relationship in terms of time of two or more activities that occur simultaneously. It is used primarily for operations that have a combination of manual operations and automatic equipment, but it can also be used for operations where two or more operators work together on the same product at the same time. For example, a good application for this tool would be if an operator loads a robotic welding station and pushes the start button, and the robot welds while the operator unloads and loads another station. We have seen many people attempt to use the Standardized Work Combination Table for all jobs, but using it to analyze a single operator who does not utilize automatic equipment is a waste of time and effort. You will not learn anything from this analysis except how to fill out the form.

Figure 6-5, above, depicts an operation with an automatic cycle robot. The shortcoming of using a simple Standardized Work Sheet analysis in this case is that it does not show what happens after the robot cycle is started. There will

TIP

The Operator Is Your Most Important Resource

The Toyota Way philosophy is that the operator, not the machine, is the most important asset. The machine serves the person, not the other way around. Toyota believes that it is disrespectful to the individual to waste his or her value by waiting for a machine to complete its cycle. The Standardized Work Combination Table is used to gain an understanding of the man/machine relationship and to effectively utilize the human asset.

likely be the waste of waiting by the operator. The operator may perform miscellaneous tasks to "keep busy," such as getting the next parts ready or "organizing" the work area (we observed one operator neatly restacking every part in the bin, which looked nice but was of no value). It is not clear what the cycle time of the robot is. The Standardized Work Combination Table (Figure 6-6) is useful for this situation.

Figure 6-6 shows the same job depicted on a Standardized Work Combination Table. Read it by following the work elements one by one from left to right, and you can see where in the cycle the operator walks to perform the next work element. In this example the operator picks up Bracket A in one second, walks to the machine in two seconds, loads Bracket A in six seconds, walks to get the next part in two seconds, and so on. By Step 11 all of the parts are loaded into the robotic welder, and you see by the dotted line that the machine cycles for 23 seconds.

#	Work Elements	Manual	Auto	Walk
1	Pick up Bracket A	1		2
2	Load in fixture	6		2
3	Pick up Bracket B	1		3
4	Load in fixture	5		3
5	Pick up Side Support	1		1
6	Load in fixture	3		1
7	Pick up Stiffener	1		2
8	Load in fixture	8		2
9	Pick up Brace	1		3
10	Load in fixture	5		3
11	Start Robot cycle	1	23	1
12				
13				
14				
15				
	Totals	33	21	23

Process Name: ___   Date: ___   Part Name / Part#: ___   Group: ___   Takt Time: 76

Standardized Work Combination Table — Manual / Automatic / Walking

Figure 6-6. Standardized Work Combination Table with one robot

This is a fairly simple job in terms of the operator-machine interface. More complex jobs may have an operator who moves within a cell and operates three or four machines. Like the Standardized Work Chart, the Standardized Work Combination Table converts the work into a visual format so the work/walk/wait time relationships can clearly be seen (the waiting time on this job should be the first improvement target!). The waiting time occurs after the operator starts the robot cycle. This time should be utilized for additional value-adding activity.

Figure 6-7, below, shows the same job with the addition of a secondary task by adding loading and unloading of a second automatic operation. Notice that the operation time "wraps around," meaning the machine operates beyond the takt time relative to the start time of the operation. The important thing to note is that the second robot completes its cycle before the operator is ready to return to reload it (the robots have an automatic unload feature, which is common in

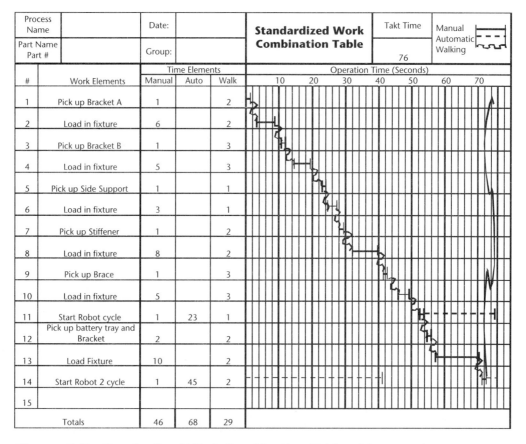

#	Work Elements	Manual	Auto	Walk	Operation Time (Seconds)
1	Pick up Bracket A	1		2	
2	Load in fixture	6		2	
3	Pick up Bracket B	1		3	
4	Load in fixture	5		3	
5	Pick up Side Support	1		1	
6	Load in fixture	3		1	
7	Pick up Stiffener	1		2	
8	Load in fixture	8		2	
9	Pick up Brace	1		3	
10	Load in fixture	5		3	
11	Start Robot cycle	1	23	1	
12	Pick up battery tray and Bracket	2		2	
13	Load Fixture	10		2	
14	Start Robot 2 cycle	1	45	2	
15					
	Totals	46	68	29	

Process Name / Date: / Part Name Part # / Group: / **Standardized Work Combination Table** / Takt Time 76 / Manual — Automatic - - - Walking

Figure 6-7. Standardized Work Combination Table with two robots

Toyota). In Toyota's view, it is acceptable to allow a machine to wait for the operator, but it is not acceptable to allow the operator to wait for the machine. Remember, the operator comes first.

Production Capacity Sheet

The Production Capacity Sheet (not shown here) indicates the capacity of machinery in the process. You must consider the cycle time of the equipment, that is, how long it takes to process each piece, but also factor in planned downtime during tool changes and changeover times. It is most applicable to machining operations that involve tooling wear and tool changes, but applies to operations such as injection molding and stamping, where changeover times must be considered. It is a useful tool for identifying bottleneck operations.

The document used is very similar to capacity planning processes used by most manufacturing engineers to specify equipment for purchase. The primary purpose is to determine if the machinery has capacity for the production requirement. Calculations are based on the available run time, the cycle time per piece, and time lost due to tool changes or other changeover requirements.

Some Challenges of Developing Standardized Work

Aside from an attempt to develop standardized work based on the myths mentioned earlier, other challenges include attempts to standardize an entire "job," versus task elements of the job, and attempting to standardize a task that has variation built in. Much of the work we see in companies today includes a variety of tasks that are performed by a single individual.

For example, an employee may have a task to build a certain product. In addition he or she will also retrieve the materials necessary and deliver the finished goods to the next operation. The task of building the product is fairly consistent and easy enough to document, but what about the other tasks? They occur randomly, or once every so many cycles. How would you weave these two distinctly different tasks together into one Standardized Work Sheet? The answer is that generally you don't. The work elements needed to build the product constitute the primary task (and the value-adding operation), and it should be standardized creating the most efficient, repeatable method. Within Toyota, operators do not typically retrieve their own materials nor transport finished product because these activities take away from the value-adding activities. The transportation of materials would be standardized for the person responsible for them, such as a material handler.

In Chapters 4 and 5 we discussed the need to isolate variation so that standardization may be achieved. The following case example illustrates the challenge of standardizing a task with built-in variation. In these cases, before the task can be standardized the variation must be separated or isolated from the remaining portion, which can then be standardized.

Case Example: One Job, Three Different Tasks

The "job" in this case example is to operate two automatic screw machines, which cut and machine long bars of steel into discrete metal parts. The operator's work includes three distinctly different tasks. The variation inherent in the three tasks makes the job nearly impossible to standardize.

The first task is to perform in-station quality checks and serve the machine (removing metal chips and moving finished product). The operator is required to perform a specific number of part inspections each hour. The inspections are repeatable in nature, and the task is repeated within a one-hour time frame (a standard cycle time).

The second task involves loading raw material as needed. This task is also repeatable in nature, but the cycle time varies, based on the part being produced and the cycle time of each part produced. The time variation is between one and two hours.

The third task is to set up and change tooling when worn and between product changes. This portion of the job is not repeatable within several hours, and the frequency of this event is highly variable.

The tasks range from fairly repeatable and consistent to very variable and inconsistent. When blended into one job, it is not possible to determine a repeatable pattern that can be standardized. To complicate matters, each operator is responsible for two machines. If one machine is in setup and the other needs material, the machine in setup will wait. If both machines are in setup simultaneously, one machine will wait for attention. In many cases this lost time exceeded several *days*. If both machines were operating normally, the first task was not enough to fully occupy the operators' time and they had considerable waiting time. This scenario created waiting time for *both* the operator and the machine.

To isolate variation, the work tasks were reassigned. The first task was assigned to one person who was now responsible for servicing 10 machines and performing the quality checks. The loading of material was assigned to one operator who was responsible for 10 machines, and the setup responsibility was assigned to two people for all 10 machines. This reassignment "freed up" an operator, and the team leader role was created to provide additional support to the line.

The reassignment also provided additional advantages, such as two people working simultaneously on setup activities, thus reducing the overall setup times. This reduction facilitated the reduction of batch sizes, increased the run frequency, and reduced the overall inventory. The team leader position ensured that each position would be filled every day and the output would be consistent. Andon signals were added to the machines to notify the material feeder before the machine ran out. The andon also included notification of impending setup and tool changes. These signals allowed the operators to prepare for upcoming tasks, verifying the readiness of tools and material *before* the actual need. These changes increased the overall output of the operation by 30 percent.

TRAP

STOP

Is Standardized Work an ISO-Controlled Operator Instruction?

Many companies today have pursued ISO certification. As organizations struggle with defining ISO requirements, this question will undoubtedly be raised when we begin to use standardized work: "Is standardized work a controlled document per the ISO requirement?" While we are not ISO experts, we have seen the result as companies struggle with the paperwork nightmare often associated with ISO. Many companies opt to refrain from posting any documents out of fear of getting "dinged" on an ISO audit or because every change to the process will require a laborious effort to update the paperwork. One company we observed removes all standardized work documents prior to an ISO audit and replaces them afterward (to appease the lean auditors). Whether standardized work is in fact a controlled document per ISO requirements depends upon interpretation.

Remember that standardized work is used as an analysis tool and establishes a baseline for continuous improvement. It is not an operator instruction, and it is not provided to the operator as a training tool (see myths, above). Management uses it to audit and verify the general steps of the job, and as such, it should be up to date. If you do make standardized work a controlled document, create a simple system that allows it to be "a living document" and makes it easy to change (e.g., one level approval process).

Auditing the Standardized Work

As mentioned, it's a common myth that standardized work is posted so the operator can refer to it while doing the job. At Toyota operations, standardized work faces out toward the aisle, where the operator cannot easily see it. It is for the benefit of the team leader and group leader who are responsible for auditing the standard work.

Isn't auditing a coercive type of management practice that reinforces the view of standardized work as the framework of a rigid bureaucracy? In an adversarial environment, auditing anything is the basis for conflict and tension. But in an environment where the focus is on eliminating waste to better serve the customer, auditing standard work is a way to maintain stability of the process. It is a cooperative venture between management and the worker. Operators often deviate from the standardized work because of a problem (creating a "work around"). Management audits uncover the root problems and ensure that they are corrected quickly and standardized work is re-established.

TIP

Allow Time for Adjustment to the New Method

A change in the work method (standardized work) will require an adjustment period. The body becomes "habituated" and will tend to return to the familiar pattern. For example, if you change from a standard-shift car to an automatic shift, you will reach for the shift lever unconsciously (and it will not be there!). It is necessary to provide continued support as the operator adjusts to the new method.

Two things trigger an audit at Toyota. First, a problem: What caused a defect? What is causing an operator to repeatedly get behind? Often, observing the operator through several cycles compared to the standard work will reveal the source of the problem. Second, it may simply be time for the audit. Toyota has a standard work auditing schedule, much as they have a schedule for preventive maintenance. You don't need to wait for the machine to break down before you maintain it at Toyota. Similarly, you don't need to wait for an operator error to audit the standard work.

Auditing allows for the discovery of deviation from the standard method. We often erroneously conclude that the operator is at fault when a deviation occurs. Upon investigation, we may find that the deviation is due to a malfunctioning piece of equipment or a problem with the product. The reason for the audit is to find the cause of the problem and to correct it.

In many Toyota operations there's a visual system set up for auditing the standard work. Each work group may have a visual board with cards called a *kamishibai* board (story book). At NUMMI, group leaders check one process each day for compliance to standardized work, watching work cycles. This brings them to each job at least once per month. The cards contain questions they complete on the performance of standardized work and the accuracy of the standardized work document. Discrepancies are noted and countermeasures described on the card. There is a card slot for every process in a team. The cards are moved to a corresponding adjacent vacant slot once the check has been performed. When a problem is noted, the card is turned with the dark side facing out, indicating that something needs correction. Assistant managers check the boards each day to verify that the checks are being made properly. They randomly select a card from the board, obtain the standardized work and conduct a check of a process with the group leader. There are approximately 90 boards throughout the shop.

Now compare this to many companies that "have" standard work. A standard work sheet is filled out and posted, perhaps by an industrial engineer. If they get really fancy, it may have photos of the work steps. It is posted so the operator can see it. No one does anything with it, but it looks good to visitors, who can say, "They look lean."

Standardized Work as a Baseline for Continuous Improvement

After the initial standardization of tasks the real fun begins. We should now ask, "Where is the next level of opportunity?" This is where the answer becomes more complex. We must reconsider our primary objective—to get more value-added activity with less cost, or in other words, to make more parts with fewer resources. Before running off and making improvements, however, we should first understand what will be done with the gain. It is important to always make improvement based on need, rather than because improvement is possible. Improvement will always be possible!

If you continue to reduce setup time, for example, what will you do with the additional time? Is it important to drive down batch sizes, to increase flexibility, or do you need the volume? Too often we see companies "do setup reduction" and reduce the time significantly, but there is no plan for using the freed up time, and the setup times slowly creep back to the original level. This same phenomenon applies to other "improvements." When improvements are made, you must change the process so that sustaining the improvements is necessary for continued success. The improved level must become the new standard, and the excess removed. If there is no need to sustain, any gains will not be maintained.

TIP

A New Standard Requires a Learning Period

It is not uncommon to see a slight drop in performance as people adjust to the new method. Do not rush to "go back to the old way." Continue observing to ensure that the method is being followed as planned and that any minor adjustments are made immediately.

Takt Time as a Design Parameter

Many people get confused about the difference between takt time and cycle time. Takt time is not a tool. It is a concept that is used to design work, and it measures the pace of customer demand. In terms of calculation, it is the available time to produce parts within a specified time interval divided by the number of parts demanded in that time interval. The number you get tells you, for instance, that a part needs to be produced every three minutes to satisfy customer demand. Seem straightforward? Yet takt time is often misunderstood. And determining it for lines that produce a variety of products with varying demands, becomes a tricky issue.

Here's an example: If the available operation time for one shift is 400 minutes, and the demand for the product is 400 per shift, the time allotted per piece (takt time) is one minute for each part. The cycle time of each operation needs to be one minute or less on average to meet the demand. If the cycle time (actual time to complete the tasks in a single job) is greater than takt, the operation will be a bottleneck and additional time will be necessary to meet the production schedule. If the cycle time is less than takt, there will be overproduction or waiting time.

A major challenge that arises is determining the customer demand. In most cases (unless you are a supplier to Toyota) the demand varies significantly. How can takt time be determined when the demand varies? You must understand that takt time is a "reference point" for designing the work, and consider what the effect of an incorrect reference point will be.

The first thing to recognize is that cycle times—the time necessary to complete the task—do not vary significantly if they are standardized. Using our example above, the machine cycle time is 23 seconds and the operator work and walk time is 56 seconds. The combined cycle time is 75 seconds and varies only to the extent that the operator can load the robot faster now and then. This means that the output from this process will be fairly consistent provided there are no losses due to equipment downtime. If the demand varies significantly, what effect does this have on the operation? None. The operation cycle time will not vary more than a few seconds. If demand increases, how will the requirement be met? The operation time can be increased (e.g., using overtime if the demand does not increase too much). The utilization of takt time will not change this reality.

So how do we determine the demand and takt time? Select a demand number that will be sufficiently *high* enough to meet the need *most* of the time. For example, suppose the demand varies from 10,000 to 20,000 per month but the average is 16,000 per month. Which number should you choose? It depends on the situation, but generally we advise a higher number. Here's why. Let's suppose we use the maximum: 20,000. If we calculate a takt time, we will get a *lower* number (less time allotted per piece). We compare the takt time to the cycle time to determine the discrepancy. Selecting a *higher* demand number will create a *larger* discrepancy. The relevance of the discrepancy is only related to the amount of improvement necessary to achieve the takt rate, and the improvement potential is based on the waste that exists in the operation.

When presented with this dilemma, a Toyota sensei would respond, "No problem," meaning that the pool of waste is large and the needed improvement can assuredly be made. The only risk of setting a demand level too large is that the amount of effort needed to achieve the takt time will be greater. You do not want to waste effort by falsely inflating the demand number (driving takt down), but it is not a major problem. If a process is improved beyond the actual need, the resources can be reduced or additional sales can be pursued.

The takt time serves as a common "beat" for all operations in the value stream. An operation balance chart is a powerful visual tool for seeing how cycle times compare to takt. In some cases it can be used for answering "What if?" questions about the capability of the process. Figure 6-8 shows an operation balance chart that was used to compare cycle times in a value stream to takt time. In this case the company wanted to increase production in order to meet possible increased demand that was only roughly estimated. They wanted to know how

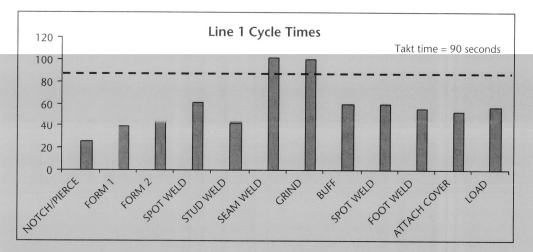

Figure 6-8. Operation balance chart to compare cycle times

much of a change would be needed to meet a hypothetical takt of 90 seconds per part. We see that two operations are currently over that estimated takt time.

If these two operations were improved, how much improvement would be necessary before the next balance "plateau" is reached? Figure 6-9 shows the next plateau. Several other jobs have a cycle time of approximately 60 seconds. Reducing the two jobs to 60 seconds would allow the entire value stream to flow at a rate of one part every 60 seconds. Does that mean we should immediately pursue this goal? In fact if we do this and the takt time based on actual demand is greater than 60 second we will be over producing—the fundamental waste.

After reducing the time it took for the two operations, it was determined that the actual takt rate necessary to meet the demand was 80 seconds. This allowed for "rebalancing" the operations and reducing their total number. In this case, after reducing the time it took to grind and buff, the total amount of work across all operations added to 645 seconds. If we divide 645 seconds of work by the takt of 80 seconds, we get a total of 8 operations at the takt time, compared to the original 12. Thus, we could reduce one-third of the operations by rebalancing to the 80-second takt. If this were manual processes, it would equate to 4 fewer operators (note: these "extra" operators could be used to develop a team leader structure as outlined in Chapter 10). It is interesting to note that if we balanced to the faster takt of 60 seconds, 11 operators would be needed (645/60 = 10.75). Thus, going faster can cost more (provided it was not necessary to go faster).

Use takt time to help make decisions about how the work will be designed and which improvements need to be made to meet the need. If you select a takt time that is too high, you will not meet the production need, which is worse than choosing a number that's too low and exceeding the need (provided you did not add resources to meet the false need). It is always easier to stop production

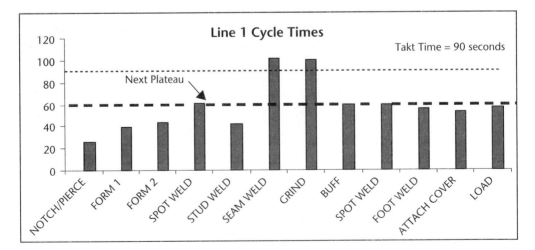

Figure 6-9. Cycle balance chart showing next level plateau

when the output is too high than it is to get more out if it's too low. When in doubt, choose a higher demand and a lower takt time.

Importance of Visual Controls

The use of visual controls is the most important step in the process of developing standardization. Unfortunately, it is also the aspect of a lean process that is most often belittled. We frequently hear, "They are just doing 5S." Perhaps this is due to the examples of visual control most often cited, namely, markings on the floor to indicate the location of trash containers and other items in the work area, which are viewed as "silly" and perhaps insulting to the intelligence of employees. Another example is signs that are used to identify the proper location of items or the type of material stored in a location. Managers and employees often respond with, "We all know what belongs there." However, when asked to identify *specific* conditions such as the standard quantity, the minimum or maximum, or the supplying operation, the response is usually less certain.

Figure 6-10 demonstrates that the primary reason for visual control is to define the desired "normal" state (standard), and then to quickly recognize any

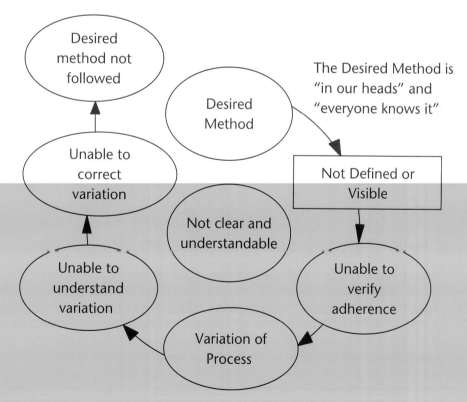

Figure 6-10. Lack of visual awareness leads to incorrect methods

deviation from that standard. As we have seen, there are many different specifications, procedures, and requirements within every work area. It is virtually impossible for every employee to remember all of these, and a written description of each in a notebook would be impractical for instant recognition.

One common condition is that people believe they "know" the standards, and any visual representation is redundant and unnecessary. Upon closer evaluation it is simple to determine the true awareness of standards. Ask different employees to explain the specific method to be followed. Is it possible for you to determine whether it's happening as it's supposed to be? The case example below on paint line loading illustrates that without the ability to quickly and easily verify adherence to standards, the abnormality will not be detected and will continue.

The following case example illustrates what happens when standards are "known" but are not visually displayed.

Case Example: Creating Visual Standards with a Paint Line Loading Pattern

This case example refers to a paint line that has three different color paint booths. The main line branches into three lines to supply all three booths. Given this branching from one main line, it is critical to the flow of product for the correct mix of product color and model to be loaded on the line to prevent overloading any booth and clogging the line. Observation of the paint line (standing in the circle) revealed that product flow to one or two paint booths was often blocked by an overload at the other. This caused the entire loading process to stop, and the total line stoppage time was substantiated by the system data. This issue was especially critical since the paint system was the constraint operation for the entire facility (it is the only operation in the plant through which *all* product passes), and the system was above maximum capacity.

The paint department manager and the loading employees agreed that the product had to be mixed properly on the line and even agreed on what the mix was supposed to be. Each person noted, however, that "they" don't always follow the rules. (The mysterious "they." Who are "they"?) A closer review of the agreed-upon mix revealed that the desired method (not a defined standard yet) was vague and general. It included descriptions such as, "No more than two of this type per hour," and "This product is supposed to follow one of these three models," and "No more than six of this color per hour." It was clear that trying to memorize this proposed sequence would be nearly impossible (there were many variables). If it were possible to memorize, it's likely that the only people who could accomplish that would be those who do it every day. This is a problem if a regular employee is absent, and it's impossible for anyone outside of that group to easily understand.

A team of three people who knew the process was assembled to develop a loading pattern that would meet all of the required constraints regarding color and model mix. It took this team nearly three days to finally determine a pattern that met all parameters and conditions. With this level of complexity, imagine the difficulty in memorizing such a pattern! Is it any wonder that the operators were not "following the rules" when the rules were so difficult to define?

The team developed an ingenious visual loading board that depicted the pattern, requiring the operators to move a color-coded magnet indicating the completion of the task. The operators responded favorably because the requirement was defined and clear and they did not get yelled at for not "following the rules." The line stoppage was reduced considerably, and the number of completed units (each unit included several subcomponents) painted per day rose from 80 to over 110. As the operators gained a deeper understanding of visual standards, they made several enhancements to the board, further clarifying the requirement and incrementally leveling the mix (detailed in the next chapter).

Standardization Is a Waste Elimination Tool

Developing standardized work is the first step. It not only provides a standard way of doing the task, but the process of doing the analysis will reveal waste that should be eliminated as part of developing the standardized work. When standard work is developed and operators are properly trained, regular audits are needed to check on whether the standards are being followed, and if not, why. Operators should be encouraged to suggest changes that will improve the process and be reflected in revisions to the standardized work.

Once standards are developed, the standard condition should be visually displayed so deviations from the standard will be obvious. The paint case example illustrates the power of making a visual standard that was visible and understandable to everyone. Visual indicators by themselves become powerful tools only when used for visual control, showing the contrast between the standard and the actual situation (Figure 6-11). Following the standard as defined "clears the clouds" and improves flow and overall performance. Toyota places a high importance on the use of visual controls to support the adherence to standards. We cannot stress enough the need to "make it visual."

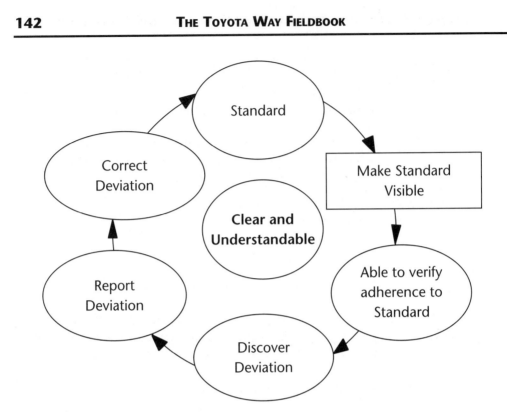

Figure 6-11. Visual standards support adherence to correct methods

Reflect and Learn from the Process

As always, begin these exercises by "walking the flow" with your current state map in hand. If you've begun implementing improvements and have established some defined connections, you have created standards as well. Begin to envision the future state and to draw the defined connections on a future state map.

1. Has customer demand been determined and takt time calculated?
    a. Identify the method currently used to monitor achievement of the takt rate at each operation.
    b. Is it possible to see and understand this standard? If not, identify a corrective action necessary to create a visual standard of takt time and add these items to your action plan.
    c. Is performance to the takt-rate standard being measured and recorded? If not, add this item to your action plan.

     d. Inability to consistently achieve the takt rate is an indicator of instability. Identify the causes and necessary corrections to reduce instability and to achieve the standard (takt rate) at least 85 percent of the time.

2. Defined, dedicated, and controlled connections between processes serve as agreed-upon expectations of performance (standards) between a supplier process and a customer process. Review your connections and answer these questions.

     a. Is there visual awareness of the standards?
        i. What is the expectation?
        ii. When is it supposed to be done?
        iii. Who is supposed to do it?
        iv. How do you know if it has been successfully completed?

     b. What is the current ability to achieve the standard (satisfy the customer)? If the performance is below 85 percent, identify necessary steps to improve performance, and make a plan to implement it.

3. Identify an operation that does not consistently achieve the standard. Stand in the circle, and observe the following conditions.

     a. Is the work method repeatable? (If it's difficult to document the work steps because of constant interruption, it is not repeatable.) If not, list the causes of variation and corrective actions necessary to stabilize the process.

     b. Is the work process interrupted more than 10 percent of the time because of equipment issues or quality-related problems? (Don't overlook small issues such as difficulty loading or unloading a fixture.) Make plans to correct the issues that interrupt the process.

4. After the major issues have been resolved and the process is reliable and stable, stand in the circle to study the job and identify waste.

     a. Use a Standardized Work Sheet to document the steps of the job.

     b. Draw a diagram of the work area and where each step is performed.

     c. Note the waste, and develop plans to improve the work process to reduce the waste.

d. Use the Standardized Work Sheet to diagram the proposed changes and show the waste elimination as a reduction of total cycle time.

e. What effect did the reduction of waste (and a cycle time reduction) have on the overall work balance and flow?

5. In the reflection questions in Chapter 5, you measured the cycle times for each operation. Identify the processes in the value stream that inhibit flow (cycle times that are over takt, or that are higher than the others), and target them for waste reduction using standardized work as an analysis tool.

Chapter 7

Leveling: Be More Like the Tortoise Than the Hare

The Leveling Paradox

The Toyota Way is full of paradoxes, and one of the most counterintuitive is the leveling paradox: that slow and steady can beat fast and jerky, like the parable of the tortoise and the hare [which the older Toyota Production System (TPS) masters often cite]. The tortoise lumbers along slow and determined while the hare sprints, runs out of breath, and takes a nap. We see a similar trend all the time in the way people work. Work, work, work to meet a deadline, and then coast for a while. Toyota would always prefer a slow and consistent pace of work.

The other side of leveling, besides a steady quantity of work, is a steady mix of work. In some ways this is even more difficult to rationalize. In manufacturing, if you're making more than one type of part, say 50-50 production between Part A and Part B, it is natural to try to get the most production possible by building large batches of A followed by large batches of B. This is particularly attractive if it takes time to set up the process to switch between A and B. Yet Toyota would prefer to make A, B, A, B . . . This leveled mix is closer to a true one-piece flow.

These days, "build to order" is all the rage. Companies like Dell Computer have led the way building just what the customer orders over the Internet and virtually eliminating finished goods inventory. Unfortunately, what is good for the assembler is not always good for the supplier. Dell expects suppliers to keep a considerable amount of inventory that the supplier is paying for in warehouses near Dell's assembly plant. From the Toyota Way viewpoint, Dell has not solved the root cause of the problem, but merely pushed the problem backward onto other companies. This will show up in a non-lean value stream and ultimately in higher costs and lower profits for someone—in this case the suppliers.

One might ask: "If Toyota is in fact lean wouldn't they build exactly what the customer orders in the sequence in which they order, like Dell?" The answer is decidedly no! Customers do not order in a stable, predictable way. Yet the foundation of TPS is a stable, leveled schedule. Another Toyota paradox is that in order to have a lean value stream, you sometimes want to hold the most expensive inventory—finished goods inventory. This allows you to ship to order but build to a leveled schedule. In this chapter we will discuss the whys and hows of leveling the schedule.

Heijunka Provides a Standardized Core for Resource Planning

The term "heijunka," as we noted earlier, means to level, or to make smooth. As with many translated words, there is some conceptual meaning lost in the translation. In most lean references, the meaning is to level the product mix over a specific time period, with the objective of producing every part every day (or even every few hours). Customers do not typically order products in specific batch sizes, but they're often produced in batches. The concept is to produce in smaller quantities more aligned with actual customer consumption.

But this is only part of the concept. Pushing a process toward an ideal smoothness in production also pushes the process to the highest degree of flexibility and responsiveness to changing customer demand.

We have never seen a situation where customers conveniently order the same mix and quantity of parts every day. If life were only that simple! Constantly changing demand creates many issues within the value stream; namely, the alignment of resources to the constantly changing need. If the demand swings are large, there will be a need to have higher levels of inventory to adjust to the swings. Equipment capacity is limited when demand swings to the high side, and is in excess when demand is on the decline. The amount of resources needed will be higher overall—generally, set at levels necessary to meet the higher demand, and excessive when the demand falls.

The swings in customer demand create a "bull whip" effect. A slight flick of the wrist by someone skilled with a bullwhip creates a tremendous destructive force at the other end of the whip. Similarly, even small variations in customer demand at the final process ripple through the entire value stream, increasing in amplitude with each successive operation. This whip effect is particularly large for suppliers or subprocesses, at the end of the whip. This magnifying effect

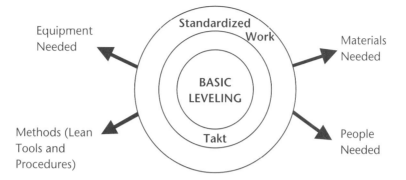

Figure 7-1. Basic leveling is the core for all resource planning

creates the need for higher levels of resources (and cost) to be able to accommodate the wide swings.

This creates a condition that makes standardized work difficult, if not impossible, to implement. Remember, in standardized work we're trying to create a precise balance of work across operations, based on the takt time, which is based on the rate of customer demand. If the takt goes up and down with the bullwhip, the work balancing and standardized work swings wildly every day. How is it possible to standardize when the takt is continually changing? This is the basis for the second form of heijunka: a self-imposed leveling for the internal benefit of the value stream (and cascading outward to suppliers as well). This leveling of demand creates a standard core onto which all resource needs are attached and aligned, as depicted in Figure 7-1.

Why Do This to Yourself?

Leveling your production is a self-inflicted choice. We say self-inflicted because it is a conscious choice, and there is a consequence. Some negative effect comes with the choice. Leveling means precise timing and being very flexible to cycle through products in small batches. This flexibility taxes the process. Any problem that causes delays will reveal itself immediately and result in a missed schedule.

For example, to level by product type means making small quantities of each item throughout the day, which means changing over from product to product. There is often some time associated with changing materials, changing a fixture, and so on. Changing over is lost production time. If the changeover process is not standardized and precise, then the large number of changeovers will lead to lost production, and the schedule will be missed. From a traditional mass production perspective, any lost production time is bad. From an overall lean system perspective, making smaller batches is good. The choice to level will leave no option but to reduce the time it takes to change over, which means having a controlled and standardized changeover process.

Some people do not like the fact that when you put this level of requirement on the process there is pressure to perform. And there's some risk of missing production numbers. Our minds are designed to naturally protect us from risks, and the purposeful creation of risk is not a natural act. This is the rub of the Toyota Way. We must put ourselves in harm's way, but not haphazardly. It requires a carefully crafted system, and diligent effort and management of the process, to minimize the risk. You must realize that when you sign up for the creation of a lean process, you sign up for life. If you want it to work, it's a permanent commitment.

So, why would you do this to yourself? If we look at any typical operation, we hear terms like "bubble" and "wave," which refer to the change in demand and the amount of work that flows through the value stream. Many managers spend time managing the waves—attempting to adjust the balance of resources and constantly fighting the fires that erupt as a result of the crashing waves. These managers are always looking for the day when they catch the wave and get things back to "normal." Unfortunately, like in the ocean, the next wave is not far behind. This continuous riding of the waves diverts efforts from the process of improvement. Management is devoting much of their time to the containment effort rather than the strengthening activity.

Smoothing Demand for Upstream Processes

What if your demand were consistent? How would that affect your process? The introduction into the value stream of consistent "customer" demand signals (the quotes signify that heijunka is not the "true" customer demand) will provide a smoothing effect for all of the processes. This smoothing allows for the standardization of resources, which greatly simplifies planning and control.

Let's revisit our value stream model introduced in Chapter 3 and depicted in Figure 7-2, below. We see that the future state value stream has a heijunka "board" or "box." This is a common approach to visually displaying the leveled schedule. Each slot in the box represents a specific time period (such as 8:00 A.M. to 8:15 A.M.) in which the material handler might pick up a production kanban, deliver it to the pacesetter as the next order, and pick up what was produced based on the previous order. In reality there are many ways to do this; for example, sometimes the orders are posted on a white board by the hour. There are several variations on the theme, but all serve the same purpose—to show the "pitch" time increment between when orders are delivered and picked up, and the quantity to produce

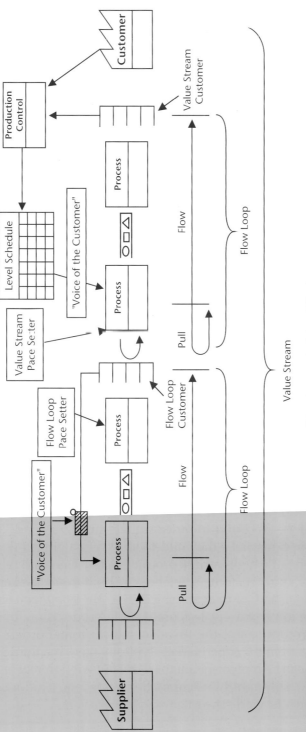

Figure 7-2. Future state value stream map with elements identified

during the pitch (see "Learning to See" for a description of pitch time). This is a mechanism that supports the leveling process. The pacesetter has a clear understanding throughout the day whether he or she is ahead or behind.

If the value stream pacesetter follows this schedule, what happens? The pacesetter will consume the components necessary to complete the task and "withdraw" them from the supermarket upstream. Since the pacesetter is leveled, this withdrawal will also be leveled. For example, say there are three different components used for assembly at the pacesetter—call them A, B, and C—and each is used for a different end product. If the assembly of end products is leveled, the consumption of A, B, and C will be leveled. That is, there will be a smooth rotation among the consumption of A, B, and C. This allows for keeping the minimum amount of inventory of A, B, and C in the supermarket. In contrast, if the assemblers suddenly spend an entire day just using part A and the supplier had put just a part of the day's worth of part A in the supermarket, the assembly would run out of A and shut down. So once the system is set up to be leveled, it's critical that the leveling process is actually followed, or you will run out of parts. When production is initiated to replenish the component supermarket, the process withdraws raw materials from the supermarket, which signals the supplier of the need for replenishment. Again, if the pacesetter is leveled, then the signals to the supplier will also be leveled, mitigating the infamous bullwhip effect in which the customer plant makes changes in schedules for its convenience only to jerk around suppliers in violent waves. With leveling, suppliers will have a good idea of what is expected of them and be able to plan with confidence. They can now balance resources to a known takt and get lean by improving quality and operating at lower cost.

We often hear companies say we cannot be level because our customers are not level. The leveled "schedule" for the first flow loop is created by production control even when the customer is not level. Note that production control has two sources of information to create the leveled schedule. There is a direct arrow from the customer—the build-to-order signal—and a second arrow from the finished goods supermarket—the build-to-stock signal. In lean systems this is a common way to handle high-variety product mixes. The relatively high-volume products that you know customers will buy are built to stock—kept in the supermarket and replenished as they are shipped to the customer using a kanban-type system. The lower-variety, less predictable products are built to customer order. Production control sees the stream of real customer orders coming in and the kanban orders from the supermarket. Typically there is a third stream of safety buffer stock that can be replenished if there are not enough real or kanban orders to fulfill in a day. Through this combination of orders, production control has the tools to create a leveled schedule.

There is no need for additional external scheduling or planning beyond this one scheduling point. For the build-to-stock items, the needs of the customer (represented by the supermarket) are visible to everyone. The kanban are used to represent the inventory position and are effectively used to control the correct quantities. Kanban can be placed on a board, and visually represent an inverse relationship of the inventory—each kanban represents a reduced level of inventory. Build-to-order items can also be placed on the board so it's clear what is being built to a real customer order, to replenish the supermarket, and to replenish safety stock. Setting priorities becomes visual and straightforward. When Toyota says, "Operators can schedule their own work," this is what they mean. The operators are not performing traditional planning and scheduling—predicting what should be produced and when—they are simply using the information that flows to them from the visual system and a defined process governs the decision making.

How to Establish a Basic Leveled Schedule

Getting to a true heijunka schedule with a steady pitch multiple times in the day is what we would consider an advanced lean practice. Some minimum amount of leveling is needed in the stability phase (see Chapter 4) to even establish a basis for calculating a takt time and setting up basic flow. During the initial stages the pitch time is generally larger, often a daily time window, which creates a basis for stability, but it is not an impossible challenge. Attempting a smaller pitch prematurely may surface too many problems and create a system that is impossible to maintain.

In addition to the pitch time increment, the three aspects that will be leveled are:

1. Product *volume*, which is simply the quantity of a given product that must be produced in a specified period of time (the pitch).
2. Product *mix*, which is the proportion of the various models that are produced during the pitch increment, the quantity of A's, B's, C's, and so forth.
3. Product *sequence*, which is the order that the product volume and mix are produced. It may be model by model, such as A, A, A, B, B, B, C, C, C, or part by part, such as A, C, A, B, A, C.

These three are listed in order of difficulty. Depending upon your starting point, you may need to begin by establishing a simple volume and mix leveling on a larger pitch time such as one shift or one day. We know that everyone is touting single-piece flow and sequenced heijunka as the epitome of lean, but that objective may be far off, depending upon the current condition of your facility. After all, it has taken Toyota 50 years to achieve their current success, and in many cases they're still striving to reach the epitome. The key is to stretch enough to make a great improvement, and to challenge your capabilities, but not so much that total failure results.

TIP

Identify the Most Important Items for the Greatest Benefit

It may not be practical to level all products, due to extremely low or sporadic demand of some items. Before beginning the analysis to identify specific products to level, it may be necessary to isolate variation (see Chapter 3) or to utilize an isolation technique we call "slice and dice," which is discussed later in this chapter. Identify key products in key areas and begin with those that will provide the greatest benefit.

Begin with a review of the actual production or sales for each specific product over the previous 12-month period. This will provide a high, low, and average volume demand. The actual numbers can be plotted on a graph to get a visual representation, which is better than the plain numbers because it's possible to see the "weighted average." Simple highs and lows represent peaks, and a few peaks may skew the average. Plotting the actual numbers on the graph allows you to use your eye to see the most appropriate leveling point.

The final decision of the level volume is somewhat subjective. In general, Toyota selects a number that is approximately 80 percent of peak demand (unless the peak was an isolated event) because the gap between 80 and 100 percent could be filled using overtime (eight hours per week). The determination of leveled demand will be used to calculate takt time. In the previous chapter, we discussed the use of takt time as a design parameter. When determining the leveled demand quantity it is better to err on the side of a slightly higher demand if you are uncertain or uncomfortable with the 80 percent level. In reality, when you determine a quantity to serve as your assumed daily level demand it will either be too high, too low, or just right (not as likely). The problem is, it's difficult to determine initially because of the variation that has been occurring in the production (a cloud). Once the process is stabilized, the clouds clear a bit and the correct level will become more evident and adjustments easily made.

TRAP

Avoid Analysis Paralysis

It's easy to slip into "analysis paralysis" at this point if you try to determine the perfect leveling point. There are a few factors at work here that make a perfect selection virtually impossible. First, as they say about mutual funds, "Past performance is not a guarantee of future performance." We are basing future plans on past results, but they will not be the same. Second, the law of large numbers means that the more data points are observed, the less influence any one point has on the overall total. When looking at yearly totals for production volumes, a random spike here and there has less effect on the overall average. In laymen's terms this simply means looking at a large enough sample, so the "noise" in the data is filtered out. Third, the information you're analyzing may be flawed. It may not show the actual demand, but rather, the orders that are generated internally by an MRP system to fulfill "demand." These order quantities are influenced by many factors, and the quantities do not necessarily reflect true demand. Finally, as you'll see below, when you attempt to level the entire product mix, there will have to be some slight adjustments made to achieve an effective balance. Our tip is to select a level volume for each item that seems to be correct and get started on leveling the process. We guarantee that you'll need to make adjustments no matter how carefully you do the analysis!

TIP

Identify the Multiple for the Level Pattern

The best pattern is based off of a multiple of two. This provides a consistent pattern of daily, every other day, every fourth day, and at most every sixth day. If the volume of an item is such that the daily demand times six is still too low to be practical, you either need to reduce setup times or shift the item to the "other" category until setup times are reduced. In our example, the pattern of every other day was established for the items that had roughly one-half the demand of the every day items, and the every four-day items had roughly one-fourth the demand of the daily items.

The first pass of leveling will remove a layer of waste associated with chasing the waves. This will provide additional capacity that was not available before. Many companies discover that the initial leveling effort allows them to "catch up" with orders, and that they are overproducing based on the initial assumptions. It is possible to either reduce the resources or to increase sales if possible.

Let's look at a specific example. The data in Table 7-1 represents a simplified version of a real situation, but the concepts can be applied to more complex situations as well. In our example we will level 10 parts, designated A through J, each with varying demands. The "Other" items that are produced in the process had low volume requirements, an average of 125, and will not be leveled by individual part. The total daily volume for all products, including the "Other" items, is leveled. In fact the "Other" items and the quantities will vary, and it is possible to make adjustments by increasing or decreasing the total running time if the actual requirement is more or less than planned. This adjustment does not alter the leveling effect for items A through J.

Based on the volume requirements for the leveled items, a production pattern is developed to minimize the negative effects of changeover (the process has improved, but the time is still greater than desired—for now). Items A

Part	Daily Average Demand
A	250
B	220
C	210
D	128
E	125
F	75
G	60
H	45
I	45
J	35
Other	125
Total	1,318

Table 7-1. Volume Requirements by Part

through C are produced every day (ED), and items D through F are produced every other day (EOD). Items G through J are produced every four days (E4D—yes, yes, we know the goal should be to produce every part every day, but we are not there yet!).

One potential pattern is shown in Table 7-2. The daily requirement of 1,318 was adjusted slightly to 1,325 just to round the numbers. As we said, this is irrelevant because there is variation in the quantity of the "Other" items. This pattern is more evenly spread and allows for production of some "Other" items daily, but on some days the quantity of the "Other" items is low. If average order sizes of "Other" items are typically greater than these amounts, another pattern may be considered.

Table 7-3 shows an alternative pattern that groups more of the ED and EOD items on the same day. The ED items are a given—they run every day. The EOD and E4D may be changed to suit the needs of the process. For example, the EOD items could all be produced on the same alternating days as in this example. There are other potential patterns as well. The objective is to achieve the best level volume across the pattern by row—leveled by individual item over a time window, and down the pattern by column—total volume, and mix per time increment (pitch). The production sequence is defined by following the patterns (A through J) in the order specified. The level across the time period is within a defined

	Day 1	Day 2	Day 3	Day 4	Day 5	Day 6	Day 7	Day 8
A (ED)	250	250	250	250	250	250	250	250
B (ED)	220	220	220	220	220	220	220	220
C (ED)	210	210	210	210	210	210	210	210
D (EOD)	256	0	256	0	256	0	256	0
E (EOD)	0	250	0	250	0	250	0	250
F (EOD)	150	0	150	0	150	0	150	0
G (E4D)	0	240	0	0	0	240	0	0
H (E4D)	0	0	0	180	0	0	0	180
I (E4D)	180	0	0	0	180	0	0	0
J (E4D)	0	0	140	0	0	0	140	0
Other	59	155	99	215	59	155	99	215
Total	1,325	1,325	1,325	1,325	1,325	1,325	1,325	1,325
Goal	1,325	1,325	1,325	1,325	1,325	1,325	1,325	1,325

ED = every day; EOD = every other day; E4D = every four days.

Table 7-2. Possible Leveled Production Pattern

	Day 1	Day 2	Day 3	Day 4	Day 5	Day 6	Day 7	Day 8
A (ED)	250	250	250	250	250	250	250	250
B (ED)	220	220	220	220	220	220	220	220
C (ED)	210	210	210	210	210	210	210	210
D (EOD)	256	0	256	0	256	0	256	0
E (EOD)	250		250		250		250	
F (EOD)	150	0	150	0	150	0	150	0
G (E4D)	0	240	0	0	0	240	0	0
H (E4D)	0	0	0	180	0	0	0	180
I (E4D)		180	0	0	0	180	0	0
J (E4D)	0	0	0	140	0	0	0	140
Other	0	225	0	325	0	225	0	325
Total	1,336	1,325	1,336	1,325	1,336	1,325	1,336	1,325
Goal	1,325	1,325	1,325	1,325	1,325	1,325	1,325	1,325

ED = every day; EOD = every other day; E4D = every four days.

Table 7-3. Alternative Leveled Production Pattern

repeating increment. In our case, the pattern has a four-day repeating sequence and each item is leveled (the totals are equal) every four days. Toyota typically uses a monthly window for leveling, but it is based on a repeating multiple of one day. Note: The main vehicle assembly line has a repeating pattern on a short pitch frequency depending on the particular mix of vehicles produced, but the supporting operations that are producing to a supermarket or "selectivity bank" are producing to a different pattern that is a derivative of the primary pattern.

Notice that in the alternative pattern the total in days one, three, five, and seven exceeds the daily goal. This is not a major problem since the amount is within reasonable limits (normally a maximum of 10 percent). In most cases when working with actual demands, the numbers don't work out as evenly as this example. For the first attempt, get the numbers as close as possible. After you've had the opportunity to produce based on a level schedule, you will gain a clearer understanding of the true need and will adjust the pattern accordingly.

It is much easier to calculate a leveled schedule than to actually produce according to the plan! At first it's likely that you will discover many obstacles that prevent adherence to the schedule. These obstacles need to be systematically identified and corrected so stability can be achieved (track causes for missing the heijunka, and use the problem-solving method to eliminate them). The leveled schedule should now be considered the "voice of the customer." It is not the true customer, but a defined agreement that represents the needs of the customer that have been smoothed for the benefit of your processes.

Since this is the "customer," you should measure and track your ability to satisfy the customer. If at any time you are unable to achieve the volume, mix, or sequence that has been defined, it is equivalent to a "missed order" (and represents a dissatisfied customer, although you may not miss an actual order). You must train people to consider the heijunka as the voice of the customer and as a primary objective of the value stream.

Incremental Leveling and Advanced Heijunka

Congratulations! Having gotten to this stage in your lean journey, you're ready for the real fun to begin. After processes are stabilized and connected, there is value stream flow, and improvements are standardized, you now begin the continuous improvement cycle. That's right, you get to go through it all again, and again, and again, forever. The good news is that each successive loop through the continuous improvement spiral will be somewhat easier, since much of the foundational learning has been done and resistance to change overcome. Any changes made from now on will yield direct benefits for the entire process. In other words, instead of "pocket" improvements that do not affect the overall result, improvements now will influence the outcome of the entire value stream.

Now the bad news. From here on, the improvement process is a continuous cycle of "tightening" and refining the operations to achieve shorter lead times and greater degrees of flexibility and capability, push inventory levels down, and strengthen the long-term position of the business. Now, the results will be incremental in nature; that is, they will be of a predetermined amount because change to standardized processes can occur within a defined portion. Because of the system that has been created, the desired outcome is identified and the result will be assured.

The method will stress the value stream, and the weakest link will snap, creating instability. When the weak link is detected, resources are gathered to attack the issues. This cycle repeats over and over as shown in the continuous improvement spiral model in Chapter 3 (Figure 3-4). Each successive cycle uncovers decreasingly smaller problems. So it's a good news/bad news scenario. The bad news is that the issues become more difficult to correct. The good news is that improvements in the process will be significant and your skill level will grow as the difficulty of issues increases.

Incremental Leveling

After the value stream is connected, the incremental tightening process is applied to specific points. Remember what happens to the value stream if the production rate of the pacesetter is changed? It establishes a new rate for every other process in the value stream. Now, if the leveled schedule product mix were adjusted, all processes would need to adjust to support the new mix.

This type of incremental leveling or squeezing of the value stream forces the improvement process. It's a planned and controlled process that will incrementally drive continuous improvement in a specific manner. If inventory in the supermarket is reduced, for example, the effect on the supplying processes should be predictable. This may force a changeover more frequently, which forces the need for shortened changeover times. Each change in a standard element of the value stream will force the need for improvement and create a specific and predetermined result.

Points of Control

Within a connected value stream there are specific "points of control" that will influence other processes in the value stream. Because of the connected nature of the value stream, an adjustment to the point of control will require an adjustment to all processes that supply the control point. And since the point of control is the primary operation within the value stream that must be closely managed in order to create consistent output of the value stream, managing it allows you to effectively understand how to maximize the entire value stream.

One key point of control is the leveled schedule. It provides a standardized core that is used to establish takt time. The pacesetter process uses this takt time to establish a beat that will be followed by all other operations. Understanding the point of control allows managers to effectively troubleshoot operations and drive continuous improvement.

If the pacesetter consistently produces the desired volume of product and is capable of producing the correct product mix and sequence according to the leveled schedule, the value stream is consistently meeting the customer requirement (the next step would be cost reduction). If, however, the pacesetter is unable to fulfill the requirement of the leveled schedule, the first place to stand in the circle is at the pacesetter. From this vantage point it is possible to evaluate whether the pacesetter is being supplied properly. If not, look upstream to find the weak link. If so, look at the pacesetter to determine if he or she is being blocked by a downstream operation. (The rules forbid overproduction, so if a downstream process is blocking the pacesetter, it will be visibly evident.) The creation of visible connections allows quick identification of flow stoppages, simplifying management of the value stream.

Point of Control for Managing Inventory

The point of control for inventory management is the kanban. Reducing the number of kanbans within the system will reduce total inventory quantity.

> **TRAP**
>
> **STOP**
>
> **Use Inventory Reduction as a Yardstick for Success, Not a Goal**
>
> Many people pursue inventory reduction as a primary goal of lean activities. There are numerous ways to achieve this goal, including manipulation of the inventory. It is better to establish a goal to create connected flow and to use inventory as a measure of success. Kanban are used to control inventory, and it's simple to measure the effectiveness of the process by regulating the kanban. Inventory control via kanban is standardized, and the possibility of false manipulation is reduced.

These reductions should be done systematically, either as improvements are made to the process or to force the need for improvements. The quantity of inventory needed to support a process can be used as a yardstick for your improvement efforts. Sustainable inventory reductions are an indication of a capable process.

Inventory turns can also be influenced by the kanban. If the part quantity per kanban (also the container quantity) is reduced, the kanban will "cycle" more frequently, moving inventory through the process at a faster rate. Reducing the quantity per kanban also provides a greater degree of flexibility in the replenishment process, and reduces the size of the work area and waste. Strange as it seems, having more kanban "in the system" is an advantage. For example, if the total inventory level of an item is 2,000 pieces, it's better to have 20 kanban of 100 pieces each than two kanbans of 1,000 pieces each. It's difficult seeing the demand with only two kanban in the system, and each time a kanban is returned, it must be filled immediately.

A Leveled Schedule Dictates Replenishment

In addition to the smoothing effect for all processes, heijunka establishes a "pitch" time. Because materials are being consumed at a standard rate during a defined pitch time, it's possible to establish a defined process for material replenishment. Material replenishment is subordinate to the primary value adding operation; therefore, establishment of material replenishment "routes" or methods should not be attempted before creating a standardized "core" in the primary process.

The following example illustrates how a leveled schedule dictates the material replenishment needs and establishes a consistent requirement. This allows

Part Name	Quantity per 8 hours	Ratio
A	200	4
B	100	2
C	50	1
D	50	1
Total	400	

Table 7-4. Quantity of Parts as a Relative Ratio

TIP

Set Your Pitch Based on Current Conditions

Unless you are well along in your lean journey, you will not likely set a one-hour pitch initially. We recommend progressing in halves. If you currently move material at a daily pitch (or it is not defined), start with a shift-by-shift pitch. Then incrementally reduce the pitch by one-half as the processes become more capable and refined.

---

the standardization of work for material handlers, including routes that are completed during the pitch time or a multiple of the pitch. Material quantities are standardized, and the quantities per container may be adjusted to match the requirement per pitch. For illustrative purposes we assume that this process is capable of advanced heijunka and produces each item in the exact sequence, and that the total available work time is eight hours. Demand is 400 total pieces, and the ratios are shown in Table 7-4.

Based on the quantity required and the ratios, the repeating heijunka pattern (which minimizes batching) would be: ABACABAD—ABACABAD—ABACABAD

The pitch time to repeat the pattern is determined by dividing eight hours by the demand of 400 pieces and multiplying by the number of pieces in a pattern (pitch):

28,800 seconds (eight hours) per day / 400 pieces = 72 seconds per piece

And:

72 seconds per piece x 8 pieces per pitch =
576 seconds per pitch (9 minutes 36 seconds) or 6.25 pitch-cycles per hour.

Part Name	Ratio	Patterns per Hour	Hourly Requirement	Quantity per Container	Containers per Pitch
A	4	6.25	4 × 6.25 = 25	10	2.5
B	2	6.25	2 × 6.25 = 12.5	5	2.5
C	1	6.25	1 × 6.25 = 6.25	5	1.25
D	1	6.25	1 × 6.25 = 6.25	5	1.25

Table 7-5. Calculation of Containers Moved per Pitch

Let's also assume that we want the material handler to move material every hour (the pitch for material replenishment). Table 7-5 shows the calculation of the number of containers that will be moved during each one-hour material replenishment cycle.

Based on the material movement requirement during a one-hour cycle time, it is possible to define standardized work, including the specific route of travel and other processes that will be serviced during the route.

Slice and Dice When Product Variety Is High

Heijunka seems straightforward enough when you are dealing with 5 to 10 products. But what happens when there are many different finished products? One company claimed to have 25,000 individual finished goods part numbers and insisted heijunka was impossible. How would it be possible to level with this kind of variety? We have to go through a process we call "slice and dice," which is a method of dividing the whole into groups of products with similar characteristics (you may also think of this as "divide and conquer").

The first "slice" separates products into value streams that have common products and processing steps. This grouping puts like items together and also reduces the overall number of items within the slice—the 25,000 may now only be 5,000. Think of your operation with the variety of products and processes in its entirety as a rectangle. The separation into value stream "families" with common characteristics and processing steps would divide the rectangle horizontally into slices (Figure 7-3). If the most important value stream overall is addressed first, the greatest benefit will be achieved from the effort.

If the slice is "diced" (Figure 7-4), the most significant items within the 5,000 are isolated, and the primary focus is reduced further. The "dicing" of the value

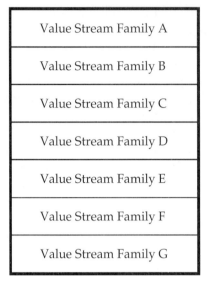

Figure 7-3. The operation sliced into value streams

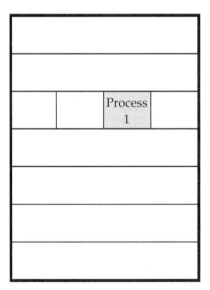

Figure 7-4. A value stream slice with a section diced

stream also includes the selection of a portion of the stream (processes) to focus on during the initial lean efforts. Usually we look at the production volumes of all products to determine where the dices should be. When the product mix is diced in this manner we invariably find that the volumes fall into three groups: a top group with the most significant demand; a second group roughly one-half the volume of the first group; and a third group, one-half again lower than the second group (the volumes in the leveling example above represent a typical example). Generally, the first group is relatively small in terms of the quantity of part numbers but large as a percentage of total volume. (If you are thinking that this is the Pareto principle in action, you're exactly right. This method allows you to isolate the "significant few" from the "trivial many.")

We began with 25,000 part numbers. The top 100 part numbers in terms of volume accounted for 35 percent of the total sales volume for the company! That is a significant reduction. An additional slice revealed that the volume for the number one item was 10 times greater than the fiftieth item. It was decided to focus on leveling production for the top 50 part numbers (out of 25,000). While looping through the continuous improvement spiral, we work on specific segments or layers (slices), and each successive pass through the cycle brings the addition of subsequent layers. After the first 50 parts are successfully leveled and the value stream is performing consistently, the next 50 parts (or more) will be initiated.

With the focus quantity reduced to 50, the magnitude of the effort is minimized and the benefit is maximized. Many people incorrectly assume that if it's not possible to level everything, it's not possible to implement heijunka. In reality, the question is a matter of simple math. Is it better to be stabilized zero percent of the time on 100 percent of the items, or to be stabilized 100 percent of the time on 25 percent of the items? This is not an all or nothing proposition.

As your operations develop greater capabilities, it becomes possible to consider leveling smaller and smaller quantities. It may never make sense to level all items. Consider the slice and dice: If 75 percent of all items are leveled—and therefore 75 percent of the total resource needs are leveled—the remaining 25 percent of the resource time (people and equipment) can be devoted to the "as needed" items. The raw materials may be shared between the leveled and non-leveled items, and the additional need can easily be factored into the material replenishment calculations.

Case Example: Leveling Workload in a Custom Cabinet Shop

The workload required at various operations in this company fluctuated greatly, depending on the product, which caused many problems, including poor quality (workers were frequently rushed), line stoppage, and unpredictable production schedules. Because of the custom nature of the product, it was assumed that standardized work for the processes was not possible.

When dealing with a situation of this nature, the apparent complexity can be overwhelming. There were many interconnected and interrelated issues resulting from the ripple effect of the workload (imagine the snake that eats the rat, and the bulge proceeds down the length of its body). As is often the case, the company had attempted to address the out-lying issues (where the "problem" was realized), creating elaborate schemes to shift labor to the bulge, but the problem originated at the core. Intuitively, they understood this, but believed it was impossible to change because every item produced was different and the size of each order and the mix of components (cabinets, doors, drawers) varied significantly. They assumed that customers dictated the schedule and there was nothing they could do to level the workload.

The first step was to stop looking at the product as "part specific" or "job specific" and to look at it based on the work content and the effect that content had on the processes within the value stream. If you step back a bit, you can see commonalities either in the product itself or in the processing. In this case, we first identified that most "jobs" or orders had some common elements that affected the workload. The primary components were: cabinets, drawers, shelves, doors, miscellaneous parts, and trim. We also determined that there were a few characteristics common to all products that had an effect on the workload, primarily the type of finish. The finishes were in two cate-gories: stains and solid colors. Further discussion revealed that within the two finish categories each had two additional separations. The stain colors had a burnished and unburnished option, and the solid colors were light and dark.

A review of the value stream revealed that the finishing line where product is stained or colored was the "pacesetter." All products converged at the finish loading area and from that operation flowed on as a complete order. Leveling the workload at the pacesetter would serve to create a smooth workload to subsequent operations (including the finish operation) and provide leveled signals to all upstream feeder operations.

Again the question surfaced: How do you level the workload when the product is always different? By standing on the circle the answer was clear. The finish type, and the surface area to be finished, affected the workload. Workers confirmed that burnished stain jobs required much more effort than unburnished ones, and that dark-colored solid jobs were much harder than light ones because the solid colors had a "polished" finish. We also saw that parts with larger surface area required more time, as did many small parts with less surface area. It was becoming clear that creating a sequenced pattern with leveled mix would be the answer. But, again the question: How do you do this when every job is different?

This group, and especially the supervisor who had struggled with the issue for years, was not easy to convince. What we needed was a variable standard; that is, we would develop a standard with an

least for the high-volume cabinets, that six-to-eight-week lead time could be reduced and level the schedule, creating a more efficient process. In fact, the plant reorganized around three product family value streams, used some finished goods inventory to level the schedule, freed up one-fourth of the plant for new business, and dramatically reduced overall inventory, lead time, and total cost.

To accomplish what appears to be a logical plan is not as easy as it sounds. The furniture manufacturer had to change the way sales people placed orders. They had to change the distribution process and the way production control scheduled the plant. These are all governed by different functional groups who had been doing things a certain way for decades. Nobody believed the new system could possibly work, and all predicted disaster. Overcoming this resistance required a strong vision of a future state and a lot of top management support.

Frequently, sales groups work to incentives based on sales targets by month or quarter. Such incentive systems lead to lumpy sales patterns with serious discounts to move product at the end of the bonus period. At Toyota, sales is aware of the importance of a leveled schedule in production. While, even at Toyota, production often complains about what sales does to them, there is a lot more cooperation than we typically see in other companies. This cooperation is encouraged by top management who understand the implications of sales patterns on the leveled schedule that is the foundation of TPS.

Thinking in systems terms and enterprise terms is just plain hard. And learning to think in value stream terms is the most critical in leveling the schedule—the foundation of lean systems.

Case Study: Leveling the Schedule in an Engineering Organization

Most knowledge work is inherently lumpy. And you cannot parcel out a schedule in units the way you can in a manufacturing process. Nonetheless, Toyota has found a way to level the workload in engineering new products to a far greater degree than its competitors.

First, you have to get some basic stability in the process. Toyota has developed a stable development process in which there are clear stages, and each one takes a standard amount of time and engineering hours.

Second, this allows Toyota to set up a planned schedule at the beginning of the program and stick to it. Roughly, Toyota freshens cars every two years and issues a major new version about every four years. Knowing this, not all cars are completely overhauled in the same way. This is spread out so that roughly one-quarter of the launches are overhauled in one year.

Third, within a vehicle program, Toyota has a clear profile of manpower over the program. The program definition phase starts off with a small number of senior engineers, the program ramps up to a peak and then comes back down to a relatively small number of engineers through launch. Again, this is based on the stability Toyota has in the process. Many of its competitors send an army of people to the plant when they launch. Toyota has such a well-planned process and does enough high-quality engineering in the concept stage that its launches are smooth and most engineers are on to another program.

Fourth, Toyota takes care of the peak of the program by drawing on its affiliates. This includes closely linked contract firms that provide technicians and computer-aided design specialists at peak times. It also includes affiliated companies like suppliers and Toyota Auto Body, which send engineers at the peaks. This allows Toyota to keep the core engineers on staff and bring in the rest flexibly. Standardized design processes and designs help Toyota engineers and affiliates come in and out of the program and contribute seamlessly.

Fifth, Toyota staggers the release of a lot of engineering information. For example, its competitors often provide a batch of all body data released at once to die engineers who then process all of this data into the design of stamping dies. Toyota releases body data as parts are developed and released directly to die design, which releases data as it goes to die making. There is a clear understanding of what body parts can be released early, before the rest are complete. This creates something like a one-piece flow and is much more level than releasing large batches of part designs.

Reflect and Learn from the Process

Basic leveling of production volume and model mix is necessary to establish process stability and continuous flow. Using your current state value stream map as a guide, identify the operations that continue to struggle with meeting the expectation.

1. Are these operations being affected by external customer variation?
   a. Does the daily requirement change?
   b. Determine the extent of the fluctuation (show the daily demand on a line graph). Variation of greater than 10 percent must be reduced.
   c. Identify current methods for aligning resources (people, material, machines) to these fluctuations, and your effectiveness in meeting the requirement (measurements of efficiency and customer delivery).

2. Establishing a "level schedule" requires up-front effort, and diligence to sustain.
   a. Evaluate the effect of the variation and decide whether leveling the product flow would be beneficial.
   b. Are you willing to make the effort to eliminate problems that currently prevent you from producing smaller quantities more frequently and consistently?
3. If you're producing a product to stock, establish a finished goods supermarket to absorb the true customer variation.
   a. Determine the average daily volume demand for your products.
   b. Determine a pitch time for each product. The highest 10 to 20 percent of products by volume (maybe more) should be set for daily production.
   c. Determine the repeating time pitch for the other products, and create a "pattern" in which to produce the product. Consider the mix of products required and the sequence to produce them for balanced flow.
4. Your leveled schedule becomes a standard for operation. Measure your effectiveness in achieving the standard and correct obstacles that prevent consistent ability to achieve the schedule. Note: Do not change the plan because the process is not capable. Correct the weakness.
5. As a process continues to achieve higher levels of capability, it is necessary to incrementally raise the bar. Evaluate your value stream, and reflect on the following questions:
   a. Do you know where the "point of control" is within your value stream?
   b. Are you measuring and managing the point of control?
   c. What changes at the point of control will impact the entire value stream?
   d. How will these changes affect the value stream (where will the chain break)?
   e. Can you implement corrective action to the weakness in the value stream prior to forcing the change?
6. Leveling is necessary to provide a "standard core" to which all resources are aligned. Build these additional elements based on your level schedule process:
   a. Material replenishment: All material supply within the facility is based on the consistent requirement at each process. This dictates the material replenishment pitch and is the

basis for a replenishment strategy, including consistent replenishment from suppliers.

b. People: The level schedule becomes the basis for determining takt time, which is necessary for standardized work. Establish standardized work for all processes, and determine the required number of people.

c. Equipment: Standardized work is also the basis for equipment requirements. Align the required equipment to the people and work based on the level schedule.

Chapter 8

Build a Culture That Stops to Fix Problems

WE ARE FREQUENTLY asked, "What is it about the way Toyota does things that makes their quality consistently better than other car companies?" While there is no one simple answer to this question, it can be said that a large part is due to the principle of building in quality and the decision to stop and fix problems as they occur rather than pushing them down the line to be resolved later. On the surface, this idea seems logical. If you have a problem, it's better to stop and take care of it. Correct it, prevent its recurrence, and make things better in the long run. In reality, when people are faced with the demand to "make the numbers," the primary focus becomes short-term results—hitting the production target every day at any cost. The focus in mass manufacturing is in getting the mass. In lean the focus is on eliminating waste.

Not that Toyota *wants* the line to stop. Excessive line stoppage would severely reduce production and profitability, so if you stop the line often the results will be terrible. If you commit to the concept of stopping the line, you will either continue to have terrible results or you'll work diligently to eliminate the problems. This commitment takes real courage and understanding of the long-term objective. Over the years, Toyota has built a system that provides the long-term benefits of stopping the line, and minimizes the negative effect by building a support structure to quickly identify, respond, and correct problems.

Developing the Culture

The demand for better quality has been on the increase for the past two decades or more. Everyone understands that survival in the marketplace depends on the ability to deliver consistently high quality. The interest in Six Sigma—and the allure of a quality level of only three defects per million products—has at least helped to create the awareness that delivering a quality product is a must in today's world. The question now is not whether the ability to deliver exceptional quality is necessary, it's: "What do we need to do to get there?" The best place to start is with yourself. If you want to learn a few lessons from Toyota, first you must develop a clear understanding of how and why Toyota accomplishes what they do.

The diagram in Figure 8-1 is similar to the models we have used in previous chapters, but it's applied to stopping the line. The traditional method of reducing per unit cost creates a mind-set of never stopping the line because higher production numbers theoretically equal lower cost per unit. Any problems that arise can be corrected later, according to this approach, and quality is controlled by additional inspection and containment. This erroneous thinking creates an attitude among the workforce that identifying problems and possible solutions is not important. People may have good ideas to solve the problems, but they "won't bother" because they've been told: "Don't worry, someone down the line will take care of that. You just worry about your job." In this environment, quality control must accept responsibility for catching problems (and for catching the offending person), and resentment often develops since the inspectors are seen as "police" or "narcs" if they report a problem. In the long run this system does not invite cooperation and mutual respect—two important ingredients of the Toyota Way.

Figure 8-2 depicts the Toyota core philosophy of eliminating waste. Notice that all the examples begin with the same core philosophy. If the thinking begins with a focus on waste elimination (in this case waste of correction), the natural extension of that philosophy is to develop a system that emphasizes getting quality right the first time. Toyota has developed an extensive support system to provide people the tools and resources to identify problems and solve them. Of course, the pressure of stopping an entire line creates a sense of urgency, and everyone must make a concerted effort to resolve problems permanently, or else the line stoppage would be excessive. People know they will be supported when a problem occurs, and with the fear of retribution eliminated, they can develop a cooperative attitude toward improving performance.

Based on the phenomenal financial performance of Toyota and the legendary quality levels they have achieved, there is no question that the "stop and fix" process works. For some reason the idea that it is better to keep the line going at all costs still pervades many organizations today. Often the "culture"

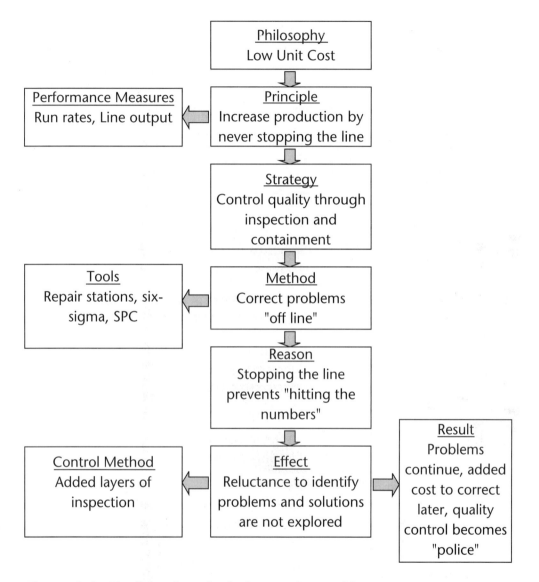

Figure 8-1. Traditional method of correcting problems

seems to be the scapegoat. How do you change a culture? How do you change the habits that have been developed since the inception of your company?

Changing a culture is a challenge. Before you run out and start creating a culture, understand that cultures don't just happen. Cultures are created over time. They arise out of need, in response to the system that exists to support them; or if there is no support structure, the culture that develops is one of self-sufficiency, "Every man for himself."

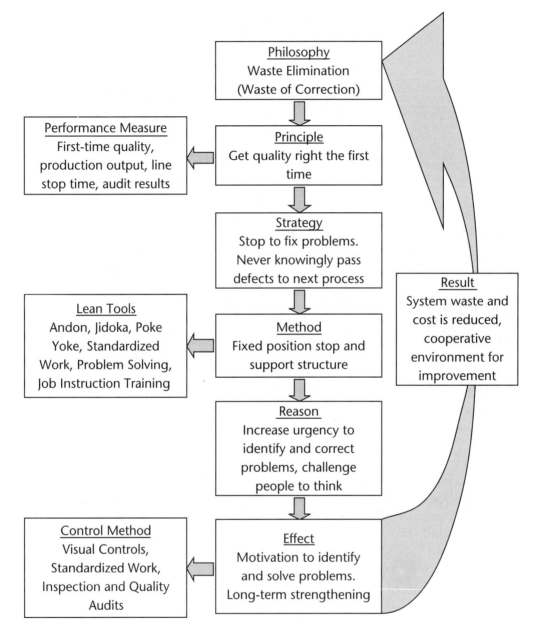

Figure 8-2. Toyota method of stopping to fix problems

Case Example: Stopping the Line Is More Than a Cord with Lights and Bells

By David Meier

The following situation occurred in an automotive assembly plant that I coached in the lean methods, which was run by one of the U.S. automakers. This situation was extremely difficult for someone conditioned in the Toyota Way, and I felt severe anxiety. The Toyota Way conditioning is similar to that of Pavlov's famous dogs. I have been conditioned to search out potential problems and to respond when called. Even though I was not in a Toyota Way facility and was not responsible for this situation, I responded the Toyota Way.

I realized I had this condition sometime after leaving Toyota. As I tour other work areas, I am constantly aware of potential problems and the need to take corrective action even before a "problem" surfaces. I notice also, with dismay, that the leadership in these facilities seems "blissfully oblivious" to the conditions around them. We walk past current problems and potential problems as if they weren't there. My mind is screaming, "Wait, here is a problem. It must be dealt with or the consequence will be large." Then I realize that the problem is "covered" and is lost in the "clouds." There is no immediate urgency to correct it. I also realize there are so many problems that I would be overwhelmed. Then I recognize that leadership is in fact overwhelmed, and that there is no support structure. Problems happen all around and people do their best to get through the day. It is then that I truly understood the value of the Toyota system.

In the course of my consulting and while observing the final vehicle assembly line (sometimes referred to as the "money line") in a Big Three plant, I noticed what appeared to be a tear in the carpet on the driver's side floor. I happened to be standing with the supervisor at the time. My first reaction was to look for a way to stop the line. Of course there was no "cord," as there is in Toyota, so I pointed out the tear to the supervisor and waited for a response. He looked and confirmed that in fact the carpet was torn, and *did nothing!* I was panicked and confused. I asked him what we should do, and he told me that the problem would be fixed in the repair area. I asked if we should look for the source of the problem in case it was repetitive and received a shrug. "They probably already know" was the reply.

This was my first experience with this kind of situation, and I did not know how to react externally, but *internally* I was very anxious. This was a potentially serious problem. At the very least the line should be stopped and this vehicle should not be completed, because all work done on the interior after this operation would need to be "undone" at the repair area. This included removal of the seats and much of the interior trim work. I know that this type of major repair, in addition to being costly, almost assuredly results in a product that is inferior to the original work. Reworking and replacing trim and seats is a significant cause of "squeaks and rattles" after time, and those issues are very annoying to customers.

In the end we completely walked away from the problem. We did not go to the end of the line to make sure the defect was identified and the repair done (preventing the escape to the customer), nor did we go to find the source to prevent further occurrence. We simply left!

I came to understand many other underlying issues later. For example, if a supervisor (or other person) finds a problem and points it out to the worker, the worker could file a complaint with the union that they were being "badgered." While the claim may be unsubstantiated, the hassle of dealing with it is greater than the the hassle of fixing the problem later. The antagonistic environment between management and the workforce that has been honed for decades prevents cooperation (although I did find out that there are exceptional people who truly wanted to make things better). This is part of the culture that would need to change if the "stop the line" strategy was going to work here.

You don't just announce to people, "Starting today, things will be different!" and suddenly the culture is changed. How do you change the supervisor who for the past 30 years has learned to survive within the old system? How do you change the mind-set about how people's performance is measured? If people are measured on output, how will they respond? There is more to this than just deciding that from now on, we will stop to fix problems.

The following list includes many of the things you will need to do in order to be able to effectively create a "stop the line" culture and system. Note that when we refer to "stop the line," we are also referring to stopping a machine or stopping the work process. It means that the work is halted when a problem is discovered.

1. Understand your current culture and why it developed.
2. Create a clear vision for change.
3. Pay attention to the respect and dignity of the people.
4. Establish a reasonable degree of stability in processes.
5. Have a method to stop the line.
6. The process must provide an audible and visual indication of the exact point of the problem. (Forget about paging systems!)
7. Have people designated to respond when the line stops.
8. Define the roles and procedure for response to problems.

9. Change the measurement process from just quantity to built-in quality.
10. Teach people to solve problems.
11. Increase the urgency, and make it necessary to fix problems.

The Role of Jidoka: Self-Monitoring Machines

Jidoka is roughly translated to mean "intelligent machines," and specifically refers to the machine's ability to detect a problem and to stop itself. It is an effort to have the machine work without continuous direct human monitoring, and it will sound an alert when there is a problem. Fortunately, many machinery manufacturers today are building self-checking capabilities into machines. As with many of the Toyota concepts, there is more to the concept of jidoka than self-stopping machines.

At the center of the Toyota philosophy is a respect for people and the value they provide. Only people can think and solve problems. Machinery is used to relieve human burden but is not a master to the person. Self-stopping machines relieve the person from the burden of constantly supervising a machine, and allow them to use their talents for more beneficial things (like adding value).

A legendary story at the Georgetown plant tells of a reporter who was doing a story on Toyota and the plant. When the reporter observed the door assembly and reattachment line, he commented about the lack of robots, which he had seen in competitors' plants. Didn't this reduce the efficiency of the plant, he wondered? The president of TMMK patiently explained that robots had limitations. They were not able to think, and they could not feel. It was important in the door installation process for a worker to sense what the customer wanted and to complete the task with the customer desire in mind. How should the door feel when it's closed? How should it sound? A robot could not be trained for these things. While the cost may be higher for labor, the total benefit gained from having this sensing ability of a human was of greater benefit.

Utilizing jidoka is a matter of understanding where waste is in any process. Do you currently have machines that need constant attention? Does this create waiting time for the operator? You may have to observe closely to understand the true condition. Long ago people realized that having an operator standing around waiting for a machine was not desirable, so in many cases the operator filled the time with "busy work." You may not see any actual waiting, so you need to look at the activity being performed while the machine is running. Is it value-added?

Notice whether you have machines idle because they need service but there is no recognition of this. We often see machines that automatically feed material and the feed gets jammed, or the material supply runs out, and the machine is waiting. This is waste also. Machines should be equipped with sensing devices and andons that sound an audible alarm and convey a visual signal to notify operators when they need service (preferably *before* they run out of material).

TRAP

STOP

Stack Lights May Not Be Effective Andons

When the concepts of andon and jidoka made their way into the general public, we started to see "stack lights" appear on machines. These are usually a small set of lights with three or four different colored lights stacked in one unit. This was to serve the purpose of an andon. There are a few problems. First we see that there is a general disregard of the lights. We can look across the work area and see many lights lit with different colors. What we don't see is any specific response to the lights. The proliferation of lights has desensitized people. Also, the lights generally have no indication as to what they mean. When we ask people to explain the meaning, we get a variety of answers. Finally, there is no audible aspect to the lights. It's relatively easy to ignore a light, but more difficult to ignore a buzzer. (By the way, Toyota's andons have a different tune for the different conditions indicated. The supervisor call, or line stop, is Beethoven's classic melody "Für Elis,"[1] for example.)

Sadly, this is a classic case of the application of a lean tool without a deep understanding of the purpose, and without *hansei* to reflect on the shortcomings. People falsely believe that because they have the lights, they have andon, or jidoka. You must evaluate to determine whether the tools you implement are serving the function for which they were intended.

The Problem-Resolution Cycle

Before you try to build a system, it is important to understand the full cycle of the problem, from recognition through resolution and prevention. Figure 8-3 depicts the problem-resolution cycle visually. This cycle is typical within Toyota.

This entire cycle is repeated many times throughout the day. Problems are constantly being surfaced and corrected, with minimal interruption to the production flow ("fixed position stop" is discussed in the section on "Minimizing Line Stop Time," and Figure 8-4 illustrates the fixed position stop system). Think of these steps as a "chain of events" with each event triggering the successive event as necessary. This process is coordinated and orchestrated as well as any basketball team executing a certain play.

1. **Recognition.** The first step of the process is the recognition that an abnormal situation exists. Recognition is possible because there are established

---

[1] This piece is designated WO o 59, or Without Opus number 59

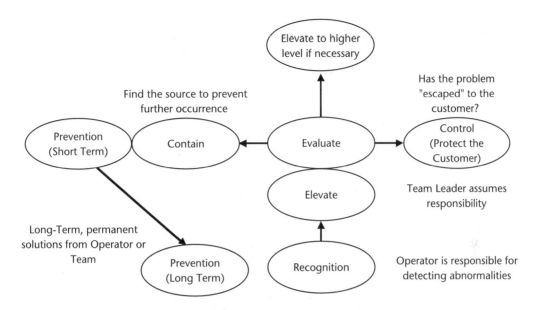

Figure 8-3. Toyota problem-resolution cycle

visible standards (see Chapter 6) that are easily distinguishable by everyone. Let's say, for example, that an operator is performing a task and realizes that he or she will not be able to finish it in the prescribed amount of time (takt time). This will be clear to the operator because the standardized work is synchronized with the line movement and demarcations on the floor indicate the step in the job. If the operator passes the line before the step is complete, he is falling behind and must request assistance.

Let's look at another example, in this case quality. First of all, if an employee is to recognize that a defect had occurred, he will need a point of comparison. You guessed it, a standard. Refer to Chapter 6 for the discussion on the importance of quality boundary samples. In addition, the operator may have some latitude to correct minor problems on his own provided he does not exceed the takt time. These "rules" are also part of the standard. The rules are an important element of the next step, which involves a decision on when the operator must make a request for assistance. This must be defined!

2. **Elevate.**   If the condition exceeds the defined span of control of the employee she must elevate the problem and request support. This is done by "pulling the cord" or another means to signal the need for assistance. The andon device is used by Toyota to quickly indicate to the designated support people (team and group leaders) exactly where the problem is

(by workstation). It typically includes an audible alarm to signal and a visual light to pinpoint location.

In many companies that try to implement an andon system, workers have a difficult time admitting they need support. They are concerned they will be held accountable. The leaders develop perceptions of workers and their abilities based on how often they need support (the "good ones" don't stop the line so often). This is a critical juncture in culture development. Leadership must develop the attitude that their role is to support and ultimately find better methods so everyone can perform the work effectively. If resentment develops by workers or by leaders, the andon will become ineffective.

When the leader responds to the request for assistance he or she must take over responsibility for the problem from the operator. The operator explains the condition, and after the leader understands, the operator will return to his or her regular regular duties. From here on out ownership of the problem belongs to the leader for containment (permanent correction of the problem cause may be a joint activity with the team).

3. **Evaluate.** When taking over responsibility, the first thing the leader must do is evaluate the condition. Is this an isolated problem or a major problem? If the problem is contained or easily controlled (such as when an operator fell behind) and the leader assumes responsibility, the first consideration is to restart the line or perhaps intervene before the line actually stops. If the problem appears to be large or the source is unknown (such as a quality problem that originates somewhere else), the line will likely stop and stay stopped until the condition can be eliminated.

   If the responding leader is unable to restart the line immediately, the situation must be elevated further. Of course, you can see by now that this repeated elevation cycle is based on predefined standards. For example, the team leader will have so many minutes to try to identify and correct the problem before he or she must elevate the situation to the group leader. When the group leader responds, there is a time limit after which she must notify the manager if the problem is not corrected. As the magnitude of a problem increases, the level of elevation must also increase. This ensures that larger problems receive the proper amount of attention, and also that upper management is not called upon to deal with smaller issues that can be handled by the appropriate leader. The role of management is to ensure that resources are available to correct problems quickly, and that corrective action to prevent recurrence is taken.

4. **Control.** The first consideration is to keep the problem within station and to ensure that the problem will not reach the customer. The leader would

typically walk downstream on the line to verify that the problem has not escaped to the customer. Stopping the line effectively controls the spread of the problem. This is the key point of the system—stop the line until the problem is effectively controlled or corrected. Stopping the line is a major decision and doing so will bring immediate attention to the problem. This is exactly the point. In traditional environments stopping the line will cause negative attention and is avoided, or if possible is done without bringing attention to the situation. The Toyota Way, in a sense, "celebrates" the fact that the problem has been forced to the surface, and everyone is encouraged because it can now be corrected. This is not to say that Toyota is happy when people make mistakes, but that when the cause of the mistake is found and eliminated, everyone understands that over the long term the process will be more robust.

5. **Containment.** The leader must identify the source of the problem so it can be contained. In the case of quality problems, the leader would begin to systematically walk the line to attempt to identify the source of the problem. Familiarity with the process aids in this procedure. For example, if a certain part is improperly installed, the leader can go directly to the operator who installs the part to find the origin. If the problem is random or sporadic, the leader must trace back at each operation until the source is located. If a defect occurs randomly, a decision may be made to restart the line while the search for the source continues. This decision is generally made by the group leader or above, and would be based on the severity of the problem.

   Another purpose of the containment effort is to identify the parameters of the problem. When and/or where did it start, and where is the end? This is important for finding the source, but also for assuring that all defective parts have been corrected. When a more serious problem is identified, several leaders respond and each assumes responsibility for a portion of the containment effort.

6. **Prevention.** After the problem has been controlled and contained and production has resumed, the focus shifts to prevention. In some cases preventive measures are short term in nature, meaning they are temporary measures until more effective permanent (long-term) measures can be implemented. The team leader implements these short-term countermeasures immediately to prevent further occurrence of the problem. If a long-term, more permanent solution is necessary, the responsibility for a solution may be returned to the entire team. All members are responsible for the development of effective countermeasures. The problem-solving process is used to find root causes and to determine effective, permanent solutions.

TIP

Develop Stability and Support Before Attempting to Implement Stop the Line

As we will see Toyota lines do not immediately stop when the andon cord is pulled. There is a very short time window (maybe 5 to 30 seconds) after the cord is pulled and before the line stops so that the team leader can respond and override the line stop if warranted. This system is very sensitive and requires a responsive support structure with high capability. Clearly, Toyota did not reach this level of capability overnight. A high level of stability was reached first so that the line does not stop continually and investments were made in developing a team leader structure to almost instantly respond to the andon calls. Move forward with your own implementation of andon in such a way as to balance the urgency to respond with the level of problems within your processes. If your processes are not reasonably stable, you will overload your support system and things will quickly unravel.

Minimizing Line Stop Time

Toyota has developed a system that allows problems to be identified and elevated without necessarily stopping the line. When a problem is identified and the cord is pulled, the alarm sounds and a yellow light is turned on. The line will continue to move until the end of the work zone—the "fixed position stop" point (Figure 8-4). The fixed position stop is especially useful for reducing actual line stops in the case of a worker who is behind in the work sequence. Markings are placed on the floor throughout the work zone that indicate the corresponding step of the standardized work. If the leader responds quickly and can reset the line by pulling the cord again before the fixed position stop is reached, the line will continue without interruption. Failure to reach the line in time or if the leader determines the problem warrants it, the line will stop when the fixed position is reached and the andon will turn red.

Many smaller problems can be corrected in this way without the annoyance of repeated starts and stops of the line. Also note that anytime the line is stopped, the problem is compounded because everyone on the line has to get resynchronized with the line when it restarts. Toyota also uses an audible alarm to signal all operators that the line is restarting.

Toyota assembly lines are generally very long and snake around corners. This can be viewed as a series of straight line segments connected by "U" shaped

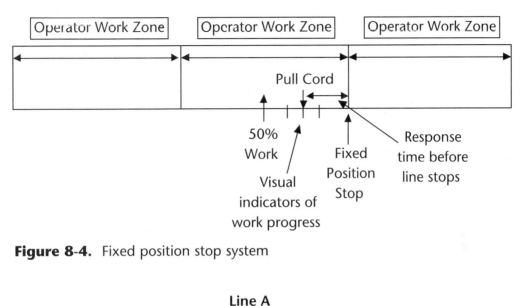

Figure 8-4. Fixed position stop system

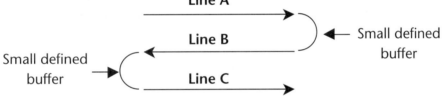

Figure 8-5. Fixed position stop and small buffering

corners. A line stop is really a line-segment stop. Each segment of the line can stop briefly without stopping the others (Figure 8-5). As we noted, small intermittent line stoppages are disruptive to the flow. Imagine traffic stopped at a red light. When the light turns green, what happens? Do the cars all move simultaneously? No, they begin to move one by one until eventually all are moving. This same phenomenon occurs when attempting to initiate flow. Small, defined buffers at the corners are used to absorb minor interruptions—no more than 10 minutes total buffer. If an operator activates the andon and the leader responds before the car has moved to the next work zone, the line never actually stops. If the problem is more significant and cannot be corrected before the end of the work zone, one segment of the line will stop (e.g., Line A), but the other lines (B and C) will continue, provided there is product in the buffer. If the stop time exceeds the capacity of the buffer, the following line will then stop due to shortage. Of course, these buffers are very small so that larger problems are not hidden by inventory.

Case Example: Making Line Stopping a Reward for Lean Maturity

General Motors has perhaps had the greatest opportunity outside of the Toyota group to learn the Toyota Production System (TPS). They co-own NUMMI, a joint venture and Toyota's first application of TPS to an assembly plant outside of Japan. General Motors has had free access to NUMMI, including sending many employees to work there for one year or more. When they first started learning about TPS, they merely copied what they saw at NUMMI. They quickly discovered that it did not work. The andon system, for instance, did not work like it did at Toyota. General Motors had invested in some of the most sophisticated technology of fixed position, line-stopping systems to no avail. Workers did not use it to stop the line and surface and solve problems.

In the Hamtramack, Michigan, plant that built Cadillacs, GM got smart. They had an andon system set up with a fixed position stop system. But they did not turn on that automatic line-stopping capability. Instead they worked on stability of the process and on teaching the various lean methods in the plant, like standardized work and disciplined use of the kanban system. They set up work teams. Then they used an assessment process to assess each individual team in the plant. It was a broad assessment of the team's discipline in using kanban, standard work, and responding to problems on the line. Only when the team achieved a strong score on the assessment could they have the automatic line-stopping turned on. This was made very visible and was celebrated by each team that achieved this milestone. Teams worked hard to achieve this honor. And the line-stopping process began to work as intended.

Build Quality Inspections into Every Job

This is an interesting paradox. Inspection is not a value-adding activity, but Toyota stresses the inclusion of self-inspection in all standardized work. On the surface this seems contradictory. A deeper look will reveal that this is somewhat of a trade-off. Inspection does not add value, but it prevents greater waste from occurring. It is important to realize that Toyota does not take the addition of any waste lightly. There is always an effort to minimize the wasteful activity. There are several methods of incorporating inspection into the work in such a way as to minimize the waste and maximize the value.

Every operator has three responsibilities regarding quality:

1. Check the incoming work to ensure that it is free of defects.
2. Verify that his or her work is free of defects.
3. Never knowingly pass defective product to the following operation.

The first item, to check the incoming work, can be accomplished while the part or the operator is in motion. For example, when the operator is completing the work cycle and returning to the next vehicle, she can visually check specific items as she walks. When a part is picked up, it is not picked up absent-mindedly, it is picked up with intent—the intent to verify that it is the correct part and that it is defect free. This inspection is an expectation for the correct performance of the job. These are not typical thorough inspections; they are very quick and specific. Thorough 100% inspections are done at the end of any subassembly or major process like body welding, body paint, or chassis production.

Targeting specific areas with a history of problems will increase the effectiveness of this checking process (use the data!). Other inspections can be performed as a part is being installed or removed. Make a point of training people to look at a specific location when performing the work. Chapter 11 has more details on job instruction training, the method Toyota uses to train employees.

In a similar manner, each person can check his or her work. Work is checked as it is removed from the machine or handed to the following operation. Specific quality "key points" are identified, and operators check them. For critical operations, or tasks that have had a history of missed steps, a *yoshi* is used. (Pronounced "yosh," it is similar to a pilot calling "Check" while going over the preflight checks.) The standardized work dictates that upon completion of the task, the operator will point (yes literally!) at the part and call out "Yoshi," signifying "I have checked this item." The pointing provides a visual cue to leaders that the check step is actually being performed (aiding in the auditing of standardized work). If this inspection were only visual, it is not possible to see if a person actually looked as instructed. Also, the physical act of pointing requires intention, and the intentional act causes the brain to engage. A step is less likely to be omitted if a yoshi is used. A similar process on parts where color marking does not matter is to use color markers and physically mark each place where a check has been done. The act of making the physical mark helps avoid missing checks.

Of course, one of the primary purposes of stopping the line is to prevent passing defects to following operations. Even with this extensive system and support available, it is one of the more difficult ideas to instill. People seem to have an aversion to admitting failure or incapability. One of the great benefits of small batch production is that if a defect is missed at one station and subsequent operators are checking incoming work, there will be a very short feedback loop from the time when the problem is created to the time when it's discovered at a downstream operation. It might be a matter of one hour or less, for example, between when a welding operation is performed on a Toyota car body and when someone trying to install parts notices a bad hole position. In a traditional large batch operation the feedback loop time could be a week or more.

TIP

Don't Give People Rules They're Unable to Follow

This tip applies in many ways, but in this case it relates to the rule of never knowingly passing defects to following processes. This involves more than just telling people not to do it. What do they do if they find a defect? Who do they call? Where do they put it? If these issues are not defined, the people will be confused and conflicted. They want to do the right thing and follow instructions, but if it isn't possible to follow the rule *and* get the job done effectively, they will choose to get the job done and violate the rule. Watch to see what happens. Try the task yourself to get firsthand experience. Don't assume that people break the rules because they don't care. Maybe there is not a good system for helping people to follow the rules.

Poka Yoke

Workers are assisted with the prevention of mistakes by the utilization of *poka yoke* methods or devices. This term is generally translated into English as "mistake proofing" or "error proofing." Error proofing is not so much a lean "tool" as it is a way of thinking and evaluating problems. It is based on the philosophy that people do not intentionally make mistakes or perform the work incorrectly, but for various reasons mistakes can and do occur.

There is a significant difference in the Toyota Way of thinking about the causes of mistakes and the thought process used within other companies. In our work with other companies, everyone unanimously agrees, "People make mistakes." It is also unanimously agreed, "If people *paid attention* they would not make as many errors." Conventional thinking tends toward identifying the cause of mistakes as "human error," while the Toyota Way always starts with the assumption that an error is a failure of the *system* and *methods* that are used to perform the work. Quite simply, errors occur because the current method allows them!

The difference in thinking shifts the responsibility for errors from the people to the method, which also shifts the blame for mistakes from people to systems. When people are released from blame, they are free to focus on creating more effective systems and actually solving problems, rather than defending themselves. It is common within Toyota for a manager to apologize to a worker when the worker makes an error, because management bears the responsibility for creating effective systems that prevent mistakes. When was the last time someone in your company apologized to a worker when the worker made a mistake?

The following case example typifies the thinking within most organizations.

Case Example: Errors in Faxing Orders

During an activity to improve order processing throughput time in an office setting, it was discovered that order approvals were often delayed by several days because of errors made during faxing to dealers. Orders were to be returned to the dealer for review and approval prior to submitting for production. The normal procedure was to return the preapproval proposal via fax to the dealer for final approval. The required response time from dealers was two workdays. If the proposal was inadvertently sent to the wrong dealer, two or three days would pass before follow-up was initiated to see if the dealer approved the proposal. During the follow-up it was discovered that the fax was never received. Investigation of the fax transmittal records showed that faxes were in fact inadvertently being sent to the wrong dealers.

Further investigation also revealed that certain employees made a higher number of mistakes, and the conclusion was that they were "more careless." As a possible "solution," instructions to employees were posted by the fax machines telling them to "Pay attention" and to "Be careful" and "Verify that faxes were sent correctly." Of course, this did not solve the problem, and the conclusion was that certain employees would always "be problems" and that more checking was needed.

When the Toyota Way of thinking was suggested, the response was, "Human error is a reality. You will never eliminate human error." Here is the issue. A person who develops a system generally understands it well and assumes that others should also. The developer (or even a person that has used it for years) believes that the system is simple and understandable. They have difficulty recognizing that others may have a different experience with the system and that people have different capabilities. Anyone who does not perform as well is considered to be incapable. Rarely does anyone consider the system. Let's look at the method in this example to find the causes of errors in the system.

Due to the large number of incoming and outgoing faxes, four machines were used. Each machine could store 100 fax numbers and use a "shortcut" code to automatically dial the phone number. A list of all dealers was posted behind the fax machines so employees could locate the dealer and the correct code (Figure 8-6). The list was separated into three sheets that were each very large (20 by 20 inches). They were also posted on the wall behind the fax machines, some distance from the employee.

When we evaluated the method in which work was performed and tried to understand why the errors could occur, we saw that while all

20 Inches across the sheet!

←——————————————————————————————————————→

Dealer Name	Dealer Region	Dealer Address	Dealer Representative	Phone Number	Fax Number	Pre-Programmed Code
A Plus Cabinets	South West	111 Short Street Anytown, AK	John Smith	888-555-1212	888-555-1213	Fax Machine 3- #49
Astounding Cabinets	East	555 West Main, Yourtown, MS	George Jones	877-222-2222	877-222-1234	Fax Machine 2- #32

Figure 8-6. Sample dealer list

information necessary to perform this task was available, it was not laid out in a manner conducive to the specific task. Let's evaluate the steps of the task.

1. Look at order and identify dealer

2. Locate the dealer on the list

3. Scan across the page to identify the fax machine and code (remember this information)

4. Find the fax machine

5. Enter correct code and send fax

Evaluating the method, we discover that errors could occur during each step. It's possible to identify the dealer on the order and then incorrectly identify the dealer on the list. When scanning from the dealer to the fax code, it's possible to cross over into another line and identify the wrong dealer (remember, the sheet was behind the fax machines, where it was not possible to track across the lines with a finger). Moving from the sheet to the fax machine, the employee had to remember the correct fax machine and the code on the machine. It was possible to get the correct machine and the incorrect code or the correct code on the wrong machine or forget the information that had been looked up.

Management concluded that employees should be careful when scanning the list and that remembering the machines and codes should be easy. When they looked at the system, they concluded that is was "easy" largely because they only had to do the task one time error free to prove the point that the system was fine. If they had to do the process hundreds or thousands of times, and sometimes were in a hurry, they would discover that they too would make numerous errors. This is a common failure of thinking by management. It may be easy to do a task one time without errors. Doing it hundreds of times without errors is another matter entirely.

To simplify this task to minimize errors, let's look at the potential causes of errors.

Error: Incorrect matching of dealer with fax machine and code.

Why does this error occur?

1. The two pieces of information used are at opposite ends of the long sheet (almost 20 inches apart).

2. There's no visual delineation between lines on the sheet, making it easy to cross into the next line.

3. The sheets are behind the machine, where the employee can't use a finger to trace across the line.

Solution: Reformat the sheet so the dealer name and the code are side by side. This minimizes the possibility of crossing lines. Also, shade every other line so it's easier to stay within the correct line, as shown in Figure 8-7.

Dealer Name	Pre-Programmed Code	Dealer Region	Dealer Address	Dealer Representative	Phone Number	Fax Number
A Plus Cabinets	Fax Machine 2- #49	South West	111 Short Street Anytown, AK	John Smith	888-555-1212	888-555-1213
Astounding Cabinets	Fax Machine 2- #32	East	555 West Main, Yourtown, MS	George Jones	877-222-2222	877-222-1234

Figure 8-7. Reformatted dealer list

Error: Employee does not use the correct fax machine identified.

Why does this error occur?

The sheets are spread out behind the fax machines and the employee has to remember the correct machine identified and locate the correct machine. Figure 8-8 shows this condition.

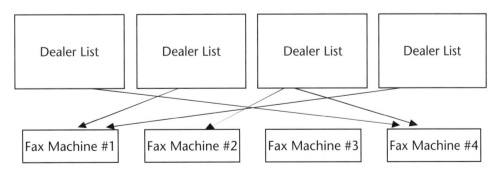

Figure 8-8. Arrangement of dealer lists by fax machine

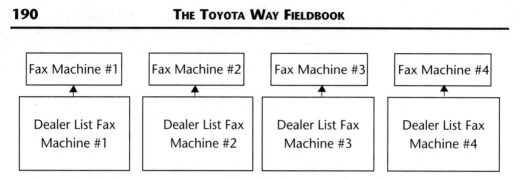

Figure 8-9. Revised layout of dealer lists by fax machine

> Solution: Separate the dealer sheets by designated fax machine and place the sheets in front of the machines so employees can trace the line with a finger. The new layout is shown in Figure 8-9.
>
> Implementing these changes reduced the errors significantly. It was also discovered that errors were made in the initial programming of codes. Even if the employee correctly identified the code, the fax was sent incorrectly.
>
> You may also ask, "Did you consider a verification process to ensure that the fax was received by the dealer?" This was in fact initiated, but bear in mind that this "solution" is similar to an inspection of product *after* it has been produced. This extra step does not address the root causes of the error, *and* it adds cost. It should only be used for critical processes, and only after root causes have been corrected.

The key to developing effective mistake proofing lies in understanding how or why the mistake occurred. Do you understand the circumstances that led to the error? Was this a random mistake or a repetitive one? Does the mistake happen with everyone or is there one person who has difficulty? If it is an individual, the answer may be to evaluate standardized work and make sure that no steps are omitted. If everyone has the problem, there may be a singular cause such as missing information or a step that is not clear. Don't make the mistake of believing every error requires a "device" to prevent recurrence.

The following case example demonstrates that there are always multiple ways to solve any problem. Encourage your employees to be creative and to seek solutions that are highly effective and low in cost. There is great power in simplicity. Look around you to apply existing solutions from other problems to your problem. The idea for Velcro was developed after an observation of "stickers," and the "problem" was converted to a solution to other situations.

Case Example: There's Always More Than One Way to Prevent Errors

In the Toyota Georgetown plant the parts were painted in a leveled color mix and sequence, meaning that one part would be painted white, the next might be blue, then black, and then back to white. It was possible to have the same color back-to-back, but the mix varied according to several conditions. The paint system required continuous circulation of paint, and only one paint gun per painter was used. Each time the color was changed, the painter would disconnect the paint line from the QD (quick disconnect) and attach it to the paint gun. The painter would flush the line momentarily and then paint the next part. Because the color changed from part to part, the painter had to disconnect and reconnect the paint line for each part. One key element of error proofing lies in understanding that people will generally behave like electricity—they'll seek the path of least resistance. In this case the painters wanted to avoid the continuous changing of paint lines.

Each paint booth had three painters. After the first painter applied color to the part, subsequent painters could visually see the colors of the parts (and the color mix) coming to them. On occasion the pattern was such that a white part was followed by a red and then another white, for example. When the painter could see that the white would be needed again, he or she would hold the white line and reconnect it after the red part (never reattaching the white line to the wall). Sometimes the painter would deviate from the rule and have multiple lines disconnected at one time, which caused the operator to mistakenly reconnect one paint-line color to a QD of another paint color. Then both colors would be mixed throughout the entire system—a big problem! This happened several times each year, and the total lost labor, materials, and waste disposal amounted to over $80,000 per year, which did not include the cost to the customer (the assembly line).

The paint line would stop while the team leaders prepared hand-mixed paint in "paint pots" for each painter so the line could be restarted. The line stoppage often created a shortage of parts to the assembly line—now a very serious problem. Previous efforts at error proofing yielded the following "solutions":

1. Notify the painters that the standardized work specified only one paint hose be removed at any time and that standardized work must be followed. As might be expected, this level of error proofing—tell the employees the correct method—is rarely effective.

2. Post a sign that stated "Only one paint hose can be removed at any time" at each workstation. This commonly applied attempt at error

proofing—to post notification of the rule or method—is also rarely effective. Most people assume that a sign, clearly in view, will prevent errors. This seems logical. People don't break the rules maliciously (most of the time), but they often rationalize, "I don't think I'll make the mistake, so it's okay if I break the rule."

3. Label the paint lines. Overspray buildup quickly obliterated any labels and made them unreadable.

4. A cover "flap" was placed over the QD for the white paint line, which required the painter to lift the cover to reconnect the hose. This countermeasure was based on the fact that the majority of incidences in the past involved white paint mixing with another color. Since 40 percent of all vehicles were white, the odds of having multiple white bumpers within the sequence simultaneously were higher. The cover over the white QD was intended to make the operator "think" before replacing the white paint line (similar to a yoshi). This "solution" also had no effect because it did not prevent connecting the wrong lines. It only made the work more difficult (lifting the cover for 40 percent of the jobs).

These four attempts at prevention represent the hierarchy of error proofing moving from telling or sharing information, to posting notices, to attempts at prevention by self-checking. The efforts may have prevented some occurrences, but they did not prevent them all.

After these attempts to eliminate the error failed, a solution was proposed to use a device known as a "peanut." This allowed the paint to recirculate at the paint gun, and eliminated the need to disconnect the paint line. This was an effective preventive device, but the negative points were additional weight on the paint gun (nearly one pound), which was an ergonomic concern, and the high cost of the devices. An installation on the entire paint line would cost over $10,000—not a low-cost solution.

It was clear from observation that the operators' inclination to deviate from the described method was not out of spite. They were deviating because of a natural desire to reduce their own burden, and they assumed that they would never make the mistake. In this case, an error-proofing method was needed that removed any need for a conscious act (following the rules). It was necessary to remove any options.

Watching the painters disconnect and reconnect the line, it looked like someone putting a key in a lock and opening a door. This was the seed for an idea. What if each paint line could somehow be made to fit only one QD? What if each QD and paint-line combination could be like a lock and a key? The QDs would need to be like locks, and the paint lines keys. A toolmaker was able to make a mock-up sample

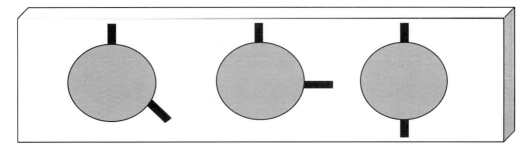

Figure 8-10. Lock and key error-proofing device

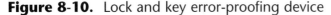

using a quarter-inch steel plate over the front of the QDs that had unique slots milled for each separate color (Figure 8-10). Then he made a sleeve that was attached to each paint line with a pin configuration that would fit the slot. Just like a lock and key! The prototype was installed at one station to test and to verify ease of use. After modifications, matching sets were made for each paint station (all were identical lock/key configurations).

Of course, this method is not completely mistake proof. In fact, it's possible to defeat the method for any system that is developed (think about computer hackers breaking into "secure" systems). In this case, if the pins were broken or removed, the device would be ineffective. To counter this possibility the team leader added a check of the pins to the daily preshift inspection to verify that everything was in correct working order.

The cost of this simple solution was about $200 for material and labor, and the sleeves only added a few ounces of weight to the operator—not a significant ergonomic impact. The device effectively prevented the problem with zero recurrences.

There are some key points that support the effort of mistake proofing. The key determinant of your success is your mind-set. Error-proofing techniques and tools are simple and easy to apply. The greatest challenge is in discovering the root cause and using your imagination to effectively eliminate it.

There is a hierarchy when it comes to the mistake-proofing effort. The highest order is to prevent the occurrence of the error completely. But complete elimination is not always feasible or practical. Any system or device that is installed can be bypassed if desired. If a prevention device is installed that is problematic or cumbersome, people will tend to "work around" it. If you create a cure that is worse than the disease, people will sidestep your cure.

If it's not possible to completely prevent the error (most of the time), then try to detect the error as it occurs. Detection devices or methods are more common

> **TRAP**
>
> **STOP**
>
> **Don't Go Overboard with Poka Yoke**
>
> Unfortunately, too much of a good thing can be bad. We've seen a trend toward higher and higher levels of mistake proofing. In many cases the devices are developed by engineers, and the actual workers have no input. The devices become extremely sophisticated and add layers of complexity. We have seen operations that take 15 seconds to perform the actual work, but an additional 25 seconds or more to engage the mistake-proofing device! In one example, a molded part has a few clips and slide rails added, then is placed in a mistake-proofing device. The part is locked in the fixture and then cycled to test for application of the correct parts. After the cycle is completed, it's unclamped and removed from the fixture. The checking takes nearly twice as long as the actual work! The sad part is that after this elaborate testing process it's possible for the parts to fall out, causing a defective part to reach the customer anyway! In addition, the sophistication of the devices creates problems with understanding how to operate them, reset after errors, and so forth. Try to find simple, effective mistake-proofing methods.

(jidoka devices fit this category). The device may detect a broken tool or signal the operator that a component is missing. The tool is already broken and some parts may be damaged, but the problem is detected and corrected quickly.

In any case, it's important to prevent any defective items (or mistakes) from affecting the customer. This is true even if an effective error-proofing device is used. There must always be protective "gates" to ensure that the customer is never compromised. As mentioned earlier, each employee acts as a "gate" by self-inspecting and inspecting key areas of others' work. More inspection points (gates) reduce the possibility of escape.

This list of possible causes of errors or omissions may not be all-inclusive, but it covers the primary causes:

1. Deviation from defined work method (work must be standardized before attempting poka yoke).
   a. Omitted steps
   b. Steps out of sequence
2. Missing parts (or components of the work)
3. Improper part (watch out for interchangeable parts)
4. Incorrect setup (wrong tools or settings)

5. Errors in information or documentation
6. Transposing type errors (watch for long number strings)
7. Misinterpretation type errors (look for similar descriptions, numbers, and appearance)
8. Recognizing the mistake but failing to segregate or correct it

Note that mistake proofing extends well beyond the prevention of defects. It applies to any work activity and to any mistake that creates a deviation from the defined standard. Perhaps the material handler forgets to pick up an item, or a designer forgets to put key information on the prints. Consider this example that we are all familiar with:

You pull into the drive-through of your favorite fast food restaurant to order lunch and notice that a screen displays your order as you call it in and the cashier enters it. The screen has a statement that says, "This screen is to ensure order accuracy." So one possible point of error is in entering the order. How could an error occur? Perhaps the cashier could not hear clearly. Perhaps the customer ordered the wrong thing or the wrong quantity (not that that would ever happen in your business!). The cashier may press the incorrect key (note that the cash registers have preprogrammed buttons for all items—an error-proofing and time-saving example), or enter an incorrect quantity.

Well, there are several possibilities for mistakes to occur, and we're only at step one! Remember in the "old days" when the order would be called back to the food preparation area? This is another opportunity for errors. Again, what if it were called out incorrectly, or heard incorrectly, or either party forgot part of the order? Many restaurants have installed monitors that display the order to the kitchen as it's keyed in. No chance to misunderstand or forget. Then comes the actual food preparation. This may be the area of greatest opportunity for error. The error rate is most likely tied to orders that "deviate" from standard (even though they promise that you can "have it your way"). Did you ask to hold the mayo or to add extra pickles? Errors might occur in the actual preparation of the nonstandard item, or the order could be prepared correctly and then a different item placed in your bag. Are the "specials" separated from the standards? How are specials visually indicated to prevent errors? With all of the possible opportunities for errors, it's a wonder the order comes out right most of the time.

Creating a Support Structure

In most traditional operations miscellaneous problems occur throughout the day, and leaders are seldom notified (based on the individual preference of the worker). We have observed machines that were not operating, defects that were piling up, and even operators who had left the work area for some reason, and there was no response. The number of problems often overwhelms the leaders because they are spread too thin.

One of the major differences between Toyota and other companies is the support structure and how it's utilized to effectively control problems and keep the system operating. The roles and responsibilities of the team and group leaders, and suggestions for selecting the right people, will be explained in Chapter 10. Suffice to say here that a critical aspect for the supporting roles is the "span of control." It is not possible for a leader to respond to the needs of several dozen people if the line or operation will be stopped each time a problem occurs. Again this is an issue of compromise—adding the waste of extra indirect workers who do not directly add value in order to eliminate or avoid much bigger wastes. The Toyota Way is full of short-term investments that result in long-term payoffs many times over.

Reflect and Learn from the Process

1. Take time to reflect on your organization's culture regarding building in quality and getting the job done right the first time.
   a. What is the cultural view of people and mistakes? Is it that people make mistakes intentionally or are careless or that there are "bad" employees? Listen to conversations and make a mental note of the comments.
   b. Do you believe that some problems are due to carelessness?
   c. How will your thinking and actions need to change in order to influence the organization?
   d. Are people in the company expected to participate in the identification and elimination of problems they detect?
2. During your "waste walks" pay particular attention to what happens when a problem occurs.
   a. How did you know there was a problem? Could you (visually) see a deviation from a standard?
   b. How did the person who detected the problem know it was a problem? Does he or she have a standard for comparison or "just know" from "experience"?
   c. How was the problem handled? Was the person able to elevate the problem from the work site, or did the person have to to find help?
   d. Was there a defined response to the elevation of the problem?

    e. Did the response include verification that the problem did not affect the customer, and if it did, was the problem contained to prevent spread to the customer?

    f. Did the response include verification of the cause of the problem and corrective action to prevent further occurrence?

    g. What is the total response time for the problem resolution cycle? What are the total losses from having an ineffective system?

    h. What actions need to be added to your implementation plan to improve your system?

3. The foundation for building quality at the source is standardized work. Evaluate your standardized work process to answer the following questions:

    a. Is the standardized work clear and understandable?

    b. Is an incoming quality check included in every job? Have specific areas been identified for checks based on historical data (check known problem areas)?

    c. Have the key quality points been identified for each job, and are they verified prior to completion of the job?

    d. Does your system allow people to stop the process if they detect a problem?

    e. Does this system automatically elevate the problem to ensure that corrective action is taken?

4. The next time a problem occurs that is caused by someone making a "mistake," evaluate the corrective action response.

    a. Does the countermeasure go beyond reminders to employees, signs, and retraining? If not, this indicates inability to find true causes and identify effective solutions.

    b. Are suggestions for solutions solicited from employees?

    c. Evaluate the mistake for the true root cause (see problem solving section). What can be done to *prevent* anyone from making the same or a similar mistake?

    d. What is the level of your attempts at mistake proofing? Are you putting up signs, detecting problems that already occurred, or preventing the problem from occurring in the first place?

    e. Add to your implementation plan details for teaching your leadership how to do root-cause analysis and error proofing.

Chapter 9

Make Technology Fit with People and Lean Processes

Back to the Abacus?

"Lean is antitechnology." "Those lean bigots are always bad-mouthing IT." "If it were up to the lean dreamers we would scrap all our computers and even our pens are too high tech—they want pencil and paper." These are examples of statements we often hear, particularly from frustrated IT professionals who are being blocked by the lean folks from implementing the technologies they had planned. The impression is that Toyota does not believe in advanced technology of any kind. They seem to imagine Toyota as a company where everyone carries an abacus on their belts.

Let's get this myth off the table immediately. The reality is that Toyota is a technology-based company. In fact, they are among the most sophisticated users of advanced technology in the world. We have not measured technology use in Toyota versus the competition, but we can tell you that they use it, and use lots of it—robots, supercomputers, desktop computers, RF scanning technology, SAP, lights-out factories, and so on. Consider the technology in Toyota products—the first company to make a mass production hybrid vehicle filled with computer chips galore—and Toyotas in Japan are filled with GPS systems for navigation.

The point of confusion is simple. It's not that Toyota avoids advanced technology, but that Toyota views technology differently. When lean experts advise a company to stop using the MRP (Material Requirements Planning) system as it is being used, or to shut down the automated storage and retrieval system, or to stop investing in that high-technology paint booth, they are not saying stop using technology but saying stop using technology in a way that produces waste. Stop using technology as a substitute for thinking.

Go back to the history of Toyota and Sakichi Toyoda, the "King of Inventors" in Japan. The company got its start as a producer of automation. Toyoda wanted to automate weaving through power looms. But he did not go out and set up an R&D lab to make the most high-tech, expensive, and exotic power loom possible. He wanted a simple and inexpensive loom that could serve the purpose of relieving some of the burden on women in the community. He built the first Toyoda looms by hand out of wood. He got his own hands dirty learning steam engine technology.

When Toyota Motor Company got into the hybrid technology business, it was not on a mission to become the world leader in advanced hybrid technology. It began with a high-powered technical team, dubbed G21, assigned to think innovatively about new ways to build cars and new ways to design cars for the twenty-first century. In the early 1990s the financial success and market penetration of Toyota was at a peak, yet chairman Eiji Toyoda took every opportunity he could to preach crisis. At one Toyota board meeting he asked, "Should we continue building cars as we have been doing? Can we survive in the twenty-first century with the type of R&D that we are doing?" This triggered the G21 team to develop a concept for the twenty-first century car. A chief engineer was assigned, and after an exhaustive search, and with prodding from new president Hiroshi Okuda, concluded that the hybrid engine was a good intermediate solution between conventional engines and the real future in fuel cells or some other renewable resource. The hybrid engine was a practical solution to a real problem—not a solution in search of a problem.

The history of Toyota has not been about avoiding new technology. It has been about putting technology into a proper perspective, one driven by a practical purpose. And then Toyota always looks at the value-added process to realize that purpose. Only then does the company consider where new technology fits into achieving that purpose. This is the lesson of lean thinking about technology.

Like most other things we have been covering in this book, there is no cookbook on how to evaluate technology or how to implement it in a "lean way." There is also no such thing as "lean technology." There are only lean systems with technology playing an appropriate role in supporting them. In this chapter we will discuss ways to think about and adopt new technology.

 ### Case Study: Is Toyota Technology Behind the Times?

Toyota has an interesting practice of allowing competitors to visit their factories. The Georgetown plant often hosted "automotive benchmarking" tours and has monthly "public information tours/seminars." Visitors were able to talk to Toyota employees and ask specific questions related to how Toyota does things. On special benchmarking tours visitors are allowed to visit the shop floor and "see whatever they want to."

On one particular tour with some Big Three plant managers, one of the visitors commented to his associates, "Get a look at this. We haven't used that technology for at least 15 years!" The outdated technology seemed to be the center of their attention. They completely overlooked other elements of the production system that they had struggled with in their plants. One of the visitors inadvertently walked into a robot cell and shut the robot down. He didn't even realize that this had happened, and a team leader came over and restarted the robot in less than a minute, before any loss of production occurred. The tour guide pointed this out to the plant manager and asked him how long it would take to restart a robot or line in his plant if it had been stopped. His response was, "Maybe 10 or 15 minutes," and then he went on complaining about the outdated technology, without understanding that it is not the technology that is critical, but rather, the people who use the technology and the total system.

Toyota robots have considerably higher reliability and uptime than those in Big Three plants. Its flexible global body line that can flexibly make trucks and minivans and car bodies in any order without missing a beat is the envy of the industry. And it is full of robots all operating in harmony. Any robot goes down and the body line goes down. But they rarely go down. Most auto makers would be concerned about old technology. Toyota believes that the worst state of the technology should be when it is out of the box and then it improves with age through regular maintenance and continuous improvement.

What Do You Believe About Technology, People, and Processes?

The starting point of thinking is what you believe. It is also what you value. If you believe that technology is the solution to your problems or if you value being the kid with the best technological toys on the block, you will not get lean.

The Toyota Way always starts with the customer. What does the customer want? Then ask what process will add value to the customer with minimum waste. Then recognize that any process you can concoct will still be full of waste. Getting out the waste takes time and experience with the process: It is a learning process of continuous improvement, and only those working in and managing the process can improve it on a day-to-day basis.

Thinking in this way is a belief system. The principles of the Toyota Way are a set of beliefs in what works. It is part of the culture of Toyota. So any new technology must fit into this broader system and philosophy:

- ◆ How will technology contribute to the value adding process?
- ◆ How will technology help to eliminate waste?

- ◆ Will the technology contribute to a flexible system that can economically adjust to ups and downs in demand?
- ◆ Will the technology support people doing the work in continuous improvement of the process?
- ◆ Have people in the system challenged themselves to accomplish the goal with the most flexible and least complex technology?
- ◆ Are people using the technology as a crutch to avoid having to think deeply about improving the process?

The cross-dock case study below illustrates two contrasting belief systems with two contrasting results. Toyota took a process-oriented view in developing a standardized cross-docking system following Toyota Production System (TPS) principles that seamlessly integrated its suppliers and assembly plant. Technology clearly took a backseat in the Toyota case. A major U.S. automaker took a technology-oriented view placing IT systems at the center, hoping the IT systems would somehow integrate a diverse range of logistics providers who were selected based on low cost bids. The result, predictably, was superior performance of the Toyota logistics system.

 Case Study: Technology Beliefs and Cross-Docks

Toyota made a serious investment in time and money to develop a lean cross-dock system in North America by establishing a joint venture: Transfreight. Toyota did not have any direct ownership stake but did involve its trading company partner, Mitsui, in a joint venture with TNT Logistics (later Mitsui bought out TNT). A cross-dock is simply like a juncture box. In this case, truckloads of parts come in at least daily from a variety of different suppliers spread around the country. The pallets of parts cross through the dock and are reloaded in mixed loads of just enough parts for one to two hours of use in the assembly plant. Shipments are going out to the assembly plant 12 times per day. It would be a waste of lots of truck space to have trucks picking up parts from all over the country 12 times per day and going directly to the assembly plant—the trucks would be mostly empty most of the time.

The Toyota belief was that the cross-dock was an extension of the assembly plant—a lean value chain from the supplier right to the person assembling parts to the vehicle. It was a complex process with many opportunities for error, with thousands of parts moving about each day. And each step in the process was based on tight time windows, with any delays cascading through the system. To get it right required a creative application of TPS. It needed to be a flow-through process with minimal waste. It needed to be a visual process so people would make the right decisions at the right time. Standardized work was needed to have consistency in timing. Truck drivers were inspectors checking that all the right parts were being collected from the suppliers.

Teams of workers needed to be highly trained, with team leaders carefully checking the work at each point to be sure no errors slipped through. And every one was a thinker driven to continually improve the process.

The result was a relatively low-tech solution. For example, a ticket system was developed. Pallets of parts from suppliers were taken off the truck and immediately tagged with a specific ticket listing critical information like the part number, quantity, and main route to the assembly plant. It was color coded according to where the part would sit in the cross-dock. Specific lanes were set up for different main routes to the assembly plants. Other physical areas were set aside for parts that needed to be repacked or parts that needed to "go to sleep" and wait more than a day to be delivered. The cards were kept in a large visual board with cubby slots by supplier subroute and assembly plant main route. As one Transfreight executive stated:

> Our process for managing the cross-docks is all manual. We use [Microsoft] Access and Excel, but it's largely manual. There's no optimization software, no RF technology to scan freight. I mean, we do have a system to calculate cube, miles, etc., but our processes are largely manual.

Now let's consider an American competitor to Toyota that set up a cross-docking system in part to imitate Toyota's just-in-time system. This auto maker also set up a joint venture, of which it owned a controlling 60 percent. When speaking to one of the executives of the joint venture, the purpose of the joint venture was described as follows:

> Our vision is [centered on] our IT. This is a global, integrated system that provides both inbound and outbound visibility so we have visibility of all material and the product. We will have database management and warehouse database management globally. We will be the central clear-inghouse for all data. We will have plug and play capability with any system that any company has, whether it is SAP, i2, CAPS, or Manugistics. The last part is supplier or logistics or partner compliance. So it is the measurement, the drive for Six Sigma, that we signed up for. We are delivering all the process management through the companies and the partners. That is our scope; that's it.

Interestingly, while Toyota invested heavily in applying TPS within each cross-dock in Transfreight, the American joint venture put each new contract for different collections of parts up for bid to competitive logistics companies that ran cross-docks. Transfreight owned the cross-docks and ran each using a uniform set of management principles.

Different logistics companies won different pieces of the work for the American joint venture and used their own approaches to cross-dock management. That is why it was so important to have "plug and play" capability—each logistics company used different software. The software was the connection between the U.S. automaker and the logistics provider. For Toyota, there was a lock-tight umbilical cord connecting the processes of the suppliers, cross-docks, and the assembly plant. Through common processes and common IT, it was not necessary to have plug and play capability.

A comparison of eight cross-docks of the U.S. automaker and five cross-docks of Transfreight on key performance indicators was conducted using measures like labor productivity, utilization of forklifts, trailer/tractor ratio, and number of time windows successfully achieved. The results showed that the Transfreight cross-docks had overall superior performance to the U.S. automaker's cross-docks. Apparently, technology was not the answer.

Tailor Technology to Fit Your People and Operating Philosophy

In the cross-dock case example above, Transfreight certainly is not using very sophisticated "supply chain solutions" software. Does that mean this software is not "lean"? On the contrary, over time Toyota has been carefully evaluating various software solutions and is gradually incorporating them into the process. But it must be carefully screened. Bringing new software into the system is a bit like transplanting an organ into the body. If it is not a match, the body might reject the organ and shut down.

Glenn Uminger has responsibility for much of the logistics system for Toyota in North America. He believed there was a role for more advanced information technology in optimizing pickup and delivery routes of trucks. A good part of this system involves Transfreight, which uses the traditional manual systems that have worked for Toyota for decades. Truck routes basically are developed manually with data from simple in-house IT systems that visually display data and routes. It is comparably easy to develop truck routes because of Toyota's passion for heijunka. If the assembly plant has stable, leveled production, it will place a stable, leveled demand on all its supply systems. If you know the quantity that will be shipped every day to the assembly plant, and the frequency of delivery, it is relatively straightforward to put together routes that will be the same every day. Yet there still are unexpected fluctuations in assembly plant production, and enough supply points that Glenn thought planning software could be faster and perhaps do a better job than the manual process. As he explained:

I personally first picked up a commercial inbound logistics software program and brought it into the Toyota world for hands-on trials with live data to judge its benefit starting three years ago. As we did this, I met much resistance from TMC (headquarters in Japan), as they did not like software for planning, were afraid Americans would come to depend on it and forget the logic and principles that stand behind it. They also thought that the human could create the best plan and then flexibly adjust it over time. I knew we were operating a very complex network and no human could consider all of the mathematical possibilities, all revolving around firm TPS principles. The facts using live data proved me right, and TMC quickly launched an internal system development project to create software with high optimization power, at the same time respecting TPS principles. During this, a relationship was formed between the TMC developers and Dr. Sean Kim of Agillence. Over time, TMC could not exceed the performance of Agillence software, so TMC is adopting the Agillence optimization engine and including it in our new route planning system (SMAP), due to go live in two months. We and Europe have been using this in a trial setting this year.

On the surface this seems like the story of a rigid bureaucracy that is controlled by leaders resistant to change: "We did it by hand in the good old days, so why can't you?" In reality the old liners in TMC are protecting the Toyota Way—the very essence of Toyota's competitive advantage. If they approve every request to adopt new software based on a simple business case, before long Toyota will be full of strung-together software and their worst fears will be realized: Toyota team associates "would come to depend on it and forget the logic and principles that stand behind it." At that point Toyota would be just like its competitors.

Instead they forced Glenn Uminger to defend his position, think hard about the issues, and present a solution that fit with TPS principles. After working on it for three years, Glenn says:

We will always search for the lowest cost solution while achieving proper application of our principles. We are not really sacrificing any service level of plant delivery frequency, lead time, heijunka from a practical view, but we are always evolving on how we achieve all objectives most effectively. Yes, we do always work on ways to reduce cost, but as we do we make sure we stay in bounds with our principles. Our SMAP system [includes the Agillence optimization engine] provides us a new tool to more dynamically plan routes, use "what if" scenarios, allows more time for study to ensure we apply the best routes considering all objectives, service, and cost. We change routes about eight times each year. We have some different ways of routing; sometimes short routes are okay at low efficiency if it frees up longer routes, so they won't be damaged by the need to include the low-volume short distance supplier, which is out of the way of the long route.

So our total system is stronger, and we also are lowering cost when considering the total system, no extra box handling, most effective routes. . . . Our group worked tirelessly to spec and functionally test/develop this tool. We will achieve a payback from the tool for all our efforts in a matter of months.

This is a different story of technology adoption than we see in most companies. It is a story of a group working tirelessly to develop a solution that fits its process and principles. This is a Toyota logistics group, not an IT group. They did not place all their faith in the outside vendor. They used the vendor's algorithm and worked with the vendor over several years to tailor it to fit TPS before finally bringing it live, including a display that meets Toyota's tough visual management standards. While the planning horizon was long, one can safely predict that the implementation will be smooth and, if successful, will migrate as a new Toyota standard globally—to be continually improved.

Contrasting Models of Technology Adoption

In reflecting on how Toyota approaches technology, we have identified contrasting models of traditional companies versus Toyota's lean approach. Broadly speaking, there are two different animals here—the case of hard automation and the case of IT systems for planning, scheduling, and decision making. We will consider each in turn.

Automation has been around for centuries. It is not a new story. Any engineer who has made a case for automation knows the drill. Do a cost benefit analysis where the cost is the amortized capital cost and the benefit is typically labor savings. If labor savings exceeds the amortized capital cost, the automation wins. In reality there is often a hidden bias in favor of the technology since automation does not talk back like people or threaten to unionize. Give a robot an order by programming it and it executes the order without further explanation. Many engineers make a living going through factories area by area and making cases for automation. The automation is typically purchased from the outside, and the engineer acts as a technical liaison for the outside vendor.

Look at the diagram of the traditional automation process in Figure 9-1. Clearly, the underlying philosophy is to lower labor cost by automating people out of the process. The strategy is to look at a cost-benefit analysis job by job and automate in those cases where it is cost justified. In this way variable labor costs are replaced by fixed capital costs. Some negative effects of this focus on taking out labor through automation are job insecurity, labor-management conflict, and a lot of complex and fixed equipment that has to be maintained. Skilled labor costs often go up, and equipment downtime becomes a problem. Moreover, if sales go down, management is stuck with the fixed technology costs.

From a lean viewpoint the technology is often unreliable, inflexible, and overproduces. It overproduces because it is not completely reliable and the company needs to justify the cost of the technology by keeping it busy. In an environment where large banks of inventory are the norm, this waste is usually ignored as long as the equipment is busily producing parts.

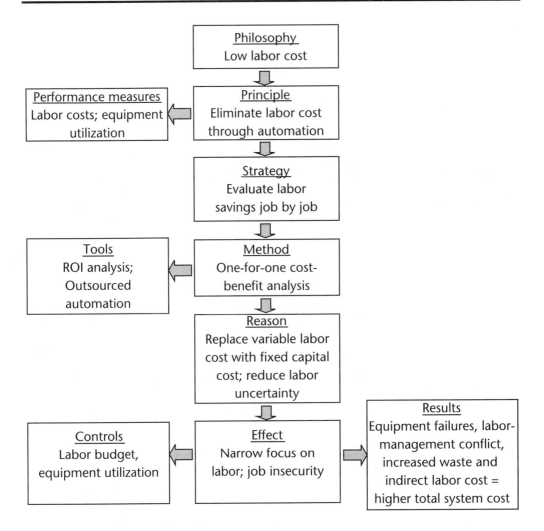

Figure 9-1. Traditional automation process

Contrast this with the lean automation process shown in Figure 9-2. Yet again the philosophy is that overall waste reduction should be the focus. The vision for any new technology is always based in TPS and viewed as a human-machine system. Equipment must support the people doing kaizen and a lean process. Any new technology must meet a specific need and fit within the total TPS system. Often that means beginning by working to improve and refine the simpler, more manual system. See what you can get out of that system before jumping into a major technology investment. Automating a non-lean system may appear to produce local cost savings but will often add waste and reduce the motivation to create a leaner system, producing more waste in the long term. When you have squeezed what you can out of the manual system, then

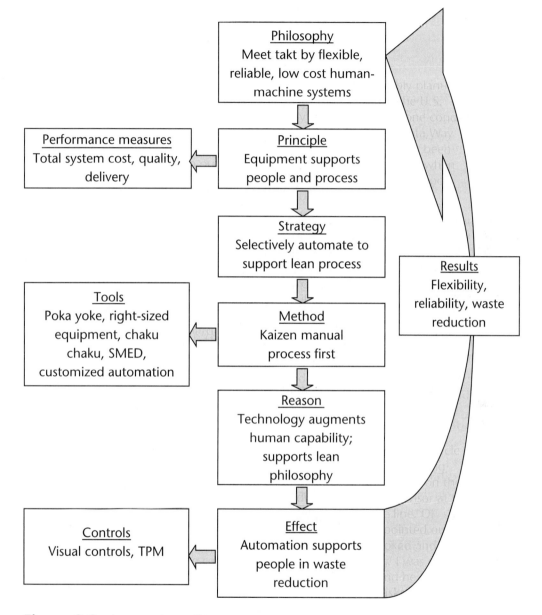

Figure 9-2. Lean automation process

ask how that system can be further improved with some specific capability. Technology offers one solution to help "meet takt time by flexible, low cost human-machine systems."

In Toyota the responsibility for bringing any new production equipment into the plant belongs to production engineering. Learning TPS is part of the initiation of any junior production engineer, and equipment is designed and selected to support TPS. For example, all equipment is extensively mistake-proofed (poka yoke) with sensors designed in to trigger an andon call when there is any abnormality in the process. The level of automation is often designed to support the worker. *Chaku chaku* refers to equipment that automatically ejects the completed part for the operator so the operator can just go from machine to machine in a cell, loading and picking up the kicked-out part. Equipment is right-sized to fit into a one-piece flow process. Equipment is also designed to support quick changeover. This all leads to the need for highly customized equipment that generally cannot be purchased on the open market. In fact, production engineering develops a good deal of the new technology used in Toyota's factory. They work hand in hand with a select group of outside vendors who are closely affiliated with Toyota and understand the Toyota Way.

Case Study: Use Right-Sized Not Super-Sized Technology

Economies of scale would lead us to believe that one huge high-tech machine would be more efficient than several smaller and simpler machines. One company that makes nuclear fuel rod assemblies manufactured metal grids to hold the fuel rods in place. After each stage of processing the grids had to be cleaned. A huge washer had pressure and heat gauges and became a bottleneck as metal parts from different processes competed to get washed.

As part of a lean transformation, the grid operation was set up as a cell and the washer was the main impediment to flow, requiring large batches. Process engineering was asked whether it was possible to use smaller and simpler washers. At first they said, "Absolutely not!" But the lean team persisted in challenging them. Ultimately they concluded that an industrial strength dishwasher would work just fine. Several dishwashers could be put in the flow, greatly reducing batch sizes and eliminating the bottleneck.

A similar story can be told when looking at other types of IT systems. Traditional IT design as depicted in Figure 9-3 is a push system. The philosophical assumption is that more information and sophisticated analysis is always better than simple human judgment. IT systems are often based on a management philosophy of top-down control of the process. With the right information and the right analysis method, the system can rationally plan and control the process.

Generic information technology is developed with some abstract purpose in mind and then pushed onto "users" who are expected to make their processes

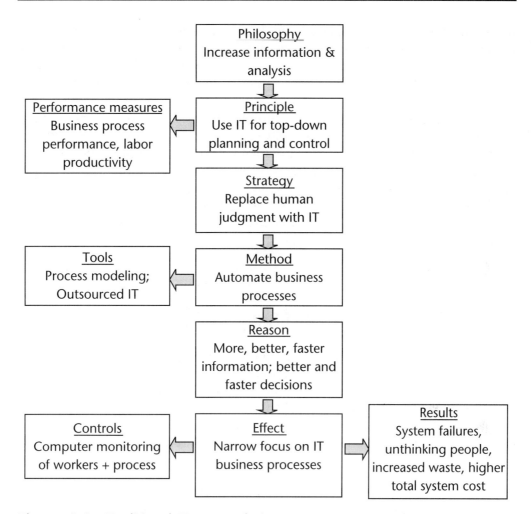

Figure 9-3. Traditional IT system design

for doing work conform to the business processes implied by the IT. The supposed "business processes" improved by IT are mostly aimed at getting the right data into the IT system (e.g., scanning in inventory every time it is moved).

The result is often a narrow focus on improving the IT business processes without closely examining the actual work process. The people become dependent on the system, which is vulnerable to failures. The people stop thinking and start following the dictates of the system. This results in less kaizen and more waste.

The Toyota Way related a story of supply chain visibility software. The software was designed to make inventory visible. When the supply chain group led a pilot of the software, they discovered that business processes in the plants were primitive and undisciplined. There were no good processes for collecting inventory data in real time. As a result, the computer system did not have a real-time picture of the inventory. The computer system was intended to show how much inventory there was throughout the plants and allow vendors to see when the inventory level reached a minimum trigger point so they could ship to bring parts up to the maximum. This was a crude type of pull system. To encourage suppliers to follow the system, a performance metric was automatically calculated, measuring what percent of the time the inventory was kept within the minimum and maximum level.

In contrast, for decades Toyota focused on putting in actual pull systems. They worked to create right-sized containers and racks to hold the containers. Strict limits were established on exactly how many parts would go in each bin

---

TRAP

STOP

Strict Reliance on IT Systems Adds Waste

A typical example of IT in companies is the desire to "track" and "understand" the actual inventory levels in "real time." Every transaction of material is "scanned" into the system (which is often performed by a value-adding operator—adding to the waste) so they can have "accurate" inventory. In fact this does not work, for a number of reasons—namely, errors and omissions—therefore it is necessary to have full-time "cycle counters" who roam the inventory and audit the levels to verify the overall accuracy and make inventory adjustments. In addition to this costly activity a physical inventory is taken one or two times per year for all items. This is a time-consuming ordeal that may take several days (sometimes on weekends).

In contrast, kanban control the inventory in Toyota, and kanban are monitored. Physical inventory is performed twice per year, and the manufacturing operation is stopped for a few hours, at most, to perform inventory (the storeroom would spend the entire day, since there are numerous items). Overall, the inventory system using "old-fashioned" cards was much less costly and more effective. Recently at Toyota, electronic kanban systems have been adopted for sending pull signals to suppliers and even for replenishing line-side inventory in assembly plants. But there is also a redundant manual system in the assembly plants to give visual indicators of parts usage.

and how many bins could be held in inventory. Kanban cards were printed to match the number of bins that could be produced. No card—no production—no more inventory. Toyota worked on equipment reliability, built-in quality, and operator training. Through continuous improvement, they had so little inventory that there was no real value to collecting real-time inventory data at each stage in the process—this is just waste. In other words, they worked on developing the true process of production and connecting production processes through simple communication vehicles and standard processes. They were less interested in non-value adding "business processes" aimed at getting data into computers. Interestingly, having worked out these manual systems Toyota has evolved to electronic kanban. But these run in parallel to a manual kanban system that provides for visual control yet with the benefits of modern computer technology.

The traditional supply chain software that promised visibility is actually based on a philosophy of top-down control. The belief is that if top management has all the information they need at their fingertips, they can control the system. The kanban system is based on a philosophy of local control. The workplace is viewed as a series of customer-supplier relationships with customers specifying just what they need when they need it through the kanban. Top management are expected to audit the system by walking down to the floor and seeing for themselves (Figure 9-4).

TIP

Always Verify the Actual Condition Yourself

We were working on a particular process to achieve stability and address operational availability issues, and the production planner on the team frequently commented that the process was "behind." Observations on the floor revealed that there was no work waiting to be processed. From a traditional Toyota standpoint, an operation can't be considered behind if an upstream process is starving it or if the customer process is full. This is all visual, and easy to determine by looking at the work area and observing the connections between operations. Confused, we asked the production planner to explain how the machine could be "behind." The answer was, "That's what the system says!" meaning that the MRP planning system showed work that was scheduled to be complete at that operation and wasn't. Simply using system information without corresponding process information can lead to false assumptions and misguided efforts to correct the "problem."

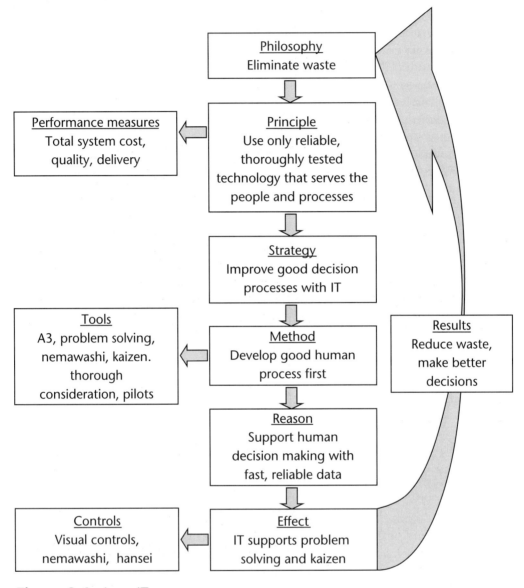

Figure 9-4. Lean IT process

As described in the Agillence software case earlier in the chapter, new IT faces a high hurdle at Toyota. The process used for adopting the Agillence software is typical at Toyota and follows the flow of logic in Figure 9-4, above, for a lean IT process. It is not enough to show in the abstract that IT can automate a process or provide more and better information. It must be clear how it will add value and support a well-thought-out and time-tested process. Typically, the process is done well manually before it is automated. The technology supports human decision making—it does not replace it. And the technology should not be used as an excuse to stop thinking and lose a focus on kaizen. Instead, the technology should support people in waste reduction.

Keep Technology in Perspective

Toyota is an engineering-driven company, and deep down it is a technology-based company. Innovative product and process technology is at the core of Toyota's success. But people are at the core in creating and successfully implementing innovative product and process technology.

The case below illustrates how "the process and people make the technology valuable." In this case a competitor we will call AmCar got considerably ahead of Toyota in technology for automating product and process design. Presentations that featured things that Toyota was not capable of doing made even Toyota a bit nervous. But the reality was far different from the hype. AmCar was not using the technology effectively and was falling further behind Toyota in development lead time, problems in new vehicle launch, and in quality. It was only after AmCar hired former Toyota employees who taught them the Toyota Way of using this technology that they began to make some positive strides.

So, again, though technology plays a critical role at Toyota, it must always be kept in context. Technology is a critical piece of the system, but the system is not just how pieces of technology fit together. The system includes the process of doing the work and the people who work in the process. It is not only a matter of what technology is selected, but of how the overall system is designed and implemented. And it is important enough to carefully plan and consider in the context of your broader philosophy of how to run the business.

Case Study: The Process and People Make the Technology Valuable

In the early 1990s the U.S. automaker we'll call AmCar began the drive toward using manufacturing simulations in the product development stage. The goal was to use computer technology to help design products that optimized the manufacturing system. Several software packages were available at the time. Delmia began to emerge as the leader in the design software race with their CATIA package, and AmCar made a commitment to this technology. There were many modules available in Delmia's software suite, but AmCar took a product-development-centered approach, focusing on design packaging—how the parts fit together without interferences in the space available. For manufacturing, the emphasis was on factory layout. Specific designs for process equipment were outsourced to suppliers who took primary responsibility for the equipment designed and did not have close interaction with the product designers.

The early promise of a truly integrated design and manufacturing system was not realized. And there was little integration between the primary functional groups (including Procurement and Supply—a large majority of component suppliers also inherited primary design responsibility for components/systems). Teams would review packaging issues, often only within functional areas (e.g., Body Engineering), and start the process very late (long after design freeze). The result was an inordinate amount of late discovery and change to both process and components, delaying product launches and leading to a long ramp-up time. In addition, there was little focus placed on developing an integrated cross-functional design review process (simultaneous engineering). The priority was placed on developing the technology, and progress became stalled despite the advancements made in software.

In 2000, a team of new employees was recruited from Toyota's North American operations to support quality improvements as a part of an effort to turn around AmCar, which at that time was losing money and struggling with severe quality problems and warranty costs. One of the Toyota employees who had experience managing product launches immediately noticed there was little activity in using computer simulations to anticipate manufacturing problems in the product development stage. Toyota called these "digital build" simulations. The car was, in a sense, built on the computer virtually, and cross-functional teams carefully evaluated problems in manufacturing and assembling the car, using Toyota's rigorous problem-solving methodology.

In late 2001 the Toyota TTC (Toyota Technical Center, Ann Arbor) participated in a joint technology sharing session with AmCar. Toyota representatives were surprised at the lack of advancement in digital design—a benchmarking session conducted in the late 1990s led Toyota to believe that AmCar was advancing rapidly in this arena. Toyota indicated that this activity was a key enabler in reducing their overall development lead time.

In early 2002 another more detailed gap analysis resulted in the recommendation by AmCar senior management to pursue the simultaneous engineering (SE) and digital assembly (DA) process. To support this, in 2002 a more stringent issues-management process was implemented, along with intense pressure to complete design/process freezes, validation activities, and overall product/process changes much earlier (using Toyota processes for each item). The groundwork was being developed to increase the level of discipline required to support SE and DA.

In late 2002 the SE and DA draft process was completed, and in early 2004 a pilot was selected and implemented. The initial process focused on the business process and behavioral aspects —not technology. Digitized photos of the parts were pulled into CATIA, and digital models of each station were created. Participants included all Engineering/Design areas, Advanced Manufacturing, Procurement and Material groups, representatives from the manufacturing plants, Quality Groups (Service, Warranty, Error Proofing), Ergonomics and Safety, and Industrial Engineering. The activities started several months prior to design freeze and continued up to the initial prototype builds (three phases). The events were very intense, and over 2,000 issues were generated in the pilot. An issues-management process was started immediately at the same intense level to record any issues observed and assign strict responsibility for their resolution by specific dates.

Initial metrics looked promising. The prototype builds for the pilot went more smoothly than usual—several significant issues were discovered and countermeasured prior to the start of prototype. The issues curve for the pilot was initiated almost nine months earlier than in previous programs. As of this writing, it was too early to have data on lead time and other performance metrics, but everyone agreed that many problems were resolved very early and launch would be much smoother.

What is interesting about this case is that AmCar was a leader in the use of CATIA technology, and as noted earlier, even Toyota was getting nervous. Yet they then fell significantly behind Toyota in the actual use of the technology. Some of the lessons that AmCar learned with the help of their recruits from Toyota were:

1. An effective process should be supported by the technology instead of trying to replace the process with the technology.

2. Build discipline through other standardized activities, then apply the discipline to the process.

3. Cross-functional involvement and input at the lowest decision-making level will lead to better use of the information made available by the technology.

4. Create a pilot/learning line to simulate results: test, test, test, then roll out.

5. Create a pull from senior management through results and supporting data.

6. Continue to kaizen the process.

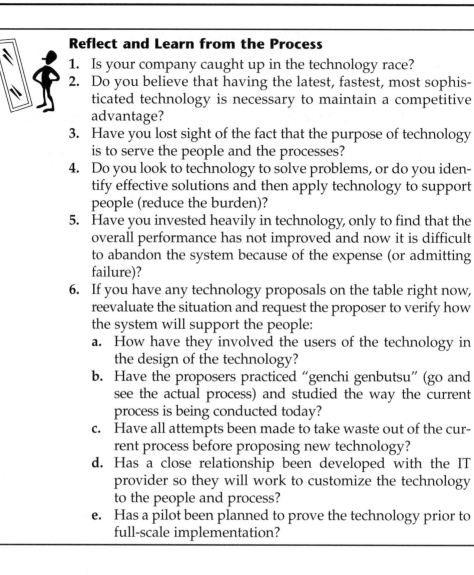

Reflect and Learn from the Process

1. Is your company caught up in the technology race?
2. Do you believe that having the latest, fastest, most sophisticated technology is necessary to maintain a competitive advantage?
3. Have you lost sight of the fact that the purpose of technology is to serve the people and the processes?
4. Do you look to technology to solve problems, or do you identify effective solutions and then apply technology to support people (reduce the burden)?
5. Have you invested heavily in technology, only to find that the overall performance has not improved and now it is difficult to abandon the system because of the expense (or admitting failure)?
6. If you have any technology proposals on the table right now, reevaluate the situation and request the proposer to verify how the system will support the people:
    a. How have they involved the users of the technology in the design of the technology?
    b. Have the proposers practiced "genchi genbutsu" (go and see the actual process) and studied the way the current process is being conducted today?
    c. Have all attempts been made to take waste out of the current process before proposing new technology?
    d. Has a close relationship been developed with the IT provider so they will work to customize the technology to the people and process?
    e. Has a pilot been planned to prove the technology prior to full-scale implementation?

Part IV

Develop Exceptional People and Partners

Chapter 10

Develop Leaders Who Live Your System from Top to Bottom

Success Starts with Leadership

When we begin to work with companies, they want us to tour their plants and see what they've done with lean. The story typically goes like this: "We started down our lean journey seven years ago. We had a consultant help us put together some training materials, and we did a project in each plant. The project focused on some kaizen events lead by the external consultant. Each plant was asked to appoint an internal facilitator to learn and keep the process going. We have one plant that went all out and has become a model in our company. We have other plants that have not done anything beyond the initial events led by the consultant."

When we query about the differences in the plants that caused this large variance in the success of the lean programs, the answer is almost always the same: "The plant manager of the model plant was very passionate and had great people skills. She and her team were absolutely committed." Unfortunately, another part of the story is often: "She then left for another opportunity, and the plant has slipped back."

It is clear that the difference between success and failure starts with leadership. This starts at the top, but ultimately the process is carried by those in the middle supporting the value-adding employees. In many organizations these "middle level managers" are seen only as a necessity to keep things in order.

People who assume these positions are often looking at them as a "step up the ladder," a temporary requirement, or rite of passage on the way to more important and lucrative opportunities. Certainly it seems that more talented or ambitious people have no desire to stay "in the trenches." Given the inherently long development period of leaders deeply skilled in TPS, this creates challenges within Toyota and other companies.

Unfortunately, in many companies today the front-line leader (middle manager or supervisor) is often viewed as a "traffic cop," or worse, as a "babysitter." True leadership, it is believed, must come from higher levels, where intelligent decisions can be made and passed down. The supervisor only needs to attend to minor problems and to keep everything under control. This shortsighted view creates a belief that the front-line leaders are an indirect cost—and thus should be maintained at minimal levels. Supervisors are thinly spread and the responsibility is far reaching (we've seen supervisors who had responsibility for over 60 people spread over multiple shifts).

Toyota has a completely different view regarding front-line leaders and places a much greater importance on them. They are viewed as crucial elements of the Toyota Way, and they must live up to much higher expectations than in most companies. Because it's expected that the group leader (supervisor) will personally develop and mentor every team member in the group, the ratio of group leaders to team members is most often one-to-20, or possibly as high as one-to-30.

In this chapter we will review some essential skills that leaders must possess or learn, and we'll look at the leadership structure at Toyota. In Chapter 20 we will focus on top leadership, but in this chapter the focus will be on the neglected middle level, sometimes negatively referred to as the "frozen middle." The buck stops at this level, where leadership from the top is translated into action. The middle managers get frozen because they are often stuck between the edicts and visions of the top and the realities of production on the front-line war zone.

Importance of Leadership Within Toyota

Toyota has a relatively flat organizational structure without many layers of management. Leaders do play a key role in the success of the company, but excessive layers of leadership are not necessary because the leaders develop and mentor others to do many of the tasks often done by leaders within other companies. While Toyota has few layers the span of control of leaders at the bottom of the organization is very small leading to more work group leaders than in competitors. The Toyota philosophy is to disperse responsibility to the lowest level possible. There is a high expectation for production associates, team leaders have a large scope of responsibility, and a group leader runs a "minibusiness." Because all leaders are expected to have a high level of responsibility, the selection and subsequent development of leaders in your organization should be one of the most important considerations.

Often, companies focus on developing leadership "duties" or "responsibilities" rather than on expectations. This is similar to attempts to implement lean tools rather than lean philosophies. People want to know, "What does a team leader or group leader do?" rather than "What are the objectives or expectations of leadership?" As a result, assignments are made to leaders such as, "Answer the andon when it goes off," or "Chart the data and post it on the board." These activities are necessary to support the system, but they are peripheral, not the essence of leadership.

At Toyota the front-line production leadership is primarily comprised of team leaders—hourly production workers with important responsibilities for direct support of the production line—and group leaders, who are salaried supervisors supporting the functions of the entire group. Team leaders and group leaders have three basic responsibilities:

1. Support for operations
2. Promotion of the system
3. Leading change

The group leader has a crucial role in the implementation and continued development of the Toyota Production System. A large number of people report to group leaders, and thus they have influence over the outcome of many people's work and progress. The group leader must take an active role in this process if it is to be successful.

The group leader role is much more than that of a "supervisor." The expectation is that the group leader is out in front, leading the way. Of course, the specific details of the group leader role may vary from area to area depending upon the process needs. But all leaders need to be flexible and willing to do whatever is necessary to achieve the desired results. The group leader position requires an ability to interpret the needs at a high level (the job responsibilities and company objectives) and to transfer that to the team to accomplish the daily objectives (leadership ability, teaching ability, and job knowledge).

The expectation of leadership at Toyota is to effectively develop people so that performance results are constantly improving. This is accomplished by instilling the Toyota culture in all employees, by continuously developing and growing capable people, and by focusing efforts on strengthening the Toyota Production System. A leader's effectiveness is based on four key performance results:

1. **Safety,** including ergonomics, reduction of injuries, and improving workplace design
2. **Quality,** including training, process improvement, and problem solving
3. **Productivity,** which encompasses consistently satisfying the customer demand and the management of resources
4. **Cost,** which means satisfying the three other criteria while controlling and reducing total cost

The assumption is that improvement in overall performance in these areas means that people's skills and abilities are improving; however, there are secondary indicators as well, such as the training plan of a group (which indicates leadership importance of skill development), the employee survey (morale), the suggestion system participation level in a group (leadership support for employee activities), and the attendance record (morale).

TIP

Focus on the Desired Outcome, Not the Daily Tasks of Leaders

Signs of effective leadership include high morale and consistent achievement of objectives within the group. The focus of leadership should be on growing people. The leader must accomplish his or her daily duties, but the real job is to develop people capable of accomplishing greater results. In effect, everyone within the group must be capable of the leadership role, even if it is only to lead their own daily activities. The leader helps to develop the correct structure for this, and also provides coaching and activities that will provide opportunities for growth.

Toyota Georgetown Production Leadership Structure

Toyota places a great deal of importance on the production-related leadership. These leaders directly support the value-adding activities, which is the central core of the organization. Toyota uses an "inverted pyramid" model for leadership, where the leaders of the organization (normally at the top of the pyramid, where they are supported by the workers) are pictured at the bottom to support the majority of the organization. We have shown the organization structure in Figure 10-1 in relation to reporting responsibilities, but in terms of support, the organization is inverted.

Production employees are assigned to groups of between 20 and 30 people, according to the needs of the work area. A group leader is responsible for the group and typically has the greatest number of direct reports of any level of management (although the team leaders are a major part of the group support structure). The group leader is the first level of "management" and is a salaried position (in the United States). Within the group are smaller teams, generally of five to seven people. The exact number varies, based on the area. Each team has

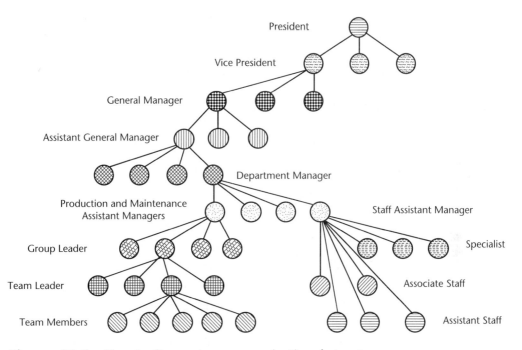

Figure 10-1. Toyota Georgetown organizational structure

a full-time team leader, which is an hourly position with a slightly higher pay rate than that of team members. These two positions—group leader and team leader—have direct responsibility for all production-related activities in the plant.

Above the group leaders are assistant managers, who are usually responsible for between four and six group leaders and are assigned to both shifts equally. All assistant managers report to one department manager. The assistant manager has direct daily responsibility for production activities and spends much of his or her time on the floor. The manager has direct responsibility for production activities, but does not tend to the daily issues. The manager is involved when issues become larger, and must be contacted in the event of any major failure in production, especially a potential shortage to the customer.

Based on the number of employees assigned to a department (e.g., assembly has more people), an assistant general manager has a different number of managers reporting to him or her. This would generally be between two and four, depending on the size of each department. A general manager often has responsibility for a "functional area," which might be all of the vehicle production, or the engine plant, or staff functions. Generally managers are not involved with the daily activities on the production floor. But they are expected to prowl the floor regularly looking for opportunities to teach and coach.

Finally, there are vice presidents and one president.

This may seem like quite a bit of management, but in actuality the quantities of leaders at higher levels diminishes rapidly (about one upper leader to three to five lower leaders). This leadership structure supports several thousand associates.

The Georgetown facility had nearly 7,000 total employees at one time, the largest facility in North America. This organizational structure was not in place from the beginning. When the plant was started there were fewer layers. There were no assistant managers, and no layers between the manager and president. Most likely this was done to allow the development of high-level leaders from within the organization, and to add responsibility as the plant grew. During the plant start-up, each member of the leadership team had a Japanese trainer assigned to support and teach them the Toyota Way. Upper level managers each had a Japanese peer who shared in the decision-making responsibility. As the ability levels grew, the need for continued Japanese support diminished, and after several years the number of Japanese managers permanently assigned had fallen to less than 2 percent.

Toyota Georgetown Staff Leadership Structure

The office staff or engineering position structure is similar to the production structure, except there are usually no group or team leaders. This structure is also similar to that used by many companies, though there are few position titles. The office staff includes "assistant staff" and "associate staff," who have responsibility for nontechnical jobs, and "specialists," who have specific technical skills and are responsible for production engineering, facilities maintenance, safety and environmental compliance, accounting, human resources, and other assignments requiring a technical degree.

Small teams of assistant staff and specialists report to an assistant manager, and several assistant managers report to a departmental manager. In the case of a production department, the manager can have responsibility for both production and staff employees. Some departments with a great deal of technical support may have a separate manager for the staff employees.

Requirements for Leaders

Toyota borrowed some of their philosophies on leadership from material originally developed in the United States by the War Manpower Commission.[1] Many of the skills that were taught by Toyota were specifically mentioned throughout the Training Within Industry (TWI) material on Job Relations, Job Methods, and Job Instruction (see Chapter 11). TWI identified five characteristics necessary for

[1] Training Within Industry Service; Bureau of Training, War Manpower Commission, Washington, D.C., 1944

leaders, and we have added a sixth, which may be the most important—willingness and desire to lead. As strange as that may sound, we do see people in leadership roles who don't have a desire to lead and are only filling the role as a path to another job. Without a desire for leadership, any of the other skills will go largely unused.

These are the five characteristics of a leader as defined by TWI, with a sixth added by us:

1. Willingness and Desire to Lead

This first characteristic may seem obvious, however, there is a difference between a desire to have a job or position and the desire to truly lead. The remaining characteristics are necessary to be a great leader, but a person need not possess all of these characteristics when they first get the job. They only need to have the desire and willingness to learn and to develop the other skills. The role of the leader today is much different than the role of "supervisor" in the past. The leader must motivate and inspire people to achieve great things.

2. Job Knowledge

This refers to the specialized kind of information and skills required to perform the work in an area. Leaders should be knowledgeable about the materials, machines, tools, and production steps. They should also possess the technical knowledge of each operation in their area, and know the correct way each operation should be performed. Without this ability, the leader cannot ensure that the work is being performed correctly to standards. This requirement is often missing from leaders outside Toyota, with the implied assumption that general management skills can overcome a lack of in-depth job knowledge.

3. Job Responsibilities

A leader must know his or her role. That is, they must keep abreast of company policies, procedures, health and safety regulations, plans and interdepartmental relationships. Leaders must understand the policies and procedures, communicate them to their team members and ensure that they are followed.

4. Continuous Improvement Ability

A leader must constantly analyze the work of the area, looking for ways to combine, rearrange, and simplify tasks to make better use of materials, machines, and manpower. The major part of a leader's role is to encourage his or her people to develop continuous improvement in thinking and action. The majority of people within the organization report to the group leader, and therefore most of the improvement and benefit comes from the group leader promoting activity within the team. It is more important to have many small daily improvements than to have few major improvements.

5. Leadership Ability

A leader must be able to work with team members so they accomplish the company goals. The leader must be able to "translate" the overall company objectives into specific activities that their team must perform in order to be successful. Like a coach, they develop the "game plan" and assist the team in how to carry it out. They must provide support and coaching to team members. The leader must have the ability to plan and schedule for training needs, as well as to follow up and ensure that training is successful.

6. Teaching Ability

One of the leader's primary duties is to teach others. No matter how much skill or knowledge a person possesses, without teaching ability the leader is unable to pass it on to others. If skill and knowledge is not passed on to others, the organization will not grow and prosper.

TIP

Some Are Born Leaders, Others Can Learn the Skills

It is true that everyone possesses different skills, and it seems that some people are born for leadership. In truth, with desire, coaching, and practice, leadership skills can be learned. Michael Jordan did not make his high school basketball team, but with internal drive and continued practice, he became one of the greatest players ever. This is true of leadership skills. It may not be possible to change a person's basic nature (being an introvert or extrovert, for example), but it is possible to learn skills and to maximize the desired characteristics, while minimizing the less desirable (this is task specific). There are many leadership "styles" that can be effective, and each leader can learn to use his or her own skill set to the best advantage. The only element that cannot be taught is desire.

Group Leader Responsibilities on a Typical Workday

For the production group leader, the workday is broken down into three distinct phases, each with a particular focus. For the leaders, the day begins prior to the shift and the start of the production line. They must ensure the readiness of all resources—people, machines, and material. The second phase of the day consists of activities and responsibilities to be performed during production, and the third phase comprises the end of production and after the shift. We won't go through the whole day, which you can see in outline form in Table 10-1, but we'll

Time	Team Members	Team Leaders	Group Leaders
	Designated team members and team leaders responsible for equipment start-up		Must arrive 30 minutes prior to shift start
15-30 Min. Prior to Shift Start	• Perform equipment start-up procedure • Perform equipment condition checks • Verify readiness of hand tools and work area • Cycle machines for production readiness • Perform first article inspection • Verify material supply levels (raw materials) • Report any problems or abnormal conditions • Assure production readiness prior to shift start	• Ensure the arrival of start-up team members • Review TL shift-to-shift logbook • Follow up on any issues from previous shift • Audit performance of start-up process • Respond to any problems with start-up • Verify condition of line from previous shift • Collect production instruction kanban • Verify daily production requirement • Determine changeover needs from kanban • Assure production readiness prior to shift start	• Review daily attendance calendar • Receive calls for absences • Make adjustments to staffing • Notify assistant manager of attendance • Review G/L shift-to-shift logbook • Follow up on any issues from previous shift • Contact maintenance if necessary • Respond to any problems with start-up • Report potential production stoppages to assistant manager. • Implement production contingency plan if necessary • Audit performance of start-up process • Verify condition of line from previous shift • Be in work area 5 minutes prior to shift start • Verify start-up, attendance, no problems
Shift Start	• Verify work placement for first period • Report to assigned job location • Be ready to work when the shift starts	• Fill in for any absent TMs (Online TL) • (Offline TLs duties) • Assure smooth start of production • Assure that all TMs are punctual and in place • Assure TM compliance with safety • Assure TM compliance with standardized work	• Verify sufficient TL coverage for production • Reassign offline TL as needed • Assume TL duties if necessary • Verify all TMs are in position on time • Record any unplanned absences or tardies

Table 10-1. Daily Activities of a Toyota Work Group

Time	Team Members	Team Leaders	Group Leaders
Shift Start to Break Time	• Perform regular job duties • Follow standardized work • Collect data regarding production as required • Perform changeovers as instructed • Activate andon when problems occur	• Respond to andon calls from TMs • Respond to any equipment stoppages • Report any problems to GL • Review production results every hour • Record results on tracking board • Perform quality audits every hour • Review scrap and rework containment area • Review production and material kanban status • Schedule any equipment changeovers • Respond to problems reported by customer process • Record any issues in TL shift-to-shift logbook	• Respond to andon calls from TMs • Respond to any equipment stoppages • Report any major problems to assistant manager • Review production results every hour • Review scrap and rework containment area • Respond to problems reported by customer process • Walk through work area to review status of: ▪ TM safety compliance and unsafe conditions ▪ Quality of product ▪ Material/Process flow— Ensure that standardized work is being followed. Pay particular attention to shortages or excesses of production (these are indications of problems). ▪ Material inventory levels ▪ 5S condition ▪ Hazardous waste storage and disposal

Table 10-1. (*Continued*)

go through the first phase of the workday for group and team leaders, prior to the shift.

The group leader (GL) is expected to arrive at work at least 30 minutes prior to the start of production. The leader is expected to set an example in all areas, but especially in promptness, attendance, and commitment to the success of the team. By reviewing the large attendance calendar, which is posted and shows all scheduled vacations, visible to the entire group, the GL is aware of any scheduled absences, and has established a plan for those on the previous day. Team members are required to call in any unscheduled absences 30 minutes before the shift. The GL then evaluates the staffing and determines what adjustments

Time	Team Members	Team Leaders	Group Leaders
Normal Production (No Problems)	• Training for TL role (set up by GL)	• Stay within close distance of work area • Update production tracking charts • Support continuous improvement activities • Prepare for Quality Circles • Verify stock of consumable supplies (gloves, safety supplies etc.) • Reorder supplies • Cross train TMs • Training for GL role	• Notify TL if necessary to leave work area • Attend daily Quality and Production meeting • Support continuous improvement activities • Process TM improvement suggestions • Complete paperwork and assignments • Prepare information for communication meeting • Record any issues in GL shift-to-shift logbook • Work on continuous improvement activities • Initiate contingency plan for major production problems
Break Time	• Breaks may be staggered if production problem • TM must finish current cycle before break • 10 minute break period • Some people play cards, Ping-Pong or other activity • May follow up on improvement suggestion • May visit with friends from other areas • Must return to break area for communication meeting.	• Breaks may be staggered if production problem • TL must attend to any line problems • 10 minute break period • Same activities as TM	• Respond to any production problems • 10 minute break period • Follow up with TMs on any requests

Table 10-1. (*Continued*)

Time	Team Members	Team Leaders	Group Leaders
Communication Meeting (5 minutes at end of break)	• Must be in break area for meeting—paid time • TMs may make announcements or requests	• TL conducts meeting in absence of GL • TL conveys information for teams	GL communicates pertinent information related to: • Company news or changes • Production, safety, and quality issues • Information relevant to the group • Continuous improvement review and changes • Hand out suggestion awards to TMs and TLs • Any other news or information
Production Restart	• Verify position for job rotation • Report to assigned job location • Be ready to work when the line starts	• Assure smooth start of production • Assure that all TMs are punctual and in place • Assure TM compliance with safety • Assure TM compliance with standardized work	• Assure smooth start of production • Verify all TMs are in position on time
Lunch time	• Same as morning break • TMs may have Quality Circle meeting • Group PT activity may be held • Resume production same as break time	• Same as morning break • TL may lead a Quality Circle meeting • Resume production same as break time	• Same as morning break • GL may attend Quality Circle meeting • Other lunch meetings as required • Resume production same as break time

Table 10-1. (*Continued*)

Afternoon Communi-cation Meeting	• Same as morning communication meeting • Resume production same as break time	• Same as morning communication meeting • Resume production same as break time	• Same as morning communication meeting • Announce daily overtime requirement (may vary by area) • Overtime work assignments
End of Shift	• Complete production requirement • Prepare work area for next shift • Complete production paperwork if required • Complete daily 5S requirement • Verify work completion with TL	• Ensure that production is completed • Verify end of day production levels • Gather production paperwork from TMs • Prepare end-of-shift production reports • Complete TL shift-to-shift logbook	• Ensure that production is completed • Complete end of shift performance tracking charts • Complete GL shift-to-shift logbook • Coordinate any repairs with maintenance • Attend monthly shift-to-shift meetings • Complete 5S of GL work area • Final walk-through of work area
Overtime if Required	• Mandatory production overtime • TMs may stay overtime to work on Quality Circle or continuous improvement activities with permission of GL	• Mandatory production overtime • Support TMs if necessary	• Mandatory production overtime • Support TMs if necessary • Attend departmental safety and quality meetings

Table 10-1. (*Continued*)

to make. The attendance is called in to the assistant manager, who has a visual attendance board for the entire department.

Many production areas have equipment that needs to be set up or cycled prior to production, to ensure equipment readiness. The GL is responsible for scheduling people to begin early and perform equipment verification checks.

Any problems are reported to the GL so they can be corrected prior to the shift start (readiness is very important because of the connected flow). Also, materials are checked and any shortages or problems corrected. This process is normally conducted within 30 minutes. (Note: At Georgetown, following extended shutdowns for holidays, several people came to work the previous weekend to test-run equipment. It is imperative that the equipment always be ready when needed.)

Team leaders (TL) are an integral part of the preshift preparations, and generally at least one TL from the group is scheduled to arrive early every day. Areas with greater amounts of equipment may require additional support during this time. The team leaders ensure that any sheets needed for gathering production data are replaced in the work area, and that all tools and supplies are available to the operators.

Also, the GL and TL each have shift-to-shift logbooks. Because of the time gap between shifts—two hours between first and second shift, and four hours between second and first shift—direct communication is not always possible, so written messages regarding safety, quality, equipment issues, issues or problems from the customer, and any other information is shared here. (Note: if you use logbooks, be sure not to put personal or confidential information regarding employees, or complaints about the work of individuals or shifts, in a place open to everyone.) Any process-related problems reported by the prior shift are investigated and corrected immediately. The logbook is a very important communication tool between the shifts.

During the 30 minutes prior to the shift, the GL greets other team members as they arrive at work and observes any potential issues. Group leaders should ask each team member in turn how they are doing to detect any problems, physical or emotional. If some members have not arrived within five minutes of the shift start, the GL may notify the TL of the need to make some staffing adjustments.

Creating a Production Leadership Structure

Many people make the mistake of comparing the Toyota leadership structure with their own, or to that of a traditional industrial organization, and mistakenly assume that the team leader is "like a floater" or "like a lead man" or "like a utility person." They also assume that the current supervisors' duties are similar to those of group leaders. While these positions do have some similarity, the differences are far more significant. The team leader does "float" and fill in for team members as needed, but only to support standardized work, since standardized work is not possible if the positions are not filled at all times. A team leader can perform all jobs in the team, and in that way is a "utility" person. In fact, team leaders may perform a job due to illness or some type of absence, but the primary essence of the job is to support and develop the team or group. If the team leader is working full or even part-time on a production job they cannot support the team and cannot respond to andon calls.

Given the centrality of this team structure to TPS, how can organizations pursuing lean duplicate the functions of this leadership structure in a very different environment? The first question is, "Where do the people come from?" It is not desirable to add cost by adding people. To build the leadership structure, we recommend starting with your current situation and finding the resources within your existing staffing.

Essentially, your staff levels were established to meet production needs. Within that plan there is "excess" to cover for both planned and unplanned absences, and many other issues, which create the seven wastes. We know, for example, that the average employee absence rate for vacation is 10 to 15 percent.

When a person is on vacation there is a reduction of available labor time and production generally suffers. When the operation is fully staffed (everyone is at work), the available labor exceeds the actual requirement, and the operation is able to "catch up" from the previous shortage. Because the operations are not standardized, it's usually possible to move people around and to do without certain operations when an absence occurs. In environments where this is not possible, companies commonly employ "floaters" to fill positions. The floater may have additional duties, but his or her primary responsibility is to fill in for absences. When there are no absences, this person is generally not utilized, and in some cases that we've seen, can spend the day reading the newspaper! In any case, the current structure has excess built in, with the expectation that people will be absent and staffing levels will average out somehow.

Additional indicators such as overtime work are used to determine whether it's necessary to add people. This is a false assumption because in a nonstandardized operation each person is not fully utilized. In fact, each person is likely to have between 10 and 25 percent (or even more) of their time available. The lack of standardization and isolation of processes makes it impossible to capture this time and to create a new structure.

We don't recommend charging into a Toyota-style leadership structure but to start by working on the operation—stabilizing, creating flow, and so on. We typically suggest the establishment of the leadership structure after the implementation of standardized work because only then can we understand the resource requirement and consolidate the portion of each person's available time until one person is released from the operation. For example, if each person has 20 percent excess available time and additional waste is removed from the operation, for every four to five people there will be one "extra." When improvements are made, the excess time is captured, and people may be removed from the operation. You may ask, "If I'm working so much overtime now, how can you say that there are 'extra' people in my operation?" The fact is, there is a considerable amount of waste in *every* operation (including Toyota), and efforts to reduce the waste will result in a reduction of needed resources. In this case, the first objective is to build a process capable of meeting the customer's needs without overtime. Successive improvements may be necessary to create excess people so the leadership structure can be created.

After the initial establishment of standardized work, it's possible to get a clear picture of the next possible improvement. Ask yourself, "If I could keep the same number of people I currently have, but by changing the structure and how they're utilized I could achieve 25 percent improvement in productivity, would that be desirable?" This would be the goal of establishing the leadership structure. Not just to have team leaders because Toyota does, but to create a structure that allows you to achieve improved results in safety, quality, productivity, and cost.

We have never seen an operation that did not have enough people within the existing staff to create a leadership structure (and we have seen quite a few operations). This is the power of waste elimination and standardized work. You must continue to make improvements until you can consolidate the waste and create the opportunity. When confronted with this challenge, the Japanese sensei would often say, "No problem." This did not mean that it would not take considerable effort to accomplish; it simply meant that the amount of waste in any system is so great that it is always possible to do.

Selecting Leaders

In Japan, Toyota employees that enter the company at the team member (hourly) level in production will remain in that position for a minimum of 10 to 15 years. Then, if they're qualified and interested, they would advance to the team leader rank. Another 10 to 15 years as team leader provides the skills necessary to be a group leader. This is the final position for many, although a few rise to the rank of general foreman (roughly equivalent to an assistant manager). The general foreman is responsible for supervising and coordinating activities of group leaders. It is rare (though it does happen) for someone from the manufacturing ranks to cross the division to the engineering or upper management side.

This system works with a company that is mature in the Toyota Way, but most companies starting out on the lean journey do not have the luxury of this much time. And even Toyota, outside Japan, often cannot retain employees long enough for this slow gestation period. During the start-up of the Georgetown plant and other Toyota plants outside of Japan it was not possible to take this much time to develop leaders prior to start-up. The new leaders required more direct mentoring until they developed capability of their own.

What we typically see in the United States is a fresh college graduate thrust into a line leadership position with little training and almost no mentoring or guidance. This problem is compounded by the fairly quick turnover time—two years seems to be a long tenure—and the fact that there is no system in place to step into. Every new leader must "learn the ropes" and develop methods for handling the day-to-day issues. We have all seen the turmoil created when a new leader steps in and places his or her own stamp on things by establishing new expectations and procedures.

The alternative is to promote from within when possible, but frankly, it's difficult to find capable willing candidates because of the challenges of the position. People who work in the company can see that the supervisors are not given the necessary tools or resources, and the hassles of the job are not worth the pay differential (in some cases the "promotion" leads to lower overall pay since overtime pay is lost).

So what can you do? The first step is to realize the importance of the group and the team leaders. These positions must be seen as more than stepping-stones or positions that no one wants. To better understand the skills that Toyota believes are important for leadership, the following case example describes the initial screening and hiring process used for the Georgetown Kentucky plant start-up.

Case Example: Screening Process for Group and Team Leaders at Georgetown

There is some advantage to starting a new plant. You get to start fresh. You get to select the most capable people possible for the jobs. You don't have any history to erase or change. There are disadvantages as well. There is a limited base of experience. The training needs are huge, and you might not end up with the right people for the jobs. Thus, everyone started fresh, but without the necessary skills.

The selection of team and group leaders was so critical for the plant start-up that an extensive and specific selection process was developed. Toyota had committed to hiring manufacturing employees from within the state. Applications quickly poured in from across Kentucky, totaling over 100,000 (this number continued to increase, but the initial pool was around 100,000). To narrow this large pool of applicants to those who possessed the basic skill set, a series of filtering processes were used.

Applicants participated in a general aptitude test, lasting about two hours, which was used as the first screening tool. A select group (we are not privy to the actual numbers) was advanced to the next level. Toyota was looking for both manufacturing and maintenance, "skilled trades" people, so those with a maintenance background were scheduled for the NOCTI (National Occupational Competency Testing Institute) test, a written technical skills test lasting six hours, and they then proceeded down a parallel path to that of manufacturing candidates.

The second major screening process was called a "day of work"—an eight hour assessment process that was facilitated and monitored by trained screeners. The focus for original candidates was to identify potential leaders, and the emphasis was on basic leadership skills. (Later, when the hiring focus shifted to team members (line workers), a major portion of the "day of work" included a simulated workplace with four hours of "work"—real physical labor.) The "day of work" included individual activities as well as team activities, with the purpose of evaluating each candidate for a specific skill set. The skills included:

- ◆ Technical knowledge (basic manufacturing practices)

- ◆ Technical skills and aptitude (use of basic tools)

- ◆ Problem solving (including problem identification and solutions, both individually and with a team)

- ◆ Team membership (ability to function on a team)

- ◆ Team leadership (ability to lead a team)

- ◆ Critical thinking

- ◆ Communication skills (verbal and written)

The top layer of candidates were skimmed off, to advance to the next step of the process, which was an additional leadership assessment. This assessment was eight-hours long (perhaps part of the test was to determine how badly a person wanted the job and whether they were willing to give this much time to the process). The activities were similar to those on the first day, but focused specifically on leadership. Those who did not make this cut were considered later for team members, or even team leaders. This advancing group was on the "fast track" because of the need to fill the group and team leader positions first. The skill set screened during this test were:

- ◆ Advanced problem solving (actual case example with written test)

- ◆ Training ability (actual training of a screener)

- ◆ Organization skills and time management (ability to plan, prioritize, and delegate)

- ◆ Facilitation skills (leading a team activity)

- ◆ Team membership (this was always observed throughout the process)

- ◆ Individual leadership (a case example exercise)

- ◆ Team leadership (ability to lead a team)

- ◆ Critical thinking

- ◆ Communication skills (verbal and written)

Finally, those who passed were scheduled for an interview. This was not an ordinary individual interview, but a group interview. Representatives from each manufacturing department reviewed candidate scores and applications, and those who were interested in a candidate participated in the interview.

The questions were specific in nature, asking for actual examples from past experience. This process was referred to as "targeted selection" because the aim was to identify and target specific skills and behaviors from the past experiences (see Chapter 11 for additional examples of this process). The idea is that specific examples of past behavior and ability will be a good indicator of future performance and ability. These were not simple questions like, "How do you think you did on that project." They were oriented to past *action*. Questions such as, "Tell me about a time when you recognized a problem on your job." "What was the problem?" "How did you recognize the problem?" "What did you do?" (Specifically—such as, "Who did you tell?" and "Did you offer a solution?" and "If so, what was it?") These questions were designed to determine a person's propensity to identify issues, and to be proactive and solution-oriented. They also look at "protocol." For example: "Did you notify the appropriate people or act without guidance?" "Did you work with others or simply work alone?" (Neither was necessarily the best answer to this, but generally people who worked well with others were preferred.)

Skilled trades applicants who passed the NOCTI exam (to test technical knowledge) also completed the day-of-work assessments and were scheduled for additional specific practical tests, such as welding, electronics, electrical, hydraulic, and pneumatic skills. These were actual hands-on tests to verify technical skills.

The total time for this process (not including driving time) was approximately 40 hours. Then, *if* Toyota was interested in making a job offer, a thorough physical and drug screen was done (another four hours!) prior to an actual commitment.

Developing Leaders

You may not be able to devote the amount of time Toyota devoted to the leadership selection process (Toyota did receive aid from the State Employment Service as part of the incentive package), but you should be able to draw from the ideas. The role of the leader is more than that of someone who knows the "job" and can do the duties. The leader must possess additional skills. If you can improve your selection process to identify the people with the best skill foundation, you can also establish a mentoring process to continually grow your leaders.

The development of leaders is not significantly different from training operators. The first step is to define the job and the necessary skills. Standardized work for leaders can be developed based on "core competencies" of the job. For example, a leader must be capable of continuous improvement. It is possible to teach a method by utilizing problem solving as a foundation, or facilitating quality circle activities. A leader must understand his or her job responsibilities. Specific duties that must be performed can be outlined. Potential leaders can be given responsibilities that will test and develop their skills in any area.

The necessary leadership skills and abilities have been identified in the previous pages. Each individual skill, activity, or duty must be identified and placed on a matrix just like a multifunction worker-training timetable (see Chapter 11). Next, the trainee's individual capabilities in each area are assessed and gaps are identified.

A specific training plan should be developed based on his or her needs. For example, for a person who has trouble facilitating team activities, more emphasis should be placed on developing that skill. They may be asked to start by leading small team activities and then move into more important activities as they develop skill and confidence.

In some cases external training may be required or necessary. Toyota has core training requirements for each leadership position (see Chapter 11), and this training may be done by the company or may include workshops or seminars. Internal development is the responsibility of the current leader. This is accomplished by daily mentoring and by allowing the "student" to assume some responsibilities with guidance from the leader (not just delegating). Honest assessment of performance and continuous feedback from the leader is necessary.

The Job Instruction Training methodology (Chapter 11) can be used as a model for leadership training as well. First the trainer (the leader) will tell, show, and demonstrate the desired skill or behavior several times. Then the student is given an opportunity to try it, with coaching from the trainer. The trainer will gauge the performance and, when ready, the student may perform some tasks on his own. The trainer will continue to monitor progress and gradually reduce the guidance.

This is a lengthy process. It is not a matter of a two-week training course and then handing off the job. If the leader works continuously to develop his or her people, they should always be prepared for the eventual need for additional leaders. If they wait until the need arises, there will not be enough time. This process must be a continual ongoing process.

> **TIP**
>
> **If You Fail to Plan, You Plan to Fail**
>
> Leadership development is based on a plan. Using the key characteristics of the Toyota screening process as the job requirements, and the abilities of leaders as defined by TWI, develop a needs assessment for potential leaders. Define specific activities and training for each of the skills, and establish a timetable for when the training will be completed. If you are unable to make a plan and to teach others the skills necessary to do your job, you will not succeed in one of the primary responsibilities you have as a leader.

Succession Plan for Leaders

The leadership development process should be based on a succession plan. Every leader should develop subordinates so that there is always a smooth transition when leadership changes are made. The primary reason for developing subordinates, however, is to strengthen the system and to have each person capable of their highest potential. This is a great advantage to you as well, since the more people who are capable of leadership tasks, the less you'll have to worry about every detail. It is also wise for the overall strength of the company to have people with the necessary skills to step into leadership positions. We recommend that a minimum of two people at each level be prepared and ready for advancement at any time. More than that would be ideal, but two would be a minimum.

Poll your people, and ask them who would like to be developed for leadership positions. Make sure that everyone who expresses an interest is considered. Sit down and discuss the plan with each person, and explain the personal sacrifices that will be required during the training process. Find out what their interests are and what they think their strengths and weaknesses are. Never assume that their skill levels are acceptable unless you've had firsthand experience with them in a specific situation.

It may be wise to at first work with those who have the fewest gaps in ability, so that at a minimum someone is ready. But always give all individuals an equal opportunity for development over the long term. This is similar to the training plan for Job Instruction Training—always look at the immediate need, and determine the least amount of effort that will fill that need. Once the immediate need is fulfilled, continue working with others to develop greater breadth of capability.

TIP

Sometimes It Helps to Put the Shoe on the Other Foot

One advantage of developing people for leadership positions is that they have an opportunity to see what it's like being the leader. They are likely to discover that it's much more challenging than they imagined, and they may gain a greater appreciation for what you do. In addition, you may gain allies who help others understand your challenges, so when someone complains that "they [management] never listen to me," they'll know there's more to it than meets the eye. People who understand the challenges are also more forgiving when mistakes are made. Don't be afraid to develop some of your "troublemakers." You may end up gaining a strong ally in the process.

Reflect and Learn from the Process

The ability to grow and develop leaders from within your organization is critical to the development of a lean culture. Toyota invests a tremendous amount of time and effort in the development of leaders because leaders support the system. The following questions will help you evaluate your commitment to developing the talent within your leaders.

1. Reflect on the capability of leadership within your company. Evaluate the methods used to grow and develop leaders. Identify and list three things you'll need to do within the next year to improve your leadership development process.
2. Develop a measurable performance expectation for your leaders that is based on:
    a. Effectiveness in developing people (how many people, what skills, by when)
    b. Ability to solve problems and make process improvement (results based on process measures)
    c. Ability to lead change
    d. Leadership and promotion of the company culture
    e. Ability to grow other leaders
3. Evaluate the depth of your leadership bench. How many people are ready to step into *each* leadership role in your organization?

a. Establish a plan for developing at least two people to fill each leadership position within the next year.

b. Include a strategy for sustaining the depth of your leadership bench (long-term plan).

4. Evaluate your current leadership selection process.

a. Identify one improvement that you'll make to the process before selecting your next leader.

b. Identify desired leadership skills and characteristics and how you plan to make them part of your selection criteria.

Chapter 11

Develop Exceptional Team Associates

"We Don't Just Build Cars, We Build People"

In most areas of life, you get out of something what you put into it. This is especially true when it comes to your associates. If you make little investment in this resource, it will provide little return. The Toyota Way is centered on the philosophy that people truly are the greatest asset. Toyota leaders are fond of saying they "build people, not just cars." What they're saying is that in the process of building cars and improving the process, people are learning and developing. Toyota uses the analogy of a garden to describe their belief in people. The soil is tended and prepared, the seeds are watered, and when the seeds grow, the soil is maintained, weeded, and watered again until finally the fruit is ready. This image is one of dedication, patience, and caring. You must be dedicated to the seeds for the entire time, be patient in waiting for the reward, and care for and nurture the plants.

It is also true that employees will fulfill the expectations that you have of them. When we work with companies, we can usually tell immediately the quality of people in the facility by simply asking the manager. We may hear comments such as, "We have trouble getting good people here," or "We don't pay enough so the quality of our people is low." Often we hear terms like "babysitting" in reference to employees. Surely these are signs that there are "bad" people working there. The thing is, it is the manager who's bad! If the manager believes that the people are not good, they will live up to that expectation.

Fortunately, we also visit companies where the manager proclaims, "We have some really good people here. We are very fortunate." When we walk with this manager you can sense the pride in the people and what they accomplish. Of course, this manager does not live in a ivory tower, nor is she living in some fantasyland. It is just a different perception of the situation. The work is not more glamorous, the pay not significantly higher (if at all), nor the benefits, yet the people are "good."

When we begin to work with people, we find that they are similar and have basic needs (see *The Toyota Way*, pages 194-98, for a discussion on motivation theory). Growing exceptional people goes beyond just providing better pay and benefits. You can throw all kinds of perks at people and still not create the proper environment for them to blossom. If you're a manager, the key is what you truly *believe* about the nature of people and what they mean to *you*. The soil must be tended and the seeds nurtured so they bear fruit that will provide sustenance and survival for you! As with all other aspects of creating the Toyota Way, it all begins with *your* thinking.

TRAP

STOP

How Do You Refer to People?

One sure sign that you and the leadership team have the wrong view of people is in how you refer to individuals during meetings and planning sessions. We often hear references to people as "heads" (as in head count), and "bodies," or worse "warm bodies" (which implies that if they are alive and breathing, that's all that is needed). These references are innocuous, and you may not even be aware of them, but they speak to your deeper level beliefs of the value of people. Are they just "bodies" with a purpose only to fill a position? Do you expect people to check their brains at the door when they come to work? Do you do more work to try to reduce your greatest asset, or to grow and develop it?

Start by Selecting the Right People

A good selection process helps to "thin the crop," to identify the people who will best fit your culture and needs. You may look at this section and think, "We already have all our people, and we're stuck with some bad ones, and there's nothing that we can do." Take heart. Even the best selection process in the world will allow some bad seeds to pass through. In the end you must work with what you have and make the best of that. The skills and traits that are targeted during the selection process are skills that can be developed. But every company has people who leave and must be replaced. Spending time up front with the selection process can help to reduce the time needed to develop these skills later.

The selection process used at the Toyota plant in Georgetown is based on the idea that a person's past behavior is a good indicator of future behavior. The selection process is long and provides many opportunities to see potential candidates in various situations so their behavior can be evaluated. These situations include simulated work activities (see Chapter 10) and an interview that concentrates on actual experience. As discussed in *The Toyota Way*, it is a multistep process, beginning with weeding out hundreds or thousands of applications and then conducting an aptitude test. We will focus here on the later stages of interviewing once a smaller subset has been identified.

The selection process targets the following skills for team associates:

- **Job-fit motivation.** Does the individual's personal motivation fit well with the company? Will the work and the environment provide them with personal satisfaction? You may find that this person would be better suited for other jobs or tasks.
- **Meeting membership.** Does the person have the ability to work with others, to participate but not dominate, and to gain the cooperation and support of others?
- **Meeting leadership.** This trait may not be as important for team associates, but it includes the ability to convey ideas to others and to get support when needed. Toyota does like to grow leaders (Chapter 10), so potential leaders are sought out.
- **Initiative.** Is this person someone who will initiate action and do more than the minimum necessary to achieve goals, or do they wait to be told what needs to be done? Do they initiate action beyond their boundaries without approval (not desirable)?
- **Ability for the work.** Has the person ever performed this type of work? If not, do they have similar experience, such as home repairs or publishing a newsletter for a church or civic group?
- **Adaptability.** The Toyota Way is founded on continuous improvement, which means continuous change. People need to be able to handle various situations, tasks, and people.
- **Problem identification and problem-solving ability.** Many people can spot problems. Are they able to provide solutions? Do they expect others to solve the problem for them?
- **Work tempo.** Toyota assesses work tempo using a simulated work experience. This allows the candidate to understand the future work requirement to make sure they know what they're in for and so Toyota can assess whether they have aptitude for the work.
- **Communication skills.** Do they speak clearly? Do they communicate ideas effectively? Are they able to understand questions and answer specifically?

Each of these traits were evaluated during simulated work exercises as described in Chapter 10, and during an interview if the candidate passed the screening process. The simulated day of work activity may be more than your company can do in terms of a selection process, and the interview will be the primary selection tool. The interview used by Toyota is a more grueling process than most. Candidates are often not prepared for the specificity of the questions and the depth of information requested. More than one person typically conducted the interview, and the team included the department interested in hiring the individual along with a member of human resources.

After the introductions and a brief overview of the candidate's work and educational background the questioning began. The purpose was to ask specific questions designed to elicit honest answers. We all know how to say the right thing during an interview! For example: Question by interviewer, "Why do you want to leave your current job?" Answer by candidate, "Well, I am just not challenged enough, and I want a job where I can use my skills and help the company." To find out more about current work relationships and conditions, the Toyota interview targets actual situations. The following are examples of typical questions. Notice that the people are asked to describe actual events and to go through the entire process surrounding the event. These are not subjective "feeling" type questions; they are objective "action" questions.

"Tell me about a time on your current (or last) job when you recognized a problem. What was the problem?" (Wait for response) "What did you do about it? Who did you tell? Did you have to get help with the solution, or were you able to do this on your own? Were you able to solve the problem? What was your solution?"

This line of questioning is geared to identify a person's ability to identify and solve problems. If you look closer, you'll see questions relating to initiative (did they take action, and was the action appropriate?), leadership, and membership. Note that there is not necessarily a "right" answer. For example, if a person said they did not solve the problem, problem-solving skills are probed with other questions. If they needed help with the solution, that was okay and showed a willingness to work with others. If they did not need help, that was okay as well. People who tried to find the "right" answer often tripped themselves up.

For example, when we asked a question related to their ability to get along with others (meeting membership), they might answer, "Oh, I get along with just about everyone. I really never have had any trouble." Now, we all know that it is virtually impossible to never have had a disagreement with *someone*. The important point is *how* they handled the situation. If a person had disagreements and handled them effectively, that was a good indication.

If the candidate just couldn't "think of anything," we would ask similar questions, such as, "Tell me about some ways that you show consideration for others at work." Again, we're not looking for opinions and feelings, but for actual situations.

This method was a surprisingly good way to determine a person's character and ability. Of course, even with all the checks and balances in this system, every now and then someone slipped through who did not fit the culture.

Assimilating Team Associates into Your Culture

When people arrive on the first day for a new job, they're generally filled with hope and have "good attitudes." It takes effort on our part to change those hopes and good attitudes into regret and negativity. Fortunately, with some effort we can sustain the positive attitude and even develop it further. As you can see, Toyota exerts a tremendous effort to identify and select the best people (choosing the best seeds). They spend just as much effort in bringing them into the Toyota culture (preparing the soil and watering the seeds). Toyota refers to this process as "assimilation," and it is conducted in two stages.

On the first day of work, a new hire will report to a training room where human resources and the training department will begin the process of introducing them to the Toyota Way. The initial stage lasts two weeks, and during this time the new hire never visits their actual work site! They are introduced to the Toyota culture, to the Toyota Production System (TPS), and to policies and procedures, including general safety and ergonomics. They also participate in a simulated work activity to "work harden" or condition them physically for the actual job. The work hardening may begin with one hour of work and two hours of classroom session. This is gradually increased over the two weeks until the person is capable of a full day's work (in stage two at the work site they will begin the actual work on a reduced basis).

There have been occasions when new hires have decided that perhaps the Toyota culture is not for them after all, and they decide to quit at that time. During the initial assimilation stage, the rules and policies are carefully explained and people understand the seriousness of the expectations.

After completing the introductory stage, the new hire is directed to their actual work area. They now begin the second stage of assimilation into the work group. There is no set time limit on this stage; however, there are expectations regarding how many jobs will be learned and what each person's participation in the group will be. The following items are covered during the assimilation process. Group leaders have a check sheet covering these items, and it must to be signed by the team member and the leader and returned to human resources.

- Welcome and introduction by the leader.
- Review of group and department policies and procedures.
- Introduction to others members of the group (there may be a "PT" activity—Personal Touch—sponsored by the company as a "get to know you" activity).

- ◆ Safety overview, including evacuation and emergency procedures.
- ◆ Develop a training plan.
  - ◆ Initial jobs are "freshman" jobs (easier jobs)
  - ◆ Begin with one or two hours of work, followed by one or two hours of offline work
  - ◆ Determine goal for training—three jobs within three months
- ◆ Long-term assimilation into team and group activities.
  - ◆ Quality Circles
  - ◆ 5S
  - ◆ Preshift and postshift duties
  - ◆ Suggestions system and continuous improvement
- ◆ Mentoring and developing.

Each group has some slight variation, depending on the needs of the group, but follows the same general format. Full assimilation into the Toyota culture might take a year or more, but there are milestones along the way, marked with progress reviews and wage increases if the progress was satisfactory. A "probationary" period of six months applied to all new hires. During this time the work progress and attendance record are evaluated (poor attendance is a sure way to get cut from the team).

Responsibility for teaching, mentoring, and coaching falls to the group leader, who sets expectations for training, but the team leader normally carries out the actual training (although the group leader is also a skilled trainer and may do some actual training). Toyota uses a very specific method called Job Instruction Training for all training.

Job Instruction Training: The Key to Developing Exceptional Skill Levels

One of the most common complaints we hear when we talk to associates at all companies is that there is a lack of effective training. We find that something as important as learning the correct way to perform work is often left to chance. No consistent method is used, trainers are not identified—and if they are, they have not received formal training—and the specific requirements for performing the work are not clearly identified. The training of employees takes a low priority on the list of leaders' duties (leaders who are often spread too thin and can't make time for the individual needs of every employee). We could probably write an entire book of stories related to poor training, but the following story sums up the problem.

During a plant tour one afternoon, we were observing an operation and trying to understand flow and the balance of operations. It wasn't completely clear what was happening so we decided to ask an operator (call her Mary) a question about her task. When approaching Mary, she had a wide-eyed "deer in the headlights" look. We asked Mary to describe some of the important points of the job. With a shocked expression, Mary said, "I just started here today, and I really don't know." This was not a problem because there was another employee working right beside her, and we assumed this must be the person responsible for training. We asked Mary, "Would your coworker know?" to which Mary replied, "She just started yesterday!" In fact, we often find a person with very little experience (skill level, knowledge of the product and quality expectations, and safety aspects) "teaching" another worker. It's hardly a surprise, then, when employees tell us, "Everyone has their own way" of performing the work.

We wonder how something as crucial to the success of an organization as the transfer of knowledge and skills can be treated so lightly. Why has an attitude developed that it's acceptable for people to pick up the necessary skills "with time"? When we confront leaders about problems in the work area, we're often told that "it takes time to learn, and normally people learn within a few months." Meanwhile, the problems continue every day, and they wait patiently for the day when the person finally gets it. Of course, if the person never does "get it," they are labeled as a poor worker, or a troublemaker, and the leader is stuck with a problem that won't go away. The leader will say, "I tried to tell them, but they didn't listen. They have their own way to do things." Of course they do! Without effective training and coaching, people will develop their own method, and it will most likely not be the "preferred" method (as in "my way").

Some common methods used for training include:

- The "sink or swim" method. This is an old-time classic that is actually used in some cases to "teach" swimming. The student is thrown into the water, and if they make is out alive they have learned to "swim." Unfortunately, it is commonly used at work as well. We have actually had employees tell us, "I had to learn the hard way, they should too!"
- The "give them time and they will learn" method. This is based on giving the new hire time to figure out how to do the job and to get better at it. It is related to the sink or swim because the person has not completely drowned yet, and if their head is above water, they will make it. Unfortunately, you will continue to pay the price of poor performance while they "learn."
- The "microwave" method. Thirty seconds and they're done! The training usually goes something like this: "First do this, then do this, then do that. Any questions?" (We often observe the "microwave" method with internal lean coordinators. Send them to a 1-2 week training class and they are "fully prepared" as a lean expert).
- The "find the best worker and follow him around" method. Unfortunately, the "best worker" may not be a good trainer. They may not want this responsibility. The other problem with this method is that there is no structure outlined. How do you know that the "trainer" is doing the work

---

TIP

Take Personal Responsibility for Training and Development

With all the talk these days about "people being the most important asset," it would seem that training would assume greater importance for managers and leaders. Many managers pass the responsibility to someone else and then hope for the best. It is important to take personal responsibility for establishing a training method and ensuring a successful outcome. Make a plan, train the trainers (yourself included), follow up personally to assure the method is sound, and verify process results. Your personal attention to this process will show people that their success is important to you.

---

correctly? How do you know that they will explain it clearly? Do they really know all the quality and safety aspects of the job?

The Toyota method for training is tried and true, and they have used it for over 50 years. It has served them well, and the basic concept is as relevant today as when it was first used in the United States during World War II. After World War II, Toyota, along with many other Japanese companies, received assistance from the United States. The Training Within Industry Service (TWI), a branch of the War Manpower Commission, supplied some of the material.[1] It was originally used to support the production of munitions and other goods during the war. At that time, many of the skilled workers were on active duty, and it was necessary to develop an effective training procedure to quickly and efficiently train unskilled people to perform the work. The TWI material included sections on Job Relations, Job Methods (which may have been the foundation for standardized work and the elimination of waste), and Job Instruction Training, which Toyota adopted as their primary training protocol.

The training method used by Toyota today is essentially a replica of the material developed in the United States in the 1940s. Toyota has made only a few minor additions, and today uses the material to effectively train thousands of workers who produce the highest quality vehicles in the world. This simple method is very powerful, yet for some reason, after the war many companies in the United States chose to forego this method, perhaps because the material was developed to train the "unskilled" workers who were taking the job of men going to war. After the return from war of "skilled" workers, it was not necessary to have such a basic training method. Toyota never viewed the method in this way, seeing it as an essential tool to use in the development of exceptional associates.

---

[1] Training Within Industry Service; Bureau of Training, War Manpower Commission, Washington, D.C., 1944.

All leaders within Toyota are required to learn the Job Instruction Training method. The course format and structure is also used for many other training courses within Toyota and is based on 5 two-hour sessions, for a total of 10 hours. The course is led by a trainer who received certification from one of Toyota's "master trainers," someone with exceptional skills and many hours of experience. The course itself is structured to follow the basic training format: First the trainer tells and shows the method, then the student tries, and the instructor provides coaching. In other words, the students are required to identify a practice job to demonstrate in the classroom with guidance from the instructor and other students. Whenever possible, the training demonstrations can be conducted in the work area. The following is the basic outline of the Job Instruction Training method. The original material is available from any major library, and there are several organizations that provide TWI specific training. We suggest that you use the following information only to gain an understanding of the method, but that you thoroughly learn the method prior to attempting to use it.

You will see that this method requires quite a bit of time and effort, both for the trainer and for the student. This may be why the method was abandoned. We hear over and over again that people are "too busy" to spend this amount of time with training. Perhaps there is an endless cycle. Poorly trained workers have more quality problems, safety problems, and less consistent performance overall. These problems consume much of the leader's time, and the leader does not have time to train. This reminds us of the old commercial for a transmission repair service where the technician proclaims, "You can pay me now, or you can pay me later." In this case, an investment on the front end will pay handsome dividends on the back end. If you elect to shortcut on employee education and training, you will be paying in perpetuity.

1. Break Down the Job

The first step of the training process is to analyze the work and develop a training aid called a "Job Breakdown Sheet" (Figure 11-1). This sheet is based on standardized work, but because the goal is to train effectively, the job breakdown is done with training in mind. The more high-level work steps on the Standardized Work Sheet, for instance, may be broken down into two or more "training steps." These more "bite-sized" steps can be taught without overwhelming the student. Breaking the job into training segments is a skill that is refined with experience. During this training, the worker is observed to determine how well he or she has learned. If the trainer sees the trainee struggling, the training method will be adjusted.

After the training steps are determined (TWI refers to them as "important steps" and Toyota refers to them as "major steps") each step is analyzed to deter-

JOB BREAKDOWN SHEET			
DATE: _____		Team Leader	Supervisor
AREA: _____	JOB: _____	WRITTEN BY: _____	
IMPORTANT STEPS	**KEYPOINTS** **SAFETY:** Injury avoidance, ergonomics, danger points **QUALITY:** Defect avoidance, check points, standards **TECHNIQUE:** Efficient movement, special method **COST:** Proper use of materials	**REASONS FOR KEYPOINTS**	
Step #			
Step #			
Step #			
Step #			

⚠ LEAN ASSOCIATES, INC.

Figure 11-1. Job Breakdown Sheet

mine the "key points." These points are the heart of the job instruction method and are developed to explain the following critical aspects of the work:

- Safety
- Quality
- Cost
- Knack or technique

Key points are essential to the successful completion of the work and must be considered carefully. In most cases they are developed based on past experience of problem areas and the correct method to perform the work in order to prevent the problem. In developing key points for new jobs or processes it is important to evaluate the work and attempt to assess potential problem areas. As the new job or process is actually performed, additional key points may be developed based on results.

TIP

Use Key Points to Positively State the Correct Way to Do a Task

Key points should be "how to's" rather than "don't do's." They're more effective as positives. For example, if there is a risk of injury on a job from a pinch point, rather than stating, "Avoid the pinch point," state, "Your hands should be placed here and here when working." During the next step of training, when the reasons behind the key point are explained, it can be said that the purpose of the key point is to "avoid the pinch point."

---

2. Present the Operation

The actual training begins with preparation of the work area and making sure that sufficient time can be devoted to the training activity. In many companies training is done "on the fly," leaving the worker feeling that their training was an afterthought. It's important that everything, including tools and safety equipment, is prepared beforehand and that the workplace is set up as you expect it to be maintained. You will be setting expectations, so if the students' first experience with the work area is clutter and disorganization, you're setting an expectation that it's acceptable to keep it that way. The message you want to convey to the student regarding you and the work area is that you're competent, prepared, and expect only top quality work, so you must demonstrate it.

There are at least three distinct phases in training the individual to perform the job: First, teach the important steps that explain *what* is done; then do the steps again while explaining each key point, which explains *how* the step is done; and then do the steps and key points yet again while explaining the *reasons* for the key points. Providing the reasons that things are done gives validity to the key points and helps the trainees understand the importance of their work.

The TWI method says "Tell, Show, and Illustrate" each important step. This means telling the students what the step is, showing them how the step is performed, and showing it in such a way as to make the actual actions clear. Exaggerating the action, pausing to allow the student to see more closely, or repeating the step provides a more clear understanding. During this first cycle, the trainer will only state the step that is being performed without any additional information. For example: "The first important step is . . ." without explanation of key points or reasons. Those are added on subsequent cycles. This can be strange to students who fear that they will see the job only one time (the microwave method) and are concerned that they won't learn the details. As the trainer, you should assure them that you will convey all important information a portion at a time, and that you will spend as much time as necessary to ensure their success. During the second cycle the job is repeated with the important steps and the key points for each step. Again, key points describe critical information related to *how* the step is performed. If the job breakdown was completed effectively, the key points have been carefully identified. Key points are essential to the successful completion of the task with minimal quality, safety, and productivity problems. They are not a matter of personal preference or style, but factual necessities based on experience. If you do a good job of identifying and conveying key points to trainees, your results will be significantly better. Don't shortcut this step!

The job is repeated and the important steps and key points are repeated this time with the addition of reasons for the key points. These reasons should include accident prevention and quality requirements, and also the effect of incorrect work on the customer or next process. Help the trainees see how their work fits into the "big picture." When you stress the importance of the work, you're stressing the importance of the individual. Everyone likes to know that what he or she does is important and that it matters.

Depending on the complexity or length of the job, it may be necessary to break the training into multiple sessions. The job instruction method stresses the importance of giving the student "no more than they can master" in any one session. The actual amount is based on many factors, but a rule of thumb is that a training session lasts about 30 minutes to an hour. More information than that in one session tends to overload the student.

3. Try Out Performance

After the job (or a portion of the job) has been presented completely, students are asked to try it themselves, without explaining what they're doing. This is a crucial time for the trainer. It is critical to observe carefully and to make any corrections or provide assistance. A student can develop incorrect methods or habits on the very first attempt, and if corrections are not made early, they are more difficult to make later. The trainer must provide coaching, but also be careful not to be overbearing. This can be a fine line, and the individual student often defines the line. This phase may be completed over several job cycles.

After the student demonstrates a basic skill in performing the work, she is asked to perform the work, and this time to explain each step. The trainer has already verified that the student can *perform* the steps, but now wants to confirm *understanding*. (The trainer has also verified that the student performs each key point correctly, but will also confirm understanding.)

The third time around, the trainer continues to provide assistance and to correct any mistakes as the student repeats the job, explains each step, and now explains the key point. During this phase the trainer must determine whether the trainee will be able to perform the work on their own and how much support they will need. Never leave an assessment of capability to the student. No one wants to give the impression that they don't "get it," so they will undoubtedly say that they understand the work. Each student will have different capabilities and will learn at different rates. The trainer must assess each situation individually.

As we said, the key points are the crucial part of the work, and they must be followed *exactly*. These are not just helpful hints or "maybe you can do this or that." The key point is necessary for the successful completion of the work. Providing reasons for the key points helps people understand the importance of *why* they do things. We find that with a lack of information, people will develop their own methods. Key points provide valid understanding for people. With this understanding, they are much less likely to deviate from the correct method.

4. Put Them on the Job and Provide Support

TRAP

🛑 **STOP**

Never Allow Students to Determine Their Own Readiness for a Task

Many trainers make the mistake of asking the trainee, "Do you think you're ready to try the job now?" The trainer should make this important decision only after careful observation of the trainee. Most trainees (especially new hires) will say they are ready because they're afraid they will be perceived as incapable if they say no, they're not ready to do the job. Asking the trainee also places responsibility for understanding on him or her. The trainer must assume responsibility for the outcome of the training.

When the student has demonstrated sufficient proficiency, he or she will be asked to perform the job. This is not, "Okay, now you're done and on your own." Usually the trainer will remain and continue to provide some assistance. In many cases at Toyota (and other companies) the student is only capable of performing a portion of the total job. They may be capable and knowledgeable, but they're not capable of performing at the required rate (line speed). In this case the student will perform a portion of the work, and the trainer will perform the remainder. This allows the trainer to stay close, to provide additional coaching if necessary, and to verify the safety and quality performance. As the students' skill level improves, they are given increasing portions of the work until they can perform entirely on their own.

The learning curve continues and the trainer will gradually reduce the support, and follow up less and less. If the trainer must leave the student, they provide someone who can support the student in their absence. The students should never be given the impression that they're "on their own." Initially, when putting the student on the job, it's important to stress the expectation that they should focus on successfully completing the task, meeting the safety and quality goals. As the student's rate of speed increases, the focus shifts to meeting the productivity targets (while maintaining safety and quality). Bear in mind that you are establishing the foundation for future expectation with these training sessions. If you have low expectations or do not clearly communicate your expectations, you will get less than the desired results.

Making a Training Plan and Tracking Performance

Understanding the needs of your area, assessing the resources and skill level available, and planning for future changes are critical steps. This cannot be left to chance or done on a "catch as catch can" basis. This is one area where Toyota made significant improvements to the TWI material. The original material presented the training plan as simply a "yes or no" for job skills, and determining dates to complete the training.

Figure 11-2 shows what Toyota calls a Multifunction Worker Training Timetable (TWI called it a Training Timetable). Because all employees at Toyota are expected to know and perform multiple jobs, the focus of the plan is geared toward creating multifunction workers.

The Multifunction Worker Training Timetable is filled out as follows:

1. The supervisor completes this section with his or her name, the group or area, and the date. Planning is usually done during the beginning of the year, but if you're starting, use today's date.
2. List the names of all employees. If there are more than 10, use additional sheets. Usually one sheet is completed for each team, which has four to seven people.
3. Fill in the process or operation names.
4. The ideal number is the number of people who need to be trained on each job to ensure that the position can always be filled. If there are three operations that are the same, for example, you'll need more than three people trained. For more difficult jobs it's also better to have more than the minimum. The supervisor determines the ideal number for each job.
5. The circle with four quadrants visually depicts each person's skill for a particular job. A blank circle indicates no training has been started.

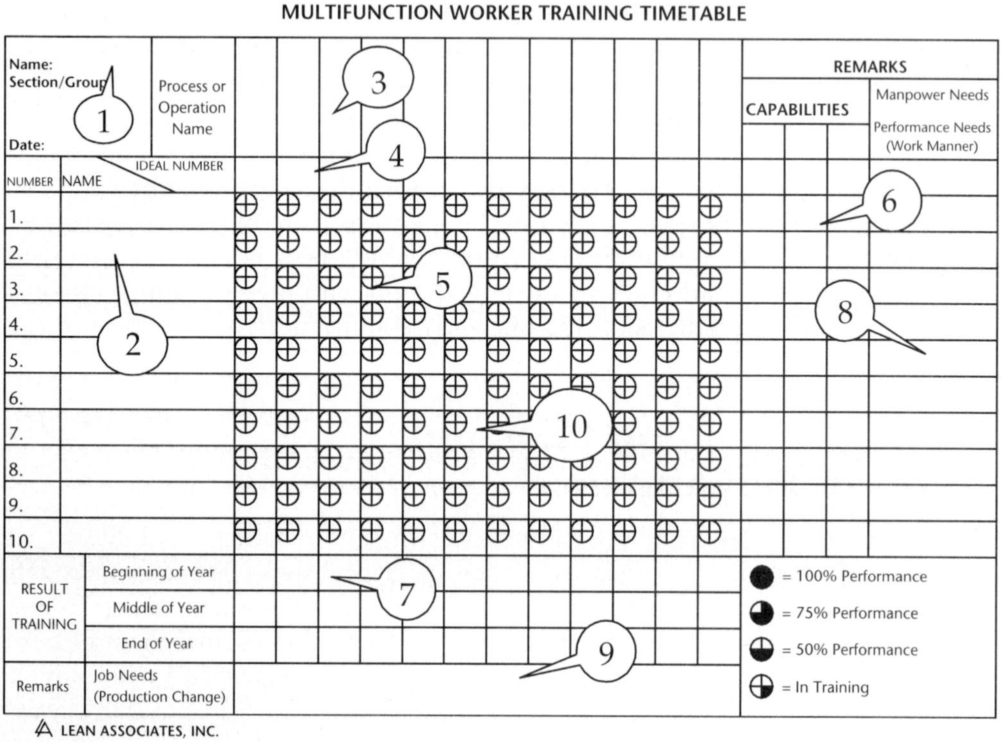

MULTIFUNCTION WORKER TRAINING TIMETABLE

Figure 11-2. Multifunction Worker Training Timetable

One-quarter indicates a person who is currently being trained. This person should never be left alone on the job, since they do not completely understand the safety and quality requirements. One-half of the circle represents a person who may be left on the job alone but requires close monitoring. This person may be too slow to completely work alone. Three-quarters of a circle represents a person who needs very little supervision but may lack complete knowledge of some aspects of the job. This person can work alone most of the time. A full circle represents a fully trained person who needs no supervision, has complete knowledge of the safety and quality rules, and can maintain the required pace. Some people use the full circle to indicate ability to actually train another person, but this requires completion of the full Job Instruction Training class.

6. Each person's capabilities are totaled and placed in the column at the end. Usually, the supervisor will make an assessment at the beginning, middle, and end of each year to evaluate whether the training plan has been achieved. This allows the supervisor to track the progress of each individual.

7. The number of people fully trained for each job are totaled and recorded at the bottom of the sheet. This allows the supervisor to monitor progress toward achieving the ideal number of people for each job.
8. Any additional manpower needs are recorded here. Some people may have only slight problems remaining on some tasks, which are noted here.
9. Any future production changes are noted in this space; for example, if production will increase or perhaps a key person will be out on leave.
10. Dates are added where there is an individual or job need that mandates training. The dates are used to schedule the actual training. The timing should be based on immediate and long-term needs.

An example of a completed form is shown in Figure 11-3. The trainer and supervisor collectively evaluate the progress and skill level of each individual. There is no benefit to the leader in attempting to make the evaluations appear better than they actually are. Poor job skills will be reflected in the performance measures, and the leaders have a vested interest in having exceptionally skilled people. Shortcutting the training process will not provide the long-term benefits

MULTIFUNCTION WORKER TRAINING SHEET

Name: Ron Coleman
Section/Group: Frame Department
Date: 8/15/2002

NUMBER	NAME	Chop Saw (2)	HPP	Glue and Dowel	Frame Clamp (2)	Prep/Inspect	Special	Busellato	Giben Panel Saw	Edgebander	Parts			Jan	Jun	Dec	Manpower Needs / Performance Needs (Work Manner)
	IDEAL NUMBER	4	6	6	6	6	6	6	6	4	4						
1.	Ron Coleman (Supervisor)													10	10		
2.	Eddie Day (Team Leader)													3	4		
3.	Jeffe Goedde (Team Leader)					12-Jul								3	5		
4.	Bradley Alvey													2	4		
5.	Tina Brooks													6	7		
6.	Clark Campbell													3	4		
7.	Willie Coleman													1	4		
8.	Dennis Daniel		1-Aug			10-Jul		25-Jul						1	2		
9.																	
10.																	

RESULT OF TRAINING

	Chop Saw (2)	HPP	Glue and Dowel	Frame Clamp (2)	Prep/Inspect	Special	Busellato	Giben Panel Saw	Edgebander	Parts
Beginning of Year	3	3	3	1	3	3	2	3	5	3
Middle of Year	5	4	4	2	4	4	3	4	6	4
End of Year										

Remarks — Job Needs (Production Change): Increase orders 10% for the year

KEY:
= 100% Performance
= 75% Performance
= 50% Performance
= In Training

LEAN ASSOCIATES, INC.

Figure 11-3. Example of completed Multifunction Worker Training Timetable

desired. Also, people get the sense that they do not matter as individuals if the leader does not place importance on the training effort. It is a sure way to create a "bad attitude."

Building Team Associates for the Long Term

Let's face it; some of the work done on a day-to-day basis can lose its excitement after time. This is especially true if the work is repetitive and does not require a high skill level. If people are going to remain actively engaged in the work process and feel a greater sense of satisfaction, they need more than a paycheck. Toyota recognizes this need and provides many additional opportunities for employees to use their creativity and to develop greater skills.

The Toyota Way promotes the growth and development of all employees. Toyota makes a tremendous investment in people, both in terms of facilities and time. The Georgetown plant has an extensive training and development department and an entire facility devoted to courses for manufacturing, office, and the skilled trades employees. There are elective courses that employees may take on their own time, and required courses that are taken during working hours (of course, when salaried personnel take a class during work, it's necessary to catch up on the work that was missed during the training). Figure 11-4 shows a training matrix of "core" (required for the job) and elective courses for each position (not including an extensive training regimen for the skilled trades).

All Toyota employees are also encouraged to participate in activities and programs. Participation is voluntary, but most people enjoy the activities because they provide an avenue to pursue personal development and to use their creativity beyond what is required to perform their job. These activities include the suggestion program, quality circles, leadership development, and various kinds of kaizen teams.

Quality Circles

Quality Circles are a vital part of kaizen at Toyota, particularly in Japan. The American quality movement in the 1980s had a brief brush with Quality Circles, which were regarded as a tool for participative management. The results were dismal. Hourly workers devoted much of the meeting to creature comforts, for example, moving the drinking fountain. There were some projects that improved quality and these were widely publicized within the company, but they were few and far between. Eventually this "management fad" died out. It was one more good idea gone bad. What was missing? Basically all of the fundamentals of the Toyota Way were missing. Well-trained employees, the team leader role, well-trained group leaders guiding the initiative, a culture of continuous improvement, and the tools of lean such as standardized work were all missing.

Training and Development Course Offerings

Courses	Length in Hours	Manager & Asst. Mgr.	Group Leader	Team Leader	Team Member	Specialist (Engineer)	Assistant Staff
Assimilation	18	C	C	C	C	C	C
Conflict Management	16	C	E			E	
Effective Meeting Facilitation	16	C	C	C	E*	C	E
How to speak so others will listen	16	E	E			E	E
Introduction to Kaizen	18	C	C	C		C	E
Introduction to Problem Solving	16	C	C	C	E*	C	C
Job Instruction Training	10	E	C	C	E*	E	
Job Relations	10	C	C			E	
Leader as Coach TPS	10	E	E	E		E	
Leadership	16	C	C	E*		E	
Listening	16	E	E	E	E	E	E
PDCA Applications	24	C					
PDCA Introduction	24	C					
Philosophies of Efficiency	10	C					
Practical Problem Solving	16	C					
Problem Solving Level II	18	C	C	C		C	E
Proposal Writing / Documents	10	C	C			C	C
Quality Circles Facilitation	8	E	E	E	E	E	E
Quality Circles Participation	8				E	E	
Quality Circles Promotion	4	C	C			E	
Intro to Standardized Work	8	C	C	C		C	E
Standardized Work, Office	8	E				C	C
Suggestion System Training	2	C	C	E	E	E	E
Targeted Selection (Interviewing)	9	E	C	E		E	E
Worksite Communications	16	E	C	E*		E	E

C = Core Course (Required)
E = Elective Course
E* = Required for Pre-promotion program

Figure 11-4. Training matrix of core and elective courses

Management was taking a top-down culture with poorly trained employees, giving them "micro-waved" problem-solving training, and suddenly expecting miraculous projects selected by the workers.

Quality Circles have never been a fad at Toyota. They have been an ongoing management tool for productivity and quality improvement for decades and are still considered a sign of a highly evolved Toyota Production System (TPS) organization. In this regard the American Toyota sites are still developing.

Participation in Quality Circles is voluntary, but many people at Toyota choose to participate because they want to take part in improving the work area. Quality Circles are a good method to improve quality, and make other improvements, and are also an excellent activity to promote teamwork and develop the capabilities of individuals. Each member of the circle is responsible for fulfilling each role on the team, such as taking minutes, keeping the meeting on time, or facilitating the meeting. A team leader usually leads the circle, but team members may elect to lead a circle as a development opportunity. The leader is responsible for establishing desired outcomes with management, planning each meeting, clearly setting expectations for the team, and coordinating activities with others, such as engineering and maintenance.

The circle is responsible for setting goals and meeting schedules, but the group leader acts in an advisory capacity. The primary role of the group leader is to ensure that the circle is addressing a meaningful issue (one that will improve the team or group) and that time is spent wisely and productively. He or she will check in with the facilitator weekly for an update and to provide any necessary support or guidance. The team is allotted one paid hour (overtime pay) per week (each person) for meeting and any assignment activity. The team may elect to meet before or after work, or in some cases during a working lunch. Most circles deal with issues in the work area so many meetings are conducted at the actual work site (*gemba*).

At the completion of an activity, the circle group prepares a short presentation for management explaining the activity and the results. This presentation is primarily a congratulatory opportunity for management to express gratitude to the team for their effort and work to improve the operation. Any suggestions implemented by the circle also qualify for a payment award in the suggestion system program (see below). In this case the members are paid for their time during the meetings and for the improvement ideas. Each year the best Quality Circle projects are selected for bronze, silver, gold, and platinum awards and make formal presentations to vice presidents of Toyota. The American plants each select a platinum award winner to present in Japan at Toyota's international Quality Circle conference. At Georgetown in 2004 there were about 22 percent of employees in voluntary circles, compared to a target in the 40 to 50 percent range. Participation of over 80 percent is not uncommon in Japan. This is a good opportunity to develop and use abilities and to be rewarded for the effort. Not a bad deal at all.

Case Example: Work Activities Help People Gain Greater Personal Ability and Satisfaction

An employee at the Toyota plant in Georgetown was very shy and did not like to speak in front of groups. Speaking in front of others is common in the Toyota culture. We had discussions daily, reported on issues in the work area, and often presented the results of Quality Circles and continuous improvement teams to members of management. Being too afraid to speak in public, this woman preferred to stay away from these activities (most were voluntary). She was interested in promotion potential, but could not get past her fear.

She was finally persuaded to join a Quality Circle, and when the time came for presentation, she was terrified. Even though she had her notes, she went entirely blank, but still managed to make it through. With a little encouragement, she tried another Quality Circle and improved her presentation at the end. Over the years, she moved to another job, and when we finally met again she told us that she'd joined the Lions Club and become the special events coordinator—a position that required her to make a report of activities at each meeting! She was proud that she'd been able to overcome her fear and participate in activities that interested her outside of work.

Toyota Suggestion Program

The Toyota Suggestion Program differs from most traditional suggestion programs in that it is based on the premise that people inherently want to improve their work environment, and that the contributions of every employee provide long-term continuous improvement. Toyota understands that the suggestions of employees ultimately contribute to the bottom line, but more important, that they provide a sense of ownership and that workers have some control over their destiny. These feelings lead to greater overall satisfaction. The suggestion program is not all about the money saved.

Some of the key elements of the program are that it is simple (in all aspects, from submitting a suggestion through the approval process), and responsibility for implementing the suggestion is maintained at the lowest possible level. In this way Toyota is able to accomplish a high submission rate (approximately 10 suggestions per person per year) and a high approval and implementation rate (over 90 percent).

Every person in the company can submit suggestions (although payment for salaried personnel is limited to suggestions outside their scope of responsibility), and suggestions may be made by individuals or groups. The submission process is simple. A one-page form is used to list the name(s) of the suggester(s), the department, and so forth, and a brief explanation of the current situation and the proposed change. The suggester is responsible for determining which areas would be impacted by the suggestion. These include safety, quality, time reduction, cost reduction, and other intangible improvements. Associates submit the form to their supervisors, who will review it with them to ensure that the idea is understood and the necessary information is included.

The supervisor plays a key role in the suggestion system process. In most cases the supervisor has the authority to approve implementation and payment of the suggestion. The supervisor can approve all suggestions with payments of up to $16, which account for approximately 85 percent or more of all suggestions. It is important to note that there is a difference between approval for implementation and approval for payment. The supervisor should approve a suggestion and support the implementation prior to submitting it for payment. The supervisor can approve implementation of most suggestions without additional approval (except for the other shift supervisor, and provided the cost to implement is within the supervisor's authority and the change does not affect current process equipment).

Many suggestions are of an intangible nature. That is, it is difficult to directly calculate the potential benefit. Suggestions for the prevention of possible safety hazards, and suggestions to eliminate possible mistakes or to eliminate current mistakes, are examples. Often, the potential dollar savings is difficult to calculate or may be small and does not justify the effort needed to calculate it. For suggestions of this value, it is not required to "cost justify" the suggestion. In all cases a minimum $10 payment is made for all approved and implemented suggestions.

If the suggestion involves more significant savings, the suggester and supervisor will compile the necessary supporting data to verify the actual savings. The suggester is responsible for gathering any data; however, the supervisor generally needs to provide guidance to ensure that the documentation is complete and accurate.

Suggestions for payments over $16 require additional levels of approval, and the greater the potential payment, the higher the level of approval required. The next level of supervision can approve payments of up to $100. A department manager must approve payments of up to $250, and the assistant general manager must approve up to $500. The Suggestion Steering Committee must approve payments over $500. The committee is comprised of area managers, general managers, accounting, and the program administrator. A suggestion valued at a payout of $500, for example, must be approved by all levels through the "chain," up to and including the Steering Committee of the entire plant. This approval process can greatly impede the payment process, but not the implementation process. If the idea is considered good by the supervisor, it is implemented immediately. The big suggestions have to be implemented and data collected for three months to verify effectiveness before the suggestion is submitted for payment.

Other details about the suggestion program at Toyota are of an administrative nature. In summary, the suggestion program is designed to be simple, intended for all employees to use, designed to remove barriers common to many programs— difficult to get and complete forms, ideas that must be "cost justified," a cumbersome approval process for all suggestions, and "little" ideas that are not widely accepted—and most of all it creates a mind-set that everyone contributes to the overall success and growth of the company by providing their ideas. Despite this focus on little ideas, the suggestion program does have a significant payback: a return on investment of seven-to-one is common.

TIP

A Process with Too Many Restrictions Will Limit Participation

There are very few restrictions placed on continuous improvement at Toyota. At many other companies management places "guidelines" or "restrictions" on ideas. These include not improving a process that will be eliminated or moved from the plant soon, and some ideas are not considered "important" enough. Toyota improves all operations up to the very end, and no idea is considered too small or unimportant. If restrictions are placed on when, what, or how important an idea is, there will not be high levels of participation. At Toyota an idea must be acceptable, but there are no other restrictions. This provides a consistent message that continuous improvement means just that—continuous and without limit. Restrictions send the message that some ideas are acceptable, but only when management decides so.

Developing Team Associates for Leadership Roles

Selecting team associates for leadership roles and developing them in those roles is a critical matter within Toyota. The leaders are responsible for teaching and coaching others in the Toyota Way. They must convey the message to the next generation. They are also responsible for sustaining the daily operation and for continuously improving. Potential leaders are carefully considered for traits that they possess and for potential to grow. Like all important decisions, Toyota makes a considerable effort to choose future leaders wisely, and the candidates, as well as the leaders, put forth much time and effort to ensure the best decision.

A team member who is interested in being promoted to the team leader position must make a formal application to participate in the prepromotion process. In order to be considered, a team member must have an excellent attendance record and must have received at least a "meets requirements" on their most recent performance review. A team member with any outstanding corrective action is not permitted to participate.

All future team leaders must attend specific training in problem solving, Job Instruction Training, and meeting facilitation (see Figure 11-4). The classes range from 10 to 16 hours in length (42 hours total), and each student attends on their own time (unpaid). Each class has a workplace exercise requirement to be completed and reviewed by the group leader and submitted to the training department for final review. A final "grade" is provided for each class, which is used to compare proficiency to other applicants.

The ability to relate with fellow team associates is a critical aspect of the team leader role, and the other team members in the work group evaluate each candidate during a peer review process. Peers rate the candidate on interpersonal skills, attendance, job knowledge, and safe working habits. The intent is not to create a popularity contest, but to allow all peers to participate in the evaluation process. In many companies the associates often complain that management will "pick who they want to." The peer review process helps balance any potential management bias.

Finally, the scores from the training classes, the peer review, and the performance evaluation are compared to other associates within the same department (in some cases the selection is limited to those individuals with specific job skills), and the top performers are selected for an interview. The interview is similar in nature to the interview previously mentioned for initial hiring and is scored. The final scores are placed on a matrix, and a final decision is made by mutual consensus between the group leader, department manager, and a representative from human resources (again preventing individual bias).

After selection, the new team leader is trained in specific aspects of the job. Many group leaders have a preselection development process that allows a team associate to develop necessary skills prior to promotion. The team associate fills in for the team leader during absences, and in many cases works directly with the team leader to learn the job. The tasks and skills required of team leaders are placed on a Multifunction Worker Training Timetable, and all prepromotion candidates are trained to perform the tasks. This allows for a virtually seamless transfer to the new leader.

Pretraining individuals for leadership roles has other advantages as well. Trainees have opportunities to experience new challenges and to grow. They also have an opportunity to "test the water" for the role to decide whether it's something they are truly interested in (this reduces the number of people who later decide the job was not for them). It also gives employees a chance to "put the shoe on the other foot" and appreciate what a leader must do. Then, even if they never get a promotion, they have more respect for the role and its difficulties.

Personal Touch Creates Stronger Bonds

One program sponsored by Toyota is called "Personal Touch," or PT. It is designed to bring team members together during a non-work-related activity in hopes of building stronger relationships. Toyota provides funds to each group (a specified amount per person every quarter) to be used as seed money for activities or to pay for them entirely. The activities are suggested on a monthly basis and can be simple, such as a pizza lunch or a daylong trip to an amusement park (with families) or event, a visit to a local restaurant, or even a charitable activity. Most groups vary the activities in terms of cost and complexity. There are usually people within the group that take the lead in planning activities, but the entire group chooses the actual activity. There are some specific rules monitored by the group leader. Certain activities, for instance, might be inappropriate and cannot be sponsored by the company.

These activities are a good way to find out about people away from work and to develop tighter bonds. Most people look forward to the monthly PT activity.

Invest in Skill in All Areas of the Company

The examples provided thus far have focused on repetitive production jobs, but the same principles apply to all jobs across the company. The Toyota Way is about behavior, which reflects attitudes. The emphasis on employee development is always on the actual "doing" of the job or the actual "doing" of the process improvement activity. It's critical to take a similar approach to the training and development of "professional" employees within the company.

If we closely examine the education and training of professionals, it starts with a college education. Presumably, they learn the fundamentals about the science of the profession, professional norms, and perhaps even professional ethics. There is still much to learn, but the basic tools of the trade have been learned in school. Then good companies provide a variety of opportunities for continuing education. These can be specific training courses on the technology used in the company (e.g., the computer system or personnel policies specific to the company). There may be a leadership or communication or problem-solving course required of certain classes of employees. And employees are often encouraged to go back to universities to update their skills on specific topics.

This is all well and good. But what specific training do individuals get on how to perform their actual jobs? What specific training does the individual get on how to improve processes in the company?

Following the principles of Job Instruction Training developed by TWI, there must be a job breakdown of important tasks, key points, and reasons. This assumes that prior to this there was a clear definition of the work, including standards for the job. Second, there must be some preparation of the jobs to be demonstrated to the trainee. Third, the trainee must have a supervised opportunity to try out the performance. Fourth, they must perform the job with supervision and support.

Does this look anything like the way professionals in your company are trained? Notice that Toyota does not assume that general education in universities creates trained professionals ready to perform their jobs. In fact, quite the opposite: Toyota often assumes they will have to untrain some of the bad habits learned prior to joining the company. Many of the assumptions and beliefs about work taught in school may be contrary to the Toyota Way.

Let's consider the example of developing a body design engineer (e.g., door engineer) at Toyota, responsible for the engineering of steel body parts. The design process begins with a styling design, which is the artistic rendering of the appearance. This is converted to computer-aided-design data, then all the structural components are designed and the work proceeds to die designers and die makers, and the product is followed through to production.

1. Engineers are selected by a rigorous process similar to what we described for hourly workers. In Japan they recruit from a few of the best universities (e.g., Tokyo, Kyoto) and let alumni working for them do some of the screening. The interviews are equally important in the hiring process.
2. Engineers are hired as a collective class before being assigned to a specialty. They go through one year of general orientation, which includes:
   a. One month general orientation to the company.
   b. Three to four months working in a Toyota plant performing manual work (preferably building the part of the vehicle they are likely to be engineering).
   c. Two to three months selling cars at a dealer (to understand the customer perspective).
   d. Assignment to the work area.
   e. A freshmen project in a work area (supervised project to get hands-on engineering experience).
3. Two years of intensive, supervised, on-the-job training in the specialty. Engineers do their own computer-aided-design, so they must learn the system in this period.
4. A minimum of three years to become a first-grade engineer within their subspecialty of body engineering (e.g., door engineer).
5. A minimum of eight years of experience to be a senior engineer with responsibility to lead others. At this point the engineer may be assigned to a related specialty (e.g., bumpers).
6. About 10 to 12 years to be a staff leader.

We call this an inverted-T model in that engineers start off with broad training for a short time and then spend time getting deep experience in their specialties. This deep experience, starting with the "freshman project," is supervised. Many things are being taught, too many to make up a job breakdown sheet for the entire job, which takes years to learn. But the job of the supervisor is to be a teacher. Then the general philosophy of doing parts and building up to doing the whole job with supervision, feedback, and support is employed for each aspect of the job. The freshman project is a challenging assignment designed to give a learning experience on how to approach an engineering project. The two years after the original orientation year are focused on the specific work of that specialty. Everything done is supervised by an experienced engineer, like the old master-apprentice relationship.

It is part of the Toyota culture that every leader is a teacher. And the teaching approach is learning by doing. "Teachers" give students specific assignments, supervise progress, and give specific feedback for improvement. Students observe teachers doing similar work and learn by observing as well. Unlike many other companies, Toyota has detailed methodologies for every aspect of engineering, which makes it more teachable. For example, there are detailed engineering checklists for door engineering, which include specific engineering features that make up a good door design from an engineering and manufacturing perspective. This greatly aids in the teaching.

What's being taught is not just the specific engineering work, but how to think about problems, how to communicate, how to get input from others, how to work in teams, how to develop A3 reports (chapter 18), how to observe a manufacturing process, how to develop standards, and so on. The learning from school on how to be a professional is too abstract for Toyota. Within Toyota you learn highly developed processes in the Toyota Way. While engineers seem to be narrowly focused on a specific part of the car, in fact they are responsible for that component through all stages of design to launch. So they are learning specific methods appropriate for each phase of this multiyear process. By the end of two to three years they have only gone through the product development process one time. Because the Toyota engineering process is so highly developed, there is a great deal to learn at each phase of the process, along with general Toyota Way approaches to problem solving, decision making, and communication. Several programs taking six to ten years are necessary to start to become comfortable with the entire process.

In short, the Job Instruction Training given to operators to perform simple manual tasks with a cycle time of one to three minutes provides a microcosm of the Toyota view of training. In any task there is a great deal to learn about the right way to do the job. And a right way has been carefully developed and standardized. So it becomes teachable. In contrast, if there is no standard, there is no choice but to throw the employee into the water and hope for the best.

Reflect and Learn from the Process

Developing team associates that fit your culture and build your system begins with a selection process and continues with assimilation once they're on board. The following questions should challenge you to honestly evaluate your commitment to hiring and developing the highest quality people.

1. Evaluate your current selection process and develop specific plans for improving weak points.
   a. Do you have a preselection process to narrow the potential candidates to the most ideal? If not, or if it isn't effective, develop a plan to improve within the next year.
   b. Make a list of the primary selection criteria used for hiring. Are the important criteria part of your selection process? If not, make a specific plan for how you will incorporate them.
   c. The criteria should be based on a predisposition to actual behavior and ability. Does your process provide awareness of desired behaviors and abilities? Identify specific changes necessary to create a selection process based on behavior and ability.

2. The expectation for future behavior concerning an individual is established within the first moments after they are hired and continues for several months afterward. Evaluate the methods used in your organization during this critical time.
   a. During the assimilation process, do you set the company's expectations from the beginning?
   b. Are new hires given personal attention and shown they're an important part of your team, or are they handed off to someone in human resources who reviews the rules and sends them to work?
   c. Are the top leaders involved in the assimilation process?
   d. Do your supervisors take personal responsibility for the assimilation of new hires into the group or do they pass responsibility to others?
   e. Is a specific training plan developed and reviewed with each of the new hires?
   f. Do you have a checklist to ensure that all aspects of the assimilation are completed?

3. Complete an assessment of your current training process.
   a. On a "strongly disagree" to "strongly agree" type scale, conduct an employee survey using the following statements to rate the overall process:

i.   I feel as though I have been adequately trained for my job.

ii. The method used to train here is effective.

iii. The person who trained me was a good trainer.

iv. My supervisor (or line leader) understands my job and is able to train others.

v.   People learn their own method of doing the work here.

b. Make a specific plan to improve your training method.

i.   Will Job Instruction Training be the primary training methodology, or will you use another process?

ii. Develop a plan to develop the training skills of all leaders.

iii. Include plans for ensuring that future leaders are trained before becoming leaders.

iv. Complete employee surveys every six months to verify the effectiveness of your plan.

4. Overall effectiveness of your selection, assimilation, and training can be ascertained by measuring retention rate and overall process capability (safety, quality, and productivity).

a. Based on these indicators, what is your assessment of your process?

b. Identify specific steps that will be necessary to improve in these areas.

Chapter 12

Develop Suppliers and Partners as Extensions of the Enterprise

Supplier Partners in a Globally Competitive World

It's a tough time to be talking about supplier "partnerships." With companies throughout the Western world looking at the prices of parts from China, India, Vietnam, Russia, Eastern Europe, and other low-wage countries, it's hard to imagine looking beyond price. Radical attempts to cut costs by suppliers, including automation, plant consolidation, and even lean techniques, seem in vain when the purchase price of raw materials for production in a typical Western company is greater than the price a supplier in a remote province in China is charging for the finished component. If the problem is competing based on cost, and the solution is to chase the lowest price in the world, then the supply chain problem becomes a straightforward logistics exercise: Get the latest software, run the optimization models, and figure out the lowest cost way of getting the best total cost of piece price plus logistics.

But the critics will argue that quality will suffer. The low-wage countries are low wage for a reason. They do not have the same high quality of labor as the developed countries and thus cannot produce the consistently high levels of quality that have become the price of entry into modern business. Even that argument breaks down. Education levels are high and getting higher in these countries, people work hard and long hours, and they are eager to learn. Their acceleration up the learning curve has been nothing short of miraculous.

So if you can't beat them, join them—right? Certainly for some commodity parts and even high value parts and tools, that will be the inevitable conclusion. But Toyota has not gone in that direction for their core components. They have invested deeply in supplier partnerships over decades, and any new suppliers added to the mix must pass stringent tests and prove they can earn their way into the partnership network slowly over time. Existing suppliers doing a good job aren't fired because of cheaper alternatives, and they have job security similar to Toyota's own employees.

Short-Term Cost Savings vs. Long-Term Partnerships

Why does Toyota make these investments? Why sacrifice short-term cost reductions for longer term supplier partnerships? This is a complex issue and there are multiple parts to the answer.

First, there's quality. Quality is more than having state-of-the-art equipment and ISO-9000 documented quality procedures. It starts with the people doing the value-added work. As we saw in Chapters 8 and 11, training your people in the specific steps required to do the job is only a small part of the equation. Training them to see quality problems, to immediately alert the team leader, to participate in root cause problem solving, and to find opportunities for improvement regularly requires building a culture of quality. Hire a firm in China to make your parts, check quality procedures, look at the equipment, and you still know very little about the people who build in quality. Toyota wants its suppliers to have a compatible culture of finding and eliminating problems through continuous improvement.

The quality movement of the 1980s, driven largely by the overwhelming success of the Japanese model, purportedly marked the end of antagonistic buyer-supplier relationships. Most big firms purchased a large portion of the products they sold, and the final quality of their products were only as good as each component part purchased from suppliers. Supplier quality became purchasing's chief marching orders. In fact, investing in quality would also produce the lowest costs, as repeated inspections, rework, and warranty costs went by the wayside. Even more important, customers will come back if the product is of the highest quality. The bottom line was that treating suppliers as *partners* in the business was a key to long-term success. The Malcolm Baldrige Award, the gold standard of quality companies, added "key supplier and customer partnering and communication mechanisms" as a major criteria for the award.

Second, there is the engineering of products and processes. Toyota has made a living on the overall quality of design and the precision, as well as the flexibility, of its manufacturing processes. The integration of product and process in the design and engineering stages has a huge impact over the life of a product.

Get it right and every unit up to the last car rolling off the line is better quality and yielding higher margins. And even for years after the last car is produced, warranty costs can kill a company if there were mistakes in engineering before the first car was ever produced. Since suppliers are manufacturing the components, high quality design and manufacturing can be best done in close concert with or even by the suppliers. Integrating engineering between Toyota and its suppliers, and integrating the engineering of the product and process of the supplier, is a critical success factor, and it takes many years of investment to get right.

Third, there is the precision and delicacy of the just-in-time system. As we have learned, JIT is not just about reducing inventory. It is about exposing problems so that people will solve them. It is a "fragile" supply chain system. Toyota extends that system and its underlying philosophy to suppliers. Suppliers are simply extensions of the assembly line, and waste anyplace in the value stream from raw materials to delivery to the customer is still waste. It must be driven out. Toyota has worked since it was founded to learn how to eliminate waste. Having suppliers who do not have this capability creates weak links throughout the value chain. Toyota wants every link to be equally strong and capable. Remember, lean is about connected flows between stable processes. The supplier needs to be stable and connected to your stable plants.

Fourth, Toyota wants innovation. The core of their long-term success has been innovation—in products, processes, and countless small improvements throughout the enterprise. Toyota sets specific targets for innovation by its suppliers. For example, Denso has done projects in radiators and alternators with the goal of putting those products at the forefront of performance relative to cost in the industry for 10 years.[1] As they approach the 10-year mark, they come up with more radical improvements to keep them ahead for the next 10 years. Toyota works with suppliers to set specific plans for investment in R&D to put innovative technologies on the shelf that will maintain Toyota as a leader in the technologies of tires, batteries, climate control systems, exhaust systems, lubricants, and so on. "On the shelf" means the technologies are proven and ready for chief engineers to pick off the shelf to design into mass-produced vehicles.

Fifth, Toyota realizes that the overall financial health of the Toyota enterprise depends on the overall financial health of each part of the enterprise. While a weak supplier may be able to inspect and build inventory and ship good parts just-in-time and provide price reductions, at some point the weak supplier will be driven out of business. Toyota wants suppliers that are strong and capable of contributing to the entire enterprise.

There is probably a sixth, seventh, and eighth reason as well. The point is, there's a huge amount of work involved to align the capabilities of suppliers

---

[1] A. Ward, J.K. Liker, D. Sobek, and J. Cristiano, "The Second Toyota Paradox: How Delaying Decisions Can Make Better Cars Faster," *Sloan Management Review*, Spring, 1995: 43-61.

with your own internal capabilities. And the huge benefits to doing so go beyond immediate savings based on undercutting price.

The best way to describe the situation facing companies today is that many are confused. Is there a payback to investing in supplier partnering? Does "partnering" truly lead to the best quality and ultimately a competitive advantage? Is partnership another way of saying we will be soft on our suppliers and they'll take advantage of us? Does supplier partnering lock companies out of opportunities to find the lowest costs globally? What does it actually take for supplier partnering to yield competitive advantage for the long term?

To address these questions, let's examine Toyota's supplier management up close. Toyota provides an object lesson in the benefits of supplier partnering. For example, working closely with their suppliers, they were able to reduce the total cost of manufacturing the Camry by over 25 percent in the mid-1990s. To deal with competition from companies in low-wage countries, Toyota asked its suppliers to reduce cost by about 30 percent by the next new model introduction in its CCC21 program. The suppliers worked hard and mostly accomplished the goal. This seems brutal, yet in the end, suppliers tell us they prefer working with Toyota (and similar customer Honda) over any other car companies.[2] How have they done it?

Supplier Partnering the Toyota Way

When Toyota first set up shop in North America there were questions about whether they could reproduce the supply system that contributed to their phenomenal success in Japan. There were many reasons to prefer local sourcing: pressure from the U.S. government, the operating philosophy of just-in-time, and a philosophy of contributing to the communities that buy their cars and trucks. Relationships built up over decades in Japan had to be developed in years in North America. In response, Toyota began to develop local sources through a combination of joint ventures with traditional Japanese suppliers and carefully selected local suppliers.

What made this task so challenging was that Toyota was not satisfied with simply finding companies that could build parts. Supplier partnering meant much more. When we began to examine the essential features of the elaborate system of supplier relations Toyota needed to establish, a picture emerged of a complex set of systems, controls, and in fact a cultural connection. Many articles written about supply chain management emphasize the use of a particular tool like target pricing or the use of kaizen workshops or inventory reductions

---

[2] According to the Planning Perspectives benchmark survey of 223 suppliers in 2004, Toyota and Honda continue to be rated as the most preferred to work with. Toyota and Honda led in every category, including more trustworthy, better communication, and concern about supplier profitability.

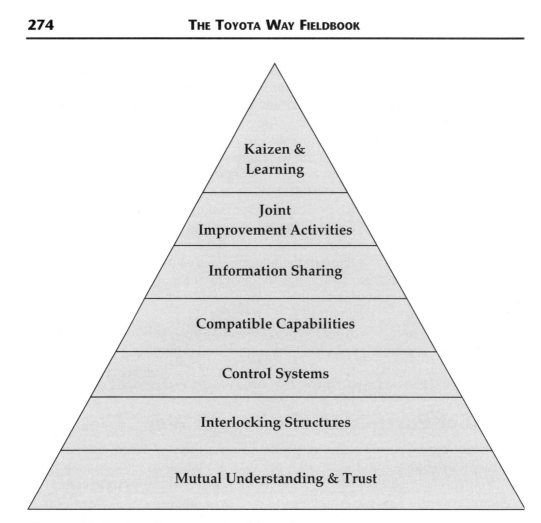

Figure 12-1. Supplier partnering hierarchy

through clever uses of information technology, but Toyota has built a much deeper foundation of relationships to allow continuous improvement to thrive.

We view Toyota's supply chain as a pyramid[3] that we call a "supplier partnering hierarchy." We use the term "hierarchy" because some of the features in the seven levels form a foundation for others (Figure 12-1).

As an example, many companies have attempted to develop supplier metrics in order to improve supplier performance. The famous balanced scorecard was

---

[3] The Toyota Way presented a similar model called the "supply chain need hierarchy." This was developed to describe the needs of suppliers in order to make them good partners. The perspective of building deep supplier partnerships that are effective for both parties, a model that applies equally well to Toyota and Honda, was first introduced in an article in the *Harvard Business Review*, December, 2004, by Jeffrey Liker and Thomas Choi, "Building Deep Supplier Partnerships," pp 104-113.

touted as a supply chain solution that would significantly improve quality, cost, and delivery. Yet in implementing the balanced scorecards, companies often did it in the context of conflicted, adversarial relations with suppliers. These conditions made the balanced scorecard a punitive measurement system to identify underperformance. Suppliers would placate the customer through short-term actions, not to solve the root cause problem, but to make the numbers look good.

In contrast, though Toyota also uses rigorous measurement systems to help control supplier performance, they do it in an environment of open communication and trust. In short, jumping up to particular control systems without a foundation of mutual understanding and a structure that supports cooperative behavior leads to game playing and short-term responses.

Of course, supplier partnering is not all fun and games. Being a partner to Toyota is not about Toyota being soft or forgiving. As pointed out in *The Toyota Way*, fairness, high expectations, and challenge characterize how Toyota treats suppliers. This is business, and the goal is to make money, but not at the expense of suppliers. As Taiichi Ohno, father of the Toyota Production System (TPS), stated:

> Achievement of business performance by the parent company through bullying suppliers is totally alien to the spirit of the Toyota Production System.

The key word is "parent." It implies leadership and long-term relationship. It connotes trust, caring, and mutual well-being, yet also signifies discipline, being challenged, and improvement.

Seven Characteristics of Supplier Partnering

What follows are the seven characteristics of Toyota's supplier partnering, as described in Table 12-1. We'll look at them from bottom to top and discuss the steps you would need to follow to bring each element of the partnering relationship to fruition.

Mutual Understanding

The basis for the relationship starts with understanding, and it does not come easily. What does it mean for a company to understand its supplier partner? For Toyota, it's genchi genbutsu (actual part, actual place), reflecting its core philosophy of going and seeing directly, to deeply understand the situation. The question is whether you are willing to hit the road, get your hands dirty, and put in the effort.

When Toyota first started to work with Metalsa, a frame and body components manufacturer headquartered in Monterrey, Mexico, they spent time with senior management and wanted to understand the company's philosophy. They appreciated the fact that Metalsa was originally a family-owned company, one

Partnering Characteristic	Key Elements
Kaizen & learning	▪ Shared lessons ▪ PDCA ▪ Annual cost reduction
Joint improvement activities	▪ VA/VE ▪ Supplier development ▪ Study groups
Information sharing	▪ Accurate data collection and dissemination ▪ Common language ▪ Timely communications
Compatible capabilities	▪ Engineering excellence ▪ Operational excellence ▪ Problem-solving skills
Control systems	▪ Measurement systems ▪ Feedback ▪ Target pricing ▪ Cost management models
Interlocking structures	▪ Alliance structure ▪ Interdependent processes ▪ Parallel sourcing
Mutual understanding	▪ Trust ▪ Commitment to mutual prosperity ▪ Respect for each other's capability ▪ Genchi genbutsu (actual part, actual place)

Table 12-1. Key Elements in Supplier Partnering

that still has significant family influence. More important, they appreciated Metalsa's emphasis on creating a positive work culture with only the best people. Hiring is a core activity for Metalsa and includes intense screening, including visiting the homes of prospective employees to see them in their family environment. Metalsa invests heavily in training its people and considers their quality its principal competitive advantage.

A team of supplier engineers from Toyota visiting the Metalsa plant were given their usual preview of frames and other products in the lobby showcase. What made it unusual was that its executives could not get the Toyota engineers out of the lobby. They pored over each and every weld, intently discussing the quality of the welds and the design of the chassis. It was apparent that there was something different about Toyota as a customer. Metalsa got major business during the engineering phase to source the entire chassis for the Tundra truck to be built in a Toyota plant that had not yet been built in San Antonio, Texas. To support the launch, Toyota asked that a large team of engineers be dedicated to the project and that they spend significant time in Japan. They asked for a full-time engineer to be stationed in Michigan near the Toyota Technical Center (TTC), and for one and later two more engineers to be stationed full-time in Japan to work alongside Toyota engineers.

It was extremely unusual for Toyota to give this much business to a brand new supplier. But Toyota had told the Mexican government they would source more product and build vehicles in Mexico in exchange for favorable tariff treatment. Once this decision was made, Toyota set out to find suppliers with compatible cultures. They then started the long and resource-intensive process of developing mutual understanding between Toyota and the supplier. This was an investment that would span decades.

Given the significant investment by Metalsa in assigning many engineers to work with Toyota, building prototypes, and investing in learning to work with Toyota before ever getting paid, one might expect a degree of apprehension. But on the contrary, Metalsa senior executives made an increase in Toyota business one of the company's top strategic objectives. They even offered to build a special plant dedicated to Toyota parts near the border (which Toyota refused). Why? They knew Toyota would be an honorable and reliable customer, their visibility in the industry would go up considerably because they supplied Toyota, and that they would learn a ton and get much better as a company.

Toyota suppliers speak in glowing terms about Toyota as reliable, capable, and that the relationship causes them to get better at supplying Toyota products and their own total business. A Toyota supplier put it this way:

> Toyota has helped us dramatically improve our production system by coming in and working with us side by side. On the commercial side, Toyota is very hands on also. They come in and measure and work to get cost out of the system. . . . We started with Toyota when they opened the Canadian plant with one component, and as we improved performance we were rewarded, so we now have almost the entire cockpit. Relative to all car companies we deal with, Toyota is the best customer.

Many companies have certain suppliers that have been with them for many years. And the customer and supplier get to know each other. But by "mutual understanding," we mean more than familiarity. Do you and your suppliers truly understand each other at a working level? Do you understand their processes in detail, enough to help them improve their processes? Do your suppliers or customers respect your ability to understand their processes and make useful suggestions? Is there trust in the relationship—trust that each party is out to help the other be successful?

Interlocking Structures

Putting out a product to bid conveys an image of a bunch of commodity suppliers who can all equally well make the product the customer wants. As homeowners, we aren't going to develop an intimate relationship with the producer of lightbulbs we buy for our house. The best the lightbulb manufacturer can do is become part of a large purchasing and retailing organization like Costco. But we might want to get to know the carpenter who will build our new addition or house. The dynamics involved in purchasing custom parts for a complex product like an automobile include an array of products, from a lightbulb to the complexity of a customized assembly like a chassis or seat.

When Toyota first decided to make cars in Georgetown, Kentucky, they needed a nearby source for seats. Seats in automobiles are big and very complex; there are a huge number of variations. So building an inventory of all possible seat combinations is not cost effective and would leave auto assemblers walking up and down the line picking the right seat. Instead, Toyota wanted seats to arrive from the supplier in the sequence needed as cars come down the assembly line. One possible way to do that is to push a ton of inventory onto the seat supplier, but if that approach were adopted, the Toyota seat supplier would not be able to meet its cost objectives. And quality problems would be hidden in mountains of inventory. Therefore, Toyota asked its supplier to actually build the seats in the sequence needed on the assembly line based on seat-by-seat orders from Toyota.

Toyota wanted to source this expensive component to an American company. After extensive discussions with many companies, they picked Johnson Controls (JCI), whose plant later became an extensively studied model for Toyota-style just-in-time production. But it is important to remember that this did not just happen without effort. It required a lot of hard work.

When Toyota first started working with the Johnson Control plant in Georgetown, JCI not only agreed to work with Toyota, but also was prepared to expand the plant to accommodate Toyota's demand. Much to JCI's surprise, Toyota said they would give them the business only if they did *not* expand the plant. They challenged JCI to reduce inventory and fit the additional volume into the existing building, which seemed impossible within JCI's mass production paradigm at the time. But with Toyota's help they accomplished it and began to understand the Toyota philosophy. From Toyota's perspective, it was not enough for Johnson Controls to deliver seats in sequence, just-in-time. JCI needed a compatible system to Toyota's—the ability to build and deliver just-in-time and continually improve their system to drive out waste over time. Only then could Toyota and the plant mutually prosper.

This became even more evident when Toyota brought on a second source of seats for Georgetown. Toyota had worked very hard to develop the Johnson

Controls plant. But Toyota's policy is to never sole source. They always want at least two to three potential sources for every component. They do not want 10, but do want intense competition between suppliers to help motivate improvement. The suppliers each get the business for a product, and they keep that business over the life of that model until a new version is introduced. At that point the next model is bid again. The incumbent may have a big advantage, unless other conditions warrant switching products around. It is possible for a poor performer to lose some share of Toyota's business and for an excellent supplier to increase its share over time.

Toyota had invested heavily in teaching the Toyota Production System to Johnson Controls and would not add a supplier of a critical component like a seat without a similar level of capability to build and deliver almost perfect quality, just-in-time, and in sequence. So they asked JCI to enter into a joint venture with Araco, Toyota's premier seat supplier in Japan, 70 percent of which is owned by Toyota. The joint venture, called Trim Masters, Inc. (TMI), was formed in 1994. Johnson Controls is the single largest shareholder, with 40 percent, but Toyota and Araco together have controlling interest.

This example and many more tell a story of interlocking structures with supplier partners. It is more like a marriage than casual dating. Technical systems, social systems, and cultural systems are all tightly intertwined. It goes beyond manufacturing to product development systems. It is not enough to be a good supplier. The supplier must act as a seamless extension of the refined lean systems of Toyota. The interlocking structure was reinforced in the case of TMI by Toyota's ownership and control. For Johnson Controls, a condition of getting the business was that they had to invest in a separate Toyota business unit with strong firewalls between it and the rest of JCI. The structure reinforces the interdependent processes with Toyota.

Investing in interdependent processes means more than a customer issuing a set of requirements to a supplier. It means the way they work fits together. If the customer is asking for just-in-time delivery of material, the supplier should have the capability to build just-in-time, not ship from inventory. If the customer has the flexibility to quickly change to a different product mix, the supplier must have that capability. If the customer picks up product in tight time windows, the supplier must have the structure in place to get the product reliably on the dock, preinspected within those time windows. In other words, the processes used to design, make, test, and deliver a product should be seamless, as if each partner is an extension of the other.

Control Systems

Partnering gives the impression of a relationship among equals. "Trust" suggests that Toyota lets suppliers do their own thing. Nothing could be further from the truth. The role suppliers play is too vital for Toyota to take a hands-off approach—they do not want to leave parts reliability and product quality to chance. To Toyota, the flip side of the same coin called trust is an effective control system. Toyota has elaborate systems of measurement, target setting, and monitoring of performance.

Toyota's command central for supplied parts is a bit like the control tower at a well-run airport. They know the status in real time of all parts suppliers. Ask for any key delivery performance indicator for any supplier, and it is at the fingertips of production control. Ask purchasing for charts and graphs of performance over time on quality, cost, and delivery, and it is there.

If there is a near missed shipment, a quality problem, incorrect labeling, or any glitch, it will surface immediately. Then Toyota is on the phone and demands the supplier come to see them and explain the cause of the problem and their planned countermeasures. They expect immediate responses to any concerns about quality, cost, or delivery, when indicators are off target, and before there are any serious performance threats to production. But these cannot be just entry-level engineers talking. They expect the highest executive levels of the supplier to get personally involved. These instances of problems are taken as an opportunity to educate the supplier.

For example, a Toyota vice president of product development relayed an example of a supplier that had a quality problem that was design related. The vice president of the supplier was asked to come to the Toyota Technical Center to discuss his countermeasures. When the VP showed up for the meeting, it was obvious that he did not have a detailed understanding of the problem, its cause, and the countermeasures. With a wink and a nod he assured the Toyota executives that he would take care of the problem immediately. The Toyota vice president was stunned that this VP would come to the meeting so poorly prepared, without seeing for himself what the real problem was. He asked him to go back and find out what the real problem was and return for another meeting.

What the Toyota vice president was doing was educating. He was not interested in this particular case. He could have had a lower-level engineer talk to a lower-level engineer at the supplier. He took the opportunity to create an object lesson in the appropriate role of an executive of a Toyota's supplier. They must take responsibility and lead by example.

Control also extends to aggressive cost reduction initiatives. Toyota not only gives the supplier a target, but carefully monitors progress in reducing costs to achieve the targets. As an example, Toyota's supplier, Trim Master, Inc., bids on every new model (about every four or five years) and is expected to decrease prices about 3 to 4 percent every year after the initial model introduction year. The cost-cutting initiative by Toyota around 2000 was so aggressive it seemed scary. The goal was to bring suppliers in America to the levels of global sources overseas. Toyota suppliers felt they should be following TPS or a similar philosophy and excel at cost reduction more than the average overseas supplier, which should make up for differences in wage levels and material costs. The program was called CCC21, and the focus was on becoming the cost leader in the world for the twenty-first century. This was not a target for existing products, but for new products being developed for the next new model launch. For TMI it meant approximately a 30 percent price reduction for the next new model launch (in about three years).

How could TMI cut prices so aggressively when they already were exceptionally lean by most standards? They had to start by accepting the fact that this was their target and it was critical that they work as hard as possible to achieve it. Next they needed a plan. The approach used was *hoshin kanri*, also called policy deployment, in which top management sets high-level objectives and the next level down comes up with objectives to support these and draws a chart showing the relationships between their objectives and the higher level. And this cascades down ultimately to the shop floor. Charts for each of the different departments with their plans and progress toward the plans are prominently displayed in a "war room."

The severe price cutting Toyota requested became the focus of this plan, and everyone knew what they had to do to support that price reduction. The group of 12 managers who were champions for their functions met weekly in the war room to review progress and the implementation of specific measures and countermeasures to achieve the plan. Since there had already been so much cost taken out of plant operations, the biggest opportunities were in the engineering of the new product, working with Toyota product development. In this workmanlike fashion TMI steadily and systematically achieved the goal. They realized that if Toyota saw a serious effort and they fell somewhat short of the target cost reduction, Toyota would not punish them. And since Toyota was closely monitoring the process, they knew that Toyota knew what kind of effort they were expending.

Target pricing is a severe form of control. It is well known that Japanese companies work backward in setting costs for the product. Instead of the typical American practice of building up costs, adding a profit margin, and setting the price, they start with the market price and figure out what costs they can bear to make the profit they want. This leads to target prices for suppliers—the piece price they can afford to pay to suppliers within the vehicle budget. American auto companies have all picked up on this practice, setting target prices, but they lack the sophistication of Toyota and Honda in setting prices within which suppliers can make a profit, and they lack sophistication in helping suppliers achieve the target costs required to meet that price. As a brake system supplier put it:

> For the Big Three, target pricing equals "squeeze the supplier until we are dead." I have asked how they have developed the target price. The answer is the following— silence. It is based on nothing. It is based on the finance guy who has divvied up money. They have no idea how we will get the cost reductions, they just want them.

Because Toyota has a rational system to set targets for suppliers, works with suppliers to reach the targets, and is reasonable with suppliers when their best efforts do not achieve the targets, they are perceived as fair customers. They are not out to simply control the suppliers or run them out of business. They are out to work with them for mutual benefit.

We will see in the case of Delphi at the end of this chapter that the backbone of this target setting system is cost management models. Toyota does not want to just manage price, they want to manage cost. They want the reality of costs to be reflected in the target price. If Toyota cuts price by 10 percent, they want the reality of the supplier to reflect an actual cost reduction of 10 percent. Toward this end, Toyota has developed realistic cost models that reflect the costs of raw materials, space, inventory, part processing, and overhead. For example, they know that processing costs for stamping are proportional to the number of strokes of the dies in the presses. They have established a relationship between these and built that into the model. The parameters of the model come from suppliers, Toyota plants, and public sources. These models allow them to estimate what the cost of the part should be. It also allows product engineers to redesign the product and estimate the cost impact. And it allows supplier development engineers to make suggestions and estimate the cost reductions of those suggestions.

Perhaps the most important source of Toyota's control is the old-fashioned free market mechanism of competition. But how can Toyota have long-term dedicated suppliers and get competition at the same time? The answer is sometimes called "parallel sourcing." Source not from one but not from many. Toyota looks for three or four top-notch suppliers for a component and keeps the business within this family. For any given car model, one of the suppliers will get this business for the life of that model. But getting it for the next version of that model is not guaranteed. If they do not perform, or their competitor, like a sibling, does a lot better, they can lose this business.

How are your control systems seen by your suppliers? Are they enabling the suppliers to get better and reach aggressive targets? Do you have enough detailed understanding of your supplier's costs to set realistic targets and understand if they are achievable?

Compatible Capabilities

These days it is popular to source in low-wage countries like China or India. We know of auto companies and their suppliers that have set multibillion-dollar targets for sourcing in China, as if that is an accomplishment in and of itself. In the near–term, at least, this is not an option for Toyota. Toyota is well known for excellence in engineering and manufacturing, and views suppliers as extensions of its technical capabilities. It is not enough to be able to make parts to specs. Suppliers must be able to innovate in the product design and process and work closely with Toyota throughout the product development process. While there are different roles in product development, ranging from being given general (black box) specifications to being asked to design the part to being given a blueprint and asked to make it, in all cases suppliers must be capable of working seamlessly with Toyota engineers.

For Toyota in Japan, close partners like Denso and Aisin can work independently on the component design, generally anticipating Toyota's needs before even receiving specifications. However, in the United States this type of approach would be considered unusual, largely because the U.S. suppliers may not have the intimate knowledge of their customers that Denso and Aisin have of Toyota, and also because they lack the specific technical capabilities. The U.S. suppliers often find that working with Toyota engineers is novel and very different from working with the Big Three. As an executive at the Toyota Technical Center in Ann Arbor, Michigan, put it:

> Some people in Japan have grown through the parent company and then moved to jobs at various suppliers, so they already know the culture. Toyota in Japan and their suppliers know each other's capability. Delphi and other large companies are going to top management in Japan and saying, "Here is what we would like to do in the U.S. with TTC," and salesmen from the suppliers will go over to Japan and tell Japanese management of Toyota what they want to hear. But the American suppliers often cannot deliver on the salesmen's promise. There is a problem of capability among American suppliers compared to what Toyota has come to expect in Japan.

It's not a matter of the American suppliers being weak technically or incapable in general, but that they do not understand the Toyota Way of product development and preparing a product for production. For example, Toyota suppliers say that Toyota often, makes things vague on specifications, especially at the beginning of a new model development. They might not spell out the exact level of drag/resistance/looseness of a hinge as it closes and opens but say something like, "This has to do with the 'feel,' and thus is hard to quantify"—it will get adjusted as they go along. Toyota in Japan is also used to giving vague specifications to suppliers. In fact, this is expected in the "guest engineer" system. First-tier suppliers typically have a significant number of design engineers who spend about three years living in Toyota's engineering offices full-time. They work alongside the parent-company engineers, learning the product development process in detail. At some point they understand the process and language intimately. They know when all of the new car programs will begin and the basic goals of those programs. They come up with ideas for the design before even being asked.

Today, Toyota has stepped up its simultaneous engineering initiative, getting input from suppliers on their manufacturing capabilities when it is still a concept and before the body is even styled. American suppliers, lacking that history and intimate knowledge, are unable to work with the vague specifications in the early stages of simultaneous engineering. A new group was set up in Toyota purchasing to help American suppliers participate in simultaneous engineering. According to an executive from Toyota's North American purchasing department:

> The degree of simultaneous engineering in Japan is so high, our engineers have to give vague specifications early in the program. Experienced suppliers know how to feed their design and manufacturing requirements to Toyota even with this uncertainty, and those less experienced do not understand the timing of that and how to do it. Our role [in North American headquarters] is to help suppliers by reviewing Toyota's technical information jointly with the supplier and trying to help the supplier fully meet the early and vague Toyota requirements. The suppliers have the technical capability if they have the information, and we help them get it and interpret it.

Not all suppliers have the capability. Their American customers do not have the same requirements for information as Toyota, and therefore do not always keep the detailed manufacturing data Toyota needs to set its design specifications—a frustrating situation for Toyota and its suppliers. As a young American auto body engineer working at the Toyota Technical Center explained:

> New suppliers are hard to work for, particularly when it comes to getting tolerance data. For fitting their parts into our body design, we want the tolerance between two points of fit. Our suppliers may come to us and say we cannot hold the level of tolerances you are requesting. We know other suppliers can hold tighter tolerances. So we ask why. They simply don't have the data. In one case recently it was clear the supplier fudged the data. They gave us data on hundreds of parts and they averaged out to exactly .5 for all the parts—we knew that was completely improbable and they fudged it. "Go and see" is the biggest thing—we live that. In the process, we teach them what our data requirements are and how we collect and analyze the data.

Toyota continues to invest heavily in teaching Americans their way, and the capabilities are gradually building in America. Toyota has made major investments in its technical center in Michigan, which is continuing to expand rapidly, and its suppliers are making comparable investments in Michigan R&D facilities. The 2005, Toyota Avalon was the first entire vehicle to be principally engineered in the United States. There was still a lot of involvement from Toyota engineers in Japan, but the development was directed out of Michigan. Developing engineering capability for North America has been an ongoing process for over 15 years and will continue for the next 15 years.

Now the question: Can Toyota simply pick up shop and transfer parts supply to a low-wage country and leave behind this investment? It is not the sunk cost that is the issue. It is that Toyota's product development process is so "leaned out" and fast that it needs suppliers who can work in lockstep and provide the critical contributions it needs every day. Losing that would mean losing a core part of Toyota's competitive advantage.

Now your turn: Is your company actively working on reducing product development lead time? Are you working to use simultaneous engineering to get the design right up front? Are you interested in the highest quality parts that work together seamlessly? If the answers to these questions are yes, it's worth taking your supplier's technical capabilities seriously. And it is the fit between your "culture of engineering" and your suppliers that is at stake. Parts are not parts, and engineering is not engineering.

Information Sharing

In the early stages of American companies learning to partner with suppliers, the approach seemed to be more information sharing with suppliers is better: "If we inundate suppliers with information, they will be informed enough to be equal partners." Toyota also believes strongly in information sharing, but of a more targeted variety. There is a high degree of structure with a specific time and place for meetings, very clear agendas, and clear formats for information and data sharing.

At the TTC in Michigan there is a "design-in" room, where competing suppliers work in the same room on the same project for Toyota. Design-in requires the most intensive level of supplier involvement. The idea is that suppliers design their components into Toyota's vehicle. It has separate rooms for the suppliers to keep themselves secure as well. However, separable body functional parts like sunroofs, mirrors, and locks are designed fundamentally by the suppliers in their own buildings. They are referred to as RDDP (Request for Design and Development Process) parts. Headliners and floor consoles might also be considered RDDP. For instance, since the Toyota management deems that suppliers garner expert knowledge of the mechanism of the locks, they ask them to work on the design and give them only basic specs. These RDDP parts can stand alone and be plugged in. Yet Toyota engineers are still deeply involved with the interface and have to work with body sheet-metal area and trim to define the boundaries of those parts. For design-in parts, suppliers must be present at TTC. But for RDDP parts, it's more hands off, and the suppliers don't have to be present. Design-in is always done on Toyota's CAD system and communication is intense, whereas RDDP can be done on the supplier's system with less intense communication.

Clearly when the supplier is involved in the "design-in" process and has engineers on site, they are in close communication with Toyota engineers. But the nature of the communication is very different from the "inundation model." Most of the communication is between the specific Toyota engineer in charge of that component system and the supplier engineer for that system. And it is highly focused on technical issues. There is much less non-value added communication than we see at other companies. Toyota expects the supplier engineer to learn Toyota's CAD system. Toyota engineers can do their own CAD work—they do not delegate the core engineering work to specialist CAD users—and they expect the same of the supplier engineers. So a lot of the time the supplier engineer is doing engineering work—something all too rare in many companies.

A great deal of information sharing is necessary in order to optimize the development and manufacturing of the vehicle. Achieving the cost reductions Toyota expects cannot be achieved through manufacturing improvements alone. For instance, Toyota estimates that 70 percent of its purchasing manpower is spent during the product development and launch phases. Particularly during the early phases of product development, the most sensitive proprietary information each company possesses is being disclosed and discussed. It can only be openly shared in an atmosphere of trust.

Has your company developed this kind of trust to openly share technical information with key suppliers? What percentage of the communication between your company and suppliers is value-added technical communication? By this we mean focused on technical issues that get immediately translated into engineering design and decisions. Is there a clear technical contact in your company working with each supplier? Are your technical contacts highly knowledgeable and authorized to make decisions about the product? Do your engineers and suppliers share a common language so communication is efficient, timely, and accurate?

Joint Improvement Activities

Many American suppliers we know celebrated when they first received business from Toyota, even if it is a small and not very profitable start-up contract. In addition to new sales, they knew as a parts supplier that they would have opportunities to learn and get better . . . and enhance their reputation with other customers. Toyota does not just purchase parts from suppliers. Toyota develops supplier's capabilities. A contract from Toyota is like getting admitted to a top university—the best in the business. Toyota's goal in teaching its suppliers lean methods is not to teach specific tools or methodologies, but to teach a way of thinking about approaching problems and about improving processes.

The approach Toyota uses is learning by doing and experiencing. Toyota has some training courses, for example on TPS. But these tend to be short overview

sessions. The preferred approach to teaching TPS is to do a project at the supplier's plant. In the 1990s, for instance, Toyota established the Toyota's Supplier
Support Center (TSSC), which was set up as a separate, wholly owned corporation to teach TPS. The approach was to work with the supplier to set up TPS
on one product line, create a model by working with a few supplier engineers
and managers, and let them discover TPS firsthand by doing it and experiencing it. After the model was implemented, it was up to the supplier to keep it
going, with occasional coaching. It's interesting that Toyota separated TSSC
from the purchasing relationship, even making it a separate corporation owned
as a subsidiary of Toyota. TSSC's goal was to teach through doing and demonstration, and Toyota did not want the suppliers looking over their shoulder,
fearing they would be asked for extra price reductions. The process took six to
nine months of intense tutelage, focusing on one product family. Typical results
were a spectacular doubling of productivity, increases in quality, and dramatic
reductions in inventory and lead time.

More recently, TSSC has shifted its focus from free consulting to fee-based
consulting, focusing exclusively outside of auto. Also, part of the old TSSC was
shifted to an internal Operations Management Development Division that focuses
on internal training of American Toyota employees in TPS. Interestingly, one
way OMDD trains internal Toyota associates in TPS is to send them to suppliers
to work on a project. They say if they do the project at Toyota and their mentor
criticizes them, it will embarrass them in front of peers, so they would rather do
the training at a supplier where they are not among peers. Obviously, suppliers
also benefit from this training.

Toyota purchasing is now responsible for supplier development, but has
still separated TPS teaching from the business relationships. There are no 50-50
splits of cost savings. A Toyota purchasing executive explained:

> We separate the cost challenge that all suppliers have anyway to reduce price from
> some improvement or support activity. We are likely to send a TPS expert to work
> with the suppliers two days a month on long-term development, and we do not
> ask the supplier to share savings based on specific improvements. Instead, that is
> part of our annual cost reduction targets for the suppliers. My engineers do not
> understand how that improvement relates to a purchasing commercial arrange-
> ment, and it is not a productive use of their time.

An example of a strategic supplier relationship comes from Delphi, the
largest automotive parts supplier. They have the size to support Toyota technically and globally, so Toyota decided to invest in training them. Delphi, set up
its own supplier development program for second- and third-tier suppliers modeled after Honda and Toyota and asked for a Toyota TPS expert to be assigned
full-time to them for three years. Toyota would not agree to three years but did
agree to assign one of their most senior experts full-time for two years. Delphi

wanted this expert housed at corporate headquarters, but Toyota insisted he be assigned to one division so he could get more deeply involved in supplier development activities on the floor. The Toyota executive in charge explained:

> We dispatched our TPS expert to Delphi to help their supplier support engineers have more of a Toyota Way of thinking and method, but we needed him back in two years. They requested to extend that assignment, and we suggested they send a senior engineer or someone from that group to our OMDD to be developed just like a Toyota engineer is developed—here is the project company, project, observe and make improvements. It is a very traditional student-sensei approach.

Complementing the supplier development activities, value engineering typically takes place in the early product development phase. Before the product is in production there are many opportunities to cut cost through common parts, simplification of the product—such as reducing the number of parts—and designing it to reduce the amount of labor required for assembly. After the product is in production, value analysis is the analogous process to redesign it to take cost out. Toyota was able to take literally billions of dollars in cost out of its vehicles over time through product redesign. They do this through their product development function, and in this case share savings with suppliers.

Clearly, Toyota's approach to supplier development is distinctive. For one thing Toyota itself is a lean model, arguably *the* lean model. So they have something to teach. But perhaps more important, the context is one of cooperation and learning, and they make suppliers better in a holistic sense. It is not just about the individual project and the savings they can extract from the project—Toyota gets its annual price reductions anyway. The teaching they do is to enable the supplier to give this price reduction to Toyota while still making money on the business.

Is your company in a position to mentor suppliers? Have you developed the internal capability so you have something to offer to your suppliers? Are you willing to make the investment in making your suppliers better so they will give you better cost, quality, and delivery performance?

Continuous Improvement and Learning

The result of working on the six base levels of the supplier partnering hierarchy is the foundation for kaizen (continuous improvement) and learning. Typically, learning is thought to occur at the individual level, and if these individuals leave the organization or move to another assignment, their learning is lost. Preserving what is learned at the organizational level is far more challenging, and learning at the enterprise level seems nearly impossible. But Toyota has developed this core competency.

With a solid foundation, the key to enterprise learning is the development of standardized processes that get refined and improved. Without standards there can be no learning. Standards go beyond documented procedures to shared tacit knowledge of the right way to do things.

Toyota views suppliers as extensions of its capabilities, but also as independent agents. At first glance this claim may appear paradoxical, but it actually is not. On the one hand, Toyota will not impose its own way or production system on its suppliers. If a supplier can use a different production system effectively to achieve the objectives required for cost, quality, and delivery, that's fine. On the other hand, the suppliers share a common philosophy of product development and manufacturing, and many specific practices. In the codevelopment of products, it's necessary to be completely synchronized on timing, testing methods, metrics to specify product performance, and even technical vocabulary. The result has been the evolution of common philosophies, language, and approaches between Toyota and its suppliers.

In the United States, suppliers quickly realize that to achieve Toyota's demanding performance requirements they must learn lean manufacturing methods. Through various supplier development activities, they end up learning from their customers, and thus a standard emerges. Many of the actions of Toyota that appear to be short-term cost-cutting initiatives are also investments in learning. Toyota thinks of CCC21 as not just a price reduction program, but a way to create a challenging environment so its suppliers will grow:

> If we go to supplier and say we want you to reduce your price by 5 percent, they will say okay and will lower the price and take a hit on profit. However, there is no way to reduce price by 30 percent and stay in business. He has to go in and revolutionize every part of the business. We will work with the supplier to make the 30 percent. We will not leave them high and dry. In some cases you cannot get 30 percent out. If it is a simple part and very little labor, you cannot get 30 percent out. Did you make a strong effort? Did you look at every step from raw material to shipping out the door? Can you get a penny here and there? Maybe we only get 20 percent out, so we are both winners. Purchasing understands the cost for every step of manufacturing from raw material on out.

Developing all of the individual suppliers to fill the North American needs for Toyota was the first step in the puzzle of creating an extended lean enterprise. Once the individual parts are in place comes the tough job of connecting these independent suppliers into a true supplier network. We call this a "lean learning enterprise."

Long ago in Japan Toyota developed *jishuken*[4], or study group, as a means of learning with its suppliers. Now they organize top suppliers into study groups. In Toyota style, these are all "learning by doing" processes. Toyota believes in keeping classroom training to a minimum. The important learning happens through real projects on the shop floor, and suppliers must take ownership of their learning.

They have set up similar *jishuken* activities with American suppliers (called Plant Development Activities) trying various configurations. They found they had to group suppliers by skill level with TPS since there was such a wide range. These Plant Development Activities afford a chance for suppliers to get

---

[4]Translated as: Ji (myself), shu (autonomous), ken (study). In other words, suppliers are responsible for taking the opportunity to learn for themselves, with mentoring from Toyota.

hands-on activity with TPS in different supplier environments. They also begin to create a bond across Toyota suppliers, almost like a club.

These activities are conducted within the context of BAMA (Bluegrass Automotive Manufacturing Association), Toyota's supplier association. It started in Kentucky when Toyota opened its first assembly plant there, but is now throughout North America. These are core Toyota suppliers who meet during the year, sharing practices, information, and concerns. There are committees that work on specific things, including joint projects. The meetings are important and allow Toyota to provide key information to suppliers. But the networking is even more important.

In sum, to be successful, a lean extended enterprise must have strong leadership from the final assembler, partnering between the final assembler and its suppliers, an established culture of continuous improvement, and joint learning among the partners. At the very least this requires a stable set of suppliers who have learned a common philosophy of operations and are part of a broader supplier network.

Building a Lean Extended Enterprise

Companies working to learn from Toyota to build high performance supply systems seem to want to skip over the hard work of developing effective supplier partnerships, looking for easy solutions through supply chain software and aggressive price reduction approaches. Toyota's approach in North America provides a model for building a successful lean learning enterprise from the ground up. The process can be summarized by the following steps.

1. Become a Role Model Lean Customer
You can't teach suppliers what you yourself have not yet mastered.
Toyota worked hard to develop the Toyota Way of management in North America, teaching American managers the philosophy. A common complaint we hear from suppliers who work for U.S. auto assemblers is that they're asked to do things that the assemblers themselves do not do or are unable to do. The complaints range from a particular way of documenting the processes to inefficient processes within the customer that drive their costs higher. For example:

> Our product development costs as a supplier are included in the piece price. But [American Auto] is redesigning themes for the vehicle two to three times after the program is officially launched, and we will spend $3 million in engineering time when we budgeted $1 million in the piece price. No one at American Auto seems to understand there is a budget out there. It can escalate. It seems free to them.

It is difficult to change fundamental operational practices and to improve. It's seductive to simply push demanding requests onto suppliers and avoid internal change. But asking suppliers to do what the customer cannot will undoubtedly appear hypocritical to suppliers. The customer should start by getting its own house in order.

2. Identify Your Core Competencies

Outsourcing entails more than simple make-buy decisions.

Outsourcing can lead to lower cost and higher flexibility. But it's also important to carefully consider what competency you should retain in-house. By focusing on core competencies, Toyota can outsource a great deal of the vehicle development and manufacturing. However, its definition of core competency is much broader than that of many auto companies. Toyota sells, engineers, and makes transportation vehicles. The key question: When Toyota outsources up to 80 percent of the vehicle to suppliers who controlled technology for them and all its competitors, how can they excel or distinguish themselves? If a new technology is core to the vehicle, Toyota wants to be an expert and best in the world at mastering it. They want to learn with suppliers, but they never transfer all the core knowledge and responsibility in any key area to suppliers.

For example, Toyota's most aggressive development project in recent times was that of the Prius hybrid vehicle. A core part of the computer system is called the Insulated Gate Bipolar Transistor (IGBT), a switching device that boosts the voltage from the battery and converts it to AC power for driving the electric motor. Toyota engineers were not experts at designing or building semiconductors, but rather than outsource this critical component, they developed it and built a brand new plant to make it—all within the tight lead time of the Prius development project. Toyota saw hybrid vehicles as the next step into the future. They wanted "self-reliance" in making that step. Once they had that internal expertise, they could selectively outsource the manufacturing.

Simply speaking, if a company does not have the internal competency to control the technology, they are at the whim of their suppliers. Since their suppliers are free agents and can supply that technology to anyone, the parent company cannot use that technology as its competitive advantage. Also, it is difficult to understand the cost structure for a particular part unless you have the capability to develop and make that part.

3. Develop Your Core Suppliers

Make sure their systems and philosophies are compatible with yours and they're at a comparable level of operational excellence

A chain is as strong as its weakest link. If your suppliers are not as capable as your own internal operations, you must develop them to that level. Obviously you can't develop hundreds of suppliers for everything from major modules to nuts and bolts. Toyota has developed a tiered structure. The top tier supplies major subassemblies or even modules that are sent to their engine and assembly plants. Toyota will work most closely with these suppliers and expect them in turn to manage lower-tier suppliers. On the other hand, Toyota will also directly manage critical lower-tier suppliers of major raw materials and components or common parts. For example, Toyota has very exacting specifications for steel and so will direct its suppliers to work with specific steel suppliers it has worked closely with to develop.

If you're starting out down this journey and are still in the process of getting lean internally, you need to start small and selectively. Your internal lean experts should first get busy fixing your own underperforming systems. You might start on selected projects with a few of your most important suppliers. Do not be surprised if they are as advanced in lean as you are and that you can in fact learn a thing or two from them.

4. Use Control Systems for Continuous Improvement
Strip down your bureaucratic systems and procedures to a critical minimum required to manage the supplier relationship.

We saw that Toyota is focused on control of the supply base, more than one might think. They use ownership in joint ventures, separate divisions dedicated to their business, meticulously kept metrics, and demanding quality expectations to keep suppliers on track. A supplier hiccup can lead to a small army of Toyota engineers swarming the supplier to find and fix the problem.

While suppliers view Big Three procedures as highly bureaucratic and coercive, Toyota, which uses equally stringent quality methods and procedures, is viewed as enabling. An American automotive interior supplier described working with Toyota in this way:

> When it comes to fixing problems, Toyota does not come in and run detailed process capability studies 15 times like the Big Three. They just say, "Take a bit of material off here and there and that will be okay—let's go." In 11 years I have never built a prototype tool for Toyota. Knee bolsters, floor panels, IPs, etc., are so similar to the last one, it's not necessary to build a prototype. When there is a problem, they look at it and come up with a solution—focus on making it better, not placing blame.

On the other hand, Toyota has a far more elaborate system for cost management than most of their competitors. Cost models, as discussed in the Delphi case at the end of the chapter, can be used to estimate what supplier cost should be and to design the product to a target cost. These cost models are very sophisticated and depend upon high-quality data from suppliers. Suppliers must believe that this data will not be misused against them.

5. Favor an Incremental Approach
Start small with selective outsourcing for a new supplier.

Giving a large chunk of business to a new, untested supplier is risky and makes it difficult for your company and supplier to learn how to work together. Once you have a capable network of suppliers who can truly collaborate on product development and manufacturing improvement, you do not want to contaminate the network with inferior suppliers. When you introduce a new supplier, you can start to train them in the lean way from the start, beginning with a small order. Test them on a less critical component and let them earn their way into the network.

At the Toyota Technical Center they gave the example of headlamps for vehicles. They would not source an entire headlight to a brand new supplier but instead started with fog lights. Valio, a French supplier with operations in North America, was first given a fog lamp and was trying to get headlights. At first, Toyota did not think they were ready for it. But Valio started performing well and being considered for headlamps for the next new model introduction.

An example of a failed Toyota project was a rear taillight given to an American company selected by purchasing because of its low bid. As it turned out, it could bid that low because it intended to build the part at a Mexican plant to take advantage of the low labor rates. This Mexican plant had never been tested to make Toyota parts. Once they got manufacturing in place, they experienced off-the-chart scrap rates for the parts. The Toyota engineers who had recommended a different supplier based on engineering and manufacturing capability were furious. Even though Toyota was not paying for the repair costs, and the supplier still wanted the business and was willing to continue at the low price point, Toyota decided to give the business to someone else. It cost a bit more, but it was worth it to get a reliable flow of quality taillights to the assembly plant. To Toyota, this became an object lesson in the folly of chasing low prices across national borders.

6. Develop Mechanisms for Joint Enterprise Learning

Learn together and capture learning in standardized routines.

The highest level of the lean enterprise occurs when partners in the enterprise are learning together and capturing the learning in standardized processes. You don't get to this level overnight. You can imitate Toyota's supplier association and find it's just one more meeting or one more visit between the customer and the supplier. In fact, this was often what Toyota's supplier association in America looked like in the early days. It was only when Toyota started to show it could add value to suppliers through improvement programs that the supplier association began to be viewed as a true source of learning and improvement.

A better structure to imitate at first than the supplier association is the *jishuken* activities of Toyota. Take three to five of your top suppliers that are not in a competitive relationship and form a kind of user group that works on projects in a plant from each company. Everyone learns and the plants get better.

Traditional vs. Lean Models of Supplier Management

There are many pressures on companies in the hypercompetitive global economy: pressures for cost reduction, unprecedented quality levels, and responsiveness to niche market demands, and all of these at hyperspeed. If a company has become big and bureaucratic and finds it difficult to adapt, it's appealing to push these requirements for change onto suppliers. This may mean using some of the new technologies for reverse online auctions or chasing parts in low-wage countries. But these short-term solutions create their own sets of problems. The supply chain infrastructure is not getting leaner and better, and in fact gets weaker. Using brute force will only work for so long before your company is paying in warranty claims and lost market share for low-quality products.

Figure 12-2 illustrates the traditional underlying model these companies follow in their relationships with "vendors." The philosophy is to seek low piece price. The assumption is that vendors are vendors, and without pressure they will seek to drive up price and drive down service. The job of purchasing agents is to counter this by being "tough" on the vendors and squeezing them on price. Mechanisms like reverse-on-line auctions are powerful price pressure methods. The supplier can directly see the competition, and in the desire to "win" continues to underbid not only the competition, but sometimes even his own costs. Delphi refers to buyers under this model as "hunters and gatherers" (see case study). They lack any significant professional understanding of the suppliers and go out with a big club to hunt up and bring home the spoils.

When suppliers are forced into low-balling the bids, they have to find ways to make money. One way is to charge for engineering changes or any special service required. Or suppliers may minimize investment in the product and process. Purchasing must try to counter this through measurement of the supplier and using the numbers to beat up the supplier. The threat is always there to pull the product and resource it to a lower-cost competitor, perhaps in a lower-wage country. The result of sourcing on price is short-term cost reduction, but there are many unintended negative effects, like parts shortages, quality problems, high warranty costs, and little investment in product innovation, which in the long term add up to higher total cost.

Toyota is not striving to be the low-price automaker. The goal is to produce cars at a fair market price that the customer would think has value. Why is this distinction so important? This philosophy suggests that cost reduction efforts should not be a one-way train toward the lowest possible cost. Toyota sets target costs, not just prices. Target costs means the suppliers must operate at cost levels that allow them to make a profit at the prices the customer pays for parts. The lean supply chain model is illustrated in Figure 12-3.

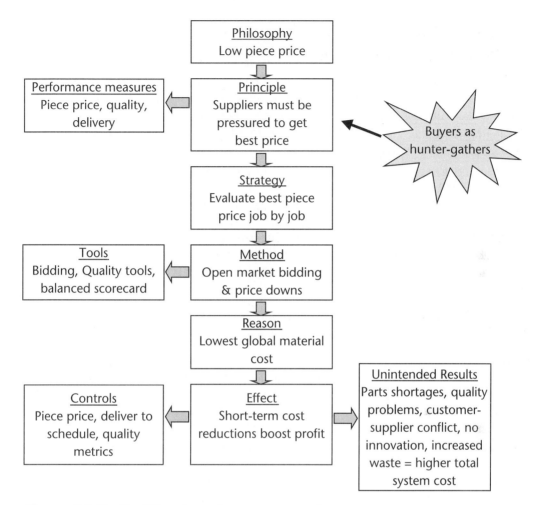

Figure 12-2. Traditional vendor management

The goal is to eliminate waste not only in Toyota plants but in the supplier plants and in the connecting processes in between (e.g., the logistics system). Suppliers are extensions of the learning enterprise participating in kaizen. For key components, Toyota selectively chooses two to three strategic partners for each component and encourages competition between them. Each will typically get an exclusive contract for that part for one car model but knows they can lose Toyota market share in the future if they do not perform. There are many tools for managing cost and improving the product, process, and supplier's capability. By investing in the partnering characteristics in the supplier partnering hierarchy, Toyota over the long term is getting the annual price reductions from suppliers that are necessary to be globally competitive, but without sacrificing quality or innovation.

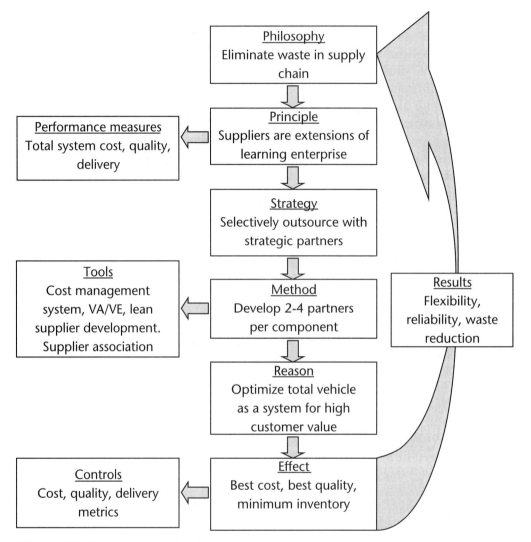

Figure 12-3. Lean supply chain process

Is Toyota actively seeking to replace American supplier partners with low-cost suppliers in China and other low-wage countries? They may purchase an occasional commodity part in these regions, but this is not a core part of their strategy. A Toyota North American purchasing executive explained:

> We get some savings from tier-two and tier-three suppliers sourcing overseas that are passed through, but it is pretty rare for us to consider it directly because of the supply chain complexity and risk. Distance and the political environment create

high levels of complexity. Our initial approach is to try to understand what that competitive level is. We have global vehicle programs so we can work with Europe and Toyota Asia Pacific and understand what is the Toyota competitive level and challenge people in North American to get to that level.

It's important to realize that there is no "one size fits all" strategy for developing these characteristics of partnering. Some companies might start out with information sharing and some with supplier development. However, they shouldn't forget the long-term vision of developing all of these characteristics as a system. The ultimate goal should be to create a lean learning enterprise.

Case Study: Developing a Lean Supply Chain at Delphi

Delphi is a world leader in mobile electronics and transportation components and systems technology with approximately $28 billion in annual sales, 185,000 employees, and 171 manufacturing sites in 40 countries. Delphi purchases from over 4,000 direct material suppliers. Since becoming an independent company in 1999, they immediately started on a lean journey. It was a top priority to shed the waste and high costs impacting Delphi's operations. As Donald L. Runkle, the former vice chairman, often stated, "Lean enterprise is Plan A! There is *no* plan B!"

Delphi's first step in becoming lean focused on its manufacturing sites. For several years they had been studying and embracing the Toyota Production System. Delphi developed and documented its own system, structure, and processes, and called it the Delphi Manufacturing System (DMS). It's a common, global production system that embraces all functional areas and focuses on creating lean products, lean purchasing, and lean internal and external manufacturing.

Though it was a rocky road, over time Delphi enjoyed considerable success, with a relatively deep penetration of lean in most of its plants. Every plant had done a considerable amount of work, and an impressive 20 different plants were awarded the Shingo prize for excellence in manufacturing. Applying for the award has been encouraged by Delphi to provide a stretch target and provide recognition for achievements, along with external visibility. The Delphi Manufacturing System was strongly supported up to the level of the chairman and CEO, J. T. Battenberg III, and the message was clear: DMS is not optional.

In 2002, Delphi hired R. David Nelson as vice president of global supply management with the charge of spreading lean through the supply base. A former vice president of purchasing for Honda of America, Nelson had a deep understanding of the "Honda Way." He brought that to

John Deere in converting a traditional purchasing organization into a lean supply chain. With that background he was well suited to help Delphi extend DMS to what it calls "outside manufacturing." Delphi avoids the term "supplier," to emphasize that the quality of manufacturing is important whether it takes place inside or outside the corporate boundaries of Delphi.

"Inside manufacturing" currently encompasses about 30 percent of the total cost at Delphi, while "outside manufacturing" makes up 50 percent. Delphi buys about $14 billion worth of goods annually. So the opportunity was clear.

Besides DMS being a well-developed system with strong training programs and internal lean expertise, Delphi had two other sources of expertise for lean supply chain. One was a set of consultants formerly with Toyota, and the second was direct support from Toyota, which has become a major Delphi customer. In fact, Toyota sent one of their TPS experts in purchasing to work full-time for two years within Delphi and to teach the Toyota Way of supplier development.

In this case study, Delphi's strategic sourcing system is illustrated as a work in progress. The case reflects Delphi's lean supply chain progress after working with the process for almost three years, when Dave Nelson's team rated themselves in an embryonic stage compared to Toyota. But Delphi felt it was headed in the right direction, and their approach is comprehensive, hitting all aspects of a lean supply chain.

Nelson learned from Honda that a cornerstone of a lean supply chain was a strong cost management system, the heart of which was a set of models of key manufacturing processes. Putting various input costs into the model leads to a predicted total cost for a component part. The models are detailed, and very accurate in reflecting actual costs to make a part. Nelson hired a former Toyota manager who had over 25 years experience in purchasing and with Toyota's cost management system. As Delphi's director of cost management, he became the internal expert, setting up and teaching a cost management system modeled after Toyota's. He was assigned a team of 30 full-time people as "disciples" to learn and spread the cost management system, which Delphi considers the cornerstone of its lean supply chain.

The Toyota veteran estimated that it would take five to six years to meet a minimum level of acceptability as a lean supply chain, and nearly three years into the program in 2004, he felt Delphi was on track. According to this cost management expert, a minimum requirement for success was to have the unwavering support of senior executives, which Delphi demonstrated through the supportive efforts of J. T. Battenberg III and Dave Nelson.

It was clear to the senior management team that Delphi had too many suppliers to have a focused, lean supply chain. Delphi was challenged to develop close relationships with like-minded suppliers dedicated to cost reduction. So they set out to identify "strategic supplier partners." This turned out to be a more onerous task than it appeared at first glance. It was a matter of meeting with the CEOs of candidate suppliers one by one and explaining the challenges associated with being a strategic supplier. In fact, about 10 percent of the suppliers interviewed chose not to join Delphi in the lean journey. It took about two years to develop an initial set of "core" and "near core" suppliers, and more work remained to be done.

In the meantime, a lean supplier development engineering group was formed, and knowing Delphi could not wait years to get started teaching lean to suppliers, developed a list of suppliers likely to make the strategic supplier list. Delphi began working with a subset of core suppliers, and in two years had done projects with 70 suppliers. The approach was modeled after Honda's best practices model and Toyota's approach, through its supplier support center.

Target model areas are selected through this approach. Lean experts from Delphi, supplemented by outside consultants who formerly worked for Toyota, act as sensei. They do not do the work for the supplier's plant, but guide them through teaching and coaching. The approach is:

1. Get a solid commitment from the supplier's CEO.

2. The CEO must appoint an internal lean champion (either full- or part-time, depending on the company size).

3. Select a product family.

4. Develop current and future state maps along with detailed action plans.

5. Post the maps, plans, and key metrics in a war room.

6. Implement.

7. The Delphi sensei visits regularly and reviews progress by walking the floor and comparing progress to plans in the war room.

8. Delphi expects to share in the supplier's cost savings resulting from the product (typically 50-50 for a specific product family only).

As Delphi anticipated, project results were similar to those of Honda, Toyota, and its own plants—double or even triple digit performance improvements on all key metrics. For traditional thinkers, lean supplier development engineering is simply about cost savings. However, for lean thinkers it's about developing relationships, trust, and building highly capable suppliers.

Most of Delphi's second-tier suppliers are comparatively small companies (e.g., $150 million in annual sales). Often, the CEO is the company founder. Typically, these suppliers are aware of lean manufacturing and have sporadically applied several of the lean tools. But the companies never experienced lean as a system and were amazed to learn firsthand of the real power of the Toyota Production System. It was a significantly different experience, leading to a collaborative "win-win" approach to operating the entire business. Delphi encouraged a number of these suppliers to apply for the Shingo prize.

The comprehensive lean supply chain approach is represented by Delphi as a model with nine interdependent gears:

1. Strategic sourcing (selecting suppliers with a broader set of expectations for R&D)

2. Lean supplier development engineering

3. Cost management (in-depth understanding of specific elements of cost)

4. New model flawless launch

5. Quality (at less than 20 ppm range at the time of the case study, and lower ppm for more serious problems)

6. Systems infrastructure (Information Technology)

7. People development (each Delphi supplier management employee has 80 hours of training in cost management and lean approaches)

8. Supplier relationships (changing the mind-set so suppliers are viewed as valued assets, not disposable commodities)

9. Communications

Many companies get enamored with some pieces of the lean process, e.g., "Let's just do supplier development." Delphi concluded that these "gears" were all interdependent strategies. It needs to have the right suppliers, with the right capabilities and the right internal purchasing group, and those suppliers must understand real cost.

The biggest challenge for Delphi is moving from its traditional price-based sourcing heritage from GM to a strategic sourcing approach learned from Toyota and Honda. Traditionally, Delphi has relied on competitive quoting to get lowest prices. It is moving to a more holistic view of extended value stream excellence. Part of this process is transitioning from a focus on price to that of a cost-based reality.

In 2004, aggressive three-year targets were set:

1. Single digit ppm quality and flawless launch

2. Thirty percent model-to-model cost savings and focus on total cost

3. Developing lean processes with core and near core suppliers

4. Investment and product coordination with business lines

5. Faster design cycle times

6. See technology early in products

7. Discontinue relationships with marginal suppliers

Moving away from marginal suppliers seems like an obvious thing to do. However, Delphi buyers were not always encouraged to do this.

To select strategic suppliers, Delphi developed a matrix and sorted commodities into four cells: core, near core, niche, and commodity. For core and near core-commodities, Delphi is gradually developing a set of strategic suppliers who sign a master supply agreement modeled after Toyota and Honda. This several page agreement lays out principles of working together (such as recall and warranty responsibility, financial terms and conditions, R&D responsibility, and long-term commitments to source from the supplier). It is not a specific contract for specific parts, but a set of detailed agreements on how each will behave. When the strategic sourcing agreement is established, purchasing decisions are almost nonevents. The cost model basically locks the supplier into a price.

Delphi's director of cost management describes the cost management concept as "reality improvement." Unfortunately price-based purchasing is not based in reality. In many instances market prices were established and buyers chose an arbitrary target for price downs (e.g., 5 percent price reductions across the board next year). Toyota's system is based on cost-management models that reflect the reality of actual costs, with target prices based on what customers are willing to pay for automobiles. Toyota sets a target profit and proceeds to develop the car to meet the cost targets necessary. Suppliers are given target costs to meet and must develop their components to meet these targets, building in their own profits. When Toyota asks for price reductions, it is based on actual knowledge of true costs, so they know where it's necessary to reduce costs and where suppliers are in danger of losing money. Price is important, but behind price is cost, and behind cost is reality.

Purchasing must look with trained eyes and see opportunities for cost reduction.

Cost-profit planning is the ultimate form of cost management. Delphi is training its buyers to be able to estimate cost more precisely, identify opportunities for improvement, and lead cost planning projects. The previous approach to buying was like the "caveman who is hunting and gathering." There were multiple rounds of bidding and poker playing. Delphi is now moving to "modern agriculture"—based on logic, science, and reality changes. The game changers are cost standards, creative improvement plans, and master supplier agreements.

In the real world, Delphi has found that suppliers' quotes are much higher than these cost models suggest they should be, even after repeated price-downs. A cost model group is producing forms on cost standards—price tables, price curves, and cost standard templates—with data drawn from suppliers, supplier meetings, government and industry data, Delphi internal sources, benchmarking, and competitive analysis data.

Price reductions should reflect reality changes—materials (challenge cost, design), labor through lean workshops, transportation (level scheduling), warehousing (inventory reduction), and so forth. The important thing is to change realities. Each buyer for each commodity must develop creative improvement plans. Nothing is left unchecked. Cost management means working very closely with suppliers to achieve these realities.

Since design impacts 70 percent of the total manufacturing cost, Delphi must involve suppliers early in the design development process. To this point, Delphi had mostly focused on the 30 percent in manufacturing because it was easier to work on. The next frontier is for suppliers working with Delphi's product engineers to move up front to product and technology development. The goal is to reach a level where engineers can use cost standards to evaluate the impact of different design options.

Delphi views this process as a major cultural change. It wants buyers to be more than just "hunters and gatherers," and instead to become change agents thoroughly versed in cost management. It has developed a list of 70 items that buyers should be able to see as they walk through suppliers' plants, and it expects them to have expertise in everything they buy. As an example, a Honda buyer came into one of Delphi's plants for two days and listed 130 items that needed to be improved. What is Delphi's key to the success? In a word: trust! Suppliers will never agree to use true costs as a basis for price setting unless they trust Delphi to think about them as true partners.

Reflect and Learn from the Process

Partnering Characteristic	Hansei Supplier Partnering Reflection
Mutual understanding	◆ Do you deeply understand your suppliers and their capabilities? ◆ Do your people go and see the supplier's processes for themselves (genchi genbutsu)? ◆ Are you and your core suppliers committed to mutual prosperity? ◆ Is there mutual trust in the relationship?
Interlocking structures	◆ Have you developed a seamless connection between your processes and your supplier's processes? ◆ Have you used appropriate alliance structures to control critical parts and processes?
Control systems	◆ Do you have effective real-time systems for measuring supplier performance that gives immediate feedback? ◆ Do you use that system for helping suppliers set challenging but realistic targets for improvement? ◆ Is competition between a small set of dedicated suppliers intense and motivating? ◆ Do you use target pricing effectively to motivate improvement so both parties win?
Compatible capabilities	◆ Are your supplier's manufacturing and logistics systems seamless extensions of your just-in-time systems? ◆ Are supplier engineers tightly integrated into your development process and speaking the same language as your engineers? ◆ Are you and your suppliers working jointly to develop innovative products and services?
Information sharing	◆ Is there accurate data collection and dissemination? ◆ Do you always set specific times, places, and agendas for supplier meetings?

Partnering Characteristic	Hansei Supplier Partnering Reflection
Information sharing	◆ Do you have clear formats for sharing information with suppliers? ◆ Is information scattershot, or targeted by specific individuals in your company with clear roles and responsibilities to work with specific individuals at the supplier?
Joint improvement	◆ Do your people have the knowledge and experience to mentor suppliers? ◆ Do you have joint improvement projects with suppliers that produce measurable results?
CI & learning	◆ Are suppliers working together in study groups to share learning? ◆ When problems occur and countermeasures are used, are there mechanisms for learning from this and sharing what is learned?

Part V

Root Cause Problem Solving for Continuous Learning

Chapter 13

Problem Solving
the Toyota Way

More Than Solving Problems

The Toyota Way seeks to identify and remove obstacles on the path to perfection. This philosophy is rooted in the Japanese cultural desire to seek perfection in every activity. As we discussed earlier in the book, the Toyota Way is a cyclical process of achieving stability, standardizing practices, and then continually squeezing the process in order to expose the obstacles (seen as system weakness). Human beings tend to seek comfort and avoid discomfort. The Toyota Way is not a natural behavior. The Toyota philosophy relies on the "system," and adhering to its concepts will force people supporting the system into uncomfortable situations. The choices presented then are to either remove the obstacles or to fail. For this reason, possessing the skills of solving problems and the ability to continuously improve are crucial to survival.

This process serves as the framework for most other aspects of the Toyota Production System (TPS) and its product development system, and is largely responsible for Toyota's tremendous success. Toyota can generate greater results, with less effort, in a shorter period of time, more consistently than any of its competitors. This process provides a structure to align resources effectively, to ensure mutual understanding of the significance of the issue, to clearly outline the necessity and benefit of resolving the issue, and, with a high degree of accuracy, to predict the actual result.

The problem-solving methodology is a skill that runs deep and strong at all levels of the organization within Toyota and across all functions, from manufacturing to purchasing to sales and the rest of Toyota. The basic method is learned in training classes, but the real learning comes from daily practical application, continued use, and evaluation by others in the organization. Technically, the methodology is fairly simple and does not require complex statistical analysis tools. Because of it's simplicity the method can be embraced and executed by all Toyota personnel regardless of education or previous experience. Toyota uses advanced statistical analysis in certain situations, but the day-to-day use of problem-solving is straightforward. This method may appear too simplistic to individuals trained as Black Belts in the Six Sigma process, but there is an elegant beauty to it. For one thing, the issues encountered by most associates on a daily basis require only basic analytical skills. More complex techniques are unnecessary and often confuse people who have a problem but are not trained in the methods. In addition, the process at Toyota can be applied rapidly, while Six Sigma and other similar processes tend to be lengthy and laborious.

This process may occur in a very short time frame (less than one minute) or may take months or even years. From the moment an operator discovers a problem on the line and signals the need for support (by pulling the andon cord, as described in Chapter 8), until the problem is controlled and corrected, may be less than one minute. At the other end of the spectrum is long-term strategy development, preparing a new product launch, process improvement, and policy deployment.

Calling this process "problem solving" may be a misnomer, since the process goes well beyond the basics of solving problems. This method encompasses a critical and logical thinking process. It requires thorough evaluation and reflection (genchi genbutsu and hansei), careful consideration of various options, and a carefully considered course of action, all leading toward measurable and sustainable goals.

With repeated use and practice, this process becomes second nature and is used in virtually every situation in which improvement is desired, when new or modified processes are added, and even as a framework for the development of a lean implementation process. Here are just a few of the situations for which this process can be used:

- Correcting weakness in skill levels and development of a training plan
- Purchasing new equipment
- Cost reduction activities
- Team improvement activities (Quality Circles, kaizen events)
- Improving productivity and process flow
- Annual planning and strategy development

Every Problem Is an Improvement Opportunity

The inverse of a problem is an opportunity. This has become a cliché and often means we don't want to deal with the fact that we have problems. It becomes real only when the organizational culture focuses on continuous improvement. Within all organizations, including Toyota, there is a virtually endless supply of problems, and thus opportunities. We may also commonly refer to these problems as "issues," and they fall into three broad categories: Large, Medium, and Small (Figure 13-1).

Many organizations fail to develop an effective process for capturing opportunity from all three categories. Quite often the Small category is overlooked entirely because these opportunities are viewed as "insignificant" or offering "not enough bang for the buck." In addition, the Medium and Large categories are not fully exploited due to the small number of people who are trained or qualified to resolve issues (Figure 13-2). In this structure, the primary impetus for improvement is management-directed and management-controlled. In this case change occurs from *outside* the process. This continues to foster the traditional we/they thinking, which implies that only management or specific individuals are responsible for improvement, and that the workers wait for "them" to correct issues. Individual efforts are not encouraged for various reasons, but primarily because there is no structure in place to support them and because managers fear a loss of control.

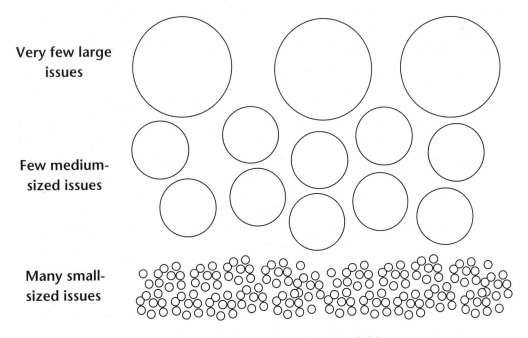

Very few large issues

Few medium-sized issues

Many small-sized issues

Figure 13-1. Typical quantities of opportunities available

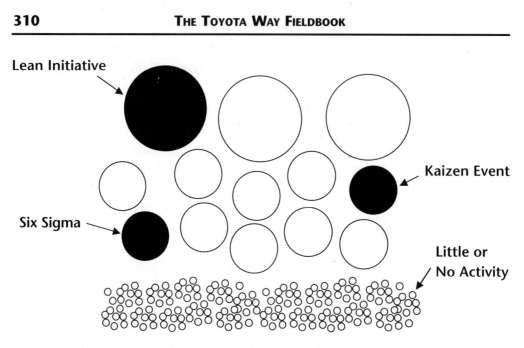

Figure 13-2. Opportunities captured by typical companies

Also, in most organizations problems are not viewed as opportunities for improvement, but as failures, and thus are hidden rather than addressed.

Toyota is able to maximize its performance using two tactics:

1. **Leverage.** Every employee is trained and encouraged to use the process daily, thus achieving tremendous leverage from the combined efforts of many problem solvers each making frequent, small, continuous improvements. This contrasts with many U.S. companies, where select individuals (such as engineers, or Black Belts) are trained and designated to solve problems; often with little or no input from those actually closest to the process.
2. **Focus.** Resources are utilized to address problems across all three levels, and the efforts can be focused, thus applying greater leverage and multiplying the results. The problem-solving process requires evaluation and comparison of issues, allowing people to focus efforts on the most significant items. In this way, a smaller amount of focused effort produces greater results by attacking the larger opportunities. In addition, individuals are able to focus efforts on the smaller items they control and that directly affect them. Toyota applies the 80/20 rule by effectively focusing 80 percent of their energy on the 20 percent of problems that will yield 80 percent of the total benefit.

The Toyota Way divides the categories and utilizes the resources appropriately for all three levels. Larger issues are generally addressed through management-directed and management-controlled activities such as Management Kaizen Training [also referred to as Practical Kaizen Training, or *jishuken* activities

(Figure 13-3)]. It is also management's responsibility to establish expectations for the organization, to identify weak points in the system, and to apply the appropriate resources. Mid-level opportunities are generally initiated by the supervisor, the team, or by an individual. These items may be based on overall company objectives for improvement or on issues of particular challenge to the group affected. Finally, Toyota is able to capture a huge opportunity by facilitating individual efforts toward improvement. The individual or small team nearly always initiates these efforts. Each person understands the process of continuous improvement and pursues that objective in his or her daily activities.

In fact, continuous improvement is so important that changes to processes are made up to the last day of production in a product cycle. This seems paradoxical until it is understood that the idea of continuous improvement truly means continuous—never ending. If people believe that improvements are only desired under the "correct" conditions, they will, in effect, not make improvements because the conditions may never be correct. We've often heard people state that a product or process will "go away" in six months, so it is not practical to spend time and money improving it. The Toyota Way suggests that a small improvement with minor effort yielding perhaps one second of time or one cent per piece saved over the six-month period is, in fact, a practical idea. It facilitates the idea that improvement must occur at all times at all levels by all individuals. Any rules suggesting appropriate times and conditions for improvement will kill the spirit of continuous improvement.

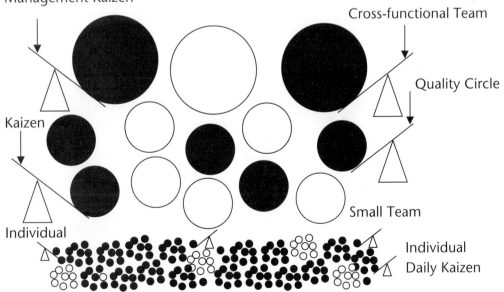

Figure 13-3. Toyota leverages opportunities at all levels

In addition, Toyota teaches basic problem-solving skills to all employees so that everyone becomes a problem solver. With thousands of people solving problems on a daily basis, Toyota can effectively leverage its people resource. For most issues encountered daily, the basic methods are sufficient. More complex techniques are unnecessary and often confuse people dealing directly with the problem. Problems of a more complex nature require a higher degree of skill, and members of management are trained via Management Kaizen events. The case at the end of this chapter on the Toyota Georgetown, Kentucky Plant illustrates the breadth and depth of kaizen activities across the organization.

Tables 13-1 through 13-3 summarize the characteristics of the three levels of issues, the typical scope of the specific issue, examples of each, and implementation methods.

Issue	Typical Scope	Examples	Implementation Process
Large issues, low quantity, high complexity and difficulty	Issues that effect the entire organization, plant, or department	• Annual planning • New model launch • Interdepartmental issues • Product development	• Management kaizen training • Cross-functional teams • Department/Plant management • Initiated and supported by plant management

Table 13-1. Toyota Approach to Large Issues

Issue	Typical Scope	Examples	Implementation Process
Medium-sized issues, moderate to high quantity, medium complexity and difficulty	Issues similar to typical Six Sigma projects or kaizen events. May affect the group or department.	• Development of new processes • Procurement of new equipment • Significant safety, quality, production, or cost issues	• Departmental, cross-functional team (production, maintenance, engineering) • Intergroup team (members of same group) • Quality Circles • Small teams or individuals • Supported by supervisor or department manager • Possible payment award through the suggestion program

Table 13-2. Toyota Approach to Medium Issues

Issue	Typical Scope	Examples	Implementation Process
Small-sized issues, virtually unlimited quantity, low difficulty to resolve	Issues that appear repeatedly throughout the day. May cause small amounts of waste every cycle. Range in opportunity from very small to fairly significant.	• Elimination of minor issues and waste • Small continuous improvement such as 5S, visual factory, or improvement of standardized work • Andon process to stop the line and fix problems immediately	• Primarily an individual effort • May be a joint effort or small team • Generally initiated by individuals or small teams • Supported largely by direct supervisor • Payment award and implementation through the suggestion program

Table 13-3. Toyota Approach to Small Issues

Telling the Problem-Solving Story

Toyota associates learn that the problem-solving process is like telling a story. Every good story has an introduction or lead-in, character development and substance in the middle, a conclusion, and perhaps a hint of a sequel . The problem-solving process has distinct chapters or steps. And like a good story, a good problem-solving process will flow smoothly between each step, with a clear connection from one to the other. The completion of one step will lead to the next step, and there will be no break in the continuity. Here are the "chapters" of the problem-solving story:

- ◆ Develop a thorough understanding of the current situation and define the problem.
- ◆ Complete a thorough root cause analysis.
- ◆ Thoroughly consider alternative solutions while building consensus.
- ◆ Plan-Do-Check-Act (PDCA):
  - Plan: Develop an action plan
  - Do: Implement solutions rapidly
  - Check: Verify result
  - Act: Make necessary adjustments to solutions and action plan and determine future steps
- ◆ Reflect and learn from the process.

There may be additional information contained in the story, but it will generally fall under one of these categories. As with good stories, each problem-solving process is somewhat different, but overall, the basic structure of the process is the same.

In Chapters 14 through 17, we'll go into detail about each chapter of the problem-solving story and developing a thorough understanding of PDCA. You will notice that Chapter 14, which focuses on understanding the current situation and defining the problem, is the longest, and subsequent chapters get shorter. This reflects the importance and level of effort in each of these phases. Getting the problem right is the most important and should be where most of the effort is made, since doing a great job of solving the wrong problem has little long-term impact. Yet in most problem-solving activities we have noticed, people are more than happy to accept a superficial definition of the problem and launch into brainstorming solutions. This brainstorming is the fun and exciting part, so they want to get to that quickly, but it's also the easiest part. Toyota's practical problem-solving methodology is a disciplined process and does not always come naturally. It requires stepping back and thinking deeply before charging into solutions and implementation.

Case Study: Kaizen at the Toyota Georgetown Plant

Toyota's first wholly owned assembly plant outside of Japan in Georgetown, Kentucky originally built only the Camry and has expanded greatly. This plant became the site of thousands of pilgrimages to see true TPS right here in our own backyard. The plant from the start began racking up J.D. Power awards that hang from the rafters, practically hiding the ceiling.

Georgetown started out as a large site, building engines, stamping, welding, painting, molding plastic bumpers and instrument panels, and assembling cars. It grew quickly as the Avalon and Sienna minivan were added, then the minivan was moved out and the Solara coupe was moved in. Through volume changes, model changes, equipment changes (e.g., a completely new body shop), and growth, it has been a busy place with little time to catch a breath. Combined with the fact that it is a favorite recruiting ground for companies that want to hire away Toyota-trained employees, it has been a challenge to maintain the lofty expectations of the plant. By 2004 the site was up to 7,800 employees, which managers felt was beyond the size where communication is truly effective. They had to switch from thinking of it as a town to thinking of it as a big city with a lot of little neighborhoods.

The growth and loss of managers led to tremendous pressure by 2000, as the J.D. Power awards became few and far between and cost pressure from the low-wage countries China and Korea pushed the plant into radical kaizen. While kaizen was part of the culture of the plant, they were used to continuous problem solving punctuated by the big changes associated with model launches and new equipment. The new competitive challenge required *kaikaku* (radical kaizen). Added to this was the pressure of becoming self-sufficient, since Toyota in Japan was spread thin, supporting plants throughout the world, and unable to afford sending additional Japanese engineers and coordinators. Georgetown had to figure things out largely with Americans.

Table 13-2, above, shows a variety of different approaches that Toyota uses for process improvement projects, including various types of cross-functional teams, Quality Circles, and work groups under a group leader. The need for radical improvement at Georgetown taxed all of these approaches and more.

There are some common characteristics of these process improvement activities at Georgetown, and Toyota generally:

1. Process improvement projects in individual areas are driven by *hoshin kanri* (policy deployment) objectives for the site that are linked to improvement objectives for North America, which are linked to improvement objectives all the way up to annual goals of the president of Toyota.

2. The process improvement project follows the steps described in Chapters 13 through 17. Ultimately it will look like the problem-solving A3 report described in Chapter 18. It may be displayed on a board, a wall, or on an A3 report, but all the elements will be included (e.g., problem statement, improvement objectives, alternatives considered, selected alternatives, justification, results, additional actions to be taken).

3. It will follow the Plan-Do-Check-Act cycle.

4. It will be part of an organizational learning process, with any key learning shared across the organization.

To support these dramatic improvements, which were needed in many Toyota facilities, Toyota established the Global Production Center (GPC) in Japan. In the past, Georgetown had a mother-child relationship with the Tsutsumi plant in Japan, which also made Camrys. The Georgetown engine plant learned from the Kamigo engine plant in Japan. They "child" plant learned some specific traits of this parent. Now Toyota wanted a global common system and developed GPC to spread TPS in a uniform way. Originally, Japanese coordinators came to each plant in North America and mentored managers one on one. It was a learning-by-doing approach. But now, with sites outnumbering coordinators, GPC had to rely on more formal training materials to spread TPS concepts. Georgetown also had the opportunity to learn from the

Operations Management Development Division (OMDD) in the United States, which taught TPS to suppliers but now was a resource internally as well. Georgetown employees can engage in a two- to three-year rotation in OMDD, doing projects at suppliers to deeply learn TPS.

One way Georgetown used OMDD was to require all managers, even at the highest levels, to lead shorter kaizen projects at suppliers and get their hands dirty in a new environment with painfully honest critiques from OMDD's TPS masters. They did a one-week process-level kaizen and then a two-week systems-level-material-and-information-flow kaizen. Managers who led the supplier kaizen activities were expected to lead four similar activities per year in their own areas back at Georgetown. To develop in-house knowledge, Georgetown set up an Operations Development Group (ODG) internally. Group leaders, area managers, and managers could rotate through for two to three years to get in-depth TPS experience doing kaizen projects in the plant. Each area of the plant has a TPS specialist who has direct experience or mentored expertise from this group assigned to work on medium-sized projects.

Through hoshin kanri, aggressive goals were set for each plant in 2003. For example, to become globally competitive on price, the engine plant set a target of reducing total cost by 40 percent by 2007. Through kaizen, the engine plant had reduced the workforce size from 1,017 to 930 people between 2000 and 2003. But cutting direct labor was not going to get a 40 percent cost reduction. That required a major analysis of all costs, for labor, depreciation, mainte-nance, indirect materials, facilities, and purchased parts and materials. Cost targets were established in each area, adding up to 40 percent when achieved. To make it more challenging, the engine plant had similarly aggressive targets in safety, quality, and product launches. The 2005 hoshin kanri was to be the best in North America at effi-ciency and effectiveness. This required breakthrough kaizen and a rededication to the Toyota Way. The Georgetown plants had the ben-efit of benchmarking their sister plants in Japan, which were already considerably ahead on these metrics. The engine plant could bench-mark the Kamigo plant, note the significant gaps, study the root cause of the gaps, and develop specific action plans to close the gap. Each plant at Georgetown used benchmarking in this way. Some of the approaches taken at the engine plant were:

◆ Minimize machine complexity through some new developments in machining technology at Toyota. This would increase operational availability.

◆ Use the "cabbage patch" approach to make operations more visual. This included a review of machined scrapped parts, laying out all the scrapped parts each day. Actual cost due to scrap is charted and a deep Five-Why analysis done. A daily board shows what the problem is, the root cause, short- and long-term countermeasures, who is responsible, and the status of the project every day.

◆ Make the line more compact through line compression. Moving operations closer together reduces waste and allows operators to add tasks in their work cycle, without adding overburden, as well as reducing travel distance to respond to andon calls.

◆ Bring subassembly operations in line with the main assembly to compress lines.

◆ Bring in a new engine on new breakthrough machining technology (Global Engine Line) that is far more flexible and at the same time simpler and easier to maintain.

◆ More local sourcing of materials and tooling to reduce shipping costs and take advantage of lower costs in America than Japan (tooling locally cut costs 30 percent).

◆ Long –term, the objective was to merge the six- and four-cylinder lines into one flexible line that would greatly reduce capital costs and provide flexibility to level the schedule as demand patterns change for one versus the other engine.

There were many small kaizen activities in the engine plant. Here are a few examples:

◆ Comparison to Kamigo showed that Georgetown was using significantly more labor, so many small projects were done using *yamazumi* (balance) charts and analysis using the Standard Work Combination Table discussed in Chapter 6. In one project a team under the group leader was able to reduce one process out of three in this way. Spread across all of the teams in the plant, this begins to add up. (Note: eliminating a "process" in many companies equates to eliminating a person's job but at Toyota the person is not let go but moved to another position. Through attrition, early retirement, and reducing temporary employees this will ultimately lead to higher labor productivity).

◆ A Quality Circle activity on tooling wear done by a team that saved 16 cents per unit.

◆ One machine was hidden from view by curtains, and uncovering it to see what was going on revealed problems of how metal chips were building up and coolant was overflowing. A better preventive maintenance system was put in place, and scrap and operational availability were charted and improved.

◆ Critical performance indicator boards were developed and the role of group leaders in TPS more clearly defined. This was accompanied by internal group leader training.

There were so many changes occurring all over the Georgetown site to meet these aggressive targets that it's hard to do justice to the magnitude of the improvement effort. Each improvement project used the same rigorous problem-solving approach, with specific measurable objectives to achieve the goals set at the next level up in the hoshin kanri. Here are a few examples:

◆ A large project was initiated to systematically work through the problems identified in the J.D. Power initial quality survey for the Camry and to implement countermeasures. The initial quality survey counted things gone wrong in six areas of the vehicle (chassis/transmission, engine/brakes, features and controls, body exterior/exterior paint, body interior). Six cross-functional "customer satisfaction teams" were established for these areas, each with a management-level lead for daily activities and a high-level "executive champion" to address external support. A visual management bay was set up on the shop floor to display information and hold weekly 30-minute stand-up meetings.

Each of the six areas has a portion of the wall to display information and project status. J.D. Power publishes results twice per year, and companies can get in-depth versions of the study comparing themselves to other companies. Toyota paid for an additional level, which gives monthly customer survey data, including verbatim descriptions of the problem and the actual Vehicle Identification Numbers of problem cars. The complete problem-solving process described in this section was followed from the problem definition to identifying alternative solutions to developing detailed action plans with what, who, and when. All of this was on the storyboards.

As an example, a detailed investigation of a steering pull problem led to some significant reengineering, while a quicker problem involved the keyless entry system, because people found it too easy to push the trunk release button unintentionally. Many of these problems cut across the company, involving corporate quality, product development, suppliers, and engineering in Japan, since there are Camry models for Europe and Japan. Georgetown took a leadership role coordinating all the activity, since they are the last line of attack and build the cars customers experience.

◆ In final assembly, benchmarking versus Tsutsumi revealed a large gap in labor costs of $187 per vehicle. A large project process, called "cost competitiveness through line simplification," was initiated at Georgetown. Many things were done to reduce the gap. One was the use of a procedure developed in Georgetown called "process diagnostics." This was a checklist process in which the total workplace of the operator is assessed and points are assigned to many aspects (part presentation, ergonomics, tool reach distance, lighting, safety, etc.). It was based on a model of an ideal workstation from the operator's perspective. By scoring an operation, the analyst gets a clear idea where there are opportunities for improvement and can measure progress as changes are implemented. A separate conveyance diagnostics instrument was developed to evaluate the conveyance process. These procedures are conducted weekly by the team leader (one process per week is confirmed in this way). This is not creating the process, but confirming that it is still working. It is initially also used to set up the process. Through repeated kaizen, the number of processes needed for the Camry (over one launch) was reduced from 628 in final assembly in 2001 to 454 in 2004.

◆ A medium-sized project focused on quality and cost in the paint shop, which has two full paint booths—one for Camry and Avalon (Assembly Line 1) and one for Camry and Solara (Assembly Line 2). In all, 730 people worked in the paint booths. The department hoshin focused on safety, environment, people development, and special productivity projects. From 2000 to 2004 intense kaizen activities were initiated. This four-year process started with trainers from Tsutsumi coming to the plant, then Georgetown managers and engineers participating in floor activities in Japan. By then, from 2002 to 2003, the hoshin required practical kaizen activities led by managers. One set of projects focused on motion kaizen, and over four years, the number of processes was reduced by 76, which put the Georgetown plant at a labor productivity level comparable to the sister Tsutsumi plant. In 2004 the focus was on how to drive all of the hoshin internally, becoming self-reliant from Tsutsumi.

◆ A more focused quality activity in paint, not based on benchmarking Tsutsumi, was a "zero paint seed" activity. Paint seeds are a common problem when dust gets on the body and paint surrounds it, forming a dust speck in the paint. This must be removed by hand. For the top-coat paint process, 180 items were identified as the main control items for the whole paint shop. By creating a clean mix room, checking items on a checklist, and root cause problem solving, quality defects were reduced by 50 percent. For example, for repairing seeds not caught in inspection they used orbital sanders, which actually created dust and caused more defects in the body. This was replaced with a simple seed knife on a dampened area, which resembles shaving. Together with standard work, this improved direct run quality from 82 to 97 percent and reduced airborne dust. In 2003 alone, the paint department changed every piece of equipment in the shop while painting cars, built a wet wall that added humidity to reduce dust, eliminated a top coat, which saved $10 per vehicle, used a balance chart across three booths to reduce labor, reduced recoats/repaints, and added the seed knife process.

♦ This medium-sized project brought a new concept in material handling to Georgetown's body shop, where subassemblies are welded and then brought to the final body station where the whole body is welded. The concept is *minomi* (parts only), which translates into something like a peanut without a shell. In this case it is transferring the part without any container. The big bulky containers moved by forklifts are gone. Steel-stamped body parts to be taken for welding are hung individually on various kinds of racks with no containers. This "parts only" storage and delivery system first developed by Toyota in Japan is a breakthrough in material handling. It eliminates containers, thus reducing the waste of loading and unloading them, gets rid of forklift trucks (using tuggers instead), presents parts better to operators—reducing motion waste, damage, ergonomics problems—and reduces the number of process steps for material handling.

One example is a hanging *minomi* in which the parts are hung on a rack on wheels as they are produced. In the traditional approach you press, convey, store, convey, and thus handle three times. Georgetown developed a cartridge system in which the cartridge is line-side in welding. The tugger slides the parts into the cartridge, which is a rack on wheels; it is brought over to the next operation; and then the parts are gravity fed to the operator one by one. Now the storage location is on the side of the line and the intermediate storage area is gone, also freeing space and reducing inventory. The process started with a model area, which Georgetown called a "schoolyard" for learning *minomi*. They selected relatively easy parts, easy to stack and to move and store. This freed up space by 150 square feet, created better visual control, eliminated a forklift, and presented parts in exactly the orientation needed for the operator. Ergonomics was improved, since the parts are loaded at the same height each time. Repacking versus this cartridge system reduced labor by 34 percent and inventory by 49 percent. Projected savings when this was spread throughout were 40 percent workability ergonomics improvement (based on a computer ergonomics model), 70 percent on racking, 5 percent on associated conveyance,

11 percent fewer forklifts, 20 percent less space and less walking in the process, and a whopping 85 percent quality improvement because of reduced damage to parts. This started in 2003, and by July 2004 was about half complete.

- ◆ On a smaller level, a team leader kaizen in stamping focused on using a *yamazumi* chart (operator work load balancing) to reduce one process from an operation. This PKA (practical kaizen activity) was designed to teach TPS by doing. The team leader used a Standardized Work Combination Table to chart what the person and machine do. He identified waste, largely from conveyance, and combined what the conveyance driver was doing with the line operator's job. There had been 499 minutes of work over a cycle of 450 minutes per day. By reducing waste by 49 minutes and bringing the workload down to 450 minutes, one operator position was removed from the operation. Safety and quality were carefully tracked and there were no problems. New standardized work was created by the team leader, an hourly employee.

These aggressive kaizen projects are being done at all levels and for big, medium, and small projects. They are being done cross-functionally and from the manager to the team associate level. Why would hourly team associates and team leaders participate in this when many of these projects lead to process reductions, which imply labor reductions? The reason is simple. Since the opening of the Georgetown plant, no full-time team associates have involuntarily lost their jobs. Those "kaizened" out are reassigned and eventually, through attrition and by reducing the use of temporary workers, the employee levels are adjusted. More recently Georgetown began to offer early retirement packages and voluntary severance packages. The drivers for these aggressive process improvements include pressure to compete in cost with China and Korea, a target to become self-sufficient from Japan, and aggressive quality improvement targets. This is constantly communicated. The goal is to be competitive and healthy for the long term.

Reflect and Learn from the Process

The ability to identify and correct problems quickly and effectively is at the heart of Toyota's success. Many aspects of the Toyota Production System are designed to surface problems quickly and at times harshly. The ability to solve these problems must exist at all levels of your organization so continuous improvement is possible. Reflect on the following questions to determine what steps will be necessary to improve the problem-solving ability within your company.

1. Evaluate the cultural mind-set toward problems within your company.
   a. Do people generally prefer to keep problems hidden or suppressed?
   b. When problems occur, are people supported in the effort to find solutions, or are they blamed for making mistakes?
   c. Does your organization promote we/they thinking because there is a cultural mind-set and structure such that some people have problems and others are designated to solve them?
   d. Identify specific steps that will shift your culture to one that views the surfacing and solving of problems to be critical to the success of the company.
2. Evaluate the problem-solving ability in your company.
   a. Are problems easily identified and resolved? (If problems continually recur, they are not being resolved effectively.)
   b. Is there a defined methodology to guide the problem-solving process?
   c. What steps are needed to change your organization so it solves problems at all three levels?
   d. What specific training will be necessary to develop problem-solving skills?
3. Evaluate your organization's ability to focus resources effectively.
   a. Does your organization leverage resources to resolve issues on all three levels?
   b. Are the efforts of your people focused effectively on the most critical issues? How do you know?
   c. Are you able to evaluate the effectiveness of your problem-solving efforts quantitatively? Can you verify that you're not spending one dollar to solve a five-cent problem?

Chapter 14

Develop a Thorough Understanding of the Situation and Define the Problem

Carefully Aim Before Firing

In Toyota's internal Toyota Way 2001 document they describe problem solving under the broad category *genchi genbutsu*—the actual part, the actual place. The discipline of carefully observing actual processes directly without preconception—with a blank mind—starts the process of truly understanding the problem. This leads to a thorough explanation of what is happening and its effect on the area, the team, the customer, or the company and reveals why the problem deserves attention. The first requirement of problem solving is to determine the merit of solving the problem. At this stage, all problems can be weighed side by side, and the most important are tackled first. Lesser problems may be assigned to small teams, such as Quality Circles, or even to individuals.

There's a saying that mocks both American and Japanese styles of problem solving. The Americans say, "Ready, fire, aim," while the Japanese say, "Ready, aim, aim, aim, fire." There is an element of truth in both of these approaches, and an element of both strength and weakness in each.

Many companies in the United States are so focused and driven by short-term (quarterly) results that improvement activities are initiated before the situation is clearly understood. These actions are completed, and a new (90-day) plan is

> **TRAP**
>
> **STOP** Avoid the mistake of putting too much effort and expense into solving insignificant problems. Carefully consider the importance and value of solving the problem prior to beginning activity. Do not exert one dollar's worth of effort to solve a five-cent problem. If the problem is relatively minor in comparison to other problems, it can be addressed by the individual or team most affected by it, rather than by a large team or member of management.

developed each quarter. This short-term "fire first and set the target later" approach leads to a "shotgun" effect, resulting in bits of improvement here and there. Often these random improvements are made to issues unrelated to the situation being addressed. Activities are completed, but the desired condition is not achieved, and because there was no defined reason for these activities, a long-term sustainment of "results" is virtually guaranteed to fail.

In contrast, the Japanese (and Toyota) can be painstakingly meticulous in the initial phase of understanding the situation, which frustrates Americans who are ready to "get started." This apparently belabored process is vital to a successful problem-solving activity for two reasons.

1. Careful consideration must be given to understanding the characteristics of the problem—by weighing the impact of the problem on customers, employees, and the company, and finally by deciding if the problem is important enough to dedicate valuable time and attention to solving. The inventor Charles Kettering said, "A problem well stated is a problem half solved." Put another way, a large proportion of the problem-solving activity should be devoted to thoroughly understanding the problem situation, which leads to focusing on the problem rather than its symptoms.
2. Focusing energy and leveraging resources is critical to achieving a higher level of success with minimal effort. This starts with reaching agreement with all affected parties on the need to pursue the issue.

Within Toyota, the question, "Why did you pick up this problem?" is often used. It means, "How did you determine that this problem deserves your time and attention?" And also, "Why did you choose this problem over the many other possible issues?" In addition, there is an implied request: "Please explain your reasoning so I can understand the situation, ensure that you've done adequate reflection, assure that we are in agreement and alignment on the issue—and so I can provide necessary support and guidelines for your process." There are many things packed into that one simple question, issues that must be examined in order to develop a thorough understanding of the situation.

This rigorous questioning often leads to frustration for Americans, who tend to feel that it questions their ability to handle the situation on their own (an American characteristic), or that their evaluation was not complete. Within Toyota, many people meticulously review the process of understanding the situation, and feedback is always given. Often, after initial rounds of questions, additional rounds of questioning ensue. This is the "aim, aim, aim" phase. Valuable insights can be gained by this repetition, perhaps bringing new things to light through various reviewers, and in the long run much time can be saved by not chasing errant issues of lesser importance.

If your organization hasn't had an effective process for making improvement, there will probably be numerous issues in the backlog. When the word "problem" is mentioned or people know that you want to improve processes and are interested in knowing what the problems are, two things will probably happen:

1. You'll be deluged with many problems, ranging from broken water fountains and fans (which should be corrected without the need for long-term problem solving) to issues that occurred years ago.
2. As soon as any "problem" is mentioned, solutions will be proposed. Since the existence of a problem has not been confirmed, any proposal of solutions is premature and a waste of time (not focused or leveraged).

Initiating this process may be like opening Pandora's box. After looking inside, you may wish you had kept the lid closed! It's easy to be overwhelmed by the magnitude of opportunity for improvement available (and necessary) and the sheer numbers of problems that will surface.

TIP

 You must be prepared to help people differentiate between issues that can and should be corrected in the short term without in-depth analysis and long-term endemic issues that affect the performance of the person, group, or company.

TRAP

 One of the signs of a "Ready, fire, aim" culture is the tendency to "jump" immediately from the "problem" to the "solution." In many cases the problem may be mentioned casually and much time spent proposing various "solutions" before the "problem" has been clearly defined. At this stage in the process it is likely that a symptom has been observed rather than a true problem.

The following is a typical conversation that might occur, indicating the trap of jumping to solutions prematurely:

Manager: We have been having trouble with defects lately. (Note the vague "definition" of a "problem".)

Employee 1: A lot of the damage is coming from handling. (Note the "root cause analysis".)

Employee 2: Why don't we get new carts? (Note the jump to a solution.)

Employee 1: Yeah, Joe had a design for one a while back. (Now the conversation gets way off track!)

Employee 3: Do you know what happened to it?

Employee 1: No, but I know he had one.

Employee 2: I saw it too, but I'm not sure what happened to it. I think he told the engineer, but nothing was ever done.

Manager: Would you ask Joe to find out about his design and see if he still has it? (Now valuable time will be wasted chasing a "solution" to an undefined problem.)

Employee: Yes, I should know something by next week's meeting.

Problem solved! Or was it? What was the problem? "Defects" is a fairly broad issue. Why did the employee jump to the conclusion that "defects" were caused by handling? That may be his personal experience regarding "defects," but it's only one possibility. Do you see how the process was so easily sidetracked? The conversation went from a general statement about defects (not a well-defined problem), to a cause (handling), to a solution (Joe's carts), to an action (follow up with Joe) in a matter of seconds. What will happen next? There will be follow-up with Joe, additional meetings when time is spent (wasted) debating why Joe's solution was never used in the first place, and then debate about whether it was actually a good design or a different design is needed. Finally, a decision may be reached to build new carts, and they will be put in place. Do you think the "defect" problem will be resolved? The sad part

---

TIP

To avoid premature discussion of solutions and to keep the process on track, record ideas for solutions with a statement such as: "Okay, that may be a possible solution and I don't want to lose your idea, so I'll write it down and we can discuss it later, when we're investigating possible solutions. However, right now we want to stay focused on identifying the problem."

TRAP

It's easy to confuse activity with results. A poorly defined problem and a rush to solution and action lead to activity without achieving the desired results. If you desire to maximize your return, a focused effort on a clearly defined problem followed by a thorough analysis will lead to significant results.

is that this group is under the illusion that they're actually getting "results," and in fact they may somewhat improve the results. But it's a case of focusing on the nickels (small causes) while the dollars (major causes) fly overhead.

Find the True Problem to Get the Most Significant Results

When beginning the process of identifying the true problem, it's a challenge to find the issue at the most significant level. Often a problem is perceived based on personal experience, but this may only be "a problem" rather than "the problem." If we ask, "What is your main problem?" the answer is likely to be an issue that is most present and frequently experienced by the person being asked. For example, an operator who experiences a persistent problem every day will likely perceive it to be "the problem." In addition, a person's role in the organization tends to skew the importance of an issue for him or her. Those in the accounting department, for example, tend to see cost issues as the most important. Those in purchasing often believe that vendors are the primary concern, and engineers tend to focus on equipment-related issues.

Toyota refers to the Five-why process (explained later) as a "causal chain," because the problems and their causes are linked together in a series of single and branched chains. In an attempt to identify "the problem," people often enter the causal chain at the problem perception point, or the "point of recognition," rather than at the level of the true problem. They have identified what they believe the problem to be, but they may be further down the causal chain rather than at the top, where the true problem resides. Finding the true problem is based on understanding its effect at the highest level, where the full impact of the issue is experienced.

When identifying any problem, Toyota views it in the context of the primary performance measures, which are safety, quality, productivity, and cost (Figure 14-1). These measures are inherently linked to one another, and it's not possible to negatively impact one of the measures without also negatively influencing another. For example, if a defect affects quality performance, it may also affect

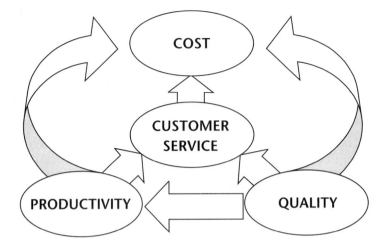

Figure 14-1. Relationship of primary performance measures

the ability to produce the desired quantity of product, thus causing customer service levels to suffer. To avoid affecting the customer, appropriate countermeasures such as increased inspection or production time may be employed to protect the customer. These extra measures will increase the cost. An operator who detects the defect may conclude that the defect is "the problem," when in fact the true problem is the affect on customer service, and ultimately on the total cost.

The placement of the measures in this model does not imply importance. In other words, cost is not the most important measure. Customer satisfaction is the most important measure. We want to achieve the highest level of customer satisfaction while maintaining the lowest possible cost.

Delivering a quality product to the customer while maintaining safety is always understood to be the number one priority. A tenet of the Toyota Way is that a defect should never knowingly be passed on to the next process. The effort to ensure the correction, containment, or control of the quality problem will have a negative impact on productivity and cost. Notice the lack of "customer delivery" or "safety." Within Toyota, all processes are closely linked to each other, and the "customer" is actually the next process. Given these tight connections and the fact that *all* processes in the plant and throughout the entire supply chain are inherently linked, if you fail to meet the customer demand (the next process), the *entire* operation will begin to stop, one process at a time (like dominos). For this reason, the satisfaction of the customer is implicitly understood and does not need to be measured separately. If a process is unable to meet the demand, it is a productivity issue. In addition, safety is an implicit expectation for everyone, and as such, may be "omitted" from the discussion of measures. Safety as the number one priority is a given.

It may helpful to think of these relationships in terms of the problem, symptoms of the problem, and the causes of the problem. Using a medical condition as an analogy: Suppose you visit the doctor and complain of aches and fever. These are not the problem. They are symptoms of the problem. The problem is that you don't feel well (and as a result may miss work or other activities). The doctor will take information and perform tests and gather facts (vital signs) that are part of the analysis, to find the cause of the aches and fever. Visually, the process looks like Figure 14-2.

Symptoms are presented to the side of the problem, as in "I have this problem, and as a result I have these symptoms." To get to the cause(s), the information is analyzed to evaluate all possibilities. The symptoms are an important piece in the overall understanding of the problem. They provide supporting evidence that a problem exists. They also provide quantifiable data showing the magnitude of the problem. In this case, a fever of 104 degrees is more significant than a fever of 100, thus increasing the need to treat the problem.

The relationship of the three primary measures will follow the same model of Problems, Symptoms, and Causes, as shown in Figure 14-3. In this case, low productivity would be the problem, poor quality a cause, and high cost a symptom or result. Using this model is important because it forces consideration of the bigger picture. We may believe that a repetitive quality problem is the true

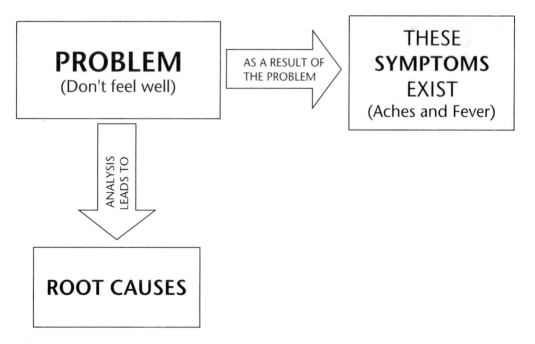

Figure 14-2. Illness symptoms versus root causes

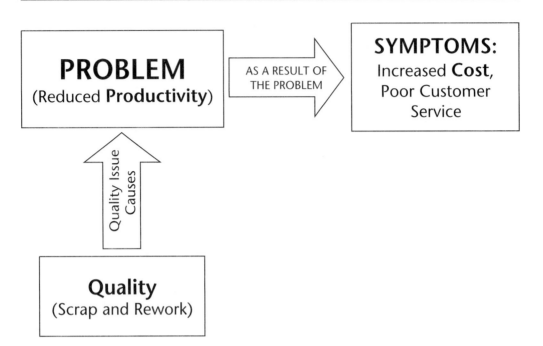

Figure 14-3. Problem symptoms versus root causes

problem, but if we look further, we find there is an issue having a greater impact (this is assuming that the rule to never knowingly pass a defect to the next process is followed). Quality is a causal factor for poor productivity.

This thought process is depicted in Figure 14-4. The problem is perceived at the point of recognition (where the problem is "found"). To consider this "problem" in a larger context, we would use a statement such as; "We have this problem, therefore, this happens." For example, suppose that the perceived problem is a machine malfunction resulting in scrap parts. The statement would be, "The machine malfunctions, therefore the part is scrap." Continuing this line of thinking we state, "The part is scrap, therefore we are losing production capacity and increasing cost. Therefore, we are not able to meet the production requirement," or, "Therefore our cost it too high." At this point we begin to understand the greater significance of the true problem.

If we do not consider the situation in a larger context, we may limit the possible solutions as well and the total impact of solving a larger problem. Thinking in this way allows us to identify the true problem and thus provides three distinct advantages:

1. Ensuring that the most significant opportunity has been captured maximizes results with minimal effort.

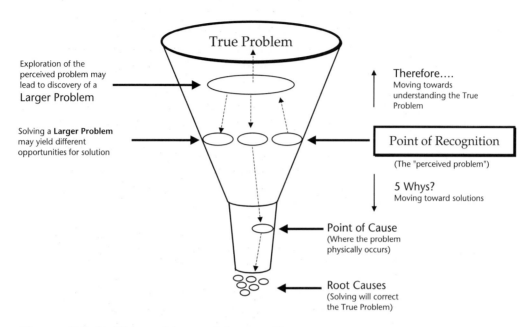

Figure 14-4. The problem-solving continuum

2. Taking a larger view opens the possibility of solving the true problem by correcting causes in addition to the ones initially identified.
3. The lower-level cause identified may be very difficult to correct (which is why it is perceived as the biggest problem), and focusing only on this difficult condition will preclude consideration of larger and easier causes, which lead to greater opportunity.

The following was an actual conversation between a Toyota *sensei* (teacher) and a process engineer at an automotive parts plant. It examines the challenge of shifting focus from the perceived problem to the true problem.

Sensei: What is the problem in your area?

Engineer: The welding robot keeps breaking down. (The perception of the "problem" is based on personal experience and the person's role.)

Sensei: Are you sure that is your problem?

Engineer: Yes. It breaks down all the time. We've tried various things to correct it but have had only limited success. We need to get a new robot. (Notice the jump to a solution.)

Sensei: I am not sure that is your real problem.

Engineer: Yes it is. It has been the problem for a long time. We have data to show how much it breaks down.

Sensei: I am sure it breaks down, but I am still not sure it is the real problem.

Engineer (a little angrily): It *is* the problem. I've been working on this for almost four years and I can tell you it is a problem. (Is it the problem or a problem?)

Sensei: Yes, I know you've been working hard on the robot; however, let me explain why it is not the real problem. When the robot breaks down, what happens?

Engineer: There is a fault at Loading Zone 3 because the weld nut does not feed. We've been working with the vendor to improve the feeder.

Sensei: Okay, what I mean is, what happens to the line when the robot breaks down?

Engineer: It stops, of course.

Sensei: When the line stops, what happens?

Engineer: Everyone stands around, and they call me to fix the robot.

Sensei: I mean, what happens to the flow of product?

Engineer: It stops.

Sensei: When the product flow stops, what happens?

Engineer: Everyone stands around.

Sensei: I mean, what happens to our ability to make parts?

Engineer: Of course we can't make parts with the line stopped!

Sensei: So we are not able to satisfy our customer with the required number of parts?

Engineer: We can't meet the demand without working overtime.

Sensei: So the real problem is that we are unable to meet customer demand without working overtime?

Engineer: No. The problem is the robot.

Sensei: Well, let's go to the line and look.

As the sensei and engineer proceed to the line, the engineer wants to take the sensei to the robot to show him the "problem." The sensei knows that line stoppage for any reason will ultimately affect the ability to meet production demand and that the robot is only *one* possibility. Therefore, it is further down the causal chain and not the high-level problem he's looking for. The sensei takes the engineer to the end of the line to observe flow. In a few minutes he notices that the flow stops.

Sensei: Why did the line stop?

Engineer: The employees are rotating positions.

Sensei: How often do they rotate?

Engineer: Every half hour, but you can't change that without causing a large problem with the employees. They all agreed on a half-hour rotation for ergonomics.

Sensei: My concern in not how often they rotate. I am concerned that when they do rotate, the line stops for about four to five minutes. That is as much as 10 minutes every hour, nearly 20 percent lost time!

They watch the line a little longer and again the flow stops. This time it is because the shipping container is full and waiting for the material handler to remove it and bring an empty one.

Sensei: Why did the line stop?

Engineer: The container was full and they needed a new one. The only way you're going to prevent that is to have a material handler here full-time, and we don't have enough material handlers for that.

Sensei: (Sternly) There is always more than one way to solve any problem. I'm sure we can design a system for exchanging the containers in a way that does not stop the product flow and does not require a material handler here full-time. Right now, though, I am just trying to *understand* the true problem.

Here is how the causal chain appears to the engineer:

Problem: The robot breaks down.

Why? There is a run fault signal in Zone 3.

Why? The nut does not feed.

Why? The equipment is not designed correctly.

Where does this path lead? It leads to a dead end! It is a dead end that can consume large amounts of time and money attempting to correct a very challenging issue. In the meantime, the "low hanging fruit" is falling from the tree!

Examining a Problem in Reverse

Now let's look at the causal chain from the sensei's point of view. First, he begins with the problem as pointed out by the engineer, and using the "therefore" method, he proceeds back up the chain until he's sure he has found the true problem, as shown below. Note that we begin at the perceived problem line and continue to state "therefore" proceeding *upward* until the true problem is identified.

Therefore: The process can't meet demand without overtime. *This is the true problem.*

Therefore: Process doesn't make parts.

Therefore: The product flow stops.

Therefore: The line stops.

The robot breaks down. Start with the perceived problem and work up to find the true problem.

Once the true problem and resulting symptoms are identified, it's possible to compare the full implications of the true problem and consider the value of proceeding with the process of solving the problem. It is still necessary to define the extent of the problem and its characteristics.

Defining the Problem

In order to be defined as a "problem," four pieces of information are required:

1. The actual current performance with some historical trend detail.
2. The desired performance (standard or goal).
3. The magnitude of the problem as seen by the difference between the actual and desired (sometimes referred to as the "gap").
4. The extent and characteristics of the problem or situation.

When presenting this information, a picture is worth a thousand words. Always try to explain the situation visually with a trend graph (Figure 14-5). The trend graph should include enough historical data to show how long the condition has existed (for long-term performance improvement opportunities a minimum of six months is recommended if available). The data should be displayed so the characteristics of the problem are seen. For example, does the problem appear to be getting better, worse, or staying the same? This understanding assists in determining the importance of addressing this problem versus other problems. If the problem is getting worse, more immediate action may be necessary, such as a short-term countermeasure. If the situation is getting better or staying

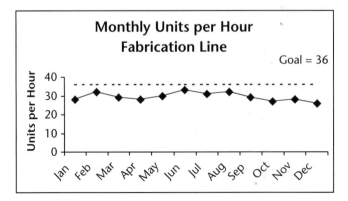

Figure 14-5. Trend chart of monthly units per hour

the same, the future results are more predictable (not likely to get worse) and the consequences of inaction (which is always a considered action) are understood.

The goal is to portray the situation so an accurate assessment is possible. This is best achieved using actual facts and not assumptions or "feelings." Be wary of data coupled with the words "I think" or " I feel"! The goal is to elevate problems and to get a clear understanding of their characteristics so we can understand what will be required to solve them and how difficult that will be. A problem that's stated in a way that makes it look better than it truly is does not help in the problem-solving process (Figure 14-9).

Also consider the stability of the problem. Are the results consistent day-to-day (or period-to- period), or are there large swings with varied good and bad results? Problems with a high degree of variation from period to period indicate a situation that is out of control. There are probably many contributing factors, and isolating the causes may be difficult. An intermittent problem is also harder to analyze because it does not occur consistently, and therefore seeing the problem firsthand is difficult and often requires an extended observation to identify the causes.

The charts in Figures 14-6 to 14-11 were generated using the Microsoft Excel charting function (primarily for ease of printing). Excel will automatically select scaling based on the high and the low data points and the variation. In most cases this scaling is effective for visually understanding the problem. Often the data is collected and charted manually (which is preferred by Toyota) and the scale is established incorrectly. The charts show some common situations encountered when charting data to develop a thorough understanding of the problem.

The chart in Figure 14-6 has an insufficient number of data points. In this example, it is not possible to get a clear understanding of the trend. Usually we need to see 6 to 12 months of history to gain a clear perspective of the trend of an issue. For the trend, a monthly summary (average) of results is preferred to show the higher-level, long-term direction of the problem.

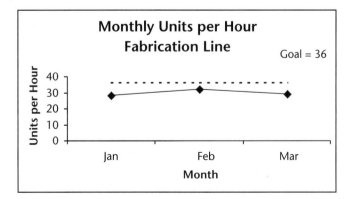

Figure 14-6. Chart with insufficient data points to see trend

Figure 14-7 shows the detail necessary to understand the daily characteristics of the problem. The performance of this fabrication process varies from day to day within a range. This process has not reached a level of stability, and the variation indicates the possibility of multiple issues contributing to the instability, thus representing a more challenging problem to solve.

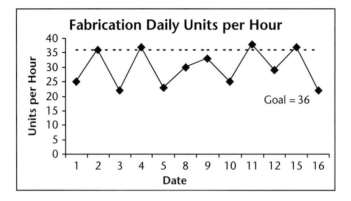

Figure 14-7. Chart with sufficient date points to see trend

Figure 14-8 shows the same data as Figure 14-7 but the variability of performance is artificially inflated due to a compressed scale on the chart. Visually, the problem appears larger than it truly is. It's important for a chart to have the correct visual impact so everyone has a clear understanding of the challenge ahead.

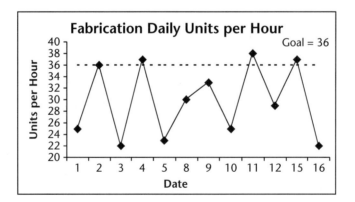

Figure 14-8. Chart with inflated appearance of variation due to scale

Figure 14-9 shows the same data as Figures 14-7 and 14-8. Notice how the variation is visually smoothed. This process appears more stable, and thus is misleading. An excessively large scale causes the artificial smoothing effect.

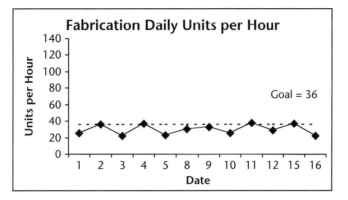

Figure 14-9. Chart with artificially smoothed variation due to scale

The chart in Figure 14-10 shows the effect of smoothing by averaging daily data on a weekly basis. The visual impact is lessened, and the daily variability inherent in this process will not be seen, thus giving a false sense of stability in the process.

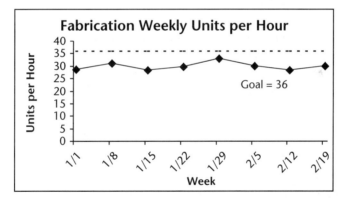

Figure 14-10. Chart with artificially smoothed variation by averaging

Collecting data is an important part of the philosophy of building a culture to stop and fix problems, as described in Chapter 8. The greatest benefit is gained by recognizing problems in "real time" and correcting them immediately. Data used to solve problems is interpreted from the perspective of long-term trends and resolving "systemic" issues.

Building a Strong Supporting Argument

As shown in the above examples, there will be symptoms that go along with problems. In the case of businesses, the symptoms will be reflected in confirming performance indicators. For example, an inability to meet customer demand will also be reflected in additional overtime, missed or late shipments, or increased backlog. These corresponding indicators provide supporting evidence of the validity of the problem and the merit of correcting it.

Toyota uses the corresponding indicators to support the process of focusing on the most important issues. Problems are evaluated to determine which require the most immediate attention using the following criteria:

- **Importance.** How important is the problem in the overall context of customer satisfaction, departmental, or company goals? Safety problems are automatically the highest-level importance.
- **Urgency.** What deadlines are dependent on the resolution of the problem, and what is the consequence if the deadline is not met? The ability to meet a change in a customer requirement deadline is considered a high urgency.
- **Tendency.** Is the problem getting worse, improving, or staying the same? When comparing problems it is necessary to consider whether every problem should be addressed.

By showing the effect of a specific problem on customer service, quality, safety, or cost, it is possible to develop a compelling argument to correct this specific problem versus other problems. This method of prioritization ensures that resources are focused appropriately on the most important and valuable problems.

Following safety concerns, problems that negatively affect the customer take precedence. This could include missed shipments, late shipments, and quality problems. Cost issues can easily be compared to ensure that the larger issues are being handled promptly. The Toyota Way necessitates building a strong rationale for attacking any problem. If a strong rationale has not been developed, the question "Why did you pick up this problem?" would surely be asked. The format for showing the supporting indicators is the same as the problem symptom model above.

A complete example of a problem statement is shown in Figure 14-11. Note that the summary statements, along with the graphs, are sufficient to thoroughly explain the problem situation and the corresponding issues. In this example the pictures tell the story and brief explanatory statements are used. Here, the true problem is the inability to meet the production requirement. As a result, overtime is used to *compensate* for the problem (increasing cost), and customer service is also declining. The problem with its supporting evidence allows us to "size up" this problem and determine the benefit if it is solved (and also determine a sensible investment to make in the solution that will provide a good return on the investment of time and expense).

Now that the problem and the effect of the problem on other performance indicators is thoroughly understood and a decision is made to correct the situation, it's time to develop a deeper understanding of the causes of the problem.

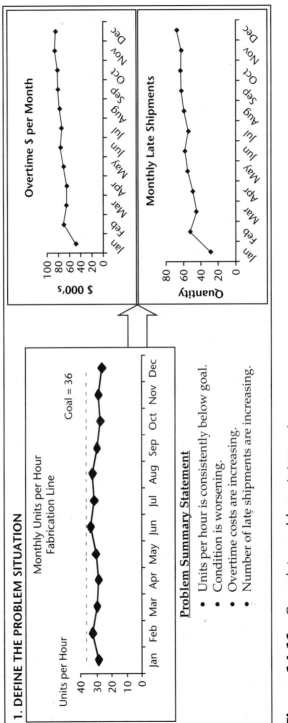

Figure 14-11. Complete problem statement

Reflect and Learn from the Process

Identify and select a problem you want to solve and use to reflect upon in Chapters 14 through 18. The problem should be significant, but not one of the most difficult problems you have. We suggest learning the problem-solving process on simpler issues before tackling more difficult ones.

1. Gather facts related to the problem and define the problem according to these criteria:
   a. Display the actual performance history (at least six months) in a line graph format.
   b. Show the goal or standard (current and/or in the future).
   c. Identify the gap between the actual performance and the goal.
2. Consider the information that you believe depicts your problem.
   a. Are you sure you have identified the "true problem"?
   b. Can you make a connection directly to a safety, quality, delivery, productivity, or cost performance measure?
3. Clarify the significance of solving this problem.
   a. Identify other issues related to this problem (items affected by this problem). Quantify them by graphing them.
   b. Can you verify that it is important to "pick up this problem"?
   c. Quantify the value of solving this problem (don't spend a dollar to solve a five-cent problem).
   d. Is it worth your time or the time of others to solve this problem?
   e. How much do you want to invest in solving this problem?
4. Based on your value quantification in the previous question, determine the most cost effective method to proceed with the problem.
   a. Will you "work the problem" personally?
   b. Will you delegate the problem to others and only follow up?
   c. Will this problem require a large team, small team, or a single individual to solve it?

Chapter 15

Complete a Thorough Root Cause Analysis

Toyota's corporate slogan is *"Yoi shina, yoi kangai,"* which means, "Good thinking, good products." This applies particularly well to the analysis portion of problem solving. Toyota places high value on the ability to think logically and creatively because a solid thinking process will produce the best results. Every Toyota manager understands, above all, the value of human creativity—that it is the single thing that will set them apart from their competition.

The analysis phase of problem solving should be an exploration into areas previously not understood. It's a bit of detective work, a bit of scientific experimentation, and an opportunity to discover new things. Analysis is the "Ah-ha" stage, the time to gather evidence, the time to repeatedly ask "Why?" and to find the source of an issue, its root. When the root causes are discovered, the "answers" to solve the problem become obvious. At this time "good thinking" will generate the best solutions—highly effective, simple yet elegant, and low cost, but not shoddy.

As Albert Einstein once said: "The important thing is not to stop questioning."

Principles of Effective Analysis

Effective analysis is crucial for finding and understanding the many potential causes of the problem. From those potential causes, it's necessary to narrow the field and focus on the most significant ones. Much of Toyota's great success stems from the ability to fully analyze a situation and understand the many causes of the problem beyond the most apparent. The following principles are a crucial part of the Toyota approach:

1. The analysis must not be clouded by preconceived ideas of the problem causes. If the cause is assumed, it will preclude a useful analysis and most likely lead to poor results.
2. Always follow the *genchi genbutsu* principle to verify the source of the problem. Do not depend on others, or on data, to find the cause. Use information to point toward the location to "go see." The point of cause must be observed firsthand.
3. Analysis is continued until it is certain that the true causes, or root causes, of the problem are discovered (using the "Five-Why" method).
4. In nearly all situations there are multiple causes for problems, and thus the analysis must be comprehensive. Toyota evaluates causes through the 4Ms: Man, Method, Material, and Machine.
5. Since there are many possible causes, it's necessary to narrow to the most significant ones. Narrowing allows the focusing of efforts to generate greater results.
6. During the analysis, the goal is to identify problem causes that can be corrected by the problem solver. This avoids the tendency to defer the problem to others and forces the question, "What can we do?"
7. A thorough and complete analysis will yield root causes that will clearly indicate specific, corrective actions. There is an observable and obvious trail leading from the problem to the causes and to the solutions.
8. Thorough and complete analysis provides factual data, allowing precise prediction of potential results when the causes are corrected. Determining the exact result is an important part of the process since it forces the evaluation of capability and effectiveness in examining a problem.

As with many aspects of the Toyota Way, the thought process is critical to success. Notice that during the following conversation, people will jump to preconceived conclusions rather than recognizing the simple but true answer to the question. Using the example in the problem statement below, we would begin the Five-Why process as follows:

Problem statement: "The fabrication units per hour is below goal."
Upon asking our group "Why?" we might get the following answers:

1. Because the machines break down.
2. Because operators are absent.
3. Because we run out of parts.
4. Because operators are not trained.
5. Because the setup times are long.

Each of these answers may be "true," as in the conversation between the engineer and the lean sensei described in chapter 14, but they are further down

TRAP

In many cases we see people attempting to force the Five-Why process into five boxes by trying to "figure out" the correct chain with five "answers." This process does not fit a predeveloped template format. The causal chain may branch at any level and yield unknown quantities of answers at each. If you are struggling to find Five Whys, most likely you're jumping across links in the chain. Take time to reflect on the simpler, more obvious answer in order to allow the discovery of all possibilities.

the Five Why chain. The first challenge is to focus solely on the direct question: "Why are the fabrication units per hour below goal?" Then the true answer would obviously be: "Because we do not make enough parts each hour." Knowing where to focus is crucial in order to train our minds to understand the *complete* chain. Skipping what appear to be obvious links in the chain will cause jumping to preconceived causes, thus overlooking other possibilities. This is one of the greatest risks and also the greatest challenges in thinking.

Proceeding with our questioning, we would ask, "Why don't we make enough parts each hour?" Again the tendency is to skip to the obvious answers, but by approaching this with a different thought process, we would see this answer: "Because we lose opportunities to make good parts." The production of any product is accomplished by utilizing the time of people and machinery, and available material. In this case there are only two main causes for a shortage of production—loss of time and loss of material (scrap). Note that this line of thinking also maintains a narrow focus that will isolate the most significant causes from the less significant ones. In the example above, the first question led immediately to a lengthy list. Once a long list is established, it's extremely difficult to narrow the focus. It is much easier to maintain a narrow focus and divide the possibilities gradually through effective questioning. At this point the Five Why chain would look like Figure 15-1.

Problem statement: **The fabrication units per hour is below goal.**

Why?
└──▶ We are not able to make enough parts each hour
    Why?
    └──▶ We are losing production opportunities
        Why?   Why?
        └──▶ Losing time   └──▶ Losing parts (scrap)

Figure 15-1. Initial Five-Why analysis

At this level the Five-Why chain has developed the first branch. Prior to asking "Why?" for both branches, it's important to understand which is the most significant. This understanding will maintain a narrower focus. For the sake of this demonstration, we will assume that the data show that scrap is very low and time is the greater loss, and proceed to show the continuation of the causal chain from this level. It is imperative to actually confirm the overall impact of each item, rather than to assume. The scrap quantity data may be available and fairly easy to quantify; however, the time losses will require a visit to the workplace (genchi genbutsu) to verify the amount of time loss.

When asking "Why?" do not jump down the chain to the deeper issues. Carefully consider the loss of time in a production process and try to keep the focus narrow by answering the direct question. Look for the broad categories under which the detailed answers will fall. Remember to use the "Therefore" method if you find yourself answering further down the chain. If the answer "Setup time is too long" arises, state "Therefore" and find the answer. In this situation it would be: "Therefore the machine is not running for a long time." The following step would be: "Therefore we are losing time." If the "Therefore" method was used on some of the other issues, it's likely that "The machine is not running" (or "The line is not running") would be a consistent theme. This is the common category we are looking for. In addition, our questioning may lead us to understand that loss of time due to excessive process cycle time is also a primary category. Now the Five-Why chain will appear as shown in Figure 15-2.

Again the causal chain is branching. At this time a visit to the workplace is absolutely necessary. In order to improve your observation ability you must learn to "look with intention." Based on the analysis thus far, what is the intention of your observation? The intention is to look to see whether there are cycle time losses or situations during which the process is not operating.

The general thinking within Toyota is to consider the cycle losses first. Cycle time losses are those losses that occur every cycle as the operation is performed;

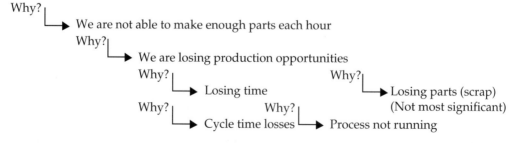

Problem statement: __The fabrication units per hour is below goal.__

Figure 15-2. Second pass Five-Why analysis

therefore, they have a "high tendency" of occurrence. The cumulative effect of these small losses can be very great. In addition, the reduction will generate an immediate and continuous payback. A small payback that can be captured immediately and will continue to pay forever is a preferred result. Small cycle time losses are also generally easy to correct. They may include excessive operator or machine motion, delays due to waiting, or overprocessing (doing more than necessary). Of course, these are all forms of *muda* (waste), and the removal of muda is a primary objective.

Visiting the workplace, you will probably see many other examples of cycle losses and process stoppages. You'll need to gather facts to understand the total impact of each issue—the importance, urgency, and tendency—and a simple way to do this is to use a value-added/non-value-added[1] breakdown list as shown in Figure 15-3. The example is from a sawing operation, but the list generated is fairly typical in most manufacturing operations. Remember, the links of the causal chain were related to losses of time, either through cycle losses or due to losses of time when the operation is not running or not adding value. The list that is generated will include both cycle and run-time losses. Since the ultimate objective is to find causes that are linked through the causal chain to the original problem, we're looking only for those activities that take time away from the value-adding task. In other words, if the operator is performing a non-value-adding task but the machine is adding value while the operator does the task, improving this item will not lead to reducing the problem, and thus is not a beneficial improvement. The first priority is to address the issues that directly reduce the time available to add value and therefore cause a loss of production.

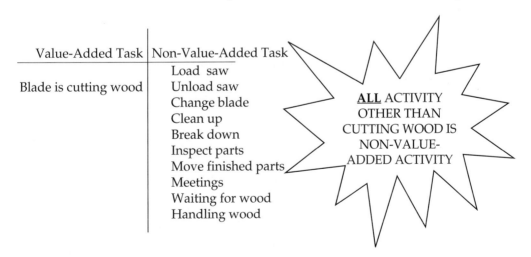

Figure 15-3. Value-added/Non-value-added analysis

For further information on the case see: Bill Costantino, "Cedar Works: Making the Transition to Lean," in J.K. Liker (ed.), *Becoming Lean*, Productivity Press, 1997.

Continuing with the causal analysis (Five-Why) process in this example revealed the chain in Figure 15-4. Follow the bold text chain to the root cause in the outlined box.

Toyota uses this process of continually narrowing, isolating (using the 80/20 rule), and focusing efforts on the items that will provide the greatest benefit. Continuing to dig until the root causes are discovered also provides causes that are both easier to improve and, when improved, will solve the original problem. We can think of it as a funnel as shown in Figure 15-5.

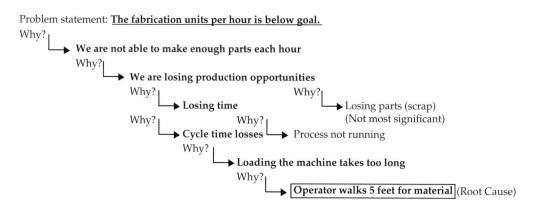

Figure 15-4. Final pass Five-Why analysis

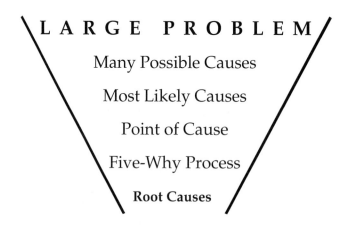

Figure 15-5. The narrowing and focusing process

Seeking Problem Causes That Are Solvable

During any process of analysis there will be a tendency to jump to predetermined causes. Predetermined conclusions are often based on issues that are not within the ability or responsibility of the person developing them. A critical thought process of the Toyota Way is the assumption of finding causes that are in the direct control of the problem solver. In any problem analysis it is always possible to find causes that originate outside the control of the problem solver. For instance, it's common to find fault with a supplier of material, or with a support group such as maintenance, or engineering (this is jokingly referred to as the "Five Who's" and the objective is to find "root blame" rather than root causes). Also, there is a tendency to accept certain causes as "the way it is," and therefore preclude the possibility of change. The following example demonstrates this phenomenon.

During the analysis of the sawing operation shown in Figure 15-3, it was determined that clean-up time was resulting in loss of production. The saws operated for three shifts, and each shift was assigned 30 minutes to clean up, resulting in a loss of 90 minutes per day. Following the Five-Why chain in Figure 15-2 above it is apparent that the operation is experiencing problems meeting the daily production requirement. There are lost time opportunities, and therefore the goal would be to capture the lost opportunities. The causal chain would appear as shown in Figure 15-6.

The cleaning activity is the "point of cause." Finding the point of cause will provide both the time and place that the problem occurs. At this stage the root causes have not been determined, and the "Why?" questioning continues.

The leader asks: "Why do we clean up?" to find the root causes.
Likely responses will be:

"It helps safety."

"It makes the work area look better."

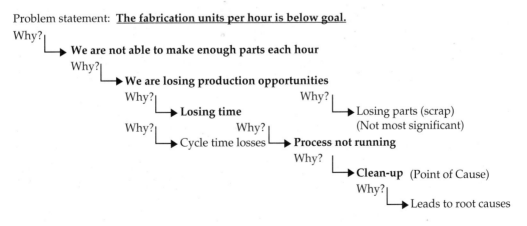

Figure 15-6. Identifying point of cause

"We like to work in a clean environment."

"Because the boss said we need to."

"It helps the quality of the product."

"It is part of our 5S program."

Each of these answers is true and valid, but tend to indicate issues that cannot be challenged: "good reasons," and therefore "the way it needs to be." Who could argue, for instance, that a clean workplace will provide a safer environment? Who would challenge the boss's request? But none of these answers support the effort to resolve the problem! They're a dead end. They presume lack of ability and responsibility for improvement. The answer to the question "Why?" *must* be related to the goal of capturing lost time opportunities and must be solvable.

Think about the issue in terms of the goal of reducing the time required for cleaning. The current loss of time is 90 minutes per day. What would the possible benefit be if the total time could be reduced to 45 minutes per day—a reduction of 50 percent? It is very simple to calculate the additional production possible with 45 extra minutes of production time available. It is possible to set a goal of reducing the total cleaning time by 50 percent and establishing a new production target. This is a key point of the analysis—the result *must* be quantifiable, and there must be a clear understanding of the impact of the cause on the problem, which is the goal.

Notice what happens when the answer to the question "Why do we clean up?" is changed to "Because it gets dirty." Continuing to ask "Why does it get dirty?" at this level would begin to yield the root causes. The objective is to reduce the time spent cleaning, so the perspective must be that of preventing the dirt, or minimizing its impact, thereby reducing the cleaning time required and enhancing the time to produce the product. A visit to the work area to see first hand how and where the dirt is generated will provide a clear understanding. Is the dirt being contained effectively? Does it leak from equipment? Identify areas that accumulate dirt: Is it possible to keep the debris from accumulating? Certain areas, such as under machines and tables, may be enclosed to prevent the accumulation. Observe the method of cleaning: Is it effective? Could the method be improved to reduce cleaning time? So you can see how the answer "Because it gets dirty" provides a perspective that yields numerous possibilities for improvement.

When the true point of cause is understood by following the genchi genbutsu method, many opportunities will surface that are well within the control of the problem solver and produce great results. Careful consideration of the causes, and by answering "Why?" in a way that will produce answers within the control of the problem solver, will generate tremendous opportunities.

Distill Root Cause Analysis to Simplest Terms

Note that any problem has many possible causes, and therefore many root causes. Attempting to list them all using the Five-Why causal chain would be tedious and time consuming. Though it's important to understand the thought process and the flow-through to the root cause level, for the sake of focusing efforts, it's better to return to the beginning and place real values on each cause along the chain, effectively isolating the most significant issues and providing tangible data that will indicate the degree of improvement possible.

A key to the Toyota process is the ability to be extremely concise in presenting massive amounts of information. Employees can then cut through the information available and communicate simply and clearly in a way that is understood by everyone. The Toyota Way forces the distillation of the information to only the most relevant details. It is always an important part of the process to review information with superiors, subordinates, and peers so guidance and support may be given. Providing reams of information that have to be interpreted or read by many individuals is considered a disservice to the readers. Imagine the waste if 10 or 20 people each had to read all the information and sift through the data to reach the appropriate conclusions!

A Picture Is Worth a Thousand Words

To be concise with the information, the analysis of the problem should be depicted graphically. This is aligned with the "visual workplace" philosophy of Toyota. To explain the loss of production capability, see the analysis depicted in the bar chart in Figure 15-7. In this situation the planned capacity would be the output if the process were operated 100 percent of the time. This may not include the hidden opportunity in cycle or scrap losses, but it captures the basic idea that losses are occurring.

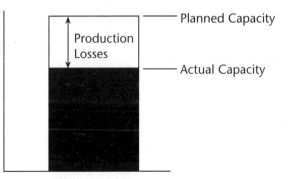

Figure 15-7. Bar chart depicting production losses

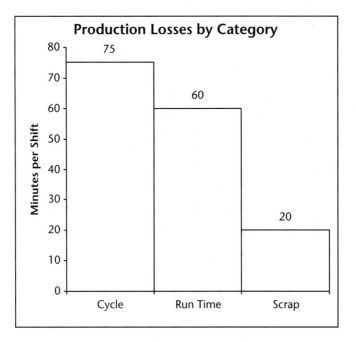

Figure 15-8. Rank order chart of production losses by category

As shown in the causal chain in Figure 15-2 above, the causes for production losses are time losses and scrap losses. This results in multiple causes, and thus a branching of the causal chain. Visually this is depicted with a rank order chart as shown in Figure 15-8.

This rank ordering analysis shows that cycle losses have the largest potential for reduction in lost opportunity. A visit to the production area for a firsthand look (*gemba*), and a brief work method analysis (utilizing the standardized work process described in Chapter 6), would reveal the basic steps of the job:

1. Pick up material (walk to machine).
2. Load machine.
3. Start cycle (walk to start button).
4. Perform inspection (walk back to inspection area).
5. Place finished part in bin (walk to bin).
6. Unload machine (walk to machine).
7. Return to start of work cycle (walk to material).

Maintaining the pattern of graphically depicting this information, the work element times are presented in a stack chart format (also called a *yamazumi* chart) in Figure 15-9.

In addition to the time required for each element, it's useful to understand the problem visually by depicting the flow of work (Figure 15-10). This pictorial flow is captured on the Standardized Work Sheet (Chapter 6).

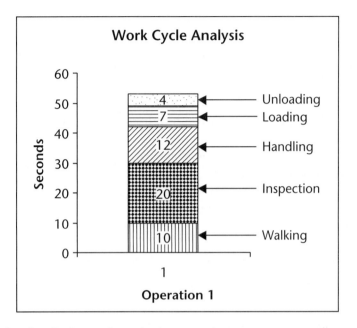

Figure 15-9. Stack chart of work element times

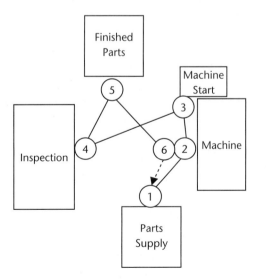

Figure 15-10. Visual depiction of work flow

Putting It All Together: The A3 One-Page Report

The analysis phase is typically where most of the problem-solving time is spent. The primary purpose of the analysis is to understand the causal relationships and to find enough causes that, when corrected, will yield an improvement sufficient to solve the problem. It is important to convey the basic findings in a way that clearly solves the problem. One method of doing this is to present them on an "A3," the name Toyota uses to describe the single-page presentation of problem-solving activities (A3 is the European designation for an 11-by-17-inch sheet of paper).

Depicting the entire process on a single sheet of paper requires concise information. Obviously, every aspect of the problem discovered during analysis could not be explained on one sheet of paper; the causal chain alone would typically fill more than one sheet of paper. Figure 15-11 shows a completed Analysis section on the A3. This would follow the problem statement shown above. (For a detailed view of the A3 report-writing process, see Chapter 18).

Dig Deeply into Possible Causes

As mentioned earlier, the problem-solving process within Toyota is a collaborative activity. Initially, the question "Why did you pick up this problem?" was used to build consensus on the need for solving the problem, as well as to ensure a clear, shared understanding. Upon completion of the analysis, the collaboration between the problem solver, the superior, and the team includes a review to make sure that all aspects of the problem were considered. During this review a common question is, "Did you consider this item?" or "What led you to that conclusion?" Questioning is especially prevalent if obvious links in the causal chain have been skipped. Often the problem solver returns to the analysis to consider additional possibilities. Toyota managers intuitively understand the importance of carefully and completely analyzing a problem before leaping into potentially fruitless "corrective" activities.

Completion of the analysis phase should provide a clear grasp of the myriad possible causes, a narrowing to root causes, and clear understanding of necessary solutions, including specific details relating to the proposed benefits of implementation.

Here's a review of the key concepts covered in this section:

- ◆ Analyze each issue with a fresh perspective and follow the genchi genbutsu principle of going to the actual work area and looking for yourself.
- ◆ Approach analysis with the intention of finding causes that can be corrected by the problem solver.

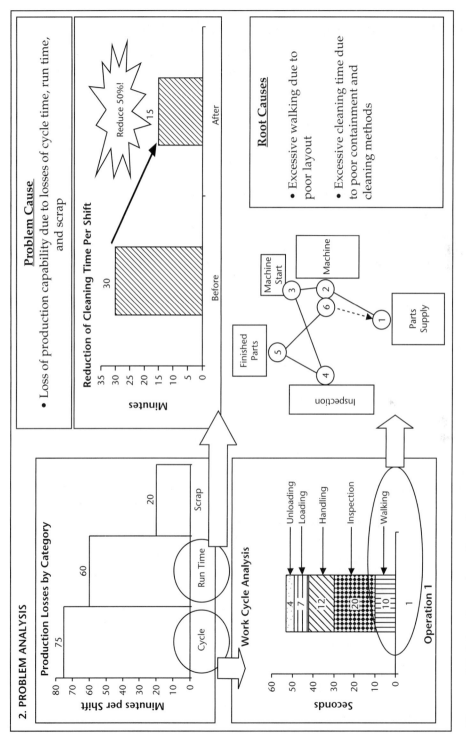

Figure 15-11. Completed analysis section of an A3 report

♦ Continually narrow to the most significant causes, and refocus the analysis accordingly.

♦ Determination of root causes should provide a clear and obvious understanding of the necessary solutions.

♦ Analysis should be fact and data based. The root causes should be quantifiable, and the effect of improvement should be predictable in advance of implementation.

Reflection Activities

Following the problem you identified in the "Reflect and Learn from the Process" section of the last chapter (remember, we told you to keep it in mind?) complete the following activities:

1. Make a list of possible causes for the problem, then narrow it to the three "most likely" causes.

2. Select one of these three causes and investigate further to determine if this is an actual cause that will lead to the "root cause(s)." Determination of root causes is the most important element in the problem-solving process. Make sure your analysis is thorough and complete prior to proceeding to the corrective actions.

   a. Go to the area where the problem occurs to see it firsthand.

   b. Observe the situation and use the Five-Why method to follow the likely cause through to the root cause. The answer to each "Why?" should be based on factual information that is seen firsthand. Do not do this based on "speculation."

   c. Use the "Therefore" method to track back to the problem statement to verify the accuracy of your logic.

   d. Is it possible to *prove* a connection between the problem, the most likely cause, and the root cause(s)? (If you can make the problem occur, or stop at will, you've proven a root cause.)

3. Locate the "point of cause" (the actual location where the root cause occurs and the problem originates).

   a. Many large problems have several root causes and thus several points of cause. Identify the three most significant ones.

   b. Keep evaluating until you find the actual point(s) of cause (you can see the problem occur).

4. Avoid the temptation to identify solutions until you have identified and confirmed the root cause(s) of the problem.
   a. Thoroughly test your conclusions and prove the root causes.
   b. Confirm that controlling the root causes will actually resolve the problem.

Consider Alternative Solutions While Building Consensus

Just as there are many potential causes and root causes for any problem, there is *always* more than one way to solve *any* problem! The creativity of the problem solver is an important aspect of the Toyota Way of thinking, so there are few absolutes regarding the best approach; however, there are some key concepts to guide the evaluation process. The typical process would include:

1. Broadly consider all possibilities.
2. Narrow the list by eliminating impractical solutions or combining similar items.
3. Evaluate based on simplicity, cost, area of control, and the ability to implement quickly.
4. Develop consensus on the proposed solution.
5. Test ideas for effectiveness.
6. Select the best solution.

Broadly Consider All Possibilities

Many a young engineer at Toyota has worked very hard to detail a solution with great pride. He or she shows the solution to his boss or mentor with great enthusiasm and a bit of trepidation, since the mentor is an expert in the field and will find some weakness in the proposal. The mentor barely bothers to go through the solution and supporting documentation but instead asks if that is the only solution considered. The young engineer explains that the documentation supports the conclusion that this is a good solution. "But could there not be even better solutions?" the mentor asks. So it's back to the drawing board to identify other potential solutions. The mentor may in fact think it is a perfectly good solution. What he or she is trying to teach is a way of thinking.

The Toyota Way documented the case of the Prius development. With intense pressure to get out this first production hybrid vehicle on an unreasonably short timeline, the chief engineer still decided to explore many possible solutions. Chief Engineer Uchiyamada asked the engine group to identify all viable hybrid engines, a total of 80, which were winnowed down to 10, and then four that were simulated on a computer before one was finally selected. Similarly, when selecting the styling for the vehicle, he held a competition among four Toyota design studios in Toyota City, Tokyo, Paris, and Calty, California, generating 20 alternative designs and then five detailed sketches, four full-size clay models, and then two exceptional designs. Those two designs were thoroughly evaluated, and the contributing studios in California and Japan were asked to make an additional round of improvements before the California design finally won.

There are many ways to generate a list of alternatives, including the use of competing groups in developing the Prius. And one useful technique for a group of people involved in a project is "brainstorming." Many companies tried it when they experimented with the "team concept," but it was viewed as only part of team activities and eventually fell out of favor. In fact, brainstorming is useful in ensuring the thorough evaluation of a subject. The failing of brainstorming is often that the problem was not well analyzed to begin with, and the process of evaluating solutions and narrowing down to a preferred solution is not well understood.

TRAP

STOP Be wary of comments such as, "There is only one way to solve this problem." In one case this comment, followed by an explanation of the proposed solution—at a cost of $10,000—led to further evaluation, and an effective solution with a cost of $200 (and savings of $80,000 per year) was implemented. There will *always* be more than one solution for every problem!

Simplicity, Cost, Area of Control, and the Ability to Implement Quickly

An evaluation whose criteria are simplicity, cost, area of control, and the ability to implement quickly will ensure implementation of the most cost effective solutions. But first, ideas that won't effectively work as countermeasures should be removed from consideration.

During the brainstorming process, many wacky or impractical ideas may be presented. This is true by design since a rule of brainstorming is that "there is no bad idea" and ideas suggested should not be evaluated until the brainstorming is complete. While a quantity of thought-provoking ideas is desirable during the brainstorming session, not every idea deserves consideration as a viable solution. Those ideas that don't should be removed from the list by either eliminating them outright or combining similar concepts into a common one. A short list of ideas can then be evaluated.

Our four criteria can now be put to use in evaluating this short list of solutions that can possibly solve the problem:

1. Is it within your control to implement? (Can you do it without outside support?)
2. Is it possible to implement the solution quickly? (Today is best.)
3. Is the solution a simple and effective one?
4. Is the solution low cost, or even better, no cost?

Each of these evaluation criteria is interdependent, and it's usually not possible to meet one without meeting the others. For example, a solution may be identified that involves purchasing a new machine ("If we had that machine, we could make more parts"). This solution would violate four of the criteria. It's unlikely that the purchase of new equipment is entirely within your control. Even if it were, the solution could not be implemented quickly and it's certainly not low cost or simple to do.

If the evaluation criteria are utilized, a pattern of certain types of solutions will begin to emerge. The types of solutions often considered first at Toyota are methodology changes. It is easy to change the method of work. Simply ask the worker to change the way the work is done. The control of work methods is generally within the direct supervisor's realm. The cost of changing work methods is minimal—it may require a new table, tool, fixture, etc.—and it can be changed immediately!

TIP

There is a tendency toward "fancy" or "high-tech" solutions to problems. Invariably the latest technology or machine is suggested. In rare cases the technology is needed; however, while waiting for the "ultimate" solution, consider a short-term improvement that can be implemented immediately.

TIP

Do not solve a five-cent problem with a one-dollar solution. (This is the fastest way to go out of business!) The advantage of solutions that are simple and low cost is that less significant causes (of which there are many) can be corrected in a cost effective manner. This improves the return on investment (ROI). It is better to spend five cents on a one-dollar problem!

TRAP

STOP

Solutions that require follow-up or input from others will extend the time before a benefit can be captured. In many cases solutions of this nature will require several weeks before a conclusion is reached. Always challenge the problem solver to implement an immediate improvement, while the ultimate solution is in progress.

Develop Consensus

Using the above four evaluation criteria will considerably narrow the list of possible solutions. It will make it easier to develop consensus on the best possible solution because of fewer choices, and personal bias and subjectivity that might influence the choice of the best solutions are removed. Now, if the choice is narrowed to two or three possibilities and it's not possible to reach consensus on one of them, proceed to the next step: Test each idea to prove its effectiveness so the merits and demerits of each will be apparent. In most cases, testing will reduce the possible solutions to the best one, making it easier to reach consensus.

It should be noted that "consensus" does not imply complete *agreement* with the proposed solution. We often hear managers discussing the difficulty of getting employees to "buy in" to the changes. This is a misguided belief that it's necessary for everyone to agree and want the change. In fact, consensus means that everyone agrees to *accept* the proposed solution, even if they don't believe it's the best one. Any disagreements regarding "my way" versus "your way" are easily resolved by agreeing to try both methods and then let everyone see "the best." There are a few exceptions where a clear winner is not obvious, in which case a vote or similar method can be used to determine the preferred choice.

The model of continuous improvement suggests that all things will continue to evolve, so any idea implemented today may be changed tomorrow. Generally, if the process has been followed carefully and everyone clearly understands the root cause, reaching agreement on a proposed solution is relatively simple. Consensus is gained at each step of the process, and by this stage most people are "on board" with the solutions and ready to implement them!

Test Ideas for Effectiveness

It's important to verify the effectiveness of the planned solution before implementing it. This is done prior to developing an implementation plan. There is little to gain from pursuing a solution that has little likelihood of success. Toyota's ability to create significant results is largely dependent on the certainty of those results, *prior* to beginning any implementation.

How does Toyota prove an idea without actually implementing it? Following the scientific method, an experiment is designed, allowing the effect of implementation to be simulated. This simulation is "real world," occurring in the workplace whenever possible. When it's not practical to test in the real world (such as machinery movement), a cardboard or even wood mock-up of the work area is used to verify the idea.

For example, take the following root cause: "Excess walking due to poor layout." For a simulation technique, the implementer can "assume the waste," with a team member presenting material to the operator "as if" it were already relocated. In this way the operator can perform the work with the waste temporarily removed. The team member can also experiment with the most effective material placement by holding the material in different positions. This allows the operator and the team member to see firsthand the most effective presentation, and it aids in the design of material presentation devices such as carts, flow racks, chutes, etc. The operator can provide direct feedback, and the team member can experience the pluses and the minuses of any method.

The operator work flow during the simulation is diagrammed in Figure 16-1. The dashed lines represent the steps of the team member who will return to the parts supply to retrieve the next part and present it to the operator at Step 1, demonstrating the effect of improved material placement. This will shorten the operator's walking time, and the resulting reduction in cycle time can easily be measured with a stopwatch.

Further tests can be conducted to demonstrate the effects of relocating the inspection process and the finished parts container. Completion of the improved work flow is shown in Figure 16-2.

It is important during a simulation to respect the needs of the person doing the work. The simulation must be accomplished without disrupting the work process or stopping the operation. It is the implementer's responsibility to be aware of the situation and stop any testing if it's having a negative impact on the operator. Of course, safety is always the first consideration, and the implementer

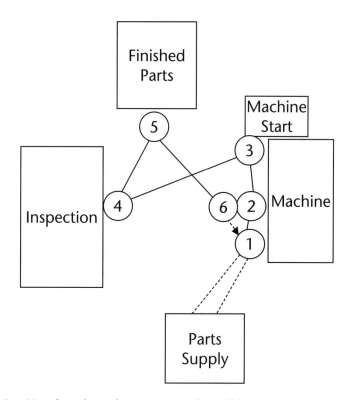

Figure 16-1. Simulated work pattern with walking removed

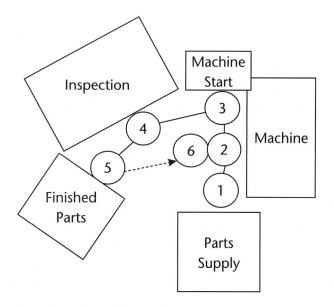

Figure 16-2. Completed work layout

must observe any changes for possible safety issues, including negative ergonomic impact.

After the basic idea has been tested and necessary adjustments made, full implementation is possible. If the solution was tested effectively, the need for further adjustments will be minimized.

Select the Best Solution

Based on the simulation, the best option among the solutions is selected and the implementation scheduled. Occasionally, an idea is tested, and it is then discovered that the idea is impractical or difficult to sustain. Discovering this during the testing stage provides the implementer with firsthand understanding of the shortcoming in thinking. (Note that Toyota would not say that an idea is "bad," but that the thinking was not complete.) The operator also sees that the implementer recognizes the shortcoming and therefore does not need to worry that an ineffective solution will be proposed (and that they will be stuck with the faulty solution). Returning to the list of possible solutions will generally provide an alternative possibility, which also must be tested and proven.

Define the Right Problem and the Solution Will Follow

You may notice that this chapter is relatively short in comparison to the previous two chapters. This parallels the reality that the bulk of the problem-solving effort is in defining a problem and analyzing it to find the root causes. If the root causes are found, the answer is often obvious and easy to understand. The greatest challenges in this stage of evaluation are keeping the solutions related to the problem at hand, focusing on the issues that are within the control and responsibility of the individual or team, and identifying simple solutions that can be done quickly (today is always best!). The leader must continually redirect the effort and ensure that it stays on track. He or she must challenge people to think creatively and explore alternatives with questions such as "Why did you select this solution?" and "What other alternatives did you explore?"

Toyota managers have mastered the problem-solving methodology and have an exceptional success rate. Careful analysis based on facts allows them to determine the benefits prior to actual implementation, and testing and verification of possible solutions allows them to completely understand the effectiveness before choosing the best options. They continually aim, aim, aim, to make certain that the target will be hit—a dead bull's-eye!

Reflection Activities

1. Present at least two potential solutions for each root cause you identified in the previous chapter. Review your proposals with others, and double the possible solutions (to at least four) for each root cause. This may challenge your thinking, but don't give up until the list is doubled.

2. Using a matrix to evaluate each solution, rank them based on the following criteria:
    a. Is the proposed solution within your control to implement?
    b. Is it simple (preferably a method change)?
    c. Is it possible to implement the proposed solution quickly?
    d. Which of the proposed solutions can be implemented for the least cost?

3. Without actual implementation, develop a method to test each viable solution that met the above criteria.
    a. Do any of the proposals need to be modified to more effectively correct the root cause?
    b. What method will be used to verify the effectiveness of each proposal?
    c. Quantify the potential benefit versus the cost for each solution.

Chapter 17

Plan-Do-Check-Act

WE HAVE FINALLY reached the implementation phase! Many people are so anxious to "get busy" with implementation that they shortcut the previous portions of the process. This is a critical mistake! Without a clearly defined problem, how would you know what you're trying to improve and how much you'll need to do to reach the goal? You would be firing at a target that does not exist. Without a thorough analysis, how would you know which target to shoot at? You'd see many targets (potential problems and causes) and even hit some of them. But would you achieve the desired result if you shot at the wrong target? Not likely. You would "fix" some things and know that you've done "good things," but the important performance indicators would not show improvement. To avoid this frustrating situation, fully complete the problem definition and root cause analysis phases before moving into implementation.

But take heart. You will actually get to implementation! In fact for some simple problems, the entire process of thinking through the problem and its causes and coming up with a solution could be done in a single short meeting. Once you are convinced you have done a good job to this point in reaching a good solution to the right problem, there is still a bit of work to do before you charge off and move stuff around, build racks, or whatever. The famous Shewhart cycle of plan-do-check-act suggests you should start with a plan. In fact, all of the work up to this point is part of the planning. But there is still the step of developing an action plan.

Plan: Develop an Action Plan

There are numerous tools and techniques to assist in the development of an action plan, including scads of project management software. Except in the case of the most complex problems, many of those tools are overkill. A common theme within the Toyota Way is that the method or tool is not as important as the thought process and the skill of the user. The development of an action plan follows this same theme. The most important objective is to develop consistent understanding of and alignment to the plan. Resources will surely be wasted and results minimized if the plan is unclear or if everyone is not aligned to the task.

Within Toyota the term "countermeasure" is used to describe the proposed solution. Toyota's philosophy is that problems are never truly "solved." The countermeasure merely mitigates the effect of the problem. Countermeasures are divided into two groups:

1. Short-term countermeasures
2. Long-term countermeasures

It's generally understood within Toyota that most countermeasures will be implemented quickly (within a week), and therefore the definition of short term, and long term refers to the overall *permanency* of the countermeasure. The primary understanding is that a short-term countermeasure refers to one that is temporary, a "Band-Aid" that will provide temporary relief until a more effective or extensive solution can be implemented. In some circumstances the temporary solution becomes permanent if a more effective solution is not found. The idea is to always consider an *immediate* action that will provide instant improvement of the problem situation.

In the case of a quality problem, for example, if the root cause is determined to be a tooling issue, and the tooling needs extensive modification to correct the issue (a long-term countermeasure), short-term countermeasures would be utilized to both reduce the creation of defects and ensure that any resulting defects are not passed to the next process (in-station process controls and error proofing—*poka yoke*). In the sawing example from chapter 15 where production output was a problem and cleaning time was an important cause, a short-term temporary countermeasure was implemented to minimize lost production time due to cleaning. Temporary workers were assigned to clean during planned line stop times such as breaks and lunch. This could be done immediately, and the benefits collected, while waiting for implementation of permanent long-term countermeasures.

Effective use of both short-term and long-term countermeasures provides Toyota with immediate benefits, and at least minimal relief from the symptoms (like an aspirin), while the "ultimate" solutions are implemented. In many cases the ultimate solution is difficult, or not possible given current capability (such as the robot failure discussed in chapter 14); much time can be wasted, and benefits lost, while waiting for an "ultimate" solution. Toyota places extremely high importance on protecting the customer (the next process in the flow) from any problem. This concept makes the implementation of short-term countermeasures critical.

Long-term countermeasures are intended to permanently eliminate the root causes. Implementation timing may extend beyond a week, or beyond months. In these cases it is best to divide the task into smaller increments. This provides two benefits:

1. Smaller, bite-sized tasks provide a smaller check frequency interval. Progress toward completion can be more closely monitored and assistance provided if the task falls behind schedule.
2. The idea's effectiveness may be tested after a small portion is completed rather than waiting until the entire process is completed and then determining that the idea was flawed.

For example, a proposal to implement a material replenishment kanban process for 2,000 individual parts is a major undertaking. The total time required may be two to three months. The team needs to analyze and determine specific design parameters regarding reorder points, container sizes, and the number of kanban required in the system. If the team analyzes all 2,000 items prior to actual implementation of physical kanban, they may discover flaws in their rationale. This discovery would occur very late in the implementation process, and many hours would be lost. In addition, no benefit would be achieved during the two- to three-month period. Essentially this is the result of "batching" the implementation instead of breaking it into a small batch flow.

Dividing the task into 25-percent segments, beginning with the 25 percent most commonly used parts (to get the greatest benefit first), would allow the team to verify their process, ensure desired results, *and* gain partial benefit earlier in the process. The team could provide feedback on their activity after three weeks, an intermediate check to verify that the entire task will be completed as scheduled (with additional feedback after six and nine weeks). Following these

---

TIP

Dividing long-term countermeasures into smaller increments is essentially the concept of *heijunka*, or leveling, applied to problem solving. In production operations the larger time frame—say one month—is first divided into smaller daily increments (usually per shift). This daily requirement is segmented further into an hourly requirement, and the production result is verified each hour. In this way, adjustments can be made throughout the day, based on the checking frequency (hourly), to ensure the successful completion of the task at the end of the period (first the day, then the month). Utilization of this leveling principle for problem solving greatly increases the likelihood of producing the desired results.

guidelines ensures Toyota immediate returns on activities, as well as verification of success for the long term.

At its core, a "plan" details what, who, when, where, and, if necessary, the how. Begin with the short-term countermeasures. Identify actions that will mitigate the effects of the problem (i.e., control the occurrence). Identify actions that will ensure that the effects of the problem do not affect others outside the area, especially customers.

Identify the person (not group) who will have responsibility for ensuring the successful completion of the countermeasure. The responsible person does not have to actually implement the action, but does have the responsibility and accountability to explain the plan, coordinate efforts, schedule additional resources, verify completion according to plan, and provide updates of progress.

TRAP

STOP

In many cases there's confusion between responsibility for making sure the countermeasure is completed successfully and responsibility for actually doing the work. More complex issues tend to be assigned to "the team" rather than to a specific individual, because of the perception that the implementation will require additional people, or that the entire group wants input or involvement. This leads to lack of individual responsibility, vague expectations, and limited results. Always identify a specific person willing to take the lead role. Others may be assigned as support if necessary, but the leader assumes responsibility. At Toyota, it is always clear which one person is responsible for results. That is the essence of accountability.

Note that in some cases the implementation of countermeasures should be "phased," or sequential. When attacking the root cause of a quality problem, for example, simultaneous implementation of multiple countermeasures makes it difficult to understand the effectiveness of each individual countermeasure. This "shotgun" approach may lead to success, but there won't be a clear understanding of *how* the success was achieved. In the scientific method, if an experiment is conducted but the results are not repeatable, no effective conclusion can be drawn. In this case the result cannot be reliably duplicated, and future problem-solving activities will be less effective because how the result was achieved is not known.

The action plan (from chapter 15 wood sawing clean up case) summary is presented in Figure 17-1. Note that this is not a completely detailed plan, with actions and responsibilities developed for the team. But this level of detail is not important

Action Item	Short-Term Long-Term	Person Responsible	Schedule			
			Week 1	Week 2	Week 3	Week 4
Temporary cleaning during breaks and lunch	ST	M. Scarpello	△			
Tape boxes to machine to collect dirt	ST	D. Danis	△			
Reduce walk time- relocate material and inspection	LT	D. Spiess	O–△			
Repostion start button	LT	M. Kissel	O——△			
Build skirt around tables to reduce cleaning	LT	M. Nicholson	O——△			
Add dust collection bin to machine	LT	P. Kenrick	O——X	△		
Modify 4 machines to catch dirt (1 per week)	LT	B. Costantino	O——X	X	X	△
		Key: Start O	Finish △		Progress Check	X

Figure 17-1. Summary action plan

for others reviewing the activity. The general idea is that if the desired results have been achieved, the action plan and its execution must have been good, and understanding every detail is not necessary. (There is no need to verify the thinking process if the desired results have been achieved.)

Do: Implement Solutions

Finally you can do something. You have arrived near the finish line. But you still may not be finished. It is common to implement a solution and then find, upon completion, an additional opportunity for improvement. This phenomenon occurs because it's not always possible to see further possibilities until initial steps are taken. Imagine yourself looking at a staircase. If you look straight ahead, it's only possible to see the step right in front of you (straight ahead). If you step up one stair, your view now changes to the next level as well. This continual climbing and revealing of the next step is the process of continuous improvement (see Figure 20-8).

Given this phenomenon, and the perpetual nature of continuous improvement, one might ask, "When is a project complete?" The answer lies in the successful achievement of the goal as established in the problem statement. If the problem is solved (as defined), the activity is officially completed. Toyota, however, will continue to make small improvements by actively pursuing all issues, at all levels, all the time (described in Chapter 13). The responsibility for sustaining the results would be passed to the people responsible for the work area.

At times the solution to one problem will "create" a lesser problem, requiring a modification. The implementer must continue to observe, and to correct until the process performs as planned.

Check: Verify Results

If you've tested your ideas as part of the selection of solutions, you have already confirmed the effectiveness, and verification of improvement has already been done. It is only necessary to collect actual process data after the change and chart it in the same way you charted the problem. It should be evident that if results are going to be presented, it's necessary to have a baseline for comparison to verify improvement. It is surprising to discover that in many cases data *prior* to "improvement" is not available! How is it possible to verify improvement if there is no point of comparison? Generally, this is due to the eagerness to rush off and solve the "problem" without fully understanding the extent. (Without data, the severity of the situation is only a subjective "feeling.")

There are two levels of results: those directly related to the root cause being addressed and those that affect the original problem. If the root causes discovered are part of the correct causal chain, an improvement in results at the root cause level should travel up the chain using the "Therefore" method and result in improvement of the original problem, as shown in Figure 17-2.

TRAP

STOP

If the process has been followed correctly, the solutions implemented will produce the desired results. Do not include "results" that are not related to the problem. For example, a discussion of improvements to the area lighting would not be relevant to the problem of not meeting the production requirement. The results presented must be directly related to the stated problem and the corresponding indicators.

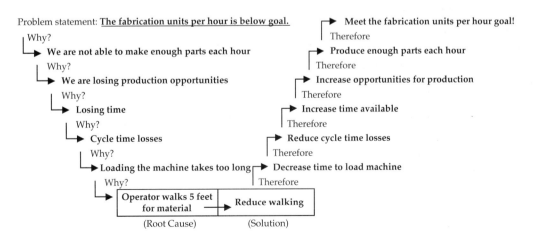

Figure 17-2. Showing the entire causal chain

The focus of the results verification should be on the high-level problems defined in the problem statement. While addressing these specific problems, unrelated benefits may be achieved. For example, the changes to the work area above will result in the reduction of floor space required. This was not a primary objective, but it provides a potential benefit that may be utilized at a later date.

Figure 17-3 shows a completed results summary.

TIP

When depicting results it is important to begin a new graph that will normally begin after you have completed analysis of the current situation. Do not simply add data to the existing problem statement graph. The dates on the graphs in the results summary section begin after the *end* of the Problem Statement section graphs. For example, in our situation the problem was "picked up" in December 2004 so the problem statement graph shows the problem up through December. The results were tracked beginning in February 2005. Of course, you will want to show a trend from before implementation through to implementation and then beyond to show sustained improvement.

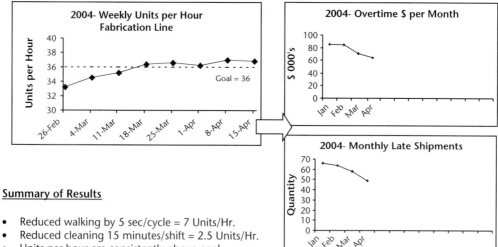

Summary of Results

- Reduced walking by 5 sec/cycle = 7 Units/Hr.
- Reduced cleaning 15 minutes/shift = 2.5 Units/Hr.
- Units per hour are consistently above goal.
- Process is stable.
- Overtime costs decreasing.
- Number of late shipments decreasing.
- Floor space reduced.

Figure 17-3. Completed results summary

Act: Make Necessary Adjustments to Solutions and to the Action Plan

As you can see, the entire problem-solving process is a continuous progression of developing a hypothesis, testing the hypothesis, measuring results, adjusting the hypothesis, retesting, measuring, and so forth, until the desired result is achieved. With continued practice, skills are improved and the first-time success rate will be increased. With a thorough understanding of the root causes, and the contribution of each to the overall problem, the effect of proposed countermeasures is easily predicted. Experimentation and simulation of countermeasures provide a clear understanding of the effectiveness of proposed solutions prior to any major investment of time or resources.

During this important phase it's critical to "stand in the circle" and observe the changes that have been implemented. Watch closely to verify that they produce the desired result. It is not uncommon for a solution to create new "problems." Sometimes these are related to people getting accustomed to the new method, and it's important to be able to distinguish "adjustment issues" from real issues. In some cases the core problem is broken into several smaller pieces, and lesser problems surface. Continue to address these subproblems until the operation runs smoothly. (Don't try to eliminate *all* problems, since that is unlikely and you could work toward that goal for a lifetime!)

TRAP

STOP

Confusing Problem Solving with Statistical Analysis

When we describe the scientific method of hypothesis, measurement, and testing . . . what will immediately come to mind for some readers is six sigma. Certainly the DMAIC methodology of six sigma is very compatible with PDCA and the problem solving method we describe here. But we have seen six sigma in the hands of novices become an exercise in statistics instead of an exercise in thinking. The problem is not well defined, months are spent carefully analyzing the wrong data, there is little go-and-see activity, and the solutions are simplistic or just plain wrong. The Toyota Way focuses on facts, most often in their purest and simplest form. As Mark Twain once said: "Facts are stubborn things, but statistics are more pliable."

Act: Identify Future Steps

The successful completion of a problem-solving activity should be celebrated and the efforts of everyone involved recognized. Members are to be congratulated on their ability to effectively identify the problem causes and for their creativity and exceptional thinking in developing countermeasures. This is not, however, a time for them to "sit back on their laurels." The nature of continuous improvement means that completion of one problem-solving activity should lead to the start of another. This is a reminder that while one problem has been resolved successfully, there are many more that need attention.

At the conclusion of a problem-solving activity the "next steps" or "future steps" are reviewed to remind everyone of this process of continuous improvement. This section should address four issues in particular:

1. Describe plans for wrapping up any "loose ends" pertaining to the current activity. These are planned items that may not have been implemented yet, or items that require some modification.
2. Explain how responsibility for *sustaining* current results and continued improvement of the issue will be assigned and supported by the leadership of the area. This item is crucial since improvement results are often not sustained because there has been no responsibility assigned. (Responsibility is often assumed to belong to leadership, but it must be clear what they will do and how and when they will do it.)
3. Identify whether any assistance is needed to resolve any issues that are beyond the control of the problem-solving team. This may include issues with a material supplier that requires support from the purchasing department, or help from an equipment manufacturer.
4. The team, or the individual, must look forward and identify the next problem to "pick up." This would generally be the next most important issue in the work area.

In addition to these four items, in some situations it is important to share the information from this activity within the organization to areas experiencing similar problems, or with similar processes. Generally, ensuring that information is shared would be the responsibility of management. Members of the team could provide the necessary technical experience to other groups.

Examples of possible future steps for the sawing example above are:

♦ Continue improving dirt containment and control activities.
♦ Implement daily 5S review by the team leader and weekly review by the group leader.
♦ Develop an automatic unloading device to further reduce cycle time.
♦ Improve handling to further reduce cycle time.
♦ Begin an activity to correct other causes of late shipments.

Finally Some Action

The implementation phase of the process is when things finally change. It is a time to develop a plan, begin to implement solutions, and verify the results.

This is the phase most people can't wait to get to. It can also be a frustrating time if change happens but the desired results do not follow! It's likely you will have to train yourself and others to develop the patience and skill necessary to thoroughly evaluate the problem and carefully analyze to find the root causes. This temporary postponement of implementation gratification (don't jump to solutions) will provide greater returns in the long run. Some key points to remember during the Plan-Do-Check-Act phase are:

- Always consider short-term temporary countermeasures for immediate benefits.
- Divide larger tasks into smaller segments, with assigned completion dates and measurements for each portion.
- Responsibility for an action item does not mean that the responsible person has to do the task. They are responsible for the outcome and for ensuring progress.
- The only way to verify results is to ensure that an effective measurement process is in place *prior* to implementation so that a before and after comparison can be made.
- Once your solutions become a reality, it will probably be necessary to make adjustments. Follow *genchi genbutsu*, and carefully observe the new process to verify that it is free from major problems.
- Always conclude your process with a look to the future. Continuous improvement means forever! Set the expectation that the process of improvement is never complete.

 Reflection Activities

Many people mistakenly place a high importance on the "action" phase of problem solving. It is thought that "making things happen" is the most important step in getting results. In fact, the most important step in getting exceptional results is in effectively identifying the root causes. If you have identified the root causes, the necessary corrective actions should be clear, and when implemented will produce the desired result. Take your time to ensure that the correct root causes have been identified prior to beginning the corrective actions.

1. Evaluate performance results in your organization. Do they show the desired improvement resulting from your problem solving activities?
2. Evaluate recent problem-solving or continuous improvement activities to determine the overall effectiveness.

a. Do you find that many items are implemented but the desired results are not achieved?

b. What part of the process is being missed that causes this situation? Look specifically at whether the problem was clearly identified and root causes were determined, or whether people just started "shooting" at the problem.

c. Were both short-term temporary and long-term permanent solutions used appropriately?

3. For the problem you've been working on, complete the following activities:

a. Make sure that defined results are predicted for each action item. This includes the specific measurement and amount.

b. Develop an action plan that includes both short- and long-term countermeasures as appropriate.

c. If the solutions require significant effort, break the activity down into quartiles, with specific actions and expectations for completion during an incremental time period. For example, a one-month activity can be broken down into 4 one-week portions each having a defined expectation for completion.

d. Clearly define who, what, when, and if necessary how each action item is to be completed.

e. As part of your action plan, define who will support the transition from the old way to the new way. Someone needs to be in the work area during the change to ensure a smooth transition.

4. Prior to implementation, determine how the effectiveness of each action item will be measured.

a. Verify that a preimprovement baseline measurement is completed.

b. Determine a measurement process and verify that results are being captured correctly.

c. Chart the results in the work area and review with everyone regularly.

d. Monitor the process regularly and determine whether adjustments to the plan are necessary (if you are not getting the planned results).

5. After the problem-solving process is "completed" (continuous improvement implies that improvement is never complete, but at some point you move on to other issues), identify appropriate future steps.

a. Complete any outstanding items from the action plan.

b. Develop a plan for sustaining the results. This includes those who will have direct responsibility for sustaining the results daily.

c. Identify whether additional support will be needed to fully correct the issue being addressed. Arrange for the necessary support.

d. Evaluate other problems, and determine which will be the next to be corrected. Make plans for correcting these issues.

Chapter 18

Telling the Story Using an A3 Report

Less Can Be More in Report Writing

Problem solving is about thinking. But writing things down can help thinking. How can you document key information and decisions at each step in a way that you can share it with others, get their input, and make appropriate modifications using their input? Documentation of a complex problem-solving process brings to mind mountains of data, reams of paper, or in this day and age, perhaps an online database, which can be queried in multiple ways. Toyota has a simpler approach. It involves pencil, eraser, and one side of a piece of paper. It is often referred to as the "A3 report." Why A3? Originally it was because much of the communication within Toyota across the various sites and across nations was by fax, and this was the largest size paper that could fit in a fax machine: 11 by 17 inches.

What can you possibly fit on one side of a piece of paper? Well, if you look at the A3 reports generated by experienced Toyota managers, the answer is a remarkable amount of information. What information is on the A3? The answer is: Only the most essential.

What is important about A3 reports is not the finesse with which you fill in the boxes and draw fancy graphics. It is the communication process. The A3 is an integral part of the problem-solving and decision-making process. It allows only the most critical information to be shared with others for careful evaluation of the thought process used, as a means of requesting support or advice, and for arriving at a consensus.

Many people outside of Toyota do not realize that the aggressive pursuit of waste elimination extends to all activities within the organization, including the presentation of information and the decision-making process based on the information. These presentations at Toyota are clear and concise, and it takes very little time to share the message. Formatting the activity in this way requires the distillation of information into a complete, clear, and easy to understand presentation. The story is told with a minimal number of words and is pictorial in nature. When properly presented, the information can be read or explained in five minutes or less so everyone understands and decisions can easily be made. A well-prepared A3 prevents a condition Winston Churchill once quipped about concerning a cumbersome report: "The length of this document defends it well against the risk of its being read."

Outside of Toyota, most presentations of lean activities we've seen have lacked a basic structure that maintained focus and direction. They tended to wander, and the usual result is that many people are presented with excessive information with no clear logical flow, and much time is wasted on side conversations and sorting through the information. Notebooks of course notes and operating procedures and discussions of lean principles sit on the shelf, never to be read. The A3 report is designed not only to be read, but to be used as part of the problem-solving process.

Determining How to Use an A3

An A3 is used for many different types of story presentations at Toyota. They are not "reports" per se, but each should tell a story with a beginning, middle, and end. Figure 18-1 shows four different common types of A3 reports. One type makes proposals; the others are various types of reporting—from a problem

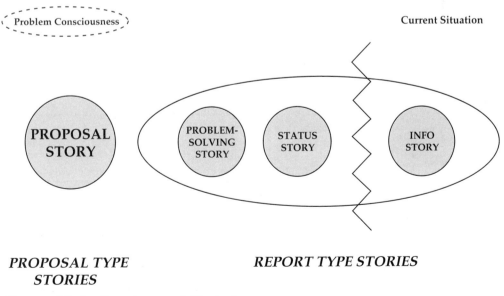

Figure 18-1. Four types of A3 stories

solving story, to a story that gives the status of a project, to an information story. There is a natural flow between these story types. Often, projects will begin with a proposal story to get approval to invest resources in the project, and then, as the project progresses, there will be a story of the problem-solving process, status stories at key milestones in the project, and an information story to present the results. Each person crafts the A3 for the specific purpose of their "story," but there are some standard formats taught within Toyota.

In some cases the A3 is used to propose a change, for example, in a process or the purchase of equipment (called "business cases" in some companies). For these "proposal stories," it is necessary to complete an A3 with the problem statement, analysis of current conditions, a proposed action (the change or purchase), and the anticipated result (both cost and improvement expected). Sufficient information should be presented so a decision can easily be made. At Toyota any major expenditure is an important decision, and if sufficient information was not presented, the A3 preparer would surely be sent back to gather additional facts. A format for the proposal story is shown in Figure 18-2.

A "status story" reports at key milestones in an important project (Figure 18-3). Examples include an annual plan, a review of a project, and a design review in engineering a new product. This story must start with clear objectives, the

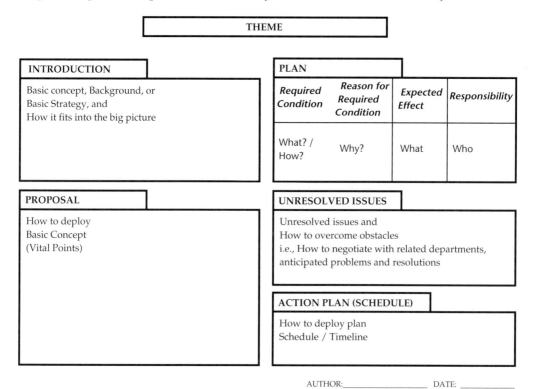

Figure 18-2. Proposal story

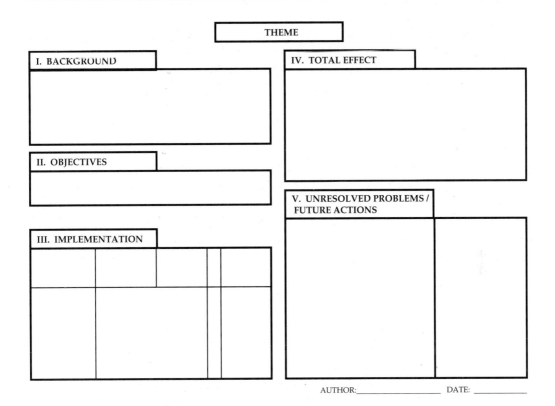

Figure 18-3. Status report story

approach to implementation, the total effect to date, and unresolved problems with accompanying actions. All proposal, problem-solving, and status A3 reports must have some action plan.

An "informational story" is intended to convey information only. There is no evaluative component. It does not require a description of a problem; the only objective is to convey general information to an audience, inside or outside the company. Visualization is very important for an informational story, and there are many possible ways of organizing this type of presentation.

An entire book could be written about each of these applications. Instead we will focus on one of the most complex and in-depth uses of an A3: problem solving.

The A3 Problem-Solving Report Process

Problem solving uses multiple formats at different stages of the process depending on *what* is being presented and *when* in the process the information is presented. There are three distinct stages in the problem-solving process. First is the *proposal* stage, when the proposal story is used. There are actually two levels during the proposal stage. The initial proposal is made to gain consensus on whether a problem should be addressed. If agreement to move forward is established, the next level of the proposal stage comes after the identification of root causes. At this time a proposal is generally made to gain acceptance and approval of the proposed solutions.

After the proposed countermeasures are accepted and implementation begins, the process moves into the second stage, the *status reporting* stage using a status report story. This stage provides information and updates to others to verify that the activity is progressing on schedule. It is also an opportunity to question and explore the completeness of thinking, and to provide additional resources if necessary to complete the activity as scheduled.

The third stage is the *final reporting* at the completion of the activity. At this time there is generally no need to further question the details of the activity itself. The focus is on the completeness of the result. Generally, the final presentation is not made until the countermeasures have successfully eliminated the problem and the desired results have been achieved. The primary purpose of the final report is to acknowledge the activity and the success of the team or individual. It is a celebration of good thinking and good process. It's also a time to ask, "What's next?" What is the next problem that will be "picked up"?

Table 18-1 shows the three stages during the problem-solving process and how the A3 is used during each. Before actually deciding to begin a problem-solving activity, it is important to evaluate the problem in the context of other issues. If the problem statement step is completed as outlined in Chapter 14, this information can easily be used for comparison. Alternatives can also be explored, such as who should work on the problem, how many people, and what time frame (depending upon the urgency of the problem). The initial proposal of a problem should bring

Before	During	After
Proposal Presentation	**Status Reporting**	**Final Report**
▪ Overall comparison with other problems ▪ Clarify objectives ▪ Provide guidance ▪ Consider other options ▪ Gain consensus and approval	▪ Progress check ▪ Verify direction of activity ▪ Provide guidance ▪ Provide additional support ▪ Provide additional resources	▪ Verify successful completion and achievement of results ▪ Celebrate success ▪ Evaluate further considerations

Table 18-1. A3 Problem-Solving Report Process

up many questions to ensure that the problem has been correctly identified and that approval to move forward is warranted.

After agreement has been reached to pursue a proposal, frequent status reports occur. Depending on the activity, it may be weekly or monthly. The initial portion of the A3 (problem statement and analysis, discussed in Chapter 15) does not change for each update. That information is of a historical nature and is briefly reviewed as a "refresher," but the data does not change (unless an additional cycle of PDCA was necessary). The A3 is used to show the status of implementation and current improvement results. The status update will include information regarding the remaining time until completion, delays in the progress and plans to return to the plan, and any challenges or issues requiring support from others. One commonly made mistake is to wait too long after the plan falls behind schedule before making a contingency plan. This can put an activity behind schedule.

Outline for an A3

Putting your story together on a single piece of paper always follows the same basic format; however, the actual content and space dedicated to each section will vary. Figure 18-4 shows the basic layout of an A3 "problem-solving story," with each section identified and the flow of information shown with arrows. Begin with a heading that has the "theme" of the activity, the preparer's name,

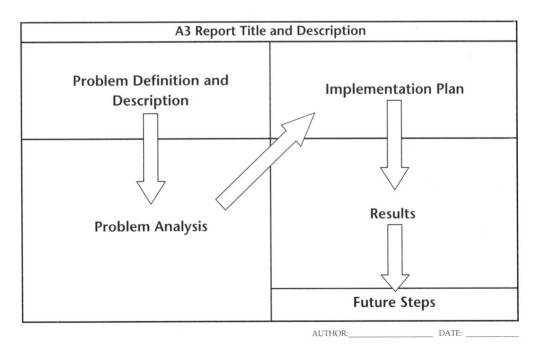

Figure 18-4. A3 problem-solving story format and flow

the date, and any other relevant information such as plant or department. Then the page is divided into two parts down the middle.

In most cases, the Problem Definition and Description (the problem statement) and the Problem Analysis fill the entire left-hand side of the sheet, as can be seen in the figure. Of this half of the paper, the bottom two-thirds is generally reserved for the analysis, and the top one-third for the problem situation. The analysis is the heart of the process, and most of the space should be dedicated to it. Without a thorough and accurate analysis, any solutions implemented will be misguided and won't yield an effective result. In some cases, if the problem is especially complex and involves many issues, the analysis may spill over to the right side of the paper. These are guidelines, not hard and fast rules because the format should fit the story, not the other way around. If a section of the story requires more or less space, then adjust accordingly.

The right-hand side of the paper is generally reserved for the Implementation Plan, as the figure shows, the Results, and the Future Steps. The results section usually fills most of the right-hand side. This represents the relative importance of each section in the process. The entire purpose of the activity is to improve results, so this should be the focus of the right side of the A3. Remember when we said that if the analysis is thorough and accurate the root causes would be obvious? If the root causes are obvious, the solutions will be as well. This connection must be clear in the story. If it is, there's less need to outline the details of implementation. Think about it this way: If you get the analysis right and have effectively implemented a countermeasure, the desired result should occur. If the result was less than expected, there is either a flaw in analysis, identification of effective countermeasures, or poor execution.

If space is at a premium for a complex problem, the future steps section can be minimized with little impact on the overall A3. Again, the actual space utilized for each section of a problem-solving activity should be based on the significance of the material to the overall story. The most important information should consume the greatest amount of space.

Formatting Tips

Completion of A3s is somewhat of an art. There isn't a single way to fill one out, but there are a few guidelines that help make the information easier to understand. We have covered many of these in Chapters 13 through 17, but they bear repeating here:

- ◆ Avoid excessive verbiage. A picture is worth a thousand words. Present data in a graphic form that is quickly and easily understood.
- ◆ Use a consistent format for similar information. Pay particular attention to the scale on charts. Similar data compared with a different scale can be visually misleading and very confusing.

- Use line graphs in the problem description section (the first section) because they show the trend of the issue. Do not use Pareto graphs or pie charts. These are analysis tools, not problem description tools.
- If you must use words, use bulleted statements rather than sentences, and keep it to three or four bullets per section to summarize the main points.
- Make sure that any charts, graphs, or wording is sized so it is easily read.
- When using a comparison tool such as a pie chart or Pareto chart, avoid comparing too many issues since this will make the data very small and difficult to read. Also, these are "separation tools" that allow the isolation of the "significant few from the trivial many." Anything past the top five is not one of the significant few and does not merit attention.
- Avoid the use of colored charts and graphs. When photocopied, the color doesn't show, and if you use color to identify elements, that clarity will be lost. Yes, we know you can use a color copier, but it's very expensive, and not everyone will have one when you want a copy! This brings up a related point: Don't try to make a poor problem-solving activity look good by using fancy, colorful material. If your A3 is all fluff and no substance, it will be obvious. As Einstein said: "If you are out to describe the truth, leave elegance to the tailor."
- While we're on the subject of charts and graphs, we must mention the use of Microsoft Excel for charting purposes. It is a handy tool, but like any tool, it's only as good as the user. The main problem is that the default settings do not always provide the best result. Settings such as scale, markers, and lines are adjustable, and you must pay particular attention to font size and style. The size may automatically adjust and be out of balance with other similar charts. Make sure you change them for clarity and ease of understanding.
- Use arrows to show the flow of information so the reader knows the relationship of each part of your story.
- Avoid acronyms and technical terminology. Remember that your audience may include people who do not know the jargon.
- Use your sense of visual balance. Make sure the story is carefully spaced and elements are aligned. It's distracting to view similar information, such as charts, in different sizes.

Final A3 Version of Problem-Solving Story

Figure 18-5 is a completed A3 of the problem case in Chapters 13 through 17. You may observe some of the problems mentioned above in this A3. If so, that's good. You can apply that learning to your own A3s. There is no perfect A3. Each time we do one we can always find ways to improve the content or the format. Our goal is not to be perfect, but to communicate information effectively.

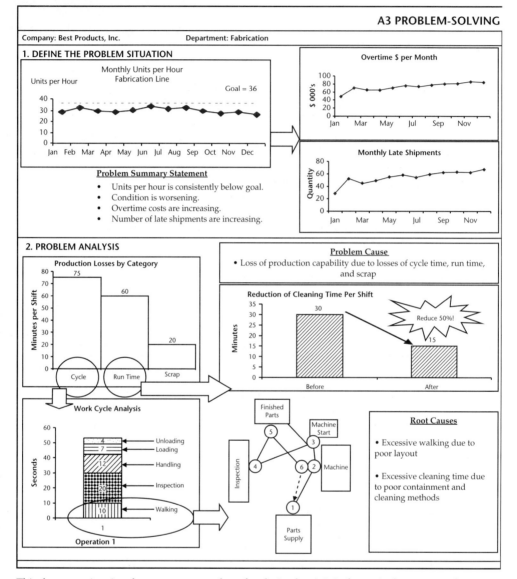

This document is printed across two pages here for clarity, but it is in fact a single one-page document.

Figure 18-5. Completed example of an A3

REPORT FORM

Date: 6/9/2004   Prepared by: David Meier

3. ACTION PLANS TO CORRECT PROBLEMS

Action Item	Short-Term Long-Term	Person Responsible	Schedule Week 1	Week 2	Week 3	Week 4
Temporary cleaning during breaks and lunch	ST	M. Scarpello	△			
Tape boxes to machine to collect dirt	ST	D. Danis	△			
Reduce walk time: relocate material and inspection	LT	D. Spiess	O△			
Reposition start button	LT	M. Kissel	O——△			
Build skirt around tables to reduce cleaning	LT	M. Nicholson	O——△			
Add dust collection bin to machine	LT	P. Kenrick	O——X	△		
Modify 4 machines to catch dirt (1 per week)	LT	B. Costantino	O——X	X	X	△

Key: Start   O   Finish △   Progress Check   X

4. RESULTS OF ACTIVITY

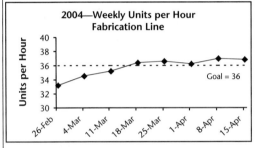

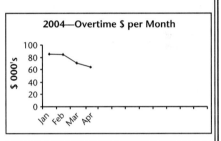

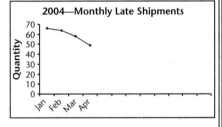

Summary of Results

- Reduced walking by 5 sec/cycle = 7 Units/Hr.
- Reduced cleaning 15 minutes/shift = 2.5 Units/Hr.
- Units per hour are consistently above goal.
- Process is stable.
- Overtime costs decreasing.
- Number of late shipments decreasing.
- Floor space reduced.

5. FUTURE STEPS

- Continue improving dirt containment and control activities.
- Develop automatic unloading device to further reduce cycle time.
- Improve handling to further reduce cycle time.
- Begin activity to correct other causes of late shipments.

Figure 18-5. (*Continued*)

Many people look at this A3 and immediately think that it is "too busy" or "complicated." This is a normal reaction to a very involved A3. There is a lot of information fit into a small space. If this A3 were presented to you, you would see that in fact the entire story can be explained in about three and a half minutes and is quite clear. The following text would be used to explain this A3, and it is presented as a reporting of results (the activity is complete):

As you can see [pointing to the trend graph in "Define the Problem Situation"], the fabrication line was consistently below goal for units per hour, and at the end of last year it had gotten worse. As a result of being under the units per hour goal [point to the overtime graph] there was approximately $80,000 per month in overtime cost, which was increasing, and also our late shipments to the customers [point to the late shipments graph] were increasing. If we did not take action, this problem most likely would have gotten worse. [End of the Problem Situation section.]

An analysis of our production losses [point to the first graph in "Problem Analysis"] showed that we were losing time during the operation cycle, and our available run time was reduced because of cleaning time. We were spending 30 minutes per shift for cleaning and wanted to reduce that to 15 minutes per shift [point to the chart]. Observation of the work area showed that contaminants were not being contained properly, causing additional cleaning time. Reducing the cleaning time by 15 minutes per shift will increase the units per hour by 2.5.

Observation and analysis of the work steps indicated 10 seconds of walking time for this operation [point to the *yamazumi*, or stack chart]. The worker flow diagram [point to the diagram] shows that the location of parts and equipment was causing excessive walking time. A reduction of one-half of the walking will be a five-second savings per cycle, which will yield an additional seven units per labor hour. [End of the Problem Analysis section.]

To get some temporary relief from this problem we decided to perform cleaning during lunch and breaks [point to each countermeasure in the "Action Plans to Correct Problems" as it is mentioned]. We had a temporary cleaning service that performed that task until we could implement the permanent countermeasure to more effectively collect the dirt. Also, we taped cardboard boxes to certain locations on the machine to capture dirt temporarily. This made the clean-up easier. These short-term countermeasures were completed immediately. During the second week we changed the layout of the work area and repositioned the start button. These changes reduced walking time and reduced the cycle time. Our permanent countermeasure was to enclose the bottom of each machine with a skirt to further reduce the cleaning requirement.

We needed to make some modifications to the dust collection system, and each machine was modified as well. This task required the support of maintenance and engineering, and we planned to complete one machine per week over a four week period. We checked progress each week to make sure we were on target. These are permanent countermeasures that will reduce the cleaning requirement to 15 minutes. [End of the Action Plans to Correct Problems section.]

We started to see immediate results when we implemented the temporary countermeasures [point to the first graph of units per hour in "Results of Activity"]. We completed a simulation of the new work layout and proved the result as well, and when the layout changes were made, the units per hour increased. For the past four weeks our units per hour has been consistently above the goal, and our process has stabilized. Also, our overtime costs and late shipments have been reduced [point to graphs]. We were not specifically targeting floor space reduction, but did get a reduction when the layout was changed [point to bulleted statements in "Summary of Results"]. [End of the Results of Activity section.]

Although these results were sufficient to achieve our goal, we have identified further opportunities for improvement [point to "Future Steps" section]. We can install an automatic unloading device on the machine and further reduce the handling time, which will reduce the cycle time. There are additional opportunities for dirt containment, and we will continue to reduce the need for cleaning in the work area. We have other issues that cause late shipments, and we have targeted that as the next improvement activity to tackle. That team will begin to evaluate the situation next week. [The end!] Are there any questions or comments?

Final Comments on A3s

A disadvantage to the 11-by-17-inch A3 is that though it is almost the size of two 8½-by-11-inch pages together, the layout is different (landscape versus portrait). This causes sizing problems when trying to copy and paste an A3 from Excel into another format. When an A3 is copied and pasted into a space with a different aspect ratio (from 11-by-17 to the layout of this book, for example), the resulting changes to fonts and graphs may not be desirable. When you print an A3 to 8½-by-11 paper, the printer will automatically adjust to 64 percent, and the resulting copy may have very small print. If you paste into PowerPoint, some details may be lost because of this aspect ratio difference. Partly for this reason, and partly to eliminate even more waste, parts of Toyota have been moving to A4 reports (8½ x 11). Most of the American Toyota associates we know who have struggled to learn to get information down to an A3 format are horrified by the thought of an A4 report.

But more important than the size of the reports and the technical details in crafting and printing them is that the A3 is only as good as the process that generates it. Without a good problem-solving process, you will not get a good A3 report. Behind the scenes, a key to generating an A3 report is *nemawashi*—the process of getting consensus. The nemawashi can be viewed as a type of *ringi sho*—a proposal being circulated. Each time a person looks at it, he or she will have some reactions and some input. If you are not open to the input, there is no point in showing it to them. The A3 is then modified as you go. In some cases it's the product of a team project, and the team must all agree to the report. By the time the A3 is presented to an executive group for decision making, everyone in the room should have seen it and agreed to it. At Toyota it is common to have just five minutes to present the report before a decision is immediately made.

Historically, the A3 was taught by the supervisor, but not in a classroom. It was part of the craft of being a Toyota professional. In the United States, Toyota discovered that American managers lacked some basic management skills taken for granted at Toyota, including A3 report writing, so a special class was designed to teach all managers. It started out as a one-day course and then was reduced to a half-day course. As the course was developed, it became clear there were prerequisites as in a college course. A prerequisite course on practical problem solving was needed.

Many companies who learn about A3 report writing find it seductive. We're all overwhelmed by the amount of paperwork in our company—whether it's physical paper or virtual reporting on the computer. One side of one sheet of paper is awfully appealing. Unfortunately, the seductive appeal of the report is also its chief weakness. It's easy to treat an A3 like a nice new toy. It becomes a dictate from management to use them. Everyone learns how and spends a lot of time outdoing each other to create fancy graphic creations, cramming more and more information on the page. This is not the point. The point is to communicate, gain consensus, solve problems, and get results.

Reflection Activities

If you've been completing the reflection section of Chapters 14-17, you will have completed your problem-solving activity. The A3 can be used as a format and guide during your activity, and as a summary report after the problem is solved. The following questions are specifically aimed at a post-problem-solving report, but could also be used to organize your ideas and information as the problem is being solved. Use the problem you completed in Chapters 14-17 and your information to complete the following tasks.

1. Starting with a blank sheet of paper, complete the heading of the A3 report. Include:
   a. Your name
   b. The theme of the problem (describe the objective of solving the problem)
   c. The name of the work area, department, facility, etc.
   d. The date of the report
2. Complete the problem situation section.
   a. Depict the problem graphically.
   b. Show the effect of the problem on other important business conditions.

    c. Use arrows to show the flow of information and lead the reader's eye along the correct path.

    d. Use no more than four bulleted statements to explain the problem situation, the effect, and the rationale for "picking up the problem."

    e. Is there a compelling reason to solve this problem? (The significance should be clear.)

3. Complete the analysis section.

    a. Use charts, graphs, and diagrams as much as possible to show the narrowing of the problem and the selection of the main causes.

    b. Avoid lists of possible causes, likely causes, etc. Use data to depict the facts.

    c. Ensure that your analysis flows step by step, progressing from the problem to the root cause(s). (It is a graphic version of the Five-Why process.)

    d. Use arrows to show the flow of information and to assist the reader.

    e. Verify that you have identified true root causes. (They must meet the four criteria outlined in Chapter 15.)

4. Complete the action plan.

    a. Identify short-term temporary and long-term permanent countermeasures.

    b. For larger tasks, were you able to break the task into smaller increments that could be completed at designated intervals?

    c. Have all actions been completely implemented?

5. Show the results of your activity in the results section.

    a. Show the effects of specific actions on the results graph (indicate implementation dates).

    b. Has the improvement been sustained?

    c. Depict the effect of the improvement on the related business indicators shown in the problem statement section.

    d. Use no more than four bulleted statements to describe the results.

6. Explain the next steps for your activity.

    a. Is it necessary to continue working on this problem?

    b. Is additional support needed from others?

    c. How will you transition responsibility for sustaining the results?

> **d.** Explain whether you will pick up another problem and what it will be.
>
> 7. Review the completed A3 with others to solicit feedback. Pay particular attention to any questions or clarification that is needed. These are indications of items that are lacking in your presentation. Use this information to improve your next A3. This is practicing the art of *hansei* (reflection and application of lessons learned).

Part VI

Managing the Change

Chapter 19

Lean Implementation Strategies and Tactics

Where Should You Start?

You know your company needs an injection of lean. There's waste everywhere. Upon serious reflection, you pretty much failed most of the tests. The culture is nowhere near the level that we describe as the Toyota Way. Leadership is not there, you don't have effective work groups, functional groups are at war most of the time, problem-solving processes are superficial, and you've tried some lean tools here and there with good short-term results but no staying power.

Welcome to most of the world. Even Toyota has to work hard to maintain the Toyota Way, and it has particularly struggled to spread the true Toyota Way outside of Japan. It is continuous hard work.

So where do you start? In this chapter we talk strategy and tactics. You need to decide where to focus actual activities implementing lean. You need a plan. There is a great deal to do and many different ways to do it.

Returning to the 4P model, we are arguing that all four levels of philosophy, process, people, and problem solving are intertwined in complex ways. It is a system. So where does that get you? Unfortunately, reality being what it is, you need to start someplace. Even if you've been at lean for some years but it hasn't taken hold, you have to start someplace to reinvigorate lean. You have at least four choices:

1. **Philosophy.** You can start with an off-site meeting of top leaders and clearly define your vision for becoming a lean enterprise.
2. **Process.** You can begin implementing lean correctly as a connected value stream, as we describe in Part III of this book.

3. **People.** You can work to train and indoctrinate your people into the new lean way of thinking, directly effecting culture change.

4. **Problem solving.** You can train people in a problem-solving methodology and give them time to meet in groups and solve problems.

All these approaches have been tried at various companies over the years with mixed success. And to some degree, you need to work on all of them. But if you have to pick one place to begin focusing your efforts, it has to be at the process layer—reducing waste in the transformation process. Having said this, there are still many choices to make.

Lean Implementation Levels, Strategies, and Tools

Another way of slicing the problem of planning implementation activity is to think about your organization in levels from the biggest slice to the smallest component.[1] In Table 19-1 we look at levels from the extended enterprise, which includes all of the organizations and companies that somehow touch your product and work down to the level of the detailed individual process. Let's consider each level, starting at the bottom with the individual process.

Process Improvement Approach

The individual process is what is done at a particular machine or by a particular worker for a manual operation: stamping or welding parts, performing an assembly, mixing a batch of paint, taking calls at a call center, entering data, etc. There should be a specific improvement objective for that process. It can be to reduce defects by 20 percent, reduce cycle time by 20 percent to improve output, eliminate work-in-process inventory by 50 percent, reduce downtime from 10 to 2 percent, and so on.

One common approach to process improvement as a lean strategy is the one-week kaizen event. The kaizen event structure (a.k.a. kaizen workshop, rapid improvement workshop, lean event, rapid improvement event) is:

1. **Prepare in advance.** Two to four weeks of advanced preparation for the workshop to define the scope of the problem, decide on a team, collect data on the current situation, decide what lean tools to use, and make logistic arrangements for the event. In some cases there is advanced purchase of tools, materials, or equipment that cannot be done in the lead time of the one-week workshop.

---

[1] Much of this discussion of implementation strategies and the figures used for the different strategies are based on a training course developed and taught at the University of Michigan by Bill Costantino, former Toyota group leader where he was an associate of David Meier.

Implementation Level	Strategy	Example Tools
Extended enterprise	Supply chain management	Contracts, alliance structures, target pricing, lean logistics, VA/VE, supplier development, supplier associations
Across enterprise	Lean office and engineering	All lean tools and approaches adapted to technical and service operations
Across manufacturing	X production system	Conceptual models, training modules, lean assessments, lean metrics, standard procedure manuals
Whole plant	Plantwide tools	5S, standard work, kanban, cell, SMED, team leaders, TPM, error proofing
	Hot projects	Constraint analysis, cost-benefit analysis, any of the lean tools
Value stream	Model line	Value stream mapping, appropriate lean tools needed to implement future state
Process improvement	Kaizen project	Kaizen event, kaizen project, Q.C. circles, task force, focused lean tools
	Six Sigma project	Six Sigma tools

Table 19-1. Lean Implementation Strategies and Tools

2. **Conduct workshop:**
   ◆ Monday: Give an overview of lean and teach any special tools needed for that week. Begin to collect data on the current process in the afternoon.
   ◆ Tuesday: Complete the current state analysis, collect data, draw a process flow map, draw walk pattern on layout, develop Standardized Work Combination Tables, etc., and develop ideas for the improved state. Perhaps detail the future state by the end of the day (Plan).
   ◆ Wednesday: First pass implementation (Do). It may be in one pilot, to try it first, or full implementation right away. Sometimes this starts by

clearing the floor of the current process, painting the floor, then moving equipment back in the new layout.
- Thursday: Evaluate process (Check), improve (Act), and keep going through Plan-Do-Check-Act (PDCA) until you have a good approach.
- Friday: Develop a presentation for management. Present to management. Celebrate. (Often the event ends after a lunch celebration.)

3. **Follow-up to the workshop**. There are always items that could not be done during the week, which are put together as a homework list sometimes called a "kaizen newsletter." An action plan for what, who, and when is prepared during the one-week workshop, and follow-up is needed to be sure the items get done.

The kaizen workshop approach has gotten a bad name in many quarters. Jim Womack used to laughingly refer to it as "kamikaze kaizen," or "drive-by kaizen." The implication was that you swoop down fast and furiously, solve some problems, and swoop back up, or drive by, take aim and fire, and you're done. The problem is not that kaizen workshops are inherently bad, but that many companies turned their entire lean process into a series of kaizen workshops along with a kaizen promotion office to administer, support, and monitor kaizen events. They may even count kaizen events as a key performance metric. There are some serious weaknesses in this approach (see Figure 19-1):

1. Kaizen workshops generally are point kaizen focusing on the individual process. Since there is no broader vision, this will not lead to flow across the enterprise.
2. The kaizen workshop generally ends with a homework list of to-do items, which often do not get done since there is no serious ownership of the process by the people in the work area.
3. While people in the work area are involved in the event and get very excited and enthusiastic during the workshop, reality sets in the week after and more often than not there is backsliding toward the pre-workshop state.
4. There is a tendency to judge kaizen events based only on short-term cost savings, which does not drive true systems change.
5. There is no lasting cultural change.

This is not to say that good companies serious about lean should ignore the kaizen event as a tool. There are some remarkable strengths of the kaizen event, including:

1. This is an exciting experience for all involved. The concentrated analysis and improvement, combined with the feeling of being part of a team, can literally change people's worldview. They can see waste and also see what is possible when waste is removed.

Characteristics	
➤ Focused process improvement	➤ Toyota uses variety of approaches
➤ Specific improvement targets	➤ Some companies use kaizen events
➤ Isolated process improvements	➤ Some companies use Six Sigma process
➤ Toyota drives with hoshin kanri	

STRENGTHS	TRAPS
• High interest/support	• Point kaizen with no overall vision/strategy
• Resources usually available	• No system to support lasting change
• Bias for action	• Risk of back-sliding
• Kaizen event approach can make radical changes quickly	• Lacks ownership if driven by staff function
• Opportunity to convince skeptics in kaizen events	• Kaizen event approach can become"the lean program"
• Six Sigma approach uses very rigorous statistical analysis	• Six Sigma can lead to analysis paralysis
• Can support value stream approach	• Typically projects look for an immediate payback which means labor costs giving lean and Six Sigma the reputation as head-cutting programs.

Figure 19-1. Strengths and traps of kaizen project approach

2. Management is enlightened on the speed with which things can be accomplished if a concerted effort is applied. Amazing things can be accomplished with proper focus and leverage of resources.
3. People learn a great deal. The intensity of the experience opens people up to learning in ways that are usually not possible in a traditional classroom approach.
4. Resources are usually made available, including management authority, cross-functional resources, and some money. So things can happen in the week that might otherwise take months of written requests, approvals, and cajoling people to help out.
5. Skeptics can be won over. In a classroom, the skeptics raise their hands and explain all the reasons lean will not work. Those same people in a workshop are making it happen.
6. As we will discuss later in the chapter, the kaizen event is a great tool for implementing aspects of an overall value stream vision.

The Tenneco example from Smithville, Tennessee, which we describe below, illustrates the positive and negative of kaizen events. In that case, radical kaizen events every other week dramatically turned around a plant. About 40 percent of the workforce were "kaizened out." Within one year they worked through every area of the plant, moving hundreds of pieces of equipment, making new shipping and receiving docks near the point of use, and basically remaking the place. The dramatic savings led to great management attention, and helped spur the CEO to invest in lean globally. We should note that an "event" is not necessarily a successful event. The Tenneco Smithville events were well-facilitated by a veteran lean coach who guided the plant and the event toward serious change. There are also events led by "kaizen coordinators" who lack the deep expertise and aggressive facilitation skills, and these can easily degrade into glorified 5S activities.

"Six Sigma" programs have some of the same strengths and weaknesses for process improvement as the kaizen workshop approach. They are generally of longer duration (e.g., several months), led by individuals who are earning or have earned "Black Belts," and focus heavily on statistical methods and measurement. The origins of Six Sigma are in Total Quality Management (TQM), but advocates argue that Six Sigma adds a bottom-line financial mentality. Projects are typically expected to save the company several hundred thousand dollars. In fact, many companies track dollars saved through Six Sigma and even report these figures to stock analysts. Train 1,000 people doing $200,000 projects and in no time huge savings pile up. While Six Sigma uses statistical tools that can be quite powerful in the right hands at the right time, there are some serious traps in the Six Sigma approach:

1. Six Sigma focuses so intensively on analyzing data, picking the right statistical procedures, validating the statistical properties of the data, and developing slick reports, that the analyst can get distracted from the true purpose of the project and lose focus on the *gemba*.
2. Six Sigma anoints individuals as Green Belts or Black Belts and gives them a special status in the organization, yet their main skills are the analysis methods and not necessarily deep understanding of the processes they are improving.
3. The Black Belts can do too much on their own, turning the projects into technical engineering projects with minimal employee involvement.
4. The result is often lack of ownership by the people doing the work, and thus the recommended changes do not stick.
5. There is no real philosophy behind the Six Sigma program except to find, measure, and eliminate variation, and save a lot of money.

The find it and measure it, and analyze it and fix it to save dollars fast approach often leads to point kaizen that may even be contrary to lean principles. We have seen the following projects that are successful in saving money on a per piece basis but actually led the organization away from lean and ultimately increased total cost:

♦ Reducing changeover time, reporting labor savings, and increasing batch sizes, instead of decreasing batch sizes (see "Case Study: Six Sigma Changeover Reduction").

+ Reducing transportation cost by filling trucks through less frequent deliveries and increasing inventory levels in the plant.
+ Reducing labor by assigning material handling and setup duties to workers in a cell, and as a result adding non-value-added activities to the core value-added workers.

"Lean Sigma" promises to provide the best of both worlds, but the "lean" in lean sigma is often narrowly construed to be a few technical tools like making a cell or developing standardized work. The result is point kaizen using both lean and Six Sigma tools without true flow and without the cultural changes necessary to support and sustain lean transformation. It has many of the weaknesses of the general process improvement approach through kaizen workshops and Six Sigma tools.

Case Example: Tenneco Smithville, Radical Kaizen, Phase I

Tenneco Automotive opened its exhaust system plant in Smithville, Tennessee, in 1994. The first customer was Toyota, and Nissan, Saturn, Honda, and Corvette followed later. In 1996 the plant was ISO 9000 certified and then QS 9000 certified and things were grand. Unfortunately, the plant was set up around Tenneco's traditional concept of process islands, with stamping, pipe bending, and different groups of welding machines together by function. Inventory of raw materials and intermediate products were everywhere, and large batches of each product type were run between changeovers. On the surface the plant was performing better than expected, and there did not seem to be a pressing need for change. It was more profitable than forecasted, and in terms of their primary measure—labor variances—they were $1 million favorable to plan.

But in 2000 trouble signs started to appear. Profits were low. Quality for Toyota was acceptable, but delivery reliability was in Toyota's words "dangerous." At one point, because of quality problems, Tenneco had to express ship parts by jet from Japan for Toyota at $30,000 a trip. It was clear they needed to do something, or they wouldn't get any future business—half the plant's business— from Toyota. At the same time, a new vice president of manufacturing, Joe Czarnecki, was brought in, and he had a completely different type of measurement. He noted that while the plant was profitable, by his calculations they should have been 20 percent more profitable. He looked at indirect labor efficiency, overtime, and inventory, which were all negative relative to his targets. Nissan was asking for a 20 percent price reduction, and Toyota was introducing a new program of price-downs. The need for change was rising fast to a crisis level.

Tenneco had recently hired a lean manufacturing expert, Pasquale Digirolamo, who agreed to dedicate almost all of his time to the plant for 8 to 12 months and treat it as a Tenneco lean pilot. Digirolamo and the plant manager, Glenn Drodge, met three times every day—a morning planning meeting, a midday review, and an end-of-day review. Digirolamo played a coaching role but was aggressive. He found the overall level of discipline in the plant to be weak and was fond of saying, "You get what you tolerate." The Japanese consulting firm Shingijutsu had trained Digirolamo to lead radical kaizen workshops. He scheduled aggressive workshops every other week, in most cases setting up a complete manufacturing cell within the week. In the first six months, all subassembly operations were converted to cells. In the second six months, all final assembly operations became cells. The entire plant was laid out almost from scratch, and about 450 pieces of equipment were moved to the new layout. New shipping docks were built near the point of use. Primarily through the radical kaizen workshops, the plant was virtually remade from the bottom up. This was *kaikaku* (radical transformation), not kaizen (continuous improvement).

In preparation for this one-year radical remaking of the plant, Digirolamo estimated that the plant had 40 percent more workers than it should have. He recommended a one time layoff before the workshops began. Mostly temporary workers were let go as the plant relied heavily on agency workers. Other workers were offered Tenneco's standard severance package, and enough took it to preclude involuntary layoffs for hourly employees. Some front-line supervisors were let go—people who did not have the management and leadership skills to perform in the new lean environment. The verbal commitment between the plant manager and Digirolamo essentially meant that Digirolamo was taking over the plant.

The bottom-line results were striking. Digirolamo came in as sensei in November 2000. Some time was spent on stability issues. In January 2001 lean deployment started seriously, led by the Smithville Lean Steering Committee. By April the plant had made a turnaround from below target to above target and other Tenneco plant managers were asking what was going on at Smithville. In the first year, labor cost was reduced by 39 percent, direct labor efficiency improved by 92 percent, total labor productivity went up by 56 percent, inventory dollars on hand were cut in half—freeing up $5 million in cash—external defects were reduced from 638 to 44 parts per million, and lead time was cut in half. In 2002 the plant for the first time received Toyota's coveted quality and service award.

In terms of the different approaches to change covered in this chapter, Smithville in this first year had used a radical version of the "kaizen project approach." It was kaizen upon kaizen relentlessly. Flow was created but mostly locally within cells. There were a few kanban systems that had been set up prior to this radical year, but the main focus of Digirolamo was on stability and cells. There was a clear bias for action, radical changes were made fast, skeptics were convinced in the plant and in other Tenneco plants, and the results were obvious. Table 19-2 summarizes the results. This plant's success also got the attention of the CEO, who raised the priority of lean implementation. On the other hand, in terms of our implementation spiral (the continuous improvement cycle shown in Figure 3-4, Chapter 3) just part of one loop—stabilize, create flow, standardize—had been made across the entire plant. There was much work to be done to get to true Toyota Production System (TPS) anyplace in the plant.

Total head count	−39%
Salaried head count	−12%
Direct labor efficiency	+92%
Total labor productivity	+56%
Inventory $ on hand	−48%
Inventory total dollars	$5 million extra cash
Floor space (on 200,000 sq. ft.)	8% freed up
External ppm (not focus)	638 to 44 (−93%)
Lead time	50%
Quality & delivery	2002 Toyota Award

Table 19-2. Smithville Lean Performance, 2001 One-Year Improvements

As we will see in phase two of this case presented later in the chapter, the plant made little progress in the next three years in lean, and some systems actually degraded. At this point they took a value stream approach and started with a model line. The current state map that reflected all of the kaizen improvements showed a bunch of push, welding cells, a bunch of push, more welding cells, and a lot of inventory. A future state map was developed and changes were implemented, resulting in another huge step up in performance. By itself, the radical kaizen events turned the plant around and greatly improved performance, but they did not lead to a sustainable culture change and did not drive true connected flow.

The kaizen project approach uses several specifically selected lean tools to address the exact process improvement purpose. Many of the problem-solving methods described in Chapter 13 are process improvement approaches. In that chapter we noted there are approaches to solving small, medium, and large problems. The medium problems are typically addressed by kaizen events or as Six Sigma projects outside of Toyota, as depicted in Figure 13-2 in that chapter. And Tables 13-1 to 13-3 show a variety of different approaches that Toyota uses for process improvement projects, including various types of cross-functional teams, Quality Circles, work groups under a group leader, and others. Depending on the project, these can be handled in different ways. It might be a very formal project assigned to a cross-functional team. It could be an assignment to an engineer who will pull together an ad hoc team. It could be a kaizen activity done by a work group with little outside help.

There are some common characteristics of these process improvement activities at Toyota:

1. They are generally driven by *hoshin kanri* (policy deployment) objectives for the site that are linked to the site improvement objectives, which are linked to improvement objectives all the way up to the president of the company.
2. The process improvement project follows the steps described in Chapters 13 to 17. Ultimately, it will look like the problem-solving A3 report described in Chapter 18. It may be displayed on a board or a wall or actually on an A3 report, but all the elements will be included (problem statement, improvement objectives, alternatives considered, selected alternatives, justification, results, additional actions to be taken).
3. It will follow the Plan-Do-Check-Act cycle.
4. It will be part of an organizational learning process, with key learning shared across the organization.

Hot Projects Approach

Every operation has some immediate and severe pain which if eliminated will make the problem solvers instant heroes. It could be a bottleneck operation that is constantly holding up schedule attainment. It could be major equipment that breaks down at the most inopportune times. Or perhaps quality problems lead to whole groups set up to do nothing but inspection and rework.

Someone well trained in lean thinking and problem solving is well-equipped to quickly reduce this pain. In some cases companies use the one-week kaizen workshop as an approach to quickly analyze and solve these types of problems. As Figure 19-2 summarizes, there are both strengths and weaknesses to the hot projects approach.

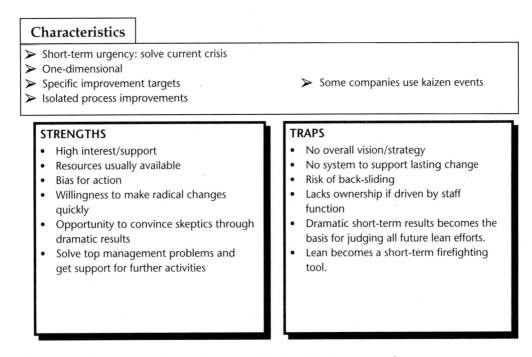

Characteristics

➢ Short-term urgency: solve current crisis
➢ One-dimensional
➢ Specific improvement targets   ➢ Some companies use kaizen events
➢ Isolated process improvements

STRENGTHS	TRAPS
• High interest/support	• No overall vision/strategy
• Resources usually available	• No system to support lasting change
• Bias for action	• Risk of back-sliding
• Willingness to make radical changes quickly	• Lacks ownership if driven by staff function
• Opportunity to convince skeptics through dramatic results	• Dramatic short-term results becomes the basis for judging all future lean efforts.
• Solve top management problems and get support for further activities	• Lean becomes a short-term firefighting tool.

Figure 19-2. Strengths and traps of hot projects approach

We've been in consulting situations where management was skeptical about lean and had a "show me" attitude. They thought lean had potential and it was worth giving it a try. But they were going to wait and see if it applied in their operation, with their culture. In cases like this we might ask, "Where is your pain? What is it about your operation that keeps you awake at night?" This will generally lead to some juicy opportunities for immediate improvements that will knock their socks off. And of course if you're working on a "hot project," as defined by the leadership, they are likely to pull out all the stops and provide open access to resources and offer their own clout to get things done. When things almost magically get better, management becomes believers.

But those who live by the sword can die by the sword. Once management sees what lean can do for hot projects, they want more. "Lets go over there, where we have another serious problem." Or: "Now let's move over here, where this darn machine has been a problem since we first installed it." And you can end up with the endless cycle of point kaizen we saw with the kaizen workshop approach. It's almost like giving the really good stuff to a drug addict. You win them over, but at what cost?

Many Six Sigma projects are "hot project" approaches. The Black Belt is under pressure to produce major savings for each and every project. The most obvious way to do this is to find a hot project. The "Six Sigma Changeover Reduction" case study below illustrates this. The hot project was intended to relieve a bottleneck—injection molding—by eliminating changeover time. The project was a success and saved almost $300,000 a year in labor cost for changeovers. Unfortunately from a lean perspective, the result of this was larger batches and a lot more inventory of molded parts and a higher total cost. And the elaborate Six Sigma approach only reduced changeovers to 1.2 hours, which is very far from world class.

This is not to say the hot project approach should be completely dismissed. First, it's a way to get some quick results and earn a license to do more thoughtful, longer-term lean system building—it's money in the bank. Second, it's something you should do anyway when you're well along on your lean journey. Once basic lean systems are in place and there is a basic level of stability, flow, and leveling, and when people are in teams and have developed good problem-solving skills, they will often be working on hot projects. These will be the objective of kaizen. But it will not be the driver for lean transformation. It will be part of a more natural process of kaizen.

Case Study: Six Sigma Changeover Reduction— Reducing Changeover Time to Break the Bottleneck[2]

In an auto parts plant that makes headlamps for vehicles, a young engineer was working toward her Six Sigma Black Belt. She selected as a project a major problem that the plant had had for years: an inordinate amount of time and resources focused on changing over plastic injection molding machines. This made injection molding the bottleneck in the process.

Detailed data were collected. The model changeovers averaged 3.5 hours. There were three changeovers per week, times 34 machines. This resulted in lost production of about 100 hours per week. The target for improvement was set at 2.5 hours per changeover, with anything longer defined as a defect. The project goal was to reduce 50 percent of the changeovers to less than 2.5 hours, thus cutting defects in half. A stretch goal was set at 90 percent.

A lot of data analysis was done to determine the probability distribution of changeovers; whether there were statistically significant differences across shifts, machines, and different molds. The system of measuring length of changeovers and process stability were both statistically verified, and a detailed process map for the changeovers was developed. Various statistical concepts were used like paired t-tests, Weibull

[2] We would like to thank Lester Sutherland and Donald Lynch, who shared this case study with us.

distributions, box plots, and a four-way probability plot. Also, more traditional lean tools were used, such as listing the process steps and determining which could be done externally while the machine was running and which had to be done internally while the machine was down. These activities were prioritized, from those taking the most time to those taking the least. A fishbone diagram of the materials, man, methods, machine, measurement, and environment causal factors effecting inefficient changeovers was developed. The top two causal factors were identified as waiting for a changeover cart and the process of heating the die, which accounted for 38 percent of the changeover time, or 1.3 hours per changeover. They also discovered 12 of 22 other steps that could be done while the machine was running (external).

The Black Belt in training generated a brainstorm of ideas for improvement with some input from the floor. This was narrowed down to action items to be implemented:

◆ Schedule mold changes to coincide with lunch breaks so the dies could be heated during lunch (they could not justify the cost of equipment to preheat the dies).

◆ Add one additional cart, which would be enough to optimize the carts needed.

◆ Assign a dedicated changeover team instead of asking operators to do it, so they could prepare a lot of the external changeover items while the machines were running.

The results exceeded the goal. Detailed data were collected, put on run charts and statistically analyzed. It showed significant improvements. The result was a 98 percent improvement resulting in 2,828 parts per million defects (defining a defect as a changeover taking more than 2.5 hours). The average changeover took 1.2 hours, well below the 2.5 hour target. Analysis of the savings focused on the reduced amount of labor for changeovers, which amounted to almost $300,000 per year. Actually, the number of changeovers done in a week was over the budgeted number, and they had a parallel program to stabilize the schedule and reduce the number of changeovers. So there were arguments about whether her project should get credit for the labor savings based on the current number of changeovers or on the anticipated reduced number of changeovers.

So this was a big success, right? Or was it? Let's consider what's wrong with this picture:

1. The total process took several months. Much of that time was spent on sophisticated statistical analysis and preparation of

presentation materials. If an experienced lean specialist did this, it could have been done within a one-week kaizen workshop.

2. The young engineer did most of the work while working mostly alone. There was little involvement or buy in of the workforce in the area.

3. The young engineer ruled out some of the most important ideas. For example, she ruled out preheating the molds, which would have had a major impact. A more experienced manufacturing change agent would have fought for this.

4. The objective of 2.5 hours is not a challenging goal, and even 1.2 hours is not a stretch objective for an injection-molding changeover. A more reasonable goal would have been 15 to 20 minutes, and a stretch objective would be five minutes, which is done routinely in lean plants. A 15-minute changeover could have allowed for more changeovers, reducing batch size, and still reduced the amount of labor significantly.

5. The overall value stream became less lean. There was no value stream map done. After the fact, a map showed that there had been five days of injected molded parts after molding, before the changeover reduction activities. By reducing the time of changeovers, doing changeovers only around lunch, and then reducing the number of changeovers, days of molded parts inventory actually increased, increasing flow days. Value stream mapping would have suggested reducing changeover in order to increase the frequency of changeovers to drive down inventory.

Plantwide Lean Tools Approach

A close cousin to the hot projects approach is what you might call the "hot tools" approach. Often when we teach professional short-courses on lean, we discover the main goals of the participants are to "learn some tools they can apply back at work." Tools seem to be the punch line, something really practical. Theories are nice, but tools work.

Again, we do not want to suggest that there is something wrong with lean tools. Carpenters, musicians, athletes, engineers, and any other professionals certainly need to master the "tools of the trade." This is not optional. What we're talking about here is whether the focus of your lean activities early in the lean process should be on mastering and broadly implementing one tool at a time.

There is a lot of attraction to going wall-to-wall through the plant implementing one tool at a time, as summarized in Figure 19-3. Or, in a multisite company, you can go across plants. Any of the lean tools can be implemented in this way,

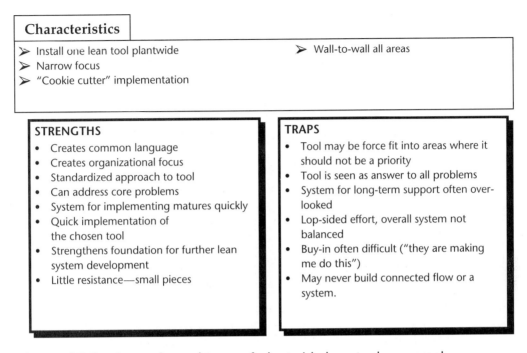

Figure 19-3. Strengths and traps of plantwide lean tools approach

including standardized work, Total Productive Maintenance (TPM), 5S, quick changeover, cells, kanban, mistake proofing, Six Sigma, and even work groups. It seems a relatively fast, easy, and inexpensive approach to learning a lot, generating a common awareness, developing standard templates for implementation, and laying the groundwork for further lean system development. Chapter 4 emphasizes the importance of developing stability before flow. So why not go across the organization implementing stability tools like TPM and standardized work?

We also emphasized, in Chapter 3, creating initial process stability in two operations in order to create connected flow between them. We've been emphasizing lean as a system, and the real benefits of lean come from creating flow in a lean system. You can see this when the system is in action. Spending years creating isolated stability in place after place will delay creating connected flows and limit the ability to learn what real lean is. If stability is like the foundation, then you are building foundation after foundation, and in the meanwhile no one sees what the house is like.

An important part of the "house" concept is that the parts mutually reinforce each other. For example, stable processes are necessary for flow, but flow lowers the water level and forces improvement in stability. Machine down time will kill flow, but why knock yourself out every day on preventive maintenance if when the machine goes down the next process keeps working off of inventory anyway? When machine shutdowns choke the next process so it also shuts down, there is a sense of urgency to fix the machine and do your preventive maintenance.

Also, the tools are there to support waste elimination, not as stand-alone tools. Take reducing changeover times, the main benefit of which is that you can change over more often, reduce batch size, and support leveled production. But as a stand-alone tool, we've seen many companies use changeover reduction to simply produce more parts and make even larger batches. This clearly sends the wrong message.

Company X Production System Approach

Now let's jump way up to the total organization level. Let's say the vice president of manufacturing decides to get serious about lean. Through reading, benchmarking visits, or a few successful kaizen events or hot projects, this executive proclaims, "We need a true lean production system." This is a noble vision and ultimately something we want with lean.

We have assisted in a number of "Company X" production system creations. One of the largest was the creation of the Ford Production System in the mid-1990s, or should we say re-creation, since TPS was originally based on Ford's system. The story in each case is the same as the summary in Figure 19-4. The consultants work with internal lean staff, with involvement of others in the company

Characteristics	
➢ Create standard operating system	➢ Typically large, multiplant organizations
➢ Focus on education and training	➢ Staff-centered deployment
-- Understanding & buy-in	➢ All advance together in standardized approach
-- Convincing upper management	➢ Focus on right lean metrics

STRENGTHS	TRAPS
• Lots of opportunity for buy-in	• VERY SLOW Progress
• Consistent message across entire organization	• $$ Expensive $$
• Common language and vision for organization	• Invites lots of useless debate, resistance
• Standarized practices as basis for kaizen	• People without lean experience may be shaping modifications and compromises of lean principles.
• "Lean" metrics promote right behavior	• Often feels overwhelming, leads to stalls
	• Bias is toward PowerPoint presentations rather than action.
	• Development before experience can lead to vacuous operating system

Figure 19-4. Strengths and traps of X production system approach

to "create" a system. While the system is based on TPS, there are modifications in language, the imagery (e.g., Ford used a five-interlocking gear model), and perhaps certain policies to fit the company. Considerable time is spent on the precise language and image. There is broad circulation of the documents and PowerPoint presentations to get agreement from senior management.

Varying degrees of standard operating procedures are put together. A lean assessment is created. The company realizes the current measurement system rewards mass production behavior, so it develops "lean" metrics such as lead-time, first-time quality capability, and overall equipment effectiveness (OEE). Worker morale is determined by conducting a survey. At Ford, key metrics were developed for each gear.

"Rolling out" the new production system (sometimes called "operating system") is a process of education and training: education on basic lean concepts and training on specific details of the operating system. For example, Ford needed a several-day course on using the new lean metrics since every plant in the world was required to begin tracking the new metrics and reporting them. The focus is on one production system standardized for all the plants. This is the way Toyota operates, and it's a good vision. It allows for easy sharing of best practices.

There are many good things that come from the effort to develop and spread a common operating system. It begins to give the organization a distinctive identity and a way to identify with its own tailored operating system. It provides a common language for communicating about progress. The lean metrics can help promote stability and flow instead of overproduction.

So what can be wrong with such an obviously good thing? The main issue is whether the cart is being put in front of the horse. The Toyota Way is based on action and learning by doing. The built-in belief is that people do not truly understand until they experience lean as a system. Otherwise, it's just an abstraction, which you may grasp with your head but not your gut. If you grasp it with your head, it's easy to intellectualize it. Basically you have three problems:

1. How can you create your production system if you do not truly understand lean?
2. Since this is often a consensus process, even if a few individuals have a good understanding of lean, others may not.
3. Developing an operating system is attractive to those with a bureaucratic mentality who love developing metrics, planning training, and envisioning the organization of the future but are eager to avoid real action.

All this amounts to a slow and expensive process of talking and developing PowerPoint presentations and teaching and talking some more. You learn lean by doing, not by talking. Or as our friend and former Toyota V.P. Russ Scafade puts it: "You can not PowerPoint your way to lean."

Value Stream Model Line Approach

You now know many things you should not do, but what should you do? Like Goldilocks and the three bears, some approaches are too narrow and specific (e.g., process, hot jobs, tools approaches) and others are too big and grandiose (like the Company X production system). We believe the value stream model line is just right for most organizations. What do we mean by this?

While hot jobs and processes are scattered across various points in the organization, value streams cut across the organization from raw materials to the customer. Lean is a value stream philosophy: Start with what the customer values and eliminate waste in the value stream. So why not focus on building lean value streams, since tools come together to create systems at that level?

Value stream mapping, described in Chapter 3, is a core tool for envisioning your lean value streams. It starts with a current state map, which provides a picture of the current situation. Waste becomes apparent, but in this approach any process kaizen to fix problems in the current state is strongly discouraged. The value stream map is not intended to determine a set of point kaizen activities. Rather, the current state is the starting point in developing a lean future state vision—a holistic picture of connected flows. Ideally, a cross-functional leadership team led by a "value stream manager" or other high-level manager creates the current state and achieves consensus on the lean future state. Action is driven by project plans to achieve the future state.

The action plans are straightforward Gantt charts. But we strongly advise that actions be organized around material and information flow loops.[3] An example of a future-state map divided into loops is shown in Figure 19-5. In this case three loops are shown:

1. **Pacesetter Loop.**   This loop is closest to the customer, and it paces all upstream operations. It is also the one schedule point in the plant. In this case, the leveled schedule is sent to Process 3 but then it flows through—first in, first out—without a break in the sequence to the finished goods supermarket. The pace of Process 3 then establishes the pace of pull from the intermediate goods supermarket, which pulls from Process 1, which pulls from the supplier.
2. **Intermediate Process Loop.**   This process supplies materials and replenishes the supermarket that holds products for its customer—the Pacesetter Loop.
3. **Supplier Loop.**   This includes the supplier of raw materials, and the replenishment loop to keep the supplied parts supermarket stocked with materials.

[3] Mike Rother and John Shook. *Learning to See* (version 1.3). Cambridge, Massachusetts: Lean Enterprise Institute, 2003.

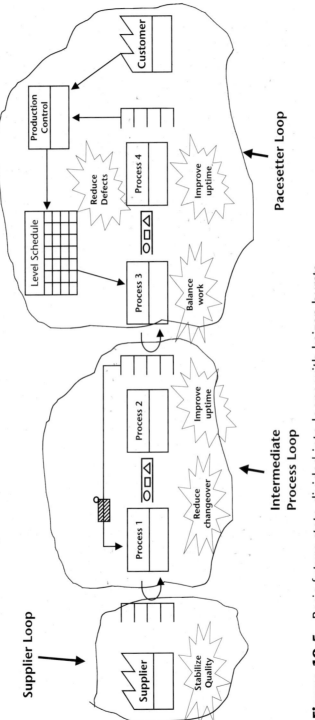

Figure 19-5. Basic future state divided into loops with kaizen bursts

Notice that each of these loops is a complete closed loop of material and information flow. Material flows toward the customer and information flows backward to trigger the next order from the immediate customer. Each loop can be independently worked on from a lean perspective, and the supermarkets buffer one loop from minor disruptions while another is being changed. A set of "kaizen bursts," specific point kaizen activities, are needed to stabilize the process.

Kaizen projects are not replaced by the value stream approach. Individual processes must be stabilized and variation removed through kaizen projects. A particularly challenging problem of process variation might benefit from a sophisticated Six Sigma project. Nor does it replace the lean tools approach since lean tools are needed to implement each piece of the future state value stream—cells, kanban, etc. What it does do is put the use of these tools and process improvements into a broader perspective—the material and information flow as a system. It also impacts the sequence in which implementation occurs. There is often a tendency to implement one tool at a time, for example, to do quick changeover across the plant. In the value stream approach you work pull loop by pull loop and do whatever is required to stabilize, create flow, standardize, and incrementally level that particular loop. In some cases you may have the resources to work on multiple loops in parallel, and in other cases you may want to work on them sequentially.

Characteristics

➤ "Learning to see" method
➤ Select product family
➤ Current & future state maps
➤ Develop detailed action plan ("loop by loop")

➤ Project management approach
➤ Visual management ("glass wall process")

STRENGTHS

• Efforts are well-integrated within a larger view
• Multiple benefits to value stream are common
• Results typically well-quantified and tangible
• Experience with lean as a system

TRAPS

• Can be time consuming
• Fluff—if no follow-up
• Requires large involvement to be effective
• Wide variability in execution
• Can be difficult to identify product families and value streams in certain contexts
• Others outside of model line are not directly involved.

Figure 19-6. Strengths and traps of the value stream model line approach

Even the hot projects approach has its place in this approach. For example, it may be that Process 1 is a severe bottleneck and regularly shuts down other operations, causing late shipments. By all means start with Process 1 and the Intermediate Process Loop. There is no lean law that says you must start with the Pacesetter Loop, but other things being equal, this loop is the logical starting point. That is, start closest to the customer and create a leveled pull at the pacesetter, beginning to create a sense of takt time in the value stream at that point.

If we return to the Tenneco case three years later, you'll see they initiated a value stream approach at Smithville. They began with a model line and value stream mapping. They found that the result of their initial foray into lean through events still left them far from a lean model. The new wave of value stream improvement got them additional results as dramatic as the initial wave of radical kaizen events.

Case Example: Tenneco Smithville, Value Stream Approach, Phase II

After the one year of radical *kaikaku* transformation through kaizen events in 2000, the plant did not make a lot of improvement, and in fact slid back from where it had been after the events. The 5S and other lean systems were not always followed, and the plant started to become less organized. This began to be seriously addressed in 2003-2004 when the plant shifted to a value stream approach emphasizing overall material and information flow across processes creating connected flows. The new approach was the "value stream model line approach." The Toyota product family was selected as the pilot. Rick Harris's firm was brought in, and the model of a purchased parts supermarket and tugger route described in *Making Materials Flow*[4] was adopted.

When Smithville mapped the current state, they found that despite the earlier radical kaizen, they had islands of lean connected by push systems. The current state value stream map is shown in Figure 19-7. Notice all of the push arrows. Basically we have inventory coming in, being pushed through various manufacturing processes, being pushed to one stage of assembly (welding of subassemblies) and then pushed to final assembly, where the muffler (brought in from outside), tail pipe, and such, are all welded to a complete exhaust system. The total lead time from steel coming in until exhaust systems were shipped out was 17 days.

The future state vision, which has been implemented, is shown in Figure 19-8. We will not go through all the details of the map, but here are some of the highlights:

[4] Rick Harris, Chris Harris, and Earl Wilson. *Making Materials Flow.* Cambridge, Massachusetts: Lean Enterprise Institute, 2003.

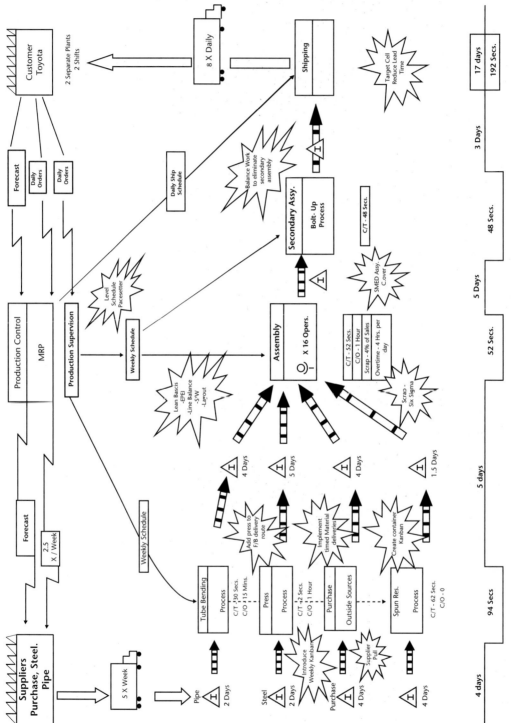

Figure 19-7. Toyota 500N center cell current state second quarter 2004

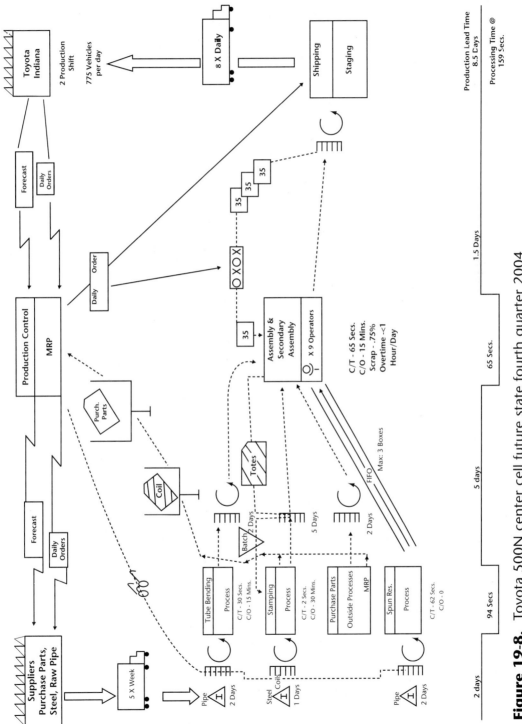

Figure 19-8. Toyota 500N center cell future state fourth quarter 2004

1. The two stages of assembly (Assembly and Secondary Assembly in Figure 19-7) were combined into a single Assembly & Secondary Assembly cell (flow where you can).

2. The manufactured component operations (Tube Bending, Stamping) and purchased components are on a pull system using a super-market and kanban (pull where you must).

3. One of the manufactured components that had been in batch mode (the Spun Res., or spun resonator) is built on a machine dedicated to Toyota with parts flowing through a small first-in, first-out buffer to Assembly. There are three boxes of inventory as compared to 1½ days in the old system.

4. A daily order goes to one place—Assembly—and is leveled, with everything else pulled to Assembly. MRP (Material Requirements Planning) has been turned off for everything except long lead-time purchased parts.

The purchased parts supermarket is modeled after Toyota's system. There is one central supermarket, and then a "water spider" makes regular timed routes from the supermarket to the various operations, delivering parts on a one-hour route. She picks up kanban and manages the entire kanban delivery system inside the plant. The route repeats over and over each hour, and there is even detailed standardized work that shows minute by minute where she will be—like a well-executed bus or train system. The result was a reduction in material handlers even though deliveries went from once a day to every hour.

The results in Figure 19-9 are impressive. Complete implementation took nine months and purchased parts inventory was cut in half, one-quarter of the floor space was freed up, parts per employee almost doubled, and overtime was reduced from 252 to 10 hours per week. Bear in mind that these levels of improvement are possible in a relatively short time because this plant had previously developed a broad base of lean capability that allowed Tenneco to work on multiple value streams simultaneously. While this value stream was being worked on, Tenneco extended the model line approach to their other main value streams, which were mostly complete about six months after the original model line. System-level changes like these are generally far more sustainable because they drive more significant cultural change.

Are there disadvantages to the value stream approach or is it nirvana? Obviously, no one approach is perfect. As seen in Figure 19-6, above, the value stream approach can be time consuming, require leadership of a cross-functional team, and a lot of involvement at all levels; and while the model is being developed, other managers and team associates are kept waiting to see how it

P-Primary S-Secondary	Metric (s)	Original State of Target Cell	1 Month Later	6 Months Later	9 Months Later
P	Assembly Lead Time in minutes (SWIP x TT)	46	13.75	12.8	11
P	Purchased Part Inventory ($)	48K	36.5K	30K	24.0K
S	Continuous Flow or Pull	0%	80% Complete	90%	100%
S	Square Footage	1896	1596	1446	1414
S	Operators/Shift	7	6	5.6	4.5
S	% Direct Labor Efficiency	61	98	101%	123%
S	Parts Per Employee Hour	5.4	9	11.25	11.25
S	Changeover Frequency	Every part Every week	Every part Every 2 days	Every part Every 1 day	Every part Every shift
S	Overtime (Hrs/Wk)	252	100	20	10
S	Non-conforming (% of total Prod.)	1.70%	0.70%	0.40%	-
S	Changeover time (mins)	>60	<25	<15	<15

Figure 19-9. Making materials flow pilot cell: D27 resonator assembly benefits

develops. We've seen ineffective execution of this method, most often when a team becomes preoccupied with mapping, creating beautiful maps with highly accurate data but little action—value stream mapping wallpaper. Some plants decide to map every product family in the plant, which can lead to endless meetings, mapping wallpaper, and no action. We believe in the principle of "no map before its time." Develop a map when you will use it for implementation—immediately!

Having the Patience to Do It Right

These approaches are not mutually exclusive. The point is to have a logical and well-planned process of deploying lean tools, which leads to lean systems and finally lean value streams. Tenneco developed a high-level, future-state value stream plan. A product family was selected, mapped, and a value stream model put in place. But soon after launching this value stream model line there are other process improvements and whole plant activities that begin. For example, kaizen workshops may be used in problem areas, tackling hot projects, and individual tools like 5S or TPM may be implemented across the plant (Figure 19-10).

The advantage of using these approaches concurrently is that you can get the strengths and reduce the weaknesses. You can get the benefit of building a pilot to go and see and learn from, and experience TPS in a holistic way. You can

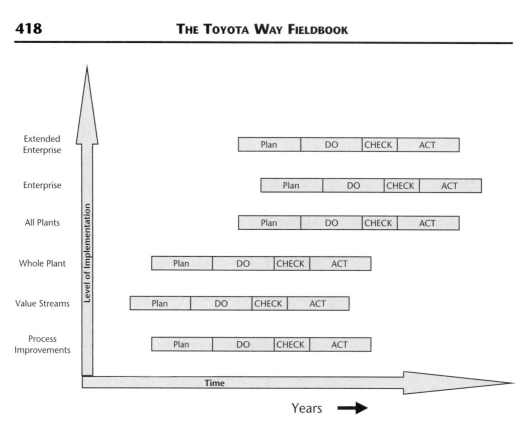

Figure 19-10. Sample lean implementation approach

also get a broader set of people involved in experiencing basic lean tools. And you can solve hot problems and get management attention and resources. The disadvantage is the very real risk of spreading resources too thin, in which case nothing gets done well or in a timely manner. You must be aware of this and be prepared to pull back on some projects if there's evidence of poor quality work or significant delays. In this case, pull back the plantwide activities and focus on the model line.

Note the Plan-Do-Check-Act cycle shown for each level of implementation in Figure 19-10. Lean implementation is about more than getting money back for an investment. Companies often invest considerable money in training and consulting support, and top management asks for the infamous "business case." When can we expect a payback? If you run the numbers for this business case, you'll probably only get credit with accounting for tangible cost savings. Mostly this means cutting heads. You might also get 10 cents on the dollar for inventory savings. The continuous improvement team, or whatever they are called, is now under the gun and transfers that to the consultants: "We need a payback in one year."

A good lean consultant can get this payback. They can reduce people, cut inventory, and make the numbers add up. But what are they really doing? In terms of the PDCA cycle, they're going through rapid successions of Plan-Do, Plan-Do. There's barely time to catch one's breath and check anything other than the resulting cost savings.

We've discussed many lean improvement strategies at many levels. The model in Figure 19-11 puts these into a framework based on two factors: Is the improvement strategy focusing primarily at the value stream level or primarily at the individual process level? Is the improvement strategy primarily aimed at applying technical tools to get short-term results, or does the goal include longer-term development of your people?

We've described the strengths and weaknesses of the process improvement approach and described the value stream approach based on value stream mapping and a model line. Both approaches are often used by companies primarily for short-term, bottom-line results. But doing this misses a much greater opportunity—to develop your people and organization so they're capable of making many of these improvements and thus multiplying the benefits. Many companies with employee involvement programs focus solely on process improvements and people development. People get team training and training in problem-solving tools but don't understand broader value stream improvement concepts. As we've seen, Toyota works on improvement in all of these quadrants, but more than most companies, they have worked to build a lean learning organization that combines value stream improvement with people development. Where is your company?

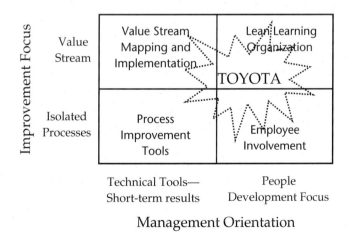

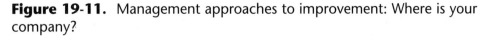

Figure 19-11. Management approaches to improvement: Where is your company?

Denso is Toyota's largest supplier and grew up with TPS along with Toyota. Yet its Battle Creek, Michigan, plant was considerably less advanced in TPS than Toyota. In the past they had implemented isolated tools, but did not put lean together as a system. As we'll discuss in the case example below, they developed their version of the Company X production system, which they call "Efficient Factory," in order to involve everyone in continuous improvement. To implement this they used real projects and the "value stream model line approach." Pilot product families were selected for each major product line and began to implement lean value streams from the customer back through to raw materials. Only when the model lines were implemented and the methodology tested did they move to other product families. Even a plant thought to be a lean model needs to periodically take stock of where it is and bring lean to another level, and the value stream model line is the recommended implementation approach.

Case Example: Denso's Efficient Factory Value Stream Approach

Denso is Toyota's biggest parts supplier, with almost $24.2 billion in sales in 2004 and 95,000 associates. Originally, the electronics division of Toyota, Denso was a spin-off, but Toyota retained a significant portion of the company (currently owning 23 percent). As TPS grew up within Toyota, Denso grew up with it, and as Toyota began to build cars in the United States, Denso built a plant (DMMI) in Battle Creek, Michigan, in 1984, to make automotive heat exchangers (radiators/condensers) and air-conditioning units. DMMI has experienced remarkable growth in a highly competitive auto parts industry year after year from its largest customer, Toyota, as well as DaimlerChrysler and General Motors. Annual sales between 2002 and 2004 went from $1 billion to $1.25 billion, and Denso's reputation for exceptional technology, high quality, and near perfect delivery placed it at the top of the list for high-performing companies. The automotive parts supply market is a difficult one in which to make a profit, but DMMI has been profitable year in and out. It would seem that Denso is an excellent example of lean manufacturing and has little more to learn. Those who don't understand the power of continuous improvement might say, "We have arrived," but DMMI knows differently.

In 2003, DMMI, Battle Creek, introduced a new activity: "Efficient Factory." DMMI is a company steeped in TPS tradition, thus, moving to a concept like "EF Activity," one might envision next generation automation, information technology, and new lean concepts. Yet, "EF" is simply DMMI's modified version of TPS. The EF symbol (Figure 19-12) has the appearance of Egyptian origin, possibly discovered on

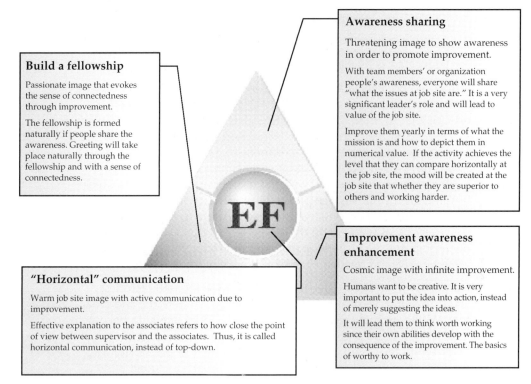

Build a fellowship

Passionate image that evokes the sense of connectedness through improvement.

The fellowship is formed naturally if people share the awareness. Greeting will take place naturally through the fellowship and with a sense of connectedness.

Awareness sharing

Threatening image to show awareness in order to promote improvement.

With team members' or organization people's awareness, everyone will share "what the issues at job site are." It is a very significant leader's role and will lead to value of the job site.

Improve them yearly in terms of what the mission is and how to depict them in numerical value. If the activity achieves the level that they can compare horizontally at the job site, the mood will be created at the job site that whether they are superior to others and working harder.

"Horizontal" communication

Warm job site image with active communication due to improvement.

Effective explanation to the associates refers to how close the point of view between supervisor and the associates. Thus, it is called horizontal communication, instead of top-down.

Improvement awareness enhancement

Cosmic image with infinite improvement.

Humans want to be creative. It is very important to put the idea into action, instead of merely suggesting the ideas.

It will lead them to think worth working since their own abilities develop with the consequence of the improvement. The basics of worthy to work.

Figure 19-12. Symbol for Denso's Efficient Factory activity

the walls of one of the great pyramids. Though the EF symbol looks intriguing, its meaning has nothing to do with advanced manufacturing technology, but everything to with people and philosophy. This symbol is also called the "Takahashi Triangle" after Denso chairman Takahashi, who retired as a Toyota senior executive. Driving it hard through DMMI is its President Akio (Alex) Shikamura, a true disciple of TPS. Certainly having a true believer at the top has been a key driver for deep change.

It is called EF Activity, not EF Program. What activities did DMMI begin in the name of EF? In the past they had many excellent technical programs to improve performance, including engineering-led kaizen through 1996, Total Industrial Engineering (TIE) from 1996 to 1997, and TPS concepts in 1998 (small lots, kanban). From 2000 to 2003 DMMI realized they needed more team member involvement so they created a program called WOW (wipe out waste). And each program had a major impact on manufacturing performance. But still, they realized they were significantly behind Toyota plants. So in 2002 they started EF activities with the following purpose:

1. Increase the "kaizen mind" of all associates.

2. Create a common target (vision).

3. Reduce costs by eliminating waste throughout the value stream.

EF focused on associate involvement to reduce waste throughout the entire product stream, from supplier DMMI to the customer. They realized that to bring TPS to the next level, they needed to invest in TPS experts in the plant. They selected Andris Staltmanis to lead the Manufacturing Engineering Department to a higher level of TPS. Andris has 18 years of production engineering and manufacturing engineering experience and was one of the originals at Battle Creek. In Yamanouchi Yutaka, vice president of Production Control and Planning from DENSO in Japan, he had a sensei to teach him. However, it was understood that the key to success was production ownership. Joe Stich (general manager of Production) was also well versed in TPS and needed to drive this activity from within.

For deployment, they split the plant into three focused factories: HVAC (heating, ventilation, air-conditioning), condensers, and radia- tors. Within each of these they selected a product family to become a model line—to go and see and improve. At first Manufacturing Engineering facilitated the model area, and then responsibility was gradually transferred to Production. The approach included basic process kaizen, floor management improvement, and value stream improvement. Some of the tools used were visual control, standard- ized work, small lot size, frequent delivery and pickup, and a *heijunka* (product load leveling) board.

Bryan Denbrock, section leader in the M.E. Department responsible for implementing the high-level model system in the HVAC plant, described establishing plantwide heijunka as particularly challenging due to the variety of products and customers. With the target of becoming a "world class" company, the HVAC model line created a system for finished goods production. This model line served as the tangible reference example for the rest of the plant.

The finished goods are shipped from a warehouse to the customer. Three hours worth of customer orders are brought to a large customer staging post. While the product is being staged for the customer, the kanban are removed. These kanban are then taken to the heijunka post. Kanban are arranged in order to level the production signal, which has a pitch of 10 minutes. This means every 10 minutes the material handler brings an order (kanban) to Production to collect the required product to be replaced in the warehouse, which represents what the customer has actually purchased. The warehouse kanban are exchanged with the production kanban, and creates the next 10 minutes worth of production. This paces the one-piece flow assembly line.[5]

When this heijunka process is applied throughout the plant (using the visual management boards known as heijunka posts), it's possible to see the state of the whole process for a whole day in one place. It is natural within the Toyota philosophy to use the material handler—or "water spider," as they are sometimes called—in this capacity, since they can see the entire material and information flow in their route. By creating this leveled condition throughout the plant, all forms of work can be standardized based on the 10-minute interval. This simplifies each operation, and it becomes immediately apparent at a glance if the standard is being followed. Once this condition is met, highly capable individuals who can carefully observe, understand, and think can understand the condition of the entire plant.

The heijunka post levels production across many part numbers. To achieve this, changeovers (fixture changes on the assembly line) were reduced to less than the takt time (takt time equals available work time divided by customer demand). A two-shift assembly line is changed from 90 to 125 times per day. The takt level is achieved through conveyor line spacing and the rebalancing of work elements for the team of associates on the assembly line. Internally there is a two-way kanban to an intermediate parts store (withdrawal) and then to a manufacturing process (production) for the parts pulled for use by the final assembly area. Kanban are brought to the store 88 times per day. Achieving these kinds of pickup and delivery frequencies requires a fine-tuned process that is highly stable. Even small problems will disrupt production and show up almost immediately. For this reason, for a company to be successful with these interruptions it must be committed to fixing problems immediately and then following up with permanent countermeasures. In terms of the continuous improvement spiral in Figure 3-4 (Chapter 3), the plant is several iterations down the spiral of stability, flow, standardization, and advanced production leveling.

Performance results on the model lines have been impressive. Product cost has been greatly reduced, while quality and delivery have risen to noteworthy levels. Most important, DMMI can utilize the success of this activity on other existing assembly lines. DMMI team associates have been directly involved and are transitioning to a new level of "kaizen mind." This allows the company to foster a new culture where associates' kaizen power can be tapped and implemented quickly.

---

[5] In fact, the process is similar to that shown in Figure 19-5, though the assembly is a true one-piece flow, and there are no FIFO lanes in the process.

Lean implementation is a learning journey, even in advanced stages. Every experience is an opportunity to learn and grow. But you have to take the time to check and then think about what actions will improve on what you've already done. We've heard statements like the following when preaching this learning perspective: "But we are in business to make money. This is the real world."

Toyota is making lots of money. But it took decades of work to get to the point where they benefited from early investments in learning. When we give this advice—to make the necessary investment—it's obvious to us that there's waste everywhere and the company can benefit from better quality, shorter lead times, more flexibility to respond to change, and increased productivity. Making some up-front investments in learning will greatly multiply long-term savings. Remember in the 4P pyramid, the base is "thinking long term, even at the expense of short-term financial considerations." Organizations that view lean as a short-term cost-cutting program are never going to achieve what is possible. They will never become high-performing organizations.

Many companies are anxious to spread lean quickly to the enterprise and extended enterprise levels. Simple analysis will show that most of the costs are typically in supplied parts. And it is well known that the impact of upstream processes like product development have multiplier effects on manufacturing that are far greater than the investment in product development. So why not start in those areas right away? Our experience is that starting enterprisewide and extra-enterprise level programs prematurely does more harm than good. There are a number of reasons for this:

1. **Lean is easier to see in physical operations.** Remember that much of the early stages of lean are about learning. It is also, unfortunately, about politics—selling the decision makers who hold the purse strings by getting visible, measurable results. This is easiest to do in routine physical processes. In pure service organizations it's easiest in the most routine parts of the business, for example, order entry, or the test labs in a hospital.

2. **There is a risk of overtaxing resources.** Management is likely to assign only so many people to lean. Focus on those from whom you'll get the best results and learning. Even if a separate staff is assigned to a "lean office," they're better off first spending some time in the trenches working on the core value-adding operation. They will start to understand lean at a deeper level, and much of that learning will transfer to the office environment.

3. **Lean service operations should support the core value-adding operations.** You can lean out a support function by making it more efficient,

but any lean project should start with the business purpose: Who is the customer? What do they need? If the customer of the service operation is some type of physical transformation process, first go see what that will look like when it's lean, so you can understand how to support it. When Glenn Uminger was asked to set up the accounting system for the Toyota Georgetown plant, he first spent a year doing TPS projects on the shop floor, which dramatically changed the way he looked at and developed the accounting system to support TPS. It was simpler, less cumbersome, and leaner.

4. **There is a risk of turning lean into the latest "program."** Often, the best lean consultants and experienced lean people are assigned to the manufacturing or core value-adding process in a service organization. Support functions are left to largely fend for themselves based on a short training program. The continuous improvement group does a superficial job, and lean starts to look like the program of the month. Doing it right is more important than doing it early.

5. **Trying to lean out suppliers before you've done it yourself is hypocritical and dangerous.** What right do you have to teach lean to your suppliers if you're not lean yourself? You need to earn that right. Also, since the lean supply chain is a hierarchy of many different elements that must be in place, if you start "developing" suppliers before you have mutual understanding and trust, suppliers will view the development as your excuse to hold them up for price reductions.

What we're preaching is patience. Think about the Buddhist monk teaching a young disciple, or the karate teacher, or for that matter any good teacher of a complex skill like a sport or musical instrument. You do not begin by playing the sport or playing songs. There are tedious exercises necessary to prepare yourself. You need basic muscle control and concentration. A top golf instructor taught by one of the world's great golfers said he spent the first three months learning golf without ever hitting a ball. Think of the Ohno circle. Stand in the circle and look. This need for patience and discipline extends to the problem-solving process. Do not race in and start implementing solutions. Take the time to find the true point of cause and then ask the Five-Whys for the root cause. Take the time to teach each employee step by step, using job instruction methods, before throwing them into the work routine. Take the time to check and audit and develop countermeasures to learn and improve. Make many little improvements, not just the big, visible ones. This patience takes vision for what can be in the long term. It takes a philosophical understanding of the purpose. It is the hardest part of lean. But in the long term, the payoff is remarkable.

Reflection Activities

Most of the readers of this book will be part of organizations that have done something with lean in the past. Many will have done quite a bit over a number of years. For those with some experience we would like you to reflect on where you have been and then develop a plan for what you should be working on next in the "process level" of the 4P model. For those complete novices here is an opportunity to work out a plan. This is a reflection that will need to be done together with a team from your organization— a team of decision makers that can legitimately set a direction for your lean initiative.

1. Take some time to list the process improvement activities you have worked on in the name of "lean."

2. Classify the most important lean activities in the 2 x 2 matrix of Figure 19-11. Where has most of your activity been located?

3. Now think about how you can build on what you have accomplished. Where should you go next in the models in Figure 19-10 and 19-11? For example, if you have mostly focused on tools or hot projects it may be time to undertake a value stream model line. If you have a good deal of experience on the left side of Figure 19-11—the tool side of the matrix—it may be time to work on the people development side. Note the lesson from Denso that working on the people side still means involving people in concrete improvement activities at the process or value stream levels.

4. Develop a high-level work plan. You can use as a framework the simple conceptual diagram in Figure 19-10 with some rough dates.

Chapter 20

Leading the Change

Can We Avoid Politics in Lean Transformation?

Changing to lean is a political process. There, we said it. Everyone knows politics are bad, right? Politics is what happens in organizations that are not being run rationally. A good, healthy organization is one in which reason rules and everyone is aligned toward a common goal. We have described Toyota as a utopian environment where everyone shares common goals, which start with the customer. So if you want to learn from Toyota, you should start with the assumption that everyone is working toward the same goals, right?

Wrong! Wrong! Wrong! Or as a harsh Japanese sensei exclaimed: "Stupid! Stupid! Stupid!" (As a young, petite woman translated from Japanese to English, to the horror of an American).

What do we mean by a political process? We mean that in any real-life organization, even Toyota, there are different people with different interests and agendas. Those who are passionate about any change in the organization have a vision. This vision will be embraced by those who see it as supporting their interests and opposed by those who do not. The degree of support and opposition will vary depending on a number of factors, such as how strongly it supports or violates interests, how strongly the interests are held, and the degree to which the organizational culture supports alignment around common goals. The political process is how these different interests work themselves out over time. Those leading the change would like to simply have everything fall into place like moving pieces on a chessboard. In reality there are always compromises to navigate through the murky waters of other people's interests. Push too hard, violate too many interests, and you will create a block of organized resistance that can stop the change process in its tracks.

Politics is about power, and power is the ability to get things done even against the will of others. Think of different people as having different pots of power: Once the pot is empty, you're done. That's a gross simplification, but power does need to be used sparingly. A wise leader knows when to give in, when to attempt to persuade, when to call in a favor, and when to use the formal hierarchy of authority to get official orders. Some leaders intuitively know how to use power, and others bobble it continually.

Leadership is about power. A leader needs to lead and is only a leader with followers. Getting people to follow you in a direction they are going anyway is not being a leader. The challenge is to get people to follow in a direction they might not otherwise go. Leaders must have a sense of direction. We sometimes call that a vision. Then they must share the vision and get others to buy into it and actively help achieve it. If they do this, especially when followers would not have done it on their own anyway, this is the definition of power.

There are a number of sources of power as described in the classic typology by the father of sociology, Max Weber[1]:

1. **Rational-legal.** This is formal authority. You are the boss in the formal hierarchy and can order things to happen, and others are supposed to obey. You have the legal right to give the orders. Your position confers the right onto you. This is often thought of as bureaucratic power.
2. **Coercive.** You can threaten negative consequences of failure to comply.
3. **Reward.** You control some type of reward and offer it contingent upon being followed. This could be a tangible reward like money or an intangible reward like praise. This was not included in Weber's original typology but it is the flip side of coercive power—instead of a threat, it is a promise that certain behavior or results will yield a certain reward.
4. **Charismatic.** When you have charisma, people simply want to follow you. There is some sort of animal magnetism that exudes a force that moves people to do as you request.
5. **Traditional.** It is the way things are done. It is part of the cultural heritage that on Sadie Hawkins day the girl asks the boy to dance and he should agree. It is part of preservation of our values and social norms.

A good leader is apt to use all of these sources of power at one time or another. Generally we think of someone as being a leader, rather than merely an administrator, if they have at least some degree of charisma. Any bureaucratic manager can use the first three sources of power. Give them a title and access to

[1] Max Weber. *From Max Weber,* translated and edited by H. H. Gerth and C. Wright Mills. New York: Oxford University Press, 1946.

formally sanctioned rewards and punishments, and they can get a lot done. But the leader is the person who has a variety of tools available and knows when and how to use them. When should I use my formal position? When should I use the hierarchy to threaten punishment? When should I use my personal charisma to meet with people one-on-one and influence them? When should I make a speech to the team that leaves them crying? When should I preside over a formal ceremony and draw on the power of tradition? Effective leaders learn over time how to use all of these sources of power effectively. Ineffective leaders are like kids with a loaded gun randomly aiming and firing.

We've had many opportunities to see large multinational companies implement lean as a corporate approach, companies like Ford, General Motors, Delphi, PPG, Boeing, Northup Grumman, the U.S. Air Force and Navy, United Technologies, and many more. In all cases there's a clear trend: Some individual manufacturing plants take off with lean and get way ahead of the pack, and many (often most) lag behind and implement lean in ritual and superficial ways. Visit individual plants and check them out. What's the difference between them? The answer is always leadership. In at least 90 percent of the cases where the lean effort has been successful, there's a plant manager who believes in lean, has a vision, and knows how to lead. In the remaining 10 percent, another high-level manager in the plant—perhaps the manufacturing or assistant plant manager—has led the charge and the plant manager did not interfere.

Leaders know how to lead, and leading means using power effectively. How do we teach that? There are many debates about what can and cannot be taught in business school. We say leadership cannot be taught in business school. The real question is if it can be taught at all or whether it's in our gene structure. In any case, companies can do a number of things to foster leadership, including:

- Carefully selecting leaders
- Mentoring potential leaders by effective leaders
- Providing opportunities to challenge people to allow leaders to emerge
- Providing leaders the support and tools to be effective

These are all things that Toyota does extremely well, from the team leader to the group leader to the general manager to the chief engineer, and to the executives of the company. Leaders are carefully groomed and carefully selected. Every leader knows one of his or her most important jobs is to develop people, and among those activities is developing future leaders. Everything about the Toyota Way is designed to challenge people to grow, and in that environment leaders emerge and blossom. And the tools of the Toyota Production System (TPS), the culture of the Toyota Way, and the unified management framework of senior executives, provide a fertile ground for natural leaders to be effective.

Leadership from the Top, Middle, and Bottom

Change is impossible without effective leaders.[2] But where in the organization should those leaders be located? The answer is that leaders are needed at the top, middle, and bottom. Let's go into each of these levels, and then look at what's involved in becoming a lean teacher, or coach.

The Role of the Top

Behavior in the trenches of the organization is a reflection of the leadership of the top. We saw in Chapter 11 that the leaders at Toyota are hands-on. They're on the floor or in the engineering offices or wherever the real action is. They have learned the art of *genchi genbutsu*, understanding how to observe deeply and see what is truly going on. Wherever they go, they are coaching and teaching.

But like all leaders, they too must work through other people. In fact, this is the definition of a leader—they have followers. We would not expect them to do a lot of the detailed design or implementation. So what exactly is their role?

Figure 20-1 shows a typical structure for a lean transformation. Each of the roles in the diagram is necessary, with the Executive Sponsor involved in two aspects of the process. On the one hand, he or she provides the resources necessary—resources that include but are not limited to money—and on the other has all the sources of power available to make things happen.

Remember, this is a political process. There is always resistance to change. There are people who will see their interests or the interests of their departments threatened by the change. Let's consider an example.

At one defense client that repairs aircraft, the labor hours of all repair workers have to be charged to accounts. To get shop floor workers involved in lean projects, they had to be taken off of their normal work and assigned to teams to participate in kaizen events. Implementation was aggressive, so a number of projects were conducted in parallel involving dozens of workers. There was a lot of pressure to get the aircraft out significantly faster to support the needs of the customer. The results of the lean transformation were impressive and moving this facility toward becoming the fastest in the business. The results were potentially worth tens of millions of dollars. But in the meanwhile the workers' time was charged to a lean account, which was falling further and further into deficit. An executive operating committee for the base was pressuring the head of the plant to stop the lean activities. Under similar circumstances an engine repair facility on that base had stopped lean events. This leader might have succumbed

---

[2] Many of the ideas and figures in this section were derived from the work of Bill Costantino, former Toyota group leader and private consultant.

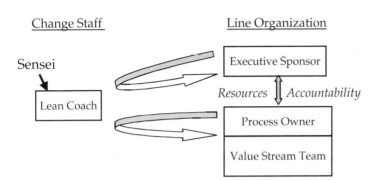

Change Staff   Line Organization

Sponsor = Executive or manager underwriting the activity of the team. Not member but provides accountability.

Process Owner = leader of the team and is personally invested in seeing the team succeed.

Relationship between Sponsor and Owner is key. Sponsor should be spending time weekly with the Owner coaching, challenging thinking and thoroughness, and providing needed support.

Figure 20-1. Role structure in the change process

were it not for the captain of the base, who authorized him to continue to use the workforce to run the events. The captain knew it was the right thing to do and was committed to lean.

It's interesting that the great "expense" of the project was an artifact of the command and control measurement system itself. All of the workers involved were hourly, but were paid a salary whether they worked on the lean project or on repair of the aircraft. In fact, with the lean activities, productivity was improving and many of the workers were not needed to work on the aircraft. There was no variable cost associated with the operators' time, but the internal accounting system that forced charging time to the lean account increased the lean account deficit. Since the executive committee managed by these numbers, they were up in arms about overspending on the lean program. They saw costs and not benefits. In reality there were large benefits but no marginal costs associated with workers' time. And the workers were learning and strongly supported the lean activities.

There will always be ongoing difficulties in making progress on lean: finances, individuals trying to block progress, lack of support from needed functions like engineering and maintenance, individuals citing rules that are being broken, etc. The executive sponsor must be able to see the bigger picture: Lean can fundamentally change the business to a high-performing organization. An effective executive sponsor running interference is the difference between progress and stagnation.

In our experience it's easy to get executives to see the benefits of lean and even get enthusiastic about it. But the difference between success and failure is the difference between head nodding and verbal support from the top and getting real action from the top. One dictionary defines "commitment" as devotion or dedication to a cause. Lean is a cause. A leader needs a vision of a lean learning enterprise and then the dedication to move toward that vision. Even in the face of opposition, the leader must press ahead and be unwavering in support. If the leader wavers, then subordinates will certainly waver. And if the leader turns every lean step into a cost-benefit analysis of whether it's worth doing, that will be seen as wavering.

A committed leader must provide the resources to keep things moving. This includes top-notch people to work on lean, financial support, and accountability for delivering results. It must be clear that this is important to the company and participation is not optional. It must be clear that the Process Owner in Figure 20-1 is responsible for success and will be held accountable. This goes both ways. The Process Owner needs to be accountable upward, and the Sponsor, as the diagram shows, must reward and encourage the Process Owner for hard work and results. This suggests that the Sponsor must know what's going on—not in the bureaucratic sense, but in the Toyota Way sense of *genchi genbutsu*. The sponsor must go and see to truly understand the status of the improvements.

TIP

Schedule Regular Reviews of Progress on the Floor

Unfortunately, top leaders get into a pattern of e-mail, meetings, and travel, and walking the floor to see firsthand lean progress is at the bottom of their priority list. Fujio Cho (quoted in *The Toyota Way*) describes getting Americans to seriously use the andon system by personally going to the floor every day to encourage them when he was president of Toyota Motor Manufacturing in Kentucky. This is a serious commitment and requires the executives to know enough to understand what they are seeing. There should be a regularly scheduled walk-through of the facility . . . or multiple facilities. There should be visual indicators of progress in the lean projects, and general metrics so it's clear when walking into the area how the projects are doing. A checklist for the executives, noting what to look for in their go and see walks, would be a good addition, at least at first. And these visits should be seriously scheduled and moved to the top of the list of priorities.

Stuck in the Middle

Pressure from the top, from the bottom, from all sides. Welcome to the life of the middle manager. We're using the term "middle manager" broadly to include everyone from the first line supervisor to the department heads. Their jobs are to turn the great ideas of the people at the top into concrete action and results. This means they must affect the lives of people at the bottom and work through these people. They must deliver daily production, be accountable for quality and service, and deal with all the "experts" management sends along to "help" them do their jobs better.

To people in the middle, lean is one in a long line of great ideas from management coming to them by way of staff. Middle management has another peculiar characteristic. Despite the formal power of people at the top of the organization, middle managers have the power to either get things done or stonewall. They can be the difference between the success or failure of lean. To a change agent, the middle managers can be less than pleasant. This is not because they are naturally stubborn, resistant folks. It's because of their position. The buck stops with them.

For a lean change agent, the middle management level poses the most serious challenges. On the one hand, this level provides the most leverage for lean transformation. It is nice to have the support of an executive sponsor, but they're not going to drive the real action. The middle manager will. In fact, we saw that the group leaders at Toyota drive most of improvement at the operating level. On the other hand, it's unrealistic to expect many middle managers to come forward and become the leaders of the lean change process in their areas. The team leaders do a lot of that at Toyota, but only after years of mentoring and coaching and creating a particular culture. And it is based on the Toyota system of group and team leaders discussed in Chapter 10.

There are some exceptions. There are particular individuals in different parts of middle management—engineering, quality, and manufacturing—who naturally relate to lean and get excited about it. If they grab it and take off, they can begin to win support upward even if senior management is not initially behind them. Unfortunately, these cases are rare. It must start at the top.

So in most cases lean transformation will rely more heavily on the lean coach using the hierarchy and power of the executive sponsor and working through middle management. Over time, if the company is successful in developing a true lean culture, there will be a flip-flop and the lean coach will be there to support middle management in driving the change.

Finding the "Sociometric Stars" at the Bottom

Organizations are "networks" in social science terms. Individuals are connected to other individuals through communication ties, social ties, and emotional ties. If you draw a picture of these connections, for example, mapping the frequency of communication, it starts to look like a big spiderweb—a network. If you look more carefully, you'll see that certain parts of the network are denser than other parts. At the center of these dense parts are particular individuals sometimes called "sociometric stars." That is the academic term for people who are popular or even natural leaders. Some people's opinions count more than others. If you can win over these opinion leaders, you can change the culture by working through them.

These leaders are not difficult to find. Since they're so well connected, you can find them in many different ways. Those in the organization generally know who they are, as do their bosses in middle management. These are the people Toyota tends to find and make team leaders.

There are many ways to involve them. The lean coach can seek them out and informally talk to them. But a better way is to formally involve them in the change process. The kaizen workshop is one great format for involving these natural leaders. If you break the larger group in this kaizen event into smaller subgroups, you might even make these individuals the head of a team. That, of course, means management must pay them to be part of the event, but it's a trivial investment in the long term, with a large payoff. Some companies will find a few of these people and make them full-time members of the kaizen promotion office. It is one thing for middle managers to come to the floor to enlist the support of the workers, and it's another for a respected peer to make a case for support. So, find these people and find ways to involve them.

Becoming a Lean Coach

The lean coach is a staff position. It is some person or group inside the company that has been assigned to be the internal expert or experts. In the transition to lean, this role is critical. Unfortunately, everyone is busy, and lean is just one more thing to do. For a full-time lean coach, this is their job, and it usually becomes a passion more than a job.

Lean needs to be driven by the line organization, not a staff organization. The line organization has responsibility and accountability for delivering results. The people doing the value-added work are in the line organization. They need to use all the lean systems, so they should own the lean systems.

Take, for example, standardized work. Going back to Frederick Taylor, the father of time and motion studies, the idea of standardizing how work gets done was thought to be a staff job. Taylor envisioned large staffs of industrial engineers who were expert in "scientific management." With their scientific management, which people on the floor did not understand, they could determine the one best way to do the job, and the foreman was required to enforce this one best way. The unanticipated result was the conflict this created between labor and management and the antagonism toward the "efficiency experts."

This led to more waste, and a separation between the goals of management and the goals of the workforce.

We saw that at Toyota standardized work is a tool used by value-added workers and their team and group leaders. It is a tool for continuous improvement. If we create a staff of "lean experts" pushing standardized work onto the workforce, we're right back to Taylor's scientific management.

Having said that, in the transition state to lean, the lean coaches are perhaps second only to top management in their importance to lean. It is the unfortunate reality that the workforce does not know enough about lean or have enough motivation to change to something they do not understand. Senior management may be "committed" but have so many other pressures they cannot focus a great deal of attention every day to driving lean change. Thus, much of the responsibility falls on the lean coach or lean team.

Given these considerations, can lean be a part-time assignment added to someone's full-time job? Presumably, if five people each spent 20 percent of their time on lean, it would be as good as or better than one person spending 100 percent. But five people with full-time jobs that always seem to expand to 120 percent of their time will not find the 20 percent to devote to lean. It is rare that we see a lot of success with lean without at least one full-time lean coach. In the last chapter we described Denso's approach to lean. As part of their Efficient Factory program, they're creating internal lean experts from their manufacturing engineering group. There is a general movement within Toyota, including NUMMI, in North America, to develop stronger TPS experts within the plant—at least two full-time TPS specialists per major process (e.g., paint, body shop, stamping, final assembly). This is a part of the recognition that outside of Japan, where TPS has become part of the culture, there is a greater need for TPS specialists to raise the bar on TPS in the plant.

The job of the lean coach includes:

1. Leading model line programs
2. Leading value stream mapping
3. Leading kaizen events
4. Teaching lean tools and philosophy (short courses and through lean activities)
5. Coaching leaders at all levels
6. Developing the lean operating system (principles, metrics, assessment approaches, standard operating procedures)
7. Internally promoting lean transformation
8. Externally learning and bringing back new ideas

The organizational structure of the lean program in Figure 20-1 that we looked at earlier suggests that the Sponsor, Process Owner, and Value Stream Team are leading the transformation, and certainly that would be ideal. Unfortunately, it's

TRAP

STOP

The Microwaved Lean Coach

Since lean tools and concepts are by design straightforward, it seems it should be easy to train a lean coach. Many universities and professional associations will certify your lean coach. But while these programs can teach useful things, they will *not* produce a qualified lean coach.

There are two kinds of knowledge: procedural knowledge and tacit knowledge. Procedural knowledge can easily be taught in the classroom—the steps to follow to develop a cell, for example. Tacit knowledge is what you learn from experience, guided by a strong coach. Knowing when a cell is appropriate, when the level of stability allows for a one-piece-flow cell, how to sell the concept to management, where the cell fits into the connected value stream, what size and shape cell will work best, and so forth, is based more on tacit knowledge. The "Tale of Two Pistons" case in this chapter illustrates how well-intentioned managers and engineers with a good deal of formal lean training ignored a true TPS expert and made many wrong decisions in setting up a machining cell. The seduction of microwaving a lean coach through immersion in a short training program is overwhelming for some managers. But resist! It takes several experiences implementing a true lean value stream as a team member and then as a leader over several years (see the model line program in Chapter 19) for an individual to begin to have a foundation to become a good lean coach. That experience should be guided by an experienced lean coach with at least 5 to 10 years of serious lean experience.

unrealistic in most cases, particularly early in the life of the lean transformation. It simply does not happen. External energy from outside lean *sensei* (consultants) is needed to keep teaching, driving, and pushing. On the other hand, when the benefits start to become clear to the line organization, there will be an increasing pull for the services of the internal lean coach: "Please come to my area next." This is a great sign of progress and makes the job of the lean coach a whole lot more fun.

Since the lean coach is so critical to the process, he or she needs to be carefully selected. Lean coaches must have the following characteristics:

1. Smart
2. Quick studies
3. Love to learn
4. Hands-on

5. Passionate about improving processes
6. Leadership skills
7. Strong interpersonal skills
8. Excellent communicators (writing, speaking)
9. Basic technical skills (comfortable with spreadsheets, graphs, data, etc.)
10. Systems thinkers (able to understand process flows, etc.)
11. Natural problem-solving skills
12. Read books
13. Open to new ideas
14. Personally organized

These are raw skills and attributes you should be looking for. But someone with these characteristics is not automatically a lean coach. The lean coach also needs to be trained. Some of this is technical training in lean tools. Reading books and perhaps taking a lean course at a university can do a lot in this regard. But the deeper training that makes a difference is on-the-job training, and it can only be done by someone who already is a strong lean coach. It is a mentoring process. This is the role of a lean sensei.

Learning from the Lean Sensei

In Japan any teacher is a "sensei." But the term connotes more than this. It connotes a relationship. The sensei is deeply respected for having knowledge and wisdom. The student wants to learn from the sensei. The sensei has walked the path before and the student is starting down the path.

Some companies are fortunate to have internal sensei, who can coach and teach. It could be someone they bring in who has been mentored in another company or a manager they hire. Some plant managers or vice presidents are former Toyota managers, for instance, and they become natural internal sensei. But more often these sensei are outside consultants who have learned through deep experiences, perhaps working for Toyota.

The most important thing about the sensei is that they are teachers. They are not the ones to come in and do it for you. Teachers are only as good as their students. Thus, picking the right internal lean coaches to learn from the sensei will determine whether you get leverage from the sensei.

There are different styles among sensei. Ohno's original approach was harsh instruction, an approach in which the sensei psychologically, and sometimes even physically, beats up the student. The sensei's job is to find fault, criticize, and ridicule the student, who learns that he or she is inferior and has to work hard to become adequate. Some hired sensei—experienced lean consultants— find they need to be kinder and gentler and go too far. They know if they are overly critical they may lose the job. So they become a member of the group and do a lot of the work themselves.

In most situations, the approach of the lean sensei should be somewhere in between harsh and soft. The lean sensei cannot become a pair of hands doing the work. They must challenge those they are training. This often means giving challenging assignments and stepping back, allowing the students to struggle and even fail. They can then step in and coach. This is the learning by doing approach. The student must be doing, and feel personally challenged, in order to learn. They will not learn nearly as much by watching the sensei.

There are different models for the frequency of visits by the sensei. It can range from full-time to leading a kaizen workshop every other week to a couple of days per month. Full-time is usually too much, and two days per month is usually a minimum.

Typically, sensei who are there full-time are doing, not coaching. This may be necessary if there are no strong students assigned full-time to the program. It also may be necessary to move fast. But it is only useful as a transition strategy. If the full-time sensei can drive enough change to demonstrate what lean can do, it will hopefully motivate management to assign a strong full-time person to work with the lean sensei. Then the sensei can reduce involvement.

The every other week workshop approach can drive a lot of change quickly (see the Tenneco case in Chapter 19). If the sensei is truly leading a kaizen workshop every time he or she comes, they are probably not doing much coaching other than on-the-job teaching through the workshops. And there is a strong value to coaching beyond the workshops.

The two-day-per-month approach is very powerful if there's a strong internal team to coach. The sensei reviews progress since the last meeting and provides challenging feedback and assignments for the next month. The sensei may demonstrate a tool or help with a tough technical issue and then leave. With this model, the sensei cannot *do,* but must teach, or nothing gets done. The students learn they cannot be dependent on the sensei.

When we put together the elements needed to make lasting change, it looks like Figure 20-2: the structure of the change process in terms of roles and responsibilities, the broad participation and ownership needed (especially within the line organization), as well as accountability, mentorship to learn by doing, and committed, knowledgeable leadership.

The importance of committed leadership cannot be overstated. The "Tale of Two Pistons" case following highlights the importance of committed *and* knowledgeable leadership. This case seemed to have everything going for it—high-level management support for lean, a good change structure, ownership by the line organization, and even one of the best lean machining experts in the world. It was a new line, so it could be developed lean from scratch. One area under one project engineer learned from the lean sensei, and the line was lean and highly

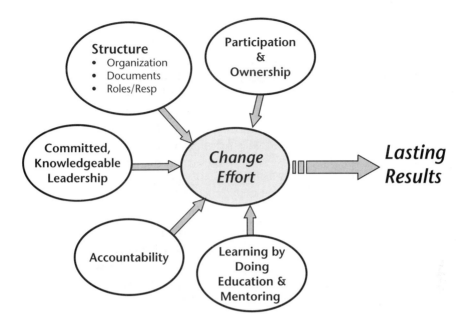

Figure 20-2. Key ingredients for change

successful. The other was led by a project engineer who did not understand or want to understand and took his lead from a plant manager who did not take the time to try to understand. The predictable result was failure.

Case Study: A Tale of Two Pistons: Toyota Machining Philosophy in an American Firm

"It's like there's a delicious glass of beer sitting there, right in front of me," explained Ishiyaki Yoshina, 30-year Toyota Motor Corporation veteran turned consultant for Engineering Integrators Company (EIC). "Every time I reach for the ice cold beer to take a drink, my hand runs into a transparent wall that has been put there in front of me." Yoshina-san spoke in the kind of metaphor that often characterizes Toyota associates. His analogy was colored with frustration over Acme Systems lack of progress toward a lean environment in the one and a half years he had been with them.[3]

---

[3] This description has been adapted from a case developed by David Ostreicher. It is based on actual events, though names have been changed and some facts modified to make the discussion points clearer; in essence, this case represents events that actually happened. Please feel free to send your feedback to David Ostreicher at djostrei@umich.edu for further clarification of the case and/or ideas to make the case a better learning resource.

Introduction

We have emphasized that lean transformation is a political process, one that requires committed, informed leadership. A great example of this was a case David Ostreicher experienced as a student intern working for Acme Systems—one of the world's largest and most diversified suppliers of automotive components. David was assigned to work with a retired Toyota engineering manager who was a leading expert on TPS applied to machining. Employed, at high daily rates, as a lean expert based on his 30 years at Toyota in production engineering, Yoshina was particularly familiar with plant launches of machining technologies. He had extensive experience with equipment installation throughout Asia during his career with Toyota, but this was his first attempt to apply Toyota methods in the United States. David was excited to further his TPS education by learning from Yoshina, and excited about the company. Acme was committed from the CEO level on down to building a lean enterprise, and had nearly a decade of experience. Yoshina was hired to launch several new product lines in what was to be a showcase for TPS applied to machining.

Two separate machining lines that made different versions of compressors were being installed in the same plant—the A1 and the X10 lines. Each had a different project engineer. As it turned out, the A1 project engineer embraced Yoshina's advice, following it to the letter with great results, while the other X10 project engineer tried to cut corners for the sake of short-term cost reduction and expediency, with poor results. Interestingly, both had the same ambitious goals and access to the same world-class lean expert.

"First Time Quality" was defined as the percentage of manufactured parts that passed all quality inspections the first time they were tested. The current First Time Quality levels were stagnant at about 85 percent, while the target called for greater than 98 percent. "Operational Availability" referred to the percentage of time equipment was available to produce parts when that equipment was required to produce parts. Machining operations at Acme typically had Operational Availability in the 60 to 70 percent range, and the team was being asked to bring this to over 85 percent. The business returns that were targeted (minimum net income, operating return, and return on net assets) were aggressive but attainable. It was obvious that there were high hopes for this new lean showcase.

The A1 project engineer was responsible for transitioning the older A1 family from an existing plant to the newer plant with completely new equipment. Simultaneously, the X10 project engineer was responsible for coming up with the best X10 line concept possible to be added to the two other X10 modules already operating in the newer plant.

Though the two lines produced pistons for different product families, the process used to create them was similar on paper.

Machine builders had already been selected for both the A1 and X10 lines. For the X10 line, the current plant manager's preference won out and the same types of machines that were already producing X10 pistons were selected for the sake of consistency. For the A1 line, Yoshina's recommendation prevailed and Toyoda Machinery Works (TMW), a relatively new player in the U.S. market for machining centers—though an established player in grinders—was selected with the hopes of initiating a long-term and more far-reaching relationship with Acme.

We will discuss some of the detailed technical decisions made by each of the two teams. This is not intended to teach a course in machining, but to illustrate some of the detailed thinking required to develop truly lean production lines.

Yoshina Meets with the A1 Team

Yoshina's approach was to provide guidance without dictating how to make all the engineering decisions required. He gave general advice and then commented on the ideas of the teams. The A1 team listened carefully to learn all they possibly could, then translated the lean concepts into decisions. One issue was how to make the material flow, given the desire to achieve one-piece flow, while considering the practical constraints they faced. The team decided that instead of one-piece flow, they would machine four pistons at a time. There were two main reasons. First, work would be balanced nicely, since four pistons would be loaded into one machine (two pistons in each of the operator's hands), a whisker switch would be activated, and then the operator would go to the adjacent machine to pick up the auto-ejected group of four pistons to place in the next process. Second, based on machining cycle times, four would be the number of pistons required per cycle to ensure that the A1 assembly area was not starved for parts; that is, to achieve the takt time required making four pistons at a time.

However, with the amount of chips produced if four parts were machined simultaneously, they were not sure how to keep the jigs that TMW was providing with their equipment clean—and without clean jigs for every part, First Time Through Quality levels would be negatively impacted. The team's current idea, brought to the table by TMW based on their process database, was to machine the pistons horizontally so centrifugal force and gravity would throw the chips away from the parts and jigs. They were not sure if this would work, and looked to Yoshina for some sort of reaction. Upon hearing this, Yoshina nodded in agreement.

The next issue concerned the footprint of the machining line. There was not much room in the proposed A1 area, but the team wanted to follow Yoshina's recommendation to maintain a straight-line flow. They recalled Yoshina's comments on the strength of this approach during an earlier meeting:

> A plant is like a show window for customers. The way the machines are laid out should make a good impression on visitors. No isolated islands are allowed. The lines and machines should be laid out straight so we can see far ahead along the neat line. The flow from receiving the material to shipping the finished goods should be simple. Only when cycle times are fairly long and the operator has to handle multiple processes and walk around a fair amount should U- or L-shaped cells be introduced to reduce the waste of walk time and distance. Always be thinking as if you were the part: Where would you want to go next? Would you want to go along a complex route from receiving to shipping, or would you prefer a simple path from supplier to customer?

Maintainability was the last topic brought up. The previous generation of A1 machines was infamous among the maintenance staff for being hard to keep running. Gauges and oil points were located all over the machines, and there was no set schedule for preventive maintenance. Struggling with this culture, the A1 team decided to take the first step and at least make the visual aspects of maintenance accessible to the staff from one place on the machine's rear side.

Yoshina took a hard look at the material that had been presented to him and seemed pleased. While he did not think that everything would go according to plan without countermeasures for issues that would arise throughout the process, he did reaffirm the team's fundamental philosophy, which underpinned each decision they had made.

Yoshina Meets with the X10 Team

The X10 team had a different view of Yoshina. It seemed everyone was of the opinion that his presence was a distraction from their more immediate deadlines. They politely listened to his ideas but then went about making decisions using more traditional criteria— mostly short-term cost.

They presented their ideas to Yoshina, beginning by touting the cost savings they were projecting by ordering jigs from a local company instead of the machine builder. The purchasing leader for the X10 product family identified an 8 percent up-front cost savings by using a local jig maker. In addition, the close proximity of the jig maker to the plant would allow for quick replenishment of damaged jigs or changes to existing equipment.

They next described their accomplishment in the area of one-piece flow. The group knew this was the ideal in lean manufacturing, based on an internal Acme workshop they had attended, and believed that Yoshina would therefore approve of their approach. The team was even prouder to report that due to the final machining cut, the initial one piece would become two individual finished pistons downstream in the process. Therefore, the line would enjoy enhanced productivity numbers, since handling one piece upstream meant two pieces of finished product downstream.

They then moved on to discuss the work flow in their cell. Everyone knew that the machine from Vendor 2 was about 66 percent faster than the machine from Vendor 5. Instead of waiting for a challenging question from Yoshina with regard to operator balance, the team anticipated the query and presented a chute concept that would be installed on several of the machines to hold a dozen pieces of work in process. Since the Vendor 2 machine was faster, it would be manually loaded and unloaded by an operator. On the other hand, due to the slower cycle time of Vendor 5, an automatic load/unload option had been purchased for that machine. In this way, it was calculated that the additional time the human operator took to load and unload parts from the Vendor 2 machine would offset its faster cycle time, thus bringing it into rhythm with the Vendor 5 machine. To complete the system, the dozen pieces of work in process would act as a buffer, just in case the automatic load/unload mechanism and the manual load/unload operator got out of sync with one another.

As for how the tool actually hit the metal, the X10 team decided to clamp the piece of metal to be machined in place, then move the tooling up and down above the piece in order to machine it. Coolant would be sprayed over the workpiece, and the plant's first implementation of standardized work would require operators to remove the chip build-up from the fixtures and tooling every hour.

These decisions enabled the new X10 module to fit into an unusually shaped space on the manufacturing floor, next to the two other X10 cells (Figure 20-3). Achieving this co-location goal was projected to save the material handlers supplying the line over 200 hours annually. The X10 team also reaffirmed the decision of previous X10 teams to keep the two metal-coating processes at an outside vendor, though their quality had taken a turn for the worse. This would increase work in process levels by 15 percent, but they would not have to invest in the $95,000 equipment and associated training.

They concluded the presentation with an update from the quality leader on the team. Due to the projected savings from various decisions throughout the design process, the team was planning to use surplus funds to invest in a data collection package that would monitor each machine's performance. Data could then be gathered at a PC with software capable of producing reports showing various metrics of interest such as down time, number of pieces produced, and machine cycle time. Collecting this sort of information was extremely important since the quality level of the current two X10 modules were not meeting targets.

With this, the presentation was over. Yoshina did not specifically comment on any of the plans presented. Instead, he approached the table and handed them a suggested layout for the X10 line that he had sketched during the presentation. They were surprised to see that Yoshina did not constrain the line to the oddly shaped space that was available next to the two current modules, but instead had sketched a straight-line layout. They agreed to discuss this proposal with the plant manager. Yoshina then thanked the group for their time and said he looked forward to hearing the layout decision.

Four days later Yoshina received an invitation to meet with the industrial engineer on the project. In the meeting, the engineer reported that after talking with the plant manager, it was decided that the layout would remain as the team had originally suggested. The plant manager did not understand why a layout that would require rearranging the proposed area to accommodate a straight-line flow was suggested. Yoshina realized that if the plant manager had taken a few minutes to go out to the floor, he would have seen the uneven risers, snakelike walk paths, and tight confines that characterized the convoluted layout he was supporting (Figure 20-3).

Upon hearing this news, Yoshina was obviously very disturbed. He could not figure out why Acme was paying his company hundreds of thousands of dollars in consulting fees for recommendations that would only be rejected. He got up from the meeting and stormed off, muttering a barely audible "*Yappari*"[4] under his breath.

Performance Results of Two Machining Lines

Which line performed better? In late 2004 both the A1 and X10 designed piston lines had been installed and were running for approximately two years. Though minimal official data exists for the performance of the A1 and X10 lines for the time they had been

---

[4] This Japanese word evokes a feeling something to the effect of "as was expected," or "just as I thought."

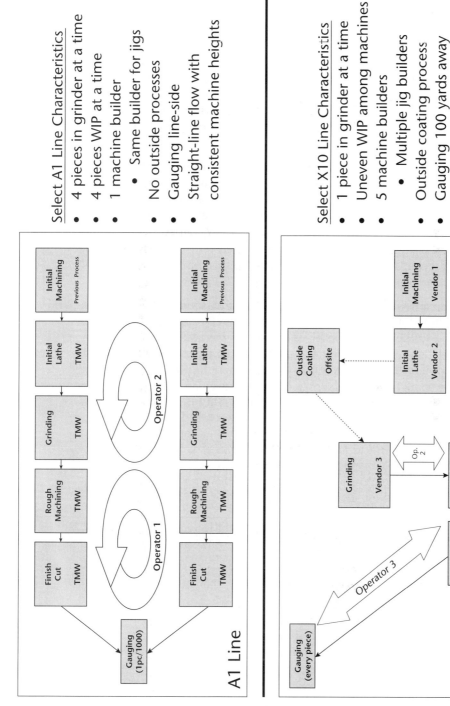

Figure 20-3. Technical characteristics of A1 vs. X10 Lines

Select A1 Line Characteristics
- 4 pieces in grinder at a time
- 4 pieces WIP at a time
- 1 machine builder
  - Same builder for jigs
- No outside processes
- Gauging line-side
- Straight-line flow with consistent machine heights

A1 Line

Select X10 Line Characteristics
- 1 piece in grinder at a time
- Uneven WIP among machines
- 5 machine builders
  - Multiple jig builders
- Outside coating process
- Gauging 100 yards away
- Confusing line flow with inconsistent machine heights

X10 Line

producing parts, interviews with operators, engineers, and managers led to the following overview:

	Equipment Downtime	Scrap Rate	Rework
X10 Line	30%	6%	15%
A1 Line	2%	1%	< 1%

The majority of downtime on the A1 line was reported as being caused by material shortages from the in-house process located adjacent to the A1 machining line that performs the previous operations, while the downtime on the X10 line was due to quality and machine breakdowns within the line. These X10 quality issues have since warranted that every finished piston is gauged in an area 100 yards from the machining line before being sent to assembly. Contrary to this, pistons made on the A1 line are gauged in sample lots every 1,000 parts.

After nearly three years' and hundreds of thousands of dollars in consulting fees, Yoshina's personal frustration became overwhelming. Despite his best efforts, he felt as though he was adding little value to the transition team and left Acme to return to Japan in mid-2003.

What Can We Learn from the Tale of Two Pistons?

1. **Knowledgeable and committed leadership is the key to successful lean transformation.** We're often asked why companies are not busily implementing everything they can learn from Toyota, given the success of the Toyota Way. Is it cultural? Is it resistance to change? This case gets to the crux of the matter. First and foremost it is leadership. This plant had all the ingredients needed for successful change: high level management support, a track record of success with lean, access to all of the lean tools and training materials, a clean sheet to work with, and one of the best experts in the world as a full-time advisor.

   The A1 project engineer believed and wanted to learn. The plant manager let him set up the line as he saw fit. We give the plant manager credit for not interfering. But when the X10 project engineer resisted the opportunity to learn and reverted to traditional thinking, the plant manager quickly sided with him in blocking Yoshina's fresh ideas, exemplified in his approving the convoluted flow to fit into the existing space, instead of stretching to achieve the recommended straight-line flow. It seemed the plant manager had everything to gain by following the advice of this expensive and knowledgeable mentor to create the showcase that would get the plant visibility throughout the company. But when push came to shove, he went with what was familiar and comfortable to him. Going to the floor to see for himself, to truly understand, was not within his definition of a plant manager's responsibility, and was not comfortable.

2. **There's a difference between a vendor and a strong technical partner**. Clearly, the A1 line benefited greatly by working with Toyoda Machinery Works. The X10 team selected the same types of machines that were currently making bad parts on existing lines—with no root cause yet identified—supposedly to get "commonality." They picked separate jigs and fixture makers because of price and locality without considering the complex interactions between these and the machines themselves. Yoshina, as an experienced practitioner of the Toyota Way, knew that spending a few dollars more on good tooling and jigs now would yield a lower total cost over the lifetime of the product. While the X10 line was created by mixing several brands of machines in a way that had caused problems in previously installed X10 lines, the A1 group relied on the experience of Yoshina and TMW as to what machines and processes to utilize in manufacturing the pistons. Yoshina and TMW were able to draw on a vast database of machines and processes that would robustly accomplish the piston manufacturing task at hand.

3. **There's a difference between learning TPS conceptually and deeply understanding**. This company had been doing lean training for years, and the vocabulary of TPS was well known. But there were specific challenges in machining that were not well understood. It was clear that the engineering teams were struggling to make the right technical choices despite their experience as engineers and having gone through TPS training.

A major difference between the X10 and A1 lines that probably led to many of the quality differences between them was how the tooling moved. The X10 tooling moved vertically, with the part clamped in the x-y plane. Due to the force of gravity, all chips and coolant would fall onto the tooling, leaving them on the parts. Over time these wastes would build up and become a big contributor to defective pistons. In contrast, the A1 tooling moved horizontally, with the part clamped in the y-z plane. With this design, though the chips and coolant would still fall due to gravity, it would not fall onto the part, but into the chip separator, for the coolant to be reclaimed and the chips recycled. This is a subtle technical difference that requires the kind of attention to detail characteristic of the Toyota Way.

Another example of the technical differences between the two lines was the misapplication of the concept of one-piece flow by the X10 team. By applying the idea too literally in a machining environment, several things happened to the X10 process. First, the operator was underutilized. In a machining environment, an operator's primary job is to check quality, change tools, and perform minor troubleshooting while picking up processed parts from one machine, setting them in the next, then pressing a cycle start button. If the person is only moving one piece at a time between machines, he or she has an extra hand free, and the process is wasting human operator potential. Moreover, the X10 team made a terrible mistake in terms of machine capacity. The machine they had purchased could make several pistons at a time, and the final product actually required four pieces, but they insisted on one-piece flow. (See the waste reduction model in Figure 5-1, Chapter 5.) The core philosophy is to reduce waste. Flow is a method used to surface problems, and single-piece flow is not always the best choice. In this case it added to waste.

4. **Don't settle for elaborate technical quality solutions when you can build in quality.** *Jidoka*, or endowing a process with the human characteristic of being able to determine a quality product has been created, is a Toyota Production System term that the X10 and A1 teams took quite differently. It appears that the data collection package the X10 group was considering would be used to make sure that no bad parts were passed on to the next process, an admirable goal. However, the system was geared toward uncovering defects, not preventing their creation altogether. This is an example of automating data collection rather than finding the root cause of a problem and quickly countermeasuring it. In comparison, the A1 line was designed to produce fewer defects, simply based on the physical machining characteristics and the process it operated within. The performance indicators of each line demonstrate that designing the process to reduce the production of bad parts from the outset vastly outweighs the results of simply catching errors that an inferior system creates.

5. **The most cost-effective short-term decision can be the most costly in the long term.** The decision to save $95,000 in up-front costs and not bring the metal-coating process in-house reduced initial capital expenditure but increased lead time and inventory. It also hindered the ability of Acme to solve problems quickly, since they were not in control of defects coming from the metal-coating process—defects that had been on the rise lately. This is another example of short-term spreadsheet-cost thinking versus total life-cycle cost minimization.

Can You Metric Your Way to Lean?

You get what you measure! How many times have we heard that? If you measure pieces per labor hour in individual departments you get overproduction. If you measure variations from budget you get people trying to increase their budgets or cutting costs even for beneficial expenditures. If you measure quarterly earnings you get companies cutting all spending at the end of the quarter to make earnings look good. These are all true statements. Narrowly measure a very specific aspect of the business, and beat them up if they miss the numbers in the short term and you get managers directing energy to making the numbers look good, even at the cost of long-term improvement.

From a lean manufacturing perspective there are many good books on "lean metrics." What are the right measures to drive lean improvements? In terms of our discussion of power, the lean metric discussion is about reward and coercive power. How can we pressure people through measures and contingent rewards or punishments to do the right thing?

We've been in the training and consulting game for many years, and the issue of the correct lean metrics always comes up. We always encourage a company

---

TIP

Use a Set of Metrics as Indicators of Progress and Problems

Let's face it, any large company is driven by metrics. There are certain metrics that get driven up top and are seen as measures of the health of the business. If these are traditional measures of labor cost variance, indirect to direct cost ratios, and such, all of the talk about lean can be for naught. We are talking one thing and measuring another. So the set of measures reviewed at the top should be broadened. The simple policy is to measure the Big Five in metrics: Quality, Cost, Delivery, Safety, and Morale (QCDSM). If all of these are measured, trends are tracked relative to targets, and top management responds to deviations from plan, you'll be well on your way to supporting lean. The key is to not get out of balance. For example, if only cost is taken seriously, managers will quickly focus only on it. And if only labor costs are tracked they will get even more out of balance. Use multiple indicators of the business and treat them as just that—indicators. When the indicator suggests a problem, go and see to investigate what the real problem is. Then, develop true countermeasures to solve the true problem.

TIP

A Standardized Process Can Be Effectively Measured and Improved

The whole point of measuring is to verify improvement. A process that is not standardized cannot effectively be measured. There is too much variation, and the resulting measure has no baseline for comparison. A process that has been standardized has *defined* agreements, such as takt rate and signals from the customer regarding demand, and the standardized use of resources ensures cost control. It's very easy to determine whether a process is fulfilling its requirement to the customer. The voice of the customer is visible. Total cost can easily be measured because the base cost is always the same. Only the time factor changes. How long the process needs to operate to satisfy the customer varies based on actual process performance. What if the customer stops pulling? To prevent overproduction, the process must stop as the agreement defines. If my process stops producing, my cost will go up and my labor efficiency will go down. That is not fair to me, right? This is why it's necessary to consider multiple measures when evaluating any process. Consistently servicing the customer at the lowest possible cost needs to be considered. Within Toyota, when a process is stopped because the customer is not pulling, the supplier process in not penalized. This time is considered "wait kanban." The operation is waiting for additional signals from the customer, and this time is deducted from the available time so that the process productivity measure is not affected.

---

to look at their measures and ask two questions: "What measures are rewarding the wrong behaviors or punishing the right behaviors from a lean perspective?" and "How can we balance this out with measures that reward the right behaviors?" This is certainly a useful exercise. Nonetheless, there are a number of reasons that we get worried when we are asked about the right "lean metrics":

1. There are more sources of power than rewards and coercion. Where are the other aspects of leadership to drive the right behaviors? Changing metrics is an easy, bureaucratic way to control behavior. It is often an excuse for failure to develop real leadership capability.

2. It is impossible to precisely measure all the right behaviors. Unfortunately, if you measure behaviors A, B, and C, you are likely to focus on those behaviors and focus less on behaviors D, E, and F, which might be equally important but difficult to measure.

or may not predict their actual behavior. For example, people can make strong claims about their lack of prejudice against minorities, but in an actual situation behave in a prejudicial manner. Sharing information and educating those individuals can influence what they say and how they say it, yet may not change actual behavior.

On the other hand, if we can change behavior, we can influence attitudes. For example, some people may not choose to work with certain minorities, but put them into a position where they must work side by side with that minority, and over time their attitudes are likely to change. One explanation for this is "cognitive dissonance" theory, which basically states that we want to bring our various beliefs into harmony. Knowing that we're working with someone in a minority group, knowing they're behaving in reasonable ways and contributing, and knowing that we do not like that minority group creates dissonance, and the easiest way to bring these facts into congruence is to change the negative beliefs about minorities: "Maybe they're not so bad."

It's not as simple as this, but the bottom line is that we're more likely to change what people think by changing what they do, rather than changing what people do by changing what they think. If we want people to understand and buy into the assumptions of lean manufacturing, let them experience it firsthand. Direct experience, with on-the-scene immediate coaching and feedback, will change behavior over time. On the other hand, trying to change what people believe through persuasive speeches, interactive video learning courses, or classroom training will not cut it. They might begin to say the right things, but it will not deeply impact beliefs or behavior (see, for example, "Tale of Two Pistons" case).

Similarly, changing culture is not going to happen because of a classroom education process. We can teach people what is politically correct to say and sophisticated ways of saying it, but not affect deeply held values and assumptions. This is the unfortunate truth, though it might seem a lot easier to change culture en masse through an educational program than to have to remake the structure and processes of organizations in order to begin to change what people think. But lean is not about doing what's easy. It is about doing what works. It is about confronting reality and having the confidence that we can shape that reality to achieve our goals.

So is it worth even worrying about culture? Ironically, you cannot directly impact culture through communications and education. Yet culture holds the key to a sustainable competitive enterprise. So it cannot be ignored.

Toyota figured this out long ago. When Fujio Cho was first creating the Toyota house to explain the theory of TPS, there are stories of Ohno tearing up the pictures. Ohno believed that you learn TPS by practicing it . . . on the shop floor. He did not believe people would understand TPS by looking at a picture of a house. In *The Toyota Way*, President Cho explained the philosophy:

There are many things one doesn't understand, and therefore we ask them why don't you just go ahead and take action; try to do something? You realize how little you know and you face your own failures and you simply can correct those failures and redo it again, and at the second trial you realize another mistake or another thing you didn't like so you can redo it once again.

From the beginning, the Toyota Production System has been about learning by doing. Anyone who has participated in or led a kaizen event experiences the intensity of the experience and the intensity of the learning. Within that team in that week, a microculture is being created. This microculture is often quite different from the culture in the everyday organization. In the microculture, trying things, sharing ideas, and even making mistakes are all valued. The group learns to see waste at a deeper level than usual and discovers it is possible to eliminate wastes they had lived with for so long. After the experience, they cannot look at things the same way again. We hear statements like, "I cannot believe I worked with that problem for the last 20 years and never did anything about it." The waste starts to stand out, and they know how much better they can make things. Friday is a celebration of the accomplishments and reinforces the microculture that evolved that week. Then something terrible often happens. After a weekend of rest, Monday comes, and it's back to business as usual.

One of the problems with the kaizen event approach is that one week is not enough to change a culture. And when the week is over, the facilitator often moves on to another area, another group, and another event. Making these short-term interventions in culture and then walking away does not penetrate deeply anyplace. The real value of the event is not the money saved that week, but the potential for learning and cultural change . . . which is often not realized.

On the other hand, the value stream project has a much better chance to affect real culture change in the area of the project. The kaizen event can be one tool in the development of the value stream, but in the value stream approach the event does not stop on Friday. It is just one in a series of repeated activities over a four- to six-month period. After the intense period of the project, management attention must continue in order for the culture change to continue and deepen. It can easily take three or more years to develop a lean culture where people understand flow, see waste, feel free to eliminate waste, and develop the discipline to sustain changes.

If you can develop a new culture in one major area of an organization, how do you spread it? Is it a matter of starting over in each area one by one? The answer is no. There can be some transfer of learning in a number of ways:

1. Management, assuming they are involved, will learn a great deal from the pilot. They will strengthen their commitment to lean and have a much clearer, stronger vision. This will carry over to the next value stream project.

2. The internal lean coaches will learn from the experience, which will help accelerate the next one and the next one.
3. People from other areas will hear about the pilot project, and some will come and see and be influenced by what they see and hear.
4. There will be opportunities for movement of personnel from the pilot, perhaps even as future lean coaches, to other areas to directly carry the culture with them.

The short of it is, the new culture will be transmitted only through people, by direct transfer of people who have experienced and been part of the cultural change. Transferring workers or supervisors is a very powerful way. In some cases jobs are eliminated in the pilot, and the people freed up can move to other areas or become part of the kaizen promotion office. What many managers miss while engaged in lean transformation is that the person whose job was eliminated is not simply waste to be eliminated. That person is an active piece of the new culture that the manager should be trying to foster. That person is extremely valuable if the value is exploited.

Toyota understands the importance of and challenge of cultural change. As they've opened operations in other countries, they place the highest importance on developing the Toyota Way culture in each operation they set up. They do this through the coordinator system. Thousands of Toyota coordinators have been deployed around the world, and their primary job is to teach the Toyota Way culture. It is not a matter of coming over for a week or two and teaching a class, but for two to three years, and mentoring every day. They challenge the student to accomplish a goal and then wait and watch for coaching opportunities.

A common question we are asked is: "Can the Toyota Way work outside of Japan since Japan's culture is so unique?" There is no question that Japan has a different culture, and in many ways it fits quite nicely with the principles of the Toyota Way. After all, the Toyota company culture evolved within the Japanese culture. The Japanese discipline, attention to detail, team orientation, dedication to company, lifetime employment, slow promotion, reflection (*hansei*), striving for perfection, and on and on, all strongly support the Toyota Way. Yet Toyota has had considerable success in moving their system to other countries. Over time, the company has learned that they cannot build the Toyota culture of Japan intact in other countries. They must allow the culture to adapt to the local culture. The result is a hybrid culture—a new combination of the local culture and original Toyota culture. But the Toyota value system is not compromised.

How much has changed in this adaptation is a matter for debate. Some might argue that the new culture is totally different. Americans, for instance, are not willing to put work before family and personal life as we see so often in Japan, are not as disciplined to follow standard processes, always want to know why they should do it this way, are individualistic, want individual rewards and recognition, are impatient, and they naturally think short term. But though there is some truth in each of these statements, Toyota has done a remarkable job of transferring many key features of the Toyota culture in Japan to countries like America, including:

- Teaching Americans to see and eliminate waste.
- Teaching practical problem solving the Toyota Way.
- Teaching the value of standardization as a foundation for kaizen.
- Teaching passion for customers and quality.
- Teaching the importance of teamwork.
- Teaching the value of people.

TRAP

Training Your Way to a New Culture

In Chapter 19 we described the "Company X Production System Approach," where X is your company name. This is often intended as an enterprise wide approach to drive a common operating system. It's a noble idea, and one to which we subscribe. The problem is when it's viewed as a top-down way of driving culture change through a staff organization. You cannot PowerPoint your way to a new culture. All the slick multicolor slides and training packages in the world will not change a culture. Simply "telling them" does little good. People will get more aware of the words and concepts that can help if there is a deeper cultural change through leadership, direct experience, and the transfer of personnel to teach and coach others into the new culture. But as a stand-alone process, training and communications do not change what people truly believe and feel and how they behave. We worked with one of our clients to develop excellent model line pilots over a one-and-a-half-year period developing strong local expertise in the process. When they decided to deploy lean from the central office they did not even promote those people involved but rather selected people with no experience to be trained in a classroom and assume lean leader roles. What a waste!

Spreading Your Learning to Partners

If partners are truly extensions of the lean enterprise, then the culture must be spread to partners. Let's take the example of Denso discussed in Chapter 19. Since Denso is one of Toyota's original *keiretsu* suppliers, partly owned by Toyota, one would think they were always thoroughly steeped in TPS. Yet they realized that they had not achieved the level of TPS they saw at Toyota plants. They had used many technical methods similar to TPS but did not have the "kaizen mind" of Toyota. The countermeasure was the EF activities represented by a triangle.

It is no surprise that this triangle is called the Takahashi triangle after Denso chairman, Takahashi, who retired as a Toyota senior executive. One of his jobs at Denso is to create a culture compatible with that of Toyota. If Toyota develops a culture of continuous improvement by all associates that is far more advanced than Denso, how can Denso keep up?

Why does Denso need to keep up as long as they give Toyota the price they ask for? As we discussed in Chapter 12, Toyota does not want to manage supplier price. They want to manage supplier cost. As Toyota reduces cost through the myriad activities of team associates solving small problems every day, they will hit the wall if their suppliers' costs reduction efforts are not every bit as intense. The supplier cost will become a bottleneck in the process. And supplier costs account for most of the cost of Toyota vehicles. If suppliers agree to price reductions but do not reduce actual costs, they will become unhealthy suppliers. They will not have the cash to reinvest in the business and in future technologies. If suppliers reduce costs by beating up employees and suppliers and other short-term cost cutting measures, the basic infrastructure of the supply base will crumble.

In Chapter 3, we talked about the process of stabilizing, creating flow, standardizing, and leveling incrementally. We said that to connect two operations in a plant, each operation needed some degree of initial stability. They could then be connected in some degree of flow. This becomes the new standard, and there's an opportunity to do some leveling. We then described the continuous improvement spiral, where this process continues at deeper and deeper levels. Instead of two operations in a plant, imagine an assembly plant and a supplier plant, and the same principle applies. Each plant's processes must be stabilized, and then they can be connected, the new process standardized and then incrementally leveled. This is repeated in a continuous improvement spiral over time.

Now consider a company like Denso sending after-market parts to a Toyota service parts warehouse. Then consider Denso's product development organization designing the heating, ventilation, and air-conditioning system along with Toyota engineers developing a new car. And how about the Toyota sales organization selling cars to dealers? In each case the principle is the same. Each partner, along with Toyota, must stabilize to a new level, create a connected flow, standardize, and then incrementally level. This is the process of continuous improvement. If Toyota stabilizes at a level well beyond that of their partners, the process stops.

Toyota wants its partners to be independent because if they're dependent and looking to Toyota for constant guidance, they will never have the strength to improve themselves. Toyota cannot drive improvement to the level they want from outside, so they say that it's fine if their suppliers have their own way, not the Toyota Way. In fact, it's encouraged . . . as long as it works. When there is a serious quality problem or a launch problem or a problem that might shut down Toyota, then the Toyota crew jumps into action and begins to teach the supplier the Toyota Way. They may not call it that, but they're teaching all the principles described in this book. In our experience, the Toyota suppliers are anxious to learn, because they know it is a better way.

So there are some strong prerequisites for changing your partners along with your internal operations to create a mutually compatible culture:

1. You must be seriously doing it yourself internally.
2. You must develop true leaders whom the suppliers want to follow and learn from.
3. You must have patience in teaching the suppliers.
4. Suppliers must want to be taught by you.
5. Suppliers must see value added to themselves by learning.
6. Suppliers' independence must grow over time; they must develop their own lean culture.

TRAP

STOP

Jumping the Gun on Teaching Lean to Suppliers

We cannot emphasize enough how important it is to be seriously doing lean yourself before trying to spread it to suppliers. We have seen truly ridiculous situations where larger companies brimming with machismo decide to bring lean to the little people—their small and inferior suppliers. The problem: The big, powerful customer has done nothing more than a lot of talking, a lot of PowerPoint presentations, and a few limited models. The suppliers, in contrast, worked hard at lean and were far ahead of their customers. Having these customers come to teach lean and then ask for price reductions was akin to hunting and gathering.

Again, Toyota wants suppliers to have their own cultures. But they want those cultures to be compatible with that of Toyota's, so the basic principles of the Toyota Way must be realized in the suppliers. For example, if the suppliers were to have a traditional large batch, top-down culture, their costs would probably be too high, and they'd risk shutting down Toyota, and Toyota would not stand for this. But if the supplier has its own version of a lean culture and it works, that's wonderful as far as Toyota is concerned.

Delphi, discussed in Chapter 12, is in the very early stages of working to develop a Toyota-style lean enterprise with its suppliers. Delphi purchasing executives realize the key to their success is winning the supplier's trust. Toward this end, they included as one of their key performance indicators a supplier survey. They contracted with Henke's Planning Perspectives company, which does the supplier surveys for all the major automakers, and requested a special survey of Delphi's suppliers working at the tier-two level. The results in 2004 were not pretty. Delphi was not perceived as a trustworthy and reasonable customer. This was not a surprise to Delphi after years of getting beat up by customers and turning around to beat up their own suppliers. Now they had to change this adversarial relationship to a win-win, cooperative relationship. Delphi is working on this supplier by supplier. They started by sending top-notch lean experts—some outside consultants and some internal—to help their suppliers lean their processes. This was a huge success and began the process of winning over suppliers. It will be some time before a large portion of Delphi's key suppliers believe and trust, but Delphi is willing to make the investment and have the patience to spend years transforming to a lean enterprise. Over time they are striving to create compatible cultures and trusting relationships internally and with their supplier partners.

Now Please Try . . . and Do Your Best

While David Meier worked at Toyota in Georgetown he was often asked to "do your best." This was not so much an instruction as a genuine request. It was expected that every individual did his or her very best. There was no need for discussion of "right or wrong" or "good or bad." Team associates all simply put forth their best efforts. It was all that was asked. We think that this request has a place in every company faced with the challenges of implementing a version of the Toyota Way. Everyone must give his or her best effort.

In addition, David would often be asked to "please try," and if for some reason he was avoiding the request, he was told to "just do." It seems some people are afraid to try things for fear of making a mistake or getting them wrong. One thing is for certain: If you never make a mistake, you're not doing anything. When a request seemed to be greater than his capability, David was simply asked to "please try." That is one of the best suggestions we can make to anyone. It's necessary to try some of the things mentioned in this book before you understand the true meaning or value.

If you're having a hard time convincing yourself or others to try, then "just do." It was after several instances of doing that David discovered the meaning of the TPS philosophy. There was no other way it could make sense to him. The only way to gain true understanding was through doing. We like to suggest to companies that when they first learn a concept, try it, then think and reflect on the result to learn more, and then try again, and again. At Toyota, team associates were always encouraged to keep trying, to keep improving, and to never stop growing and developing.

Sometimes the simplest lessons provide the most profound education. We have been fortunate over the years to work with many exceptional teachers of the Toyota Way. It has not always been an easy education. On one particular day David's mentor, Mr. Takeuchi, was insistent that he complete a particular task immediately. David was fairly busy and had his attention on other issues. He explained that he would take care of Takeuchi's request in a few weeks (he said "*Atto dei,*" which means "Later" in Japanese). But Takeuchi gently suggested that David complete his request immediately—*ima* in Japanese. This tug of war went back and forth, with David insisting he would take care of it later and Takeuchi suggesting that he would prefer immediately. One thing about Mr. Takeuchi is that he is both patient and persistent. Ultimately his persistence won out over his patience. Finally, he motioned David to the nearest meeting room where there was a white board, drew a stair step diagram (Figure 20-6) and said, "Dave-san, our job is, every day, little up."

Figure 20-6. Every day, little up!

Drawing an arrow parallel to the stairs, he said, "Then, over time, we up!" (Figure 20-7).

In a moment like this, valuable lessons are often lost. In this case David just wanted to get Takeuchi off his back, so he complied with his request. Sometime later David realized the power within this simple message. Toyota simply strives to make small gains continuously, every day. If they can make these improvements consistently over time, the company will grow stronger. It was the leader's responsibility to ensure that everyone was making some contribution

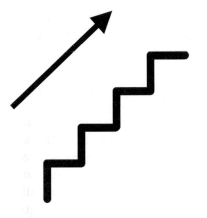

Figure 20-7. Then, over time, we up!

every day, no matter how small. These contributions would surely lift the group and company over time. David came to understand how strongly this philosophy ties to Toyota's philosophy of long-term thinking and planning. They are clearly in it for the long haul. They understand that a tortoise who methodically moves forward will not only finish the race, but also can beat the speedier, inconsistent hare.

Another lesson also became clear. It's necessary to take a first step up the stairs before it's possible to see the next step, or to see the potential benefit of moving forward. We've said this before, but it bears repeating: Imagine that you are standing on the stairs. If you look straight ahead, you only see the visible step. As you take a step up, new opportunities become visible (Figure 20-8).

"Every day, little up"

"Until you take the first step, it will not be possible to see the next step."

Figure 20-8. Continuous improvement never ends

This also applies to the change process. Some potential improvements will remain hidden until you take initial steps. Then suddenly opportunities appear that you never saw before. So there is this paradox: If you do not take steps, the opportunities may not present themselves to you. It is a natural incremental process of learning by doing. You start the journey and then adjust it as you go.

Unfortunately, it's not always easy for people to try and risk failure. A University of Michigan professor, Fiona Lee, and her colleagues have been studying the phenomena of trying.[5] They have been doing psychological experiments in which subjects need to try a lot of alternatives and learn from success and failure if they want to get through a type of maze. It is a rug on the floor full of squares with some electronics hidden underneath in a pattern. If they step on the wrong square, they trigger a loud "beep." But by trying a lot of squares and getting beeps, they learn the pattern and can get through the maze. They find that often people just get stuck and refuse to keep moving forward because they're afraid to trigger the dreaded "beep." This is to some degree cultural. Americans, who have been raised to believe in rugged individualism, hate to fail. There is a stigma of appearing incompetent, and American culture discourages experimenting, trying something new, reflecting on failures, and asking for help—even when they desperately need help and help is available. These results are true of American male and female professionals in Lee's experiments—there is no significant gender difference.

The piecemeal changes that David was learning, one step at a time, can be quite threatening. Do something new each day. Take a risk each day. Risk a beep. This may explain another phenomena we have observed. When we first start to work with companies, they often ask: "Is there a company like ours that has implemented lean that we can go visit?" This can be as specific as wanting to see a low-volume, high-mix decorative toilet seat company, or a prototype design shop for prosthetic devices, or a low-volume medical lab that does specialized blood tests, or a highly automated glass-making plant, or name your type of company. Unfortunately, there is not one of everything in the world that is a lean model—there are all too few lean models outside Toyota and its suppliers. What we think they're telling us is: "Paint me a detailed picture of exactly what the destination will look like in my business before we start the journey." The other question asked is: "What exactly can we expect in terms of cost savings and what will it cost to go lean?" In other words, put in numbers precisely what we can expect so we don't have to take a risk. Fear of taking this step by step and figuring it out as we go is one reason there are so few good lean models, and overcoming that fear requires a leap of faith.

---

[5] Fiona Lee, A. Edmondson, S.. Thomke, and M. Worline, "The mixed effects of inconsistency on experimentation in organizations," *Organization Science, 15*(3) (2004), 310-26.

Fiona Lee and her colleagues also discovered another interesting finding in their experiments. Inconsistency in messages about taking risk kills the drive for innovation. People are more likely to take the risk if the failures are not punished *and* there is support that failure is acceptable—you need both of these things combined. Interestingly, if there are supportive statements about how taking risks is valued but then people are punished, or if they're not punished for failing but get the message that failure is unacceptable, they are less likely to take any chances and more often get stuck. In fact—and this is the most interesting finding—if they're told that taking risks is unacceptable, and they're punished for taking risk, they are still more likely to take risks then if they get inconsistent messages. This is startling. It seems that the worst thing is *inconsistency*.

In many organizations we've worked with there are too many inconsistent messages. Trying and experimenting are supported in the kaizen event but not in daily work. Top management is preaching change but middle managers are preaching production and business as usual and punishing any production disruptions. Management is preaching to stop and fix problems to achieve high quality, but in the heat of production workers are instructed to put their heads down and get production out at all costs. Management says it's okay to innovate and experiment, but then punishes people for failing. This threatens feelings of individual competence and superiority—both highly valued in Western society.

TIP

Consistent Messages Will Dictate Behavior

In Chapter 11 we referred to continuous improvement within Toyota and how a consistent message regarding what "continuous" means is critical to the thinking and resulting action. We see other companies attempt to model continuous improvement and then place several criteria on when the improvements are acceptable. Many improvements are overlooked because it isn't clear if they are "worthy" or acceptable. This is how the process gets bogged down and innovation dies. If you say you want continuous improvement, you must literally mean continuous, all the time, under all conditions, without regard to merit, complexity, or significance. No improvement is too small, and the right time is always now.

None of this is easy. It's all very risky. We can only imagine that *The Toyota Way* and *The Toyota Way Fieldbook* are a little overwhelming. People are inspired and excited about the possibilities, but there is so far to go. Virtually every aspect of every process and every aspect of the culture needs work. Yet, if you think of it that way, you are apt to get frozen. Then you will only be looking at the visible step ahead . . . or even worse, looking down at the step you're on. About the best advice we can give is to "please do" . . . and "please try your best." Remember, "Every day, little up!"

Reflection Activities

This is the most serious reflection of all. We are asking you to reflect on whether you are serious about getting started on a real lean journey. We have worked to paint a picture in this book of what that looks like in detail. It is clearly much more than the technical trickery of many lean programs. It is a serious lifetime commitment to building a culture of continuous improvement. Are you ready? This question would apply whether you are brand new to lean or have been at it for 10 years but not in the deep sense of the Toyota Way. Ask yourselves the following questions and begin on whatever path you choose. We use the term "you" not to refer just to the reader but to a critical mass of leaders in the organization.

1. Does your organization have top leaders who are seriously dedicated to becoming a lean learning enterprise? If not, do they at least seem seriously coachable?
2. Are you committed to this process for the long term (forever)?
3. What steps will you need to take to prepare yourself for this process?
4. Are you willing to make enough of a commitment to take time to learn, to observe deeply (genchi genbutsu), and to participate in continuous improvement?
5. How will you mentor others? Do you have the personal tools to do that?
6. How will your organization get the sensei support needed for this transformation?
7. Is your organization full of conflicting and inconsistent messages? If so, develop a communication plan for beginning the process of sending consistent messages.
8. What will be necessary to change the culture so that a singular, consistent message develops?

Index

Page numbers followed by n indicates note(s).

About the Authors

Dr. Jeffrey K. Liker is Professor of Industrial and Operations Engineering and Director of the Japan Technology Management Program at the University of Michigan. He is author of the international best-seller, *The Toyota Way: 14 Management Principles from the World's Greatest Manufacturer*, McGraw Hill, 2004 (winner of the 2005 Shingo Prize and the Institute of Industrial Engineering 2005 Book of the Year Award). Previously he edited *Becoming Lean: Experiences of U.S. Manufacturers* (Productivity Press, 1997), winner of the 1998 Shingo prize (for excellence in manufacturing research). He has also won Shingo prizes for his research in 1995, 1996, and 1997. Other books by Dr. Liker include *Engineered in Japan*, (Oxford University Press, 1995); *Concurrent Engineering Effectiveness: Integrating product development across organizations* (Hanser-Gardner, 1997), and *Remade in America: Transplanting and Transforming Japanese Manufacturing Methods* (Oxford University Press, 1999). His most recent book, with James Morgan, is *High Performance Product Development: How Toyota integrates people, process and technology to create a revolutionary lean product development system* (Productivity Press). Dr. Liker is active as a keynote speaker, speaker for executive retreats, and lean consultant, independently and through a company he cofounded—Optiprise, Inc. Recent clients include DaimlerChrysler, Metalsa, Danfoss, Rio Tinto Mining, Caterpillar Asia Pacific, Benteler Automotive, Amcor, Federal Mogul, PPG Industries, Johnson Controls, Tenneco Automotive, Framatome Technologies, Northrop Grumman Ship Systems, Jacksonville Naval Air Depot, the U.S. Air Force, and Portsmouth Naval Ship Yard.

David Meier learned the Toyota Production System (TPS) as one of the first group leaders hired at Toyota's Georgetown, Kentucky facility in the plastics molding department. He was trained and mentored in Japan and Kentucky over a ten-year period by TPS experts including full-time coaching by several Japanese coordinators. After leaving Toyota, David founded Lean Associates, Inc., a consulting firm that is dedicated to supporting companies that are pursuing implementation of the Toyota Production System.

David wrote two chapters for *Lean Manufacturing: A Plant Floor Guide (Society of Manufacturing Engineers*, 2001) and has been a trainer and speaker for over eight years. He has presented training workshops on Standardized Work, Value Stream Mapping, and Introduction to Lean Fundamentals for the Society of Manufacturing Engineers, and the Shingo Prize Conference. David has supported many companies in a variety of industries including automotive, aerospace, wood and plastic products, chemical processing, metal machining, fabricating, welding, and assembly operations in both manufacturing and non-manufacturing work areas. He specializes in developing TPS expertise within organizations so that they become capable of achieving lean transformation.